ALSO BY JOHN THORNE

Simple Cooking

Outlaw Cook

Serious Pig

Pot on the Fire

Home Body

MOUTH
WIDE OPEN

MOUTH WIDE OPEN

A COOK AND HIS APPETITE

JOHN THORNE

WITH MATT LEWIS THORNE

NORTH POINT PRESS

A DIVISION OF FARRAR, STRAUS AND GIROUX

NEW YORK

North Point Press
A division of Farrar, Straus and Giroux
18 West 18th Street, New York 10011

Copyright © 2007 by John Thorne
All rights reserved
Distributed in Canada by Douglas & McIntyre Ltd.
Printed in the United States of America
Published in 2007 by North Point Press
First paperback edition, 2008

The chapter in this book entitled "The Marrow of the Matter" was originally published in slightly different form in *Gourmet* magazine, and the chapter entitled "American Eats" first appeared in *The Art of Eating*, edited by Edward Behr.

Grateful acknowledgment is made to the following for permission to reprint copyrighted material: Rolando Beramendi, for permission to print the description of wild fennel pollen that appears on the website of Manicaretti Italian Food Importers, www.manicaretti.com. Fratelli De Cecco di Filippo Fara San Martino S.P.A., for permission to reprint the recipe "Fusilli with Tomato and Green Olive Sauce." The editors of www.gourmet.gr, for permission to print a passage from "Greece's Lake District: Prespes," by Diana Farr Louis, as published on their website. Houghton Mifflin Company, for permission to reprint "Mushroom Pot Roast," from *How to Read a French Fry*, by Russ Parsons, copyright © 2001 by Russ Parsons; Reprinted by permission of Houghton Mifflin Company; All rights reserved. Bob Lucky, for permission to quote a passage from a letter to the authors. Bruce C. Moffitt, for permission to print a passage from the essay on *menudo* that appears on his website at www.premiersystems.com /recipes/mexican/menudo.html. Joan and David Peterson, for permission to reprint their list of satay variations originally published in *Eat Smart in Indonesia*, published by the Ginkgo Press in 1997. Charles F. Swett, Jr., for permission to quote two passages from a letter to the authors. Elisheva S. Urbas, for permission to quote a passage from a letter to the authors. Ari Weinzweig, for permission to print two passages about wild fennel pollen that appeared in his essay on the subject published in the November/ December 2000 issue of *Zingerman's News*.

The Library of Congress has cataloged the hardcover edition as follows:
Thorne, John.
    Mouth wide open : a cook and his appetite / John Thorne ; with Matt Lewis Thorne.
        p.   cm.
    Includes bibliographical references and index.
    ISBN-13: 978-0-86547-628-8 (hardcover : alk. paper)
    ISBN-10: 0-86547-628-4 (hardcover : alk. paper)
    1. Cookery.   I. Thorne, Matt Lewis.   II. Title.

TX652.T457 2007
641.5—dc22
                                                                                2007019137

Paperback ISBN-13: 978-0-374-53143-0
Paperback ISBN-10: 0-374-53143-9

Designed by Jonathan D. Lippincott

www.fsgbooks.com

1   3   5   7   9   10   8   6   4   2

For David
best of friends

CONTENTS

COOKING THE BOOKS

LIST OF RECIPES

INTRODUCTORY NOTE

Anyone familiar with my writing will already know that, for the most part, creating recipes is not something that greatly interests me, and I am even less interested in curating any but the most historical. What I do is look for recipes with the potential for a lively conversation—a friendly argument, if you like, between two cooks. As I explain further on in "The Reviewer and the Recipe," I don't follow recipes; I interact with them. Because of that, when a source is provided (as it often is) for a recipe that particularly attracts you, consider seeking out the original version. That way you can clearly see what the argument was all about . . . and have two cooks to converse with instead of one.

As to the recipes themselves, one day last year I found myself balking when typing "freshly ground black pepper" into a recipe ingredient list. True, when I keyed in "black pepper" instead, the naked plainness insinuated that I might be so boorish myself as to actually use an ordinary, vulgar pepper shaker.

Well, to tell the truth, I do use them all the time: very few of the greasy spoons I frequent have gotten around to putting pepper mills on the table—and the food doesn't seem any the worse for it. True, I usually grind my pepper at home, cook (even fry) with extra-virgin olive oil, and almost always prefer fresh minced garlic to the powdered stuff. Still, look on my spice shelf and you'll find dried onion, leek, and bell pepper flakes, curry powder, and celery salt. Elsewhere, there are cans of soup and corned beef hash, bags of frozen vegetables.

Chances are, your kitchen is like that, too. Learning to talk isn't simply about mastering vocabulary and grammar, it also requires that we master one way of talking to our parents and another to our friends, and, later, to our teachers and our bosses. Even home cooking has its several dialects. So you don't need me nagging you to buy artisanal bread or to use unsalted butter when you cook. Cooking changes best by epiphany; advice is best when it merely prods these into happening.

In any case, so much of what we do in the kitchen is very different from appreciating the best ingredients. In her autobiography, *Zami: A New Spelling of My Name*, the poet Audre Lorde rhapsodizes about the smell of onions frying in margarine. I knew just how sweet such a memory could be. Cooking is about doing the best with what you have . . . and succeeding. The rest is nothing but frosting. So I've done my best to winnow out those little peremptory qualifiers in the ingredient list.

However, I do want to note that Matt and I cook with pure, coarse kosher salt (which means if you substitute fine-grained salt—kosher or not—reduce the amount called for in our recipes by half, and adjust from there). We use an inexpensive but fruity extra-virgin olive oil from Spain, Greece, or Italy, depending on the market, and prefer peanut oil by far when olive oil isn't appropriate.

We use a lot of chiles in our kitchen, sometimes fresh, sometimes dried and flaked or powdered, ranging from mildly hot to mouth-searing. But we don't own any "chili powder," the commercial blend of powdered chile, toasted cumin, Mexican oregano, and other things. So, when we call for any kind of powdered chile, we mean just that—the result of grinding up dried chile pods.

Other, specialized ingredients are detailed in the recipes that call for them, including (where possible) ordering information. This was all updated when this book was about to go to press, but, sadly, small merchants—especially—do come and go, online and in situ. If you find this to be the case, get in touch with us at johnthorne@outlawcook.com— we may have been able to find another merchant.

A
Amato's Italian Sandwich: see Sandwich, Amato's Italian

B
Baeckeoffe: see Casserole, Alsatian, with pork, lamb, and beef
Bagel *mit wiener Salswasser* (bagel dipped in German wiener
    brine)   319

AUTHOR'S NOTE

Although the "I" that speaks from these pages is mine in every chapter of this book, my wife, Matt Lewis Thorne, has also considered every word of every draft I have written, reacting, suggesting, amending, and, hence, reshaping what appears herein. As I have noted in each of our collaborations, starting with *Outlaw Cook*, this means that the subjective self who speaks out of these pages is a larger, braver, much more interesting person than I am alone—and I honor her for it.

As in my four previous food books, *Mouth Wide Open* assembles a selection of essays written over the past several years, most of them originally published in our food letter, *Simple Cooking*. Those who read this book with pleasure might also be interested in subscribing to it. Either write to us at P.O. Box 778; Northampton, MA 01061—or, better yet, visit our website: www.outlawcook.com.

—John Thorne

THEN AND NOW—
BY WAY OF A PREFACE

It was a hot day, summer, the late sixties. I was sitting at a kitchen table across from a friend and fellow faculty member at the small independent school where I was then teaching English. He was about to show me how to make mayonnaise . . . on a plate . . . with a fork.

I later was to find out that making it this way was considered a tricky business. But in his hands it was astonishingly simple. He used the fork first to mix a little splash of vinegar into an egg yolk, seasoning this with salt and pepper. Next, stirring briskly all the while with the tines of the fork, he began to whisk in olive oil.

He covered the bottle's mouth with his thumb and lifted it high enough so that he could keep his eyes focused on the egg yolk. He shifted his thumb slightly, releasing the oil, at first drop by drop, then in a steady golden stream, as slender as a thread.

For the first few minutes, the egg yolk simply absorbed the oil, which gave it a bright yellow, greasy sheen, neither appetizing nor very promising. But the fork went on squeaking across the plate, the oil kept dripping down, and the collation began to thicken, lighten, mount up.

The result was initially flabby-looking, like a scoop of vanilla pudding. But in another minute or two, the tines began leaving a distinct trail. It didn't last for long, but it was there. By now the golden thread of falling oil had become a thin stream.

"How much will it absorb?" I asked.

"A lot more than I'm going to pour in," he answered. "A cup, at least. I'm still adding it because I want to tone down the taste of the egg yolk."

"Here," he said, finally, holding out the fork to me, a clot of the mayonnaise roosting at the end.

I tasted. The experience wasn't rapturous, but it was, in its way, illuminating. This was mayonnaise with attitude—all the more so after a childhood where, whether one opted for Cains or Hellmann's (almost as big a decision as deciding between Coke and Pepsi), what one tasted was a certain bland unctuousness, perked up by a sharpness that, depending on the brand, might be vinegar or might be lemon.

This mayonnaise asked you not to choose but to decide if you were ready to move on, the way you might from cola to wine. The real thing, it turned out, didn't even pretend to be everybody's pal. It was what it was, and you were either up to that or you weren't. So, no, I wasn't swoony with delight. I was busy recalibrating my palate to make sense of a forthright mouthful of creamy olive oil and egg, with all the flavor notes lingeringly plangent.

This, I discovered, is what mayonnaise is all about—the emulsifying of oil into egg yolk. In her own lesson on preparing it,* Elizabeth David forbids the addition of mustard, frowns on the use of salt and pepper, and allows only a whisper of wine vinegar or lemon juice. Everything else only gets in the way.

That experience—and my subsequent success at replicating it—is what comes to mind whenever I'm asked what "simple cooking" means, and why I chose it to name the food letter I've now been writing for more than a quarter of a century. Making mayonnaise this way may not be effortless—the synonym many people associate with "simple"—but it is "fundamental and straightforward," which is to say the greatest effect conjured out of the fewest possible means—a plate, a fork, an egg yolk, some olive oil, a touch of wine vinegar, and (apologies, Elizabeth) a pinch of salt.

In this sense, the phrase became the motivating force of my adventures in the kitchen. Without really noticing it, I lost interest in complicatedly impressive dishes (the hallmark of my earlier efforts at "considered" cooking) and turned my attention to the often unremarkable-seeming foods that have, ever since, been the ones to capture my heart.

The reason I'm telling you this, however, isn't to pat myself on the back. Instead, what impresses me most, looking back from a perspec-

---

*In *Masterclass: Expert Lessons in Kitchen Skills,* edited by Jill Norman.

tive of twenty-five years, is how much this aesthetic, so important to me and my writing, turns out to be almost entirely the product of its time and place, its particularity shaped by my idiosyncratic personal history.

I grew up as an army brat, and thus was completely sheltered from the economic forces—and resulting stresses—that shape most American lives. No one we knew risked losing their job because of a downturn in the economy or the whim of a new boss, or possessed conspicuous wealth or even an enviably higher standard of living. Medical treatment and (quite decent) housing were free. Those who made the army their career felt they were motivated by duty, a sense of patriotism, even if, like my father, they were drawn to military life because it offered someone without many prospects a way into a respected profession.

To be sure, the ethos of the armed forces is fired by idealism, and although, even as a child, I resisted the rah-rah aspect of this, I was still indelibly affected by its pervasiveness. I also have always had a hard time grasping why people want to make lots of money and, once they have it (or even before), why they buy many of the things they do.

This isn't a moral position. I don't *care* that people do these things; I just don't get it. And this, by itself, has left me woefully unprepared to grasp the changes that have swept through the food world in recent decades. These, I don't think anyone would deny, have been determined largely by money—and I mean the desire both to make it and to impetuously spend it.

Spending real money on everyday food was a novel idea when I started cooking. It wasn't that people weren't interested in good food, but their perception of its possibilities was still largely determined by the Depression and the world war that followed. A roast chicken or a plateful of flapjacks was plenty enough for most people, whose image of "fancy" eating was the groaning board laid out each time a holiday rolled around—turkey at Thanksgiving, ham at Easter—or when company came to dinner.

Those who think that we Americans knew nothing of imaginative cooking before the sixties haven't read their history. It's just that our appetite was waking up then from a long slumber, and had forgotten much of what it once knew. An extended period of denial may whet the appetite, but it withers imagination, until what is longed for has calcified into an emblem of itself. Dry-aged steaks were mythic, if you had heard of them at all; quality chocolates were known by the liqueur in their centers; butter was butter, salted, please, to keep it from spoiling the long time it sat waiting in the refrigerator, while margarine was passed around the family table.

True, you could find things then that you can't now, like beef tongue or fresh goose or small crimson strawberries, full of flavor and juice, brought up from the Carolinas in the late spring. But these were happy exceptions. Mushrooms came in cans, garlic existed as a powder, and if you wanted any fresh herb apart from curly-leaf parsley, you had to grow it yourself.

If a recipe called for anything faintly exotic, your best bet (and by no means a sure one) was to search for it at the gourmet store, or, if you happened to live near one, the local Italian market. These, as I remember them, were often nothing special—most likely a repository of Italian-American canned goods, *salumi*, and pastas, with maybe some whole, string-wrapped, dusty balls of provolone hanging from the ceiling.

If you were lucky, they might also have rounds of crusty bread sprinkled with sesame seeds, and a butcher, who could provide you with a stuffed veal roast or a whole rabbit. My own prize find was the tins of murky, green-gold olive oil. That it was imported from Sicily was imprimatur enough—the term "extra-virgin" was almost completely unknown in this country until well into the seventies.

In fact, the maps available at the time for anyone setting off on their first voyage into the world of food were covered with empty spaces marked "terra incognita"—how much so it would take me decades to discover.

However, two good consequences sprang from this, the first being that—unless you were a member of the small coterie of epicures—a tight budget was not at all incompatible with pursuing an interest in food. In those days, even the top food writers were often pressed for cash, and several wrote books on how to eat well without much money (a genre that has now pretty much disappeared).* Others, like Elizabeth David, wrote about foreign cuisines where cooks knew all manner

---

*Including M.F.K. Fisher's *How to Cook a Wolf* (1942); James Beard's *How to Eat Better for Less Money* (1954); Sylvia Vaughn Thompson's *Economy Gastronomy* (1963) and *The Budget Gourmet* (1975); and Ann Rogers's *A Cookbook for Poor Poets and Others* (1966).

of ways to make *cucina povera* good enough for a king, and certainly for a hungry private-school teacher.

Second, because culinary discoveries were then so isolated and unique, they tended to resonate in the imagination for a long time. My first bunch of fresh basil is fixed in memory partly because of its resinous intensity, partly because a whole year passed before I got my hands on another. Other gemlike memories include my first encounter with fresh brown mushrooms, authentic Parmigiano-Reggiano, just-made mozzarella dripping with whey, Kalamata olives, and applewood-smoked duck.

Today, of course, it's another world. The local supermarket sells fresh basil the year round and offers several sizes of fresh mozzarella floating in little tubs. Its deli offers genuine Italian prosciutto; the cheese department, sublime sheep cheeses from French Basque country; the grocery section, a whole shelf of extra-virgin olive oils, including some bottled under the store's own label. The list goes on and on—indeed, it may be endless, since items are constantly being added to it. And this in a form of generalized food retailing that may soon become passé.

Now we have large markets that specialize in natural and organic foods, others that feature high-end foodstuffs, and still others that offer carefully selected quality foods at bargain prices. Local farm stands no longer have to promote themselves as tourist traps to stay in business (although it still helps if they make their own ice cream). And, in many places, farmers' markets have made a strong comeback.

In other words, we (middle-class Americans) inhabit a world where culinary pleasure knows no boundaries. Choosing has become a lost art; you can heap your plate with anything you fancy. This, of course, isn't the absolute truth, but it's true enough—certainly to the extent that the culinary aesthetic that shaped me as a cook is of little use at all to anyone launching their little barque today. And whereas aspiring cooks of my generation and the one that followed it turned to food writers for inspiration, today's cooks seek it among the chefs.

• • •

Many years ago, it occurred to me that the popularity of spy thrillers with white-collar readers derived from the fact that spies also worked

in offices and dealt with unimaginative, even willfully obstructive supe-
riors. But spies also got to go on missions where they could break the
law, bribe and steal, and, best of all, kill people. They got to be the cops
and the robbers.

In today's information-centered corporate world, chefs have it all
over spies. Chefs churn out one brilliant idea after another, thrilling
their clientele while cranking out big bucks for their backers (and taking a prime cut for themselves). Their names can become household
words (at least in the households that count). Chefs also work long
hours, but in a testosterone-charged, genuinely dangerous workspace,
crowded with guys wielding razor-sharp knives and intentionally
bumping into each other. To many, this appears to be the very ideal of
a job. And, don't forget, there's the food, too.

It's no accident that the center of today's culinary ethos is the chef.
Being a chef is as much about money as it is about food, if not more so.
As Michael Ruhlman noted in *The New York Times* (June 4, 2006):

> Fewer and fewer chefs, it seems, strive to be the single-restaurant
> artist-monk. "I don't want to just stay in one kitchen," [Geoffrey]
> Zakarian said on the opening day of Country, dressed in street
> clothes while tasting dishes brought to him by a sous-chef. "I have
> way more interests than just cooking." He continued, "There are
> so many ways to enjoy this métier"—everything from multiple
> books [money] to opening a boutique cooking school [money] to
> developing kitchen products [money] to designing kitchens for
> other chefs and operators [money].

More than anyone else, chefs know that there's so much good food
around these days that only a fool takes any of it seriously for longer
than a moment. One's eyes must always be fixed on the horizon for the
appearance of the next best thing. Their recipes are a restless amalgam
of many ingredients, looking for a combination potent enough to seize
the eater's fickle attention. In such a milieu, simplicity only commands
respect when it exudes its own particular extravagance—impressively
costly ingredients, infinite preparation time.

Admittedly, my gut reaction to the nation's current obsession with
chef-oriented cooking has been far from positive. In fact, I out and out
hated its intrusion into the home kitchen. From my own perspective, it
turned quiet but pleasurable experiences into overly competitive and
embarrassingly egocentric ones.

Recently, however, a sobering realization set in. Suppose (I thought) I was in the position of, say, John Sebastian of the Lovin' Spoonful,* looking down the decades at Eminem, Yung Joc, and the Pussycat Dolls, and wondering "What *happened*?" The thing is, Sebastian, even though he's been off the charts for eons, is still around, still recording albums, and still into jug-band music—which is, speaking analogously, just what you could say about me.

Pushing this train of thought still further, I had to admit that even if what I believe about chefs is true, that doesn't mean it is *all* the truth. On the contrary, as chef culture continues to spread, my attitude toward it has turned me more and more into an outsider, uninterested in and out of touch with important changes in America's culinary life. In other words, without really noticing it, I'd become an old fossil. Maybe the time had come to stop staring, mouth agape, at the antics of Bobby Flay, Mario Batali, Emeril Lagasse, Anthony Bourdain, and company—and to try to comprehend what my cooking aesthetic would be like if I found them a source of inspiration.

This was hard to do, and it wasn't accomplished in a day, or a week, or even a month. I'm an old dog and I was being asked not to learn a new trick but to imagine myself as a puppy again. But the more I thought about chefs and their ways, the more I found to like—and the more I found myself transferring my previous negative feelings about them to the universe of cookbooks and those who mostly write them.

When I started cooking, the food writers I admired were, essentially, literary—in the sense that they kept popular culture at bay, while attempting to hold to a culinary aesthetic that embraced authenticity, respect for ingredients, clarity of flavor, and mastery of craft. Like serious reading, this sort of cooking was something that you did alone, in private, in engrossed communion with the writer who was inspiring you.

Writing like this was never mass-marketable, and the books written by the writers who practiced it—Elizabeth David, Jane Grigson, Madeleine Kamman, Richard Olney, Patience Gray—sold accordingly. But then Julia Child came along and showed that the right personality could make serious cooking a form of entertainment, draw an audience, make money.

---

*Their hits included "Daydream," "Do You Believe in Magic?," "You Didn't Have to Be So Nice," and, my own fave, "Summer in the City"—especially as covered by Joe Cocker in *Have a Little Faith*, 1994.

Consequently, she brought into being an endless number of cook-books written by virtuoso instructors whose natural stage was not the printed page but the dais of the cooking school. It was only a matter of time before these, in turn, were increasingly supplanted by chefs—whose performances were all the more virtuosic because they knew much more about what they were doing. (Stop the press. According to Bill Buford, writing in the October 2, 2006, issue of *The New Yorker*, the chefs are now being supplanted by personalities like Rachael Ray, television producers having decided that the former were making cook-ing look too much like work. As Judy Girard, a television executive Bu-ford quotes, puts it: "You need television talents. You can't run a network with chefs." To make truly serious money, you need Rachael Ray, who makes cooking seem as effortless as eating, and *lots* of fun.)

All this has meant the kiss of death for a certain kind of food writ-ing—wholeheartedly devoted to cooking but meditative, teaching al-most by osmosis, rather than by being determinedly helpful and instructive. What passes for "literary food writing" (always a danger-ous term) has become a subset of autobiography—my life, with recipes. This sea change has been profitable and successful, and has drawn many people into the kitchen. But it has been terrible for anyone who wants to think seriously about cooking. What a lively personality may bring to life in face-to-face instruction almost always translates on the page as a monotonous, cheerily hectoring tone, a belief that no recipe is too familiar to not be enthused about and no culinary platitude too fa-tigued to not be worth repeating—over and over and over again.

For example, the notion that we ought to "eat with the seasons" has been with us now for decades. Yet it's still feverishly preached as if it were something just this moment discovered—despite the fact that, for the most part, the adjuration is meaningless. What, for exam-ple, is the "season" for carrots or bananas or eggplant or celery or parsley or . . . the list goes on and on. Conversely, are there any be-nighted souls left who have yet to learn that sweet corn, tomatoes, green peas, and asparagus are best when just picked—ideally from one's own garden?

Then there's food writing's nonstop stream of well-meaning but hysteria-powered health advice. You may be better able than I to win-now out what is truly useful from the partial truisms and patent falsehoods with which we are all bombarded.* But perhaps you'd agree that the never-ending insistency that we "eat well" has inextricably linked eating *with* health—thus intensifying rather than toning down our current obsession with food. We have become, rather pathetically, a nation of the overweight convinced that it can somehow gobble its way out of obesity.

Since the cooking that chefs do is considered the exception, not the rule, they have a free pass to heap on the calories as they will. Surely this, too, helps explain the magnetic attraction that food entertainment holds for its audience. Within the magic circle, you get to eat (or at least imagine eating) *all* the good things, without being called to task for it. Given the pervasiveness of nutritional dogma, this safe harbor seems both necessary and blessed, whether one experiences it while eating in a restaurant or cooking chef-inspired dishes at home.

This isn't to say that chefs are entirely immune to all the proselytizing. But by keeping it at arm's length, they have gradually, and perhaps even profitably, internalized it. The classic, knee-jerk addition of butter and heavy cream has (often enough, at least) segued into the drizzle of *jus*, the fruit-intensive coulis, the cilantro-infused vinaigrette. Hedonism, it turns out, can use nutritional wisdom to its own ends, given time and scope enough.

To my mind, food writing is only worth reading when it has something interesting to say, and instruction, while it can be informative, is rarely interesting after the first time around—who, for example, ever goes back to read the notes taken during even favorite college courses? Chefs, on the other hand, are interesting mainly in what they do. And doing something well over and over doesn't leach it of interest—sometimes, it is precisely this repetition that makes it interesting.

Or consider this real-world example: the sustainable agriculture movement. I think it is a wonderful thing. It provides continued awareness of local farmers, be they of the traditional sort or the new breed of independent entrepreneurs who forage for wild mushrooms; who cultivate flavor-intensive vegetables and greens (sometimes organic, sometimes not); who put cattle out to graze on grass, rather than stuffing them with corn in the feedlot.

---

*My own rule of thumb, for what it's worth, is to try to eat moderately, graze widely—and, most importantly, let others volunteer to be the zeitgeist's guinea pigs.

Food writers have, of course, busily promoted all this. But no amount of effusive prose and glossy photos are of much help to their subjects, who tend to live in out-of-the-way places or whose products don't marry well with farmers' markets. For example, those who have a flock of hens and a few dozen eggs to sell every day would prefer to have customers come to them. People who raise food animals or run small smokehouses usually want to sell in bulk rather than by the lamb chop or pound of bacon.

Here, while food writers talk the talk, chefs walk the walk. Because they can spread the cost among many diners, they are more than willing to buy all the eggs, the side of pork, the basket of mushrooms, in one quick transaction, and not be flattened by the price. For small producers, that makes all the difference.

Chefs are equally adept at handling the touchy matter of quality. Matt and I have been going to farm stands and farmers' markets for a long time, both here and in Maine, and we're quite familiar with farmers who have next to no interest in critically tasting what they've raised. Some soil is better suited for cabbage than carrots; superior varieties of fruits and vegetables are often more challenging to grow or to harvest. And some farmers insist on trying to sell what ought to have been heaved onto the compost pile.

Chefs, partly because of their buying power and partly because they know what "good" is, are in a much better position to get what they want, by getting suppliers to want to give it to them. In our part of central Massachusetts, where the number of sophisticated upscale restaurants barely makes it into the double digits, local chefs still make a real effort to track down and nurture small producers. Because of that, there's not only more locally grown food available, but more of it that's truly worth seeking out.

• • •

The best chefs are simultaneously sensualists and disciplinarians. You can do the job with just one of those qualities, but you won't rise to the top. Chefs have to force their ingredients—not always the best—to pull off some fantastic tricks. They constantly have to browbeat their underlings, their suppliers, even their bosses, to get things done right. Chefs, in fact, can be threatening people to get close to—which is one good reason why there's such a thing as a waiter.

I remember looking at the photograph of Daniel Boulud, one of New York City's most acclaimed chefs, on the cover of his first cookbook,* and thinking that it would take guts to cook with this guy. Partly it was his smile, just this side of a grimace, and the tension in his pose, waiting for this picture-taking nonsense to be over so that he could get back to his kitchen. Mostly what struck me were his hands: solid, muscular, and hard-used, two highly disciplined, unquestioningly obedient slaves.

What those hands bear witness to is that professional cooking is hard work, and mastering it is a toughening experience that ultimately leaves you standing on your own two feet. Most food writing, however, isn't intended to lead you to that sort of independence—instead, it leaves you with the need to buy another cookbook. Once out of culinary school, chefs learn by hanging out in other chefs' kitchens, not by poring over cookbooks—and these, when consulted, tend to be either technical and/or written for chefs by other chefs.

That's why I can watch a good chef going about his or her business all day long, but can't spend more than a few minutes reading most cookbooks. Usually I just quickly leaf through them, scanning the recipes for anything interesting. The best food writers have always been cooks who are especially gifted in articulating what they do in their own kitchen, and not only make that seem worth doing but also worth thinking about. The rest fall back on instruction—and you can't learn cooking, any more than carpentry, by following numbered directions from a book. You have to work much harder than that, and you have to choose books that make you do so.

Unfortunately, few chefs write their own cookbooks. Instead, they let a professional food writer reconstruct their dishes into recipe-speak, which strips them of any real interest. (The regal exception to this is Richard Olney's explication of the cooking of Lulu Peyraud.†) Most readers, if they cook from these books at all, use them to reproduce trophy dishes by carefully connecting all the dots. Sous-chefs, on the other hand, even though they're required to spend their day making replications, have their boss looking over their shoulder, tasting, adjusting, commentating—which is to say, teaching.

Cooking is a métier that demands that you learn to think with your

---

* *Cooking with Daniel Boulud* (Random House, 1993).
† *Lulu's Provençal Kitchen.*

senses and articulate with your hands. Tasting, smelling, prodding, kneading, even listening—at bottom, kitchen work is just not a verbal activity. Fortunately, as a home cook, I don't need much in the way of disciplinary chops, but I do have to get down, mano a mano, with the onions and potatoes. Real cooking takes place in real time with the laying of hands on real food—and it is there that its lasting pleasures lie.

This, of course, is cooking as I see it—and, albeit in a more complicated sense, how I see chefs doing it, as well as an ever-shrinking tribe of interested home cooks. As for everybody else—well, I think that the recent craze for culinary entertainments may be signaling the end of home cooking as we know it. For the past hundred years, an enormous amount of commercial effort has been invested in making cooking progressively less of a chore. On the whole, I think, it has failed. No number of conveniences can change the fact that many people just don't have enough time in the day to accomplish all that they need to do, let alone what they would really like to.

Because of this, the historical and cultural reasons that once compelled us to cook are waning fast. Even the very word "cooking" has been pared and twisted to the point where it no longer has a clear, straightforward meaning. Is heating something up cooking? Heating up two different things and serving them together? As the prepared-meal counter at markets like Whole Foods gets longer and longer, "cooking" becomes a matter of selecting something among all this food to bring home for dinner.

Before the phonograph and the radio, people learned to sing or play instruments if they wanted to listen to music. Now, for the most part, the chief motivation to learn the ways of an electric guitar is the hope of playing in a rock band. Entertainments like *Iron Chef* and the Food Network are similarly transforming kitchen work into spectacle. When we want music, we play a CD; one day soon, perhaps, when we want to eat, we'll pop a favorite chef's signature dish into the microwave— David Waltuck's seafood sausage for you; Gordon Ramsay's cappuccino of white beans with grated truffles for me.

Granted, these meals won't be nearly as good as they would be if eaten at the restaurant, let alone as something lovingly made from scratch at home. But that's not the point. All they *have* to be is better than (or at least as good as) what most people prepare for themselves, most of the time. The moment cooking became a form of entertainment, its aura of virtue evaporated, and there was no reason left not to let others do the heavy lifting.

• • •

Cooking has always been too pleasurable a part of my life for me to consider it a virtuous enterprise (like making the bed)—let alone the sort of boring task that I'd be happy to relegate to someone else (like making the bed). On the other hand, the whole world can dine on microwave dinners, for all I care, as long as I can still scrounge up an onion and a chunk of butter.

Simple cooking. It's worth remembering that a chef—Escoffier, no less—said it first: "Above all, make it simple!" He was in revolt against the obtuse over-ornamentation of dishes—which is why the phrase continues to resonate with professional chefs today. Culinary overkill has its moments, to be sure, but, in the long run, creativity does its best work when struggling against restraint.

However, as I've grown older and become increasingly set in my ways, the nature of the struggle has changed. Calcification should never be confused with simplicity, and what this meditation has shown me is that it's time for me to embrace a bit more complexity. I need to

1. Try to become more comfortable with waste. I find it hard to shake the idea that I ought to eat all the food I buy to make a particular dish, or at least save it for another day. This means that there are many dishes I wouldn't even *think* of making, even once, out of mere curiosity.

2. Shop less at supermarkets. I've survived their ever-increasing cacophony and bogusness by mentally stuffing my ears and donning blinders, which can only have a dampening effect on my cooking. Ethnic markets are full of junk as well, but their sheer foreignness keeps me alert to what is wondrous and different and worth a try. And shopping well at a farmers' market *really* tests one's mettle.

3. Keep narrowing my focus. Three decades ago, I yearned to learn everything I could about a range of

foreign cuisines. But now, despite the ever-increasing number of cookbooks, cooking schools in situ, and imported ingredients, authentic connection seems even further away. Times of scarcity produce generalists; times of abundance, specialists—and that means persistently seeking out ingredients and techniques that resonate with one's cooking and relentlessly weeding out what doesn't.

4. Continue to strive to be a "single-kitchen artist-monk." Eaters are browsers by definition, but cooks who browse will always be slaves to their cookbooks. By keeping an eye open for connections, by adapting one dish according to what I learn from another, I may grow old but my kitchen will stay young.

Whenever you hold the past up to the present, one or the other always suffers. Looking back at the time I began cooking, it's hard for me not to feel embarrassed by how ingenuous it all was. Salt was salt, wine vinegar was just another kind of vinegar, an egg was just an egg. Even imported olive oil seemed no more than a hard-to-find, slightly classy kind of vegetable oil. The one used by my friend was light and delicate, yet unmistakably pressed from olives. It gave the mayonnaise its flavor, its presence—even as the egg made it thick. It was the first time I really *noticed* olive oil, but it didn't seem at all as rich with signification as it soon would become.

Indeed, it's only because of the bottle's unique shape that I know, even after all these years, that it was bottled by James Plagniol, and that it came from Provence. Recently, I went to our local gourmet emporium to see if I could purchase some, wondering whether its taste would summon back anything of the old enchantment. There, I discovered that the sole Provençal oil they carried was a seventeen-ounce bottle of Arnaud extra-virgin, AOC Vallée des Baux de Provence—blended of Salonenque, Grossane, Verdale, Picholine, and Aglandeau olives. It couldn't be more echt Provençal, but priced at the princely sum of thirty-three dollars, it was neither simple nor affordable.

As for James Plagniol, he was nowhere to be found—not here, not on those burgeoning supermarket shelves. I did an online search, and the only place I found offering it for sale was a market and garden center in New Jersey. They didn't do mail order, so, back at the super-market, I chose a pale, "grove-pressed" extra-virgin olive oil from Argentina. Then I made the mayonnaise—with a fork, by hand, on a plate, with a raw egg yolk. Everything went perfectly—as I'm sure it will for you, if you just make sure the egg is fresh and at room temp-erature.

No, it didn't carry me back to 1969. It just stayed what it was, a glowing emulsion of egg and olive oil on a plate. What it did do was remind me again of how much fun such kitchen work can be—controlling the release of the oil, chasing after every droplet with the fork to get it mixed into the yolk, feeling the suspense build, until that delicious moment when it suddenly all comes together, and there you are.

MOUTH WIDE OPEN

THE MARROW OF THE MATTER

I was nine years old. I had been helping set the table for Christmas dinner, covering it with the freshly ironed linen cloth, setting out the good china and the carefully polished silverware. I had just added the finishing touch—my mother's prize pair of silver candelabra—and was now hanging out in the kitchen, standing beside the baked ham resplendent on our largest platter. As my mother mashed the potatoes, I stealthily pulled off little bits of crusty fat from around the ham's edges and popped them into my mouth. As I did this, my attention wandered from the edges of the ham to the bone in its middle, or, more precisely, to the pinkish stuff inside it. I didn't know what it was or even if you were "supposed" to eat it. But there was something about the soft, luscious look of it that drew an exploratory finger. I scooped a little out, tasted it . . . and found myself transported to heaven. Forty-eight years later, I still remember that moment—not my earliest culinary memory, but the first where a single taste would change my life.

To this day, I think ham marrow is one of the most delicious—certainly one of the most *neglected* delicious—things in the world. If my palate ruled, smokehouses would sell it in little jars that would have the status, if not the price, of caviar. Ham marrow is as delicately flavored and as easily spreadable as butter, but it has none of butter's spinelessness. Instead, its oddly resilient texture resists melting even while it so delectably does. The difference can be put so: Butter is solidified cream; marrow is the ethereal distillation of meat.

The first time I noticed beef marrowbones in a supermarket, I was thirty-something, living in a Boston neighborhood called Jamaica Plain.

I did my grocery shopping in an old-fashioned A&P, the sort with cramped, narrow aisles, low ceilings, and harsh fluorescent lights. The bones were at the very end of the meat case, wrapped in packages labeled "Soup Bones." Some contained a single large knuckle; others held sawed shinbones with centers full of marrow. None had a shred of meat attached—strange, I thought, as I had watched the butchers regularly toss bones with gobbets of meat still attached into the offal barrel. A package of the marrowbones quickly made its way into my basket, but I couldn't help asking one of the butchers about this peculiar discrepancy—why throw away the meaty bones and sell the bare ones for making soup? He gave me a look. "Those," he said, pointing to the packages, "are meant for dogs. Customers don't want dog bones with meat on them—they make too much of a mess." When I stared at him blankly, he added, his voice dropping a little, "If we call them dog bones, people get upset finding them in with the meat they're buying for themselves." He glanced down the aisle before adding in an even lower tone, "And, anyway, if we labeled them 'Dog Bones,' people would expect to get them for free." I bore this information back home with me along with my groceries. I was, it seemed, in love with dog food.

• • •

The eating of bone marrow, to be sure, is hardly unknown. The French use it to give a glossy delicacy to sauces, and it is a featured element in that Italian classic, osso buco. In Georgian England, cooks would saw an end off a beef shinbone, cover the opening with pastry, bake the thing in the oven, and then send it, wrapped in a napkin, to table, where it was eaten with a special silver spoon. Victorian eaters—for the most part, exclusively male—would scoop out the marrow and spread it on toast. American mountain men, after killing a buffalo, roasted the bones and drank the marrow from them as if from flagons.

However, when I started my own search, I quickly learned that— outside of ethnic neighborhoods—we marrow lovers were out of sync with the culinary majority. I remember looking up the topic in Waverley Root's culinary encyclopedia *Food*, which appeared in 1980, at the height of my marrow passion. Root, who had already chronicled the regional cooking of France and Italy, was no stranger to the odd mouthful. But his definition of marrow reads: "the rather mucilaginous matter which fills bones and is considered a particular delicacy by cannibals."

Cannibals! This hit a little too close to home, all the more so because my own way of eating beef marrow was not to poach it—the usual preparation—but to dig it raw from the bone and spread it onto a hot English muffin. The latter's heat softened the marrow's tallowy consistency until it was almost as smooth as butter. This raw stuff roused a much more visceral reaction in me than ham marrow ever did—a provocative mixture of pleasure and fear. From the perspective of today's health concerns, of course, there are good reasons to avoid raw bone marrow. But back then, mad cow disease was unknown and cholesterol-intensive fare had only just made the top of the food police's "Most Wanted" list. No, what made me uneasy was the simple fact that, unlike poached marrow (which tastes mostly of bone), raw marrow, even if tempered by the heat of toast, has the delicate but unmistakable tang of blood.

Interestingly, the full-throated potency of blood sausage makes me gag; it's the only offal-related food that I'm completely unable to eat. But bone marrow is different. It is not blood. It is what produces blood. There is no deeper, darker part of the body than the interior of our bones. To eat the soft, fatty, helplessly vulnerable vascular tissue that hides there is to put into your mouth the source of life itself. Ultimately, this fearsome intimacy proved too much for me. And I dealt with it the way the subconscious disposes of many problematic issues—by pushing it out of mind. Years would pass without even a sign that marrow had once been one of my favorite foods.

Then, recently, I began noticing marrowbones for sale at our local supermarket. They were large, and the marrow packed inside them smooth and creamy. Something in me stirred; I took a package home. How had I prepared these, anyway? I couldn't remember. So I searched through some cookbooks and learned how to cap the ends with foil and roast the bones in the oven. I brought them to the table and spread their contents on sourdough toast. I ate with relish, but also bemusement. Why had I been so unsettled by this stuff? It was rich, sure, but it was also delicious, and a little went a long way.

I was so delighted with our reacquaintance that I decided to acquire an authentic marrow spoon. I went online to eBay, and after considering a lovely silver one made by William Chawner II in 1830 for the mess kit of a military officer—the bidding had reached a little more than 300 dollars—I settled for an undated spoon by Cooper Brothers of Sheffield. Bidding was desultory; I nailed it for fifteen bucks. It was a full nine inches in length, with a long narrow scoop at one end and an equally long but even narrower scoop at the other—an admirable example of form in hot pursuit of function. I was thrilled with it.

Even so, I wasn't entirely happy. This beef marrow was a little greasier, a little soupier, than I remembered. I didn't realize why until we happened to buy some country ham slices and I was able to savor ham marrow again. It was thick and unctuous . . . somehow I had gotten beef marrow to be that way as well. And then it came to me: I used to eat it raw. I was appalled. Eating raw marrow was one of those things—like driving a sports car down a moonlit empty road with the headlights turned off—I didn't exactly regret doing but knew I could never do again.

• • •

I was also reminded that the marrow in the ham bones had been cured and smoked. Might there not be some circumstance in which beef bones were prepared that way, too? I returned to the Internet, went to my favorite search engine, and typed in "beef marrowbones smoked." To my astonished delight, I soon found myself at the website of a country smokehouse that specialized in beef bones. They were treated with a real maple-sugar cure and smoked over hickory, then sealed in Cryovac and frozen. They were also amazingly inexpensive—$3.50 a bone. There was, as it happens, a very good explanation for this (which is why I'm not revealing the name of the smokehouse): these bones were being marketed for dogs.

I pondered this. During my first marrow phase, I actually had a dog, a Siberian husky named Mick. He would sit patiently while I ate my toast, knowing his turn would be coming soon. It was a companionable thing; his utter interest in the proceedings helped make the meal. It would be an insult to his memory to let the phrase "canine treat" stand in my way now. The people at the country smokehouse took real pride in their bones; the only thing that kept them aimed at dogs was the cost of USDA inspection and the lack of demand for them as "human" treats.

I sent my order in.

You'll want to know, perhaps, how they were. Really, all I'd hoped. Since the bones were already fully cooked, I had only to warm them to room temperature. The marrow was—if not exactly like that of a ham bone—rich and silky, with a whispery taste of smoke. I felt the little stab of guilt that these days is an inescapable part of eating rich food, but nothing that put me off my feed. On the contrary. As I scoured out the last of the marrow, I caught myself thinking how nice it would be to now lie down on the living room rug and gnaw awhile on the bone.

BAGNA CAÔDA

> Bagna caôda is a dish for cold weather, to be made at least a
> month after the grape harvest, when the wine has all been safely
> cellared and a barrel of the new vintage is finally ready for
> broaching . . . Or, to put it another way, [it] is to be made at the
> beginning of the season when the peasant starts his rest, for this
> dish also celebrates the arrival of that short time of respite in a life
> of hard and endless work.
>
> —Giovanni Goria, *"La Bagna caôda"*

I first sampled *bagna caôda*—which literally means "hot bath"*—back
when I was young, freshly awakened to the adventure of eating, and in-
satiably alert to things good and new. It was a highly romantic evening.
Not for me, the guest, but for the couple who had invited me over; it
was their first social dinner since they had moved in together. There
was candlelight, there was wine, and there was this bubbling pot of
creamy, rich, but also subtly piquant sauce—the hot bath—into which
we dipped small pieces of raw vegetable and bits of bread.

I was already familiar—even overfamiliar—with both meat and
cheese fondues, but what I was eating that night seemed several degrees
more sophisticated, and not simply because it was so new. Even the
uninitiated could grasp what fondue was all about: Welsh rabbit eaten
as dip; quick-frying your own strips of beef. But *bagna caôda* was

---

*Caôda is dialect for *calda*, the feminine form of the standard Italian word for hot. *Caôda* is
now mostly spelled *cauda*, but I like the implacable foreignness of the circumflex, its hint of a
distant corner of a language where words still taste of local speech.

something you had to take on faith . . . that you would like it, that you would "get it," that it would, by the end of the meal, have filled you up.

Well, as Meat Loaf used to sing, two out of three ain't bad. I did like it—very much so—and it did—rather to my surprise—fill me up. That was enough at the time to persuade me that I also understood what was going on. But, on reflection, I'm not at all sure I did. Because, as much as I enjoyed it, as easy as it seemed to make, *bagna caôda* has always floated just beyond my grasp.

We all know dishes like this—where the ingredients are at hand and the appetite interested, but where any tentative movement toward them comes to a halt almost as soon as it begins, running smack up against some psychic tree branch that has fallen down and blocked the path . . . or, in this instance, a whole pile of them.

Bagna caôda is to the Piedmont region of Italy what chili con carne is to Texas or *feijoada* to Brazil: a dish that has become the embodiment of regional identity. However, its bare-bones simplicity can easily tempt the unwary outsider into understanding it too quickly, which is just what had happened to me. To grasp *bagna caôda*, I had to step away from the dish and look around—because, when eaten on its native turf, it is more than a meal; it is an event.

So Howard Hillman discovered when, exploring Piedmont one autumn, he stopped to watch the grape harvest at a small vineyard.* As he stood there, the owner of the plot drove up in his truck, emerging from it with

> an earthenware crock half-filled with a hot olive-oil-and-butter sauce, accented with anchovies and garlic. He also brought half a dozen liter bottles of hearty red wine and two wicker baskets— one overflowing with bread sticks and the other with fresh, raw vegetables, including scallions and cardoon stalks. All was neatly placed on a grassy patch under a venerable oak tree.
>
> The workers quickly assembled themselves around the fare, leaving a sitting space for me. Following the lead of my new-found friends, I selected a vegetable, dipped it in the hot sauce,

---

*He tells this story in *Great Peasant Dishes of the World*, a carefully detailed and often insightful collection of hearty simple dishes, many personally gathered by the author from almost everywhere in the world—an undeservedly neglected book that is well worth chasing down.

and savored the morsel. After quaffing some of the wine, I dipped into the sauce my next food choice, a crusty bread stick for which Piedmontese bakers are famous. With some practice, I was able to transfer each piece of food to my mouth without allowing a single drop of the clinging sauce to fall in my lap.

To get at the essence of *bagna caôda*, then, you must imagine yourself tired, famished, sitting in a field somewhere surrounded with comrades, a raw scallion in one hand and a tumbler of equally raw red wine in the other. The scallion is already half eaten, a dip and a bite at a time; the contents of the tumbler have been replenished more than once. The air is thick with the smell of garlic; every taste bud in your mouth is wildly pounding its tambourine; your body glows in the warmth that comes from ingesting an overload of butter and oil. Life, for the moment, is nothing but unalloyed delight . . .

Now try to imagine the transmogrifications necessary for this same dish to be set down before guests at a quiet little dinner party in a city townhouse. Or, more to the point, since this is the destination I wish to arrive at, for it to become a simple meal for two.

• • •

The Piedmontese do not usually serve the bagna cauda at meals, but at any time of the night or day they may feel hungry and thirsty, for it is a dish which essentially needs the accompaniment of plenty of strong coarse red wine, such as the local Barbera. It is also excessively indigestible, and is indicated only for those with very resistant stomachs. For garlic eaters it is, of course, a blissful feast.

—Elizabeth David, *Italian Food*

The issue of indigestibility we will get to in due course. For the moment, we have enough on our hands. First of all, notice that phrase "plenty of strong coarse red wine." *Bagna caôda* is as much about drinking as eating, and the dish itself is superbly engineered to encourage both. Taking a nip of olive oil before a bout of heavy drinking is reputed to impede for a time the body's absorption of alcohol—and for anyone who has shifted into full *bagna caôda* consumption mode, that nip is consumed in the first few bites. *Bagna caôda*, in other words, is serious partying fare.

Elizabeth David has a point, I suppose, about the garlic (more about this later, as well), but the single most important ingredient in this dish is the salted anchovies. (Note that—as is explained in detail in the advisory on pages 24 to 26—all preserved anchovies are salted. Those that come oil-packed in cans or jars have also been cleaned and filleted for consumer convenience.) And the same salty piscatory pungency that powers all that eating and drinking is also what pushes *bagna caôda* beyond the pale for eaters who can take a dish supercharged with garlic completely in their stride—although they may happily consume those same anchovies in sauces where their presence provides a piquant depth of flavor without any hint of its source.

Bagna caôda, however, has no such subtlety. In the world of the Piedmontese peasant, where the food, even when plentiful, was bland, starchy, and monotonously dull, the rare dish enlivened with the plangent presence of something like salted anchovies was an intensely desired event. Unlike today, when the fish's tiny rack of bones is carefully pulled away and discarded, in the last century it was considered a crunchy delicacy—as well as proof that the dish had been made with actual anchovies and not just the semisolid, powerfully flavored sludge retrieved from the bottom of the barrel.

That salted anchovies are so central to a peasant dish that originated in Piedmont—a mountainous, landlocked region far from the sea—is one of those culinary paradoxes that make food historians lick their lips. (By most accounts, the use of olive oil—another non-native ingredient—is relatively recent, that oil having gradually edged out butter and walnut oil as Piedmontese cuisine became more "Italian.") In *A Passion for Piedmont*, Matt Kramer explains that the Piedmontese taste for anchovies

> goes back five hundred years, to the expulsion of the Jews from Spain in 1492, a consequence of the Spanish Inquisition. Dispersed through Europe, the Spanish Jews—many of whom were traders and merchants—sought new homelands. Piedmont became one of them, notably the town of Cherasco, which for centuries had been a major stop on itinerant traders' routes through Europe. It was one of Piedmont's significant trading centers. Jews settled in Cherasco, and elsewhere, bringing with them their tastes and trade connections. One such taste was for anchovies. They were easily imported as they shipped well, packed in salt.

Here, once again, we find the classic pattern of peasant feasting. The bulk of the meal is made up of readily available, homegrown ingredients; the magic touch that pulls it all together is special without being either exotic or inordinately expensive. Typically, too, the amount used is—proportionately—quite small, not out of stinginess but because the dish requires no more.

These anchovies also satisfied something that reaches so far into the past that it predates humankind itself: the craving for salt. For much of Piedmont's history, salt was brought on muleback from the distant seacoast, a costly and heavily taxed commodity, a fact that gave value even to the briny sludge in which the anchovies were preserved. Tinged a rusty red by the fishes' entrails, it was carefully drawn from a bunghole set into the bottom of the cask and used as a ready-made seasoning, the Italian equivalent of Thailand's *nam pla*. The Neapolitans affectionately call it *la colatura*—which is to say, "the drippings."

As with garlic, there are sexual overtones to salted anchovies—certainly I can think of no better way to describe their aggressively clinging smell and viscerally pungent flavor. But "sexual" also embraces their peculiar asocial effect on the eater—they are so vitally crude that they transport you to a place where propriety simply doesn't exist. *Bagna caôda*, for those who originally feasted on it, was as loaded with gustatory significance as it was with calories—a potent dish made to satisfy appetites that, almost all year round, were gnawed at by never-satiated desire.

• • •

Everyone I spoke to from Piedmont had important advice for me about bagna cauda, focusing on digestion, breath, ingredients, and technique. Eat it with friends. Scramble eggs in the pot when most of the dip is gone and top with a grating of white truffle. Finish the meal with a bowl of broth to aid digestion. Sleep with the window open! One expert insisted on three-year-old anchovies, melted unboned into the dip, but told me I'd never find any and I didn't. Most recipes stuck to the formula of one head of garlic per person, peeled and cooked whole, sliced, or minced, in milk, cream, or even wine. Extra-virgin olive oil was used alone or combined with butter. A few walnuts were added to the dip. I tried them all and we ate bagna cauda at home with friends for a week. And slept with the window open.

—Faith Willinger, *Red, White & Greens*

On the whole, I think I was fortunate in not having any Piedmontese neighbors eager to advise me when I set out to make my first round of *bagna caôda*. Otherwise, I might never have realized how simple a matter the whole thing really is. Although I've always found the idea of roasted heads of garlic appealing, the practice reduces the cloves to the status of sour-tasting midget squashes, and the thought of simmering them into that state was even less inviting. However, I recalled Waverley Root's comment in *The Food of Italy* that "you have to be born in Piedmont to be able to make it successfully; a Milanese cook told me he had tried to produce it, but always wound up with a slimy thin unappetizing liquid," and I worried that the mass of puréed garlic was the necessary thickening agent. Thickener it surely must be, but it is neither necessary nor, as it turned out, traditional.

I had already started doing some research into the proportions of anchovy, garlic, butter, olive oil, and other ingredients used by various writers on the subject (see chart on page 14). Taking a quick glance down the list, which is organized in chronological order, you'll note— perhaps not unexpectedly—that olive oil has come to shoulder aside butter almost entirely as the primary fat and—here, I was surprised— that garlic has replaced anchovies as the dominating savory presence, to the point where recipes now call for a whole head of it per person.

Where, I wondered, did this notion come from? Browsing through Internet sites in Italy for more information, I happened upon an entire manifesto on *bagna caôda*,* written by Giovanni Goria, *vice-presidente nazionale dell'Accademia della Cucina Italiana*. As is the case with such documents, it is charged with passionate hyperbole, both in praise of the dish and in condemnation of those who in their attempts to civilize it have instead betrayed what is, in effect, he says, the Piedmontese national flag. And he particularly directs his thunder against those fellow countrymen who, for reasons of misdirected delicacy, either omit garlic from the dish altogether ("no garlic, no *bagna caôda*!") or— perhaps more insidiously—render it impotent by a long soaking and/or cooking in milk.

That such things are now ordinary practice in Piedmont is indisputable. Here, for instance, are directions for preparing garlic for

---

*It is, of course, written in Italian. With the help of various Internet translation services, I have rendered what follows into English (as I did the long quotation from Goria at the beginning of this essay).

Recipe Source	Serves	Butter	Olive Oil	Garlic	Anchovy	Liquid	Et Cetera
Best Food from Italy, Countess Morphy (1954)	not given	¾ cup	½ cup	4 cloves	6 whole salted	none	pinch salt, 1 white truffle (optional)
Italian Cooking, Elizabeth David (1965)	not given	3 oz.	3 oz.	3 oz.	3 oz.	none	none
Michael Field's Cooking School (1965)	6	¼ cup	none	1 tsp.	8 fillets	2 cups heavy cream	⅛ tsp. cayenne, 1 white truffle (optional)
Italian Regional Cooking, Ada Boni (1969)	not given	1 cup	¼ cup	4 cloves	6 fillets	none	salt, 1 small white truffle (optional)
Piemonte in Bocca, Alberta Lantermo (1979)	not given	¼ cup	½ cup	12 cloves, 4 crushed and 8 sliced	3½-oz. can	none	½ cup walnut oil
Gastronomy of Italy, Anna Del Conte (1987)	4	¼ cup	scant cup	4 cloves	5 whole salted	none	salt, 1 white truffle (optional)
Seasons of the Italian Kitchen, Darrow and Maresca (1994)	4	none	½ cup	1 to 2 heads[a]	4 small fillets	1 cup milk	
Red, White & Greens, Faith Willinger (1996)	4–6	none	1 cup	3 to 4 heads cooked in milk and then puréed	⅓ cup fillets	½ cup milk	2 tbs. chopped walnut meats
Recipes from Paradise, Fred Plotkin (1997)	6	1 cup	¾ cup	4 cloves	12 fillets	none	1 small piece of white truffle
The Man Who Ate Everything, Jeffrey Steingarten (1997)	not given	¼ cup	½ cup	1 large head	8 to 10 fillets	1 cup full-bodied red wine	
A Passion for Piedmont, Matt Kramer (1997)	1	1 Tbs.	½ cup	1 small head	2 whole salted	¼ cup milk	
A Passion for Piedmont, second recipe	1	1 Tbs.	none	1 large clove	1 whole salted	½ cup heavy cream	

[a]Peeled cloves are cooked in milk until soft, then puréed.

bagna caôda taken from a recipe at the website of a *grissini* manufacturer located in Alba, a small city in the heart of the province:

> Peel the garlic and place each clove to rest in part of the milk in a pot. Leave to stand for one night. This takes away any bitterness and adapts the flavor for the delicate palates of the year 2000, without betraying the original of the dish. Pour the fresh milk into a terra-cotta pot. Slice the garlic and add it. Cook gently for an hour or so. The garlic will turn into a cream.

Recipes like this help explain the note of desperation in Goria's voice when he admonishes his compatriots to remember that "garlic is not bad for you but actually beneficial to your health" and that "the odor of garlic is not unpleasant to the intelligent and open-minded but only to the ignorant and prejudiced." Then he himself, when he presents his own recipe, directs that the garlic, after it has been peeled and cut into tiny strips, be left in cold water—or, even better, in cold running water—for a few hours!

The mind, as they say, reels. And all the more so because what is going on here is not (as the phrase "delicate palates" suggests) a dislike of strong flavor so much as it is—and here I can think of no more politic way of saying this—sheer terror of garlic breath.

It is hard not to savor the frisson of pleasure that comes from discovering that Italians, who for decades have been held up to us as models of insouciant garlic consumption, are in truth as squeamish about it as your average Iowa farmer. (Even *Ricette di osterie di Langa*, a collection of Piedmontese inn recipes published by that august, terroir-affirming organization Slow Food, can't help remarking of *bagna caôda* that it "makes an excellent meal, unless you have a business or amatory engagement afterwards.")

However, the joke may yet be turned on us. This soak-and-simmer garlic treatment—despite the fact that it runs counter to the robust character of the dish—has already begun to percolate into the most up-to-date American accounts of Piedmontese cooking, where it is presented as the "real thing." Which only goes to show that authenticity, slippery as an eel, can never be grasped for long . . . unless you're willing to slam its head against the side of a table.

But this fearless garlic eater was not unnerved at the prospect of consuming a few cloves that had been minced, sautéed, and then allowed to dissolve into a simmering creamy mixture (and, more important, this lazy cook was not about to peel two whole heads of garlic for a casual supper for two). I was more interested in having as much of the sauce as I wanted without also ingesting my week's allotment of butter and olive oil at a single sitting.

This brings us back to the matter of indigestibility, and perhaps also of an aging digestive system. Had I been twenty years younger, I would have been thrilled by the idea of devouring, *solo mio*, half a cup of extra-virgin olive oil and a head of garlic, tempered by some butter and salt anchovy . . . and with a bottle or two of wine alongside. These days, however, I leave such feats of heroic consumption to those who still truly enjoy them; my more prosaic ambition was simply to feel comfortable sitting in at the feast.

To this end, I cast back to a rather *primitivo* version described by E. A. Reynolds-Ball eighty years ago in his *Unknown Italy: Piedmont and the Piedmontese*:

> Among the peasantry a favourite delicacy (often eaten on Sundays and festas) is a sauce popularly known as *bagna del pover omm*. It is composed of crushed garlic, anchovies, and milk, while a little pepper and salt are added. It is served with *cardi* (a vegetable resembling celery) or hearts of cabbages, and is eaten cold. Sometimes it is served hot in a *stufetta* (earthenware pot). This is placed in the middle of the table and each person tips his *cardi* into the *stufetta*.

Well, milk seemed maybe a step too far in the other direction, but it did appeal more to me than the heavy cream called for in dairy-intensive *bagna caôda* recipes, such as the one in *Michael Field's Cooking School*. I decided to start out using half-and-half, leaving open the option to move up a notch to light cream if this proved necessary. That way, I'd be consuming at most a quarter of the calories of an equal amount of olive oil.* Now it was time to sort out the vegetables.

• • •

As with most poverty-inspired dishes, when *bagna caôda* was reinvented for consumption in middle-class households, most of its

---

*For the sake of comparison, half a cup of olive oil contains about 960 calories, light cream, 240, and half-and-half, 160.

metaphoric significance was rubbed away. Where once *bagna caôda* had been the feast, now it became no more than the precursor to one. Still, despite having been demoted to the role of appetizer, *bagna caôda* appears to be pretty much the same. The *intingolo*—dipping sauce—is made from the same garlic and anchovies and oil, and vegetables are dipped into it, just as before. The only change seems to be the quantity that the eaters will ultimately consume.

Even so, something as simple as a change in quantity can radically affect the logic of a dish. Observe the effect it has had on the choice of vegetables—as, for instance, in those recommended in the recipe for *bagna caôda* that appears in the volume on Italy in Time-Life's *Foods of the World*: cucumbers, carrots, sweet red and green peppers, romaine, cherry tomatoes, and fresh mushrooms, with the option of substituting fennel, cauliflower or broccoli flowerets, white turnip wedges, or red or white radishes.

Such a selection would have astonished Piedmontese peasants even as it would have seemed to them laughably beside the point. However, when *bagna caôda* is eaten as an appetizer, its intake is measured by the mouthful—first a cherry tomato, next a piece of carrot, then a slice of green pepper or a rolled leaf of lettuce . . . a colloquy of individual tastes, each followed by an appreciative pause. A little of this goes a long way—that, after all, is the idea of an appetizer. But a whole meal made up of such mouthfuls would be tiresome to eat and difficult to digest. What was it about cardoons, I wondered, that produced an entirely opposite experience?

Fortunately, autumn is the time when cardoons appear—if they do at all—in American supermarkets, and I was able to find some in both of the stores near us. My reaction to them, though, was mixed. In Italy, the choicer specimens are grown with dirt piled up around the stalks to keep them tender and white. But this is too labor-intensive for American farmers, which results in a cardoon with a noticeably bitter taste that does not really cook away.

Still, I was glad to have had the opportunity to sample them, because Italian cookbooks don't give all that clear an idea as to what they're like. Cardoons may resemble celery in appearance, but in taste they have more in common with their close relation the artichoke. In texture (apart from their tough strands of celery-like fiber, which should be pulled away), they are nearer to, say, bok choy—that is, the stalks are both crisp and extremely succulent. That inherent juiciness makes cardoons easy to eat. And, because they are mostly water, a lot can be consumed before they fill you up.

What I wanted, then, was a selection of vegetables whose relationship to the dipping sauce would be one of affable concord. They should have sufficient character to stand up to their creamy coating but not so much as to impede the motion toward the next mouthful. Think, for example, of the difference between a raw red pepper and a roasted one, and you'll see what I mean—as you will if you give mushrooms, scallions, or broccolini a few minutes on a brazier or in a skillet. Add to these the other vegetables one would want to cook anyway—shallots, artichoke hearts, potatoes, and so forth—and I had plenty enough to place beside the bubbling pot.

It was time for the first trial run. As it happened, Matt was away for a few days on a family visit. So I made a quick foraging trip to the supermarket by myself, returning with a container of half-and-half, a little jar of anchovy fillets packed in olive oil, a huge portobello mushroom, a box of frozen artichoke hearts, a head of Belgian endive, a jar of roasted peppers, a handful of shallots, a potato, and a loaf of crusty Tuscan-style bread. Garlic, of course, we always have on hand. With all this prepped and spread out on the counter, I started making the sauce itself.

Anyone who has never made *bagna caôda* before will be amazed at the wonderful transformation that takes place as its few simple ingredients start to meld. I minced the garlic, then heated it to translucency in a small amount of butter as I worked the anchovy fillets and a little of the half-and-half into a paste with the back of a wooden spoon. I stirred this paste into the rest of the half-and-half, then into the butter-garlic mixture, and began to reduce it over a gentle heat. Even this brief treatment substantially altered the taste of the anchovies, smoothing their coarse rawness while barely muting their full, meaty flavor. I like preserved anchovies well enough, but I simply loved the taste of this.

At that point, unexpectedly, I found myself propelled back to the refrigerator for a small piece of steak. Even now, I'm not sure why that first lick of the spatula prompted me do this, or why I then sliced an edge from the raw meat and dipped it into the sauce as it cooked. All I know is that the tender and silken beef coated with that dark-edged luscious sauce was a flavor marriage made in heaven.

Admittedly, this was a perverse sort of homage—steak is *not* a traditional accompaniment to *bagna caôda*. In fact, one could easily argue that the presence of steak subverts the dish's meaning as much as its reincarnation as an appetizer. The moment that meat steps on the stage, the sauce has, at best, to share the spotlight; at worst, it gets shoved into the shadows. I should have been—I *was*—ashamed of myself. But this was one of those instances when my palate seized control of the throttle, moral or intellectual reservations be damned. And—as the saying has it—if you must sin, sin greatly. Tender strips of grilled steak dipped in *bagna caôda* might not be worth eternal damnation . . . but a few years in food-world purgatory, absolutely.

Happily, as good as the steak was, it didn't overwhelm or even outshine the other ingredients. The mushrooms were ravishing, the artichoke hearts delicious, as were the roasted red peppers and the shallots. The potato I didn't try—I was just too full. *Bagna caôda*, a stranger to my table for all those years, had come back to stay.

• • •

There are different ways to read the moral of this story, if indeed there is one. From one perspective, my experience should caution me not to poke too much fun at Italian garlic squeamishness—the currents of cultural determinism rarely run smoothly or clearly, and we can only swim against them for so long before we find ourselves marooned on a rather desolate sandbank. It's one thing to love the image of Italian peasants swigging wine and downing piles of cardoons dunked in anchovy sauce; it's another to think I could—or would even want to—replicate such communal feasting at my own kitchen table.

On the other hand, dishes as venerable as *bagna caôda* are still around today because they have learned that they must adapt in order to survive. Consider: As I type these words, a cold rain is falling outside our windows, and the light has that dull, flat grayness that comes when thick clouds block the rays of a feeble late-November sun. Inside, the furnace puffs and grumbles; outside, the last of the autumn leaves are being stripped from the branches and swept into the gutter. Matt, stepping out for a loaf of bread, feels the damp chill through layers of flannel and a water-repellant jacket.

Here in New England, we have plenty of food that offers succor on days like this—everything from baked beans to boiled beef. However, behind these dishes stands the memory of the old cast-iron woodstove, a massive presence casting off a veritable wall of heat. *Bagna caôda* speaks of another, more vulnerable world where heat reaches only partway into a room and cooking takes place over an uncertain and easily quenchable flame.

Ironically, for those of us whose lives are now so unthreateningly warm and cozy, it is the meal prepared at table in tiny clay pots heated by candle flames that creates the stronger sense of comfort. Where baked beans link the eater back to the salt-pork barrel, the molasses jug, and the burlap sack of dried beans—which is to say, to determined self-reliance in the face of long, hard winters—*bagna caôda* speaks more gently of a time of seasonal rest, of friends and family gathered together around the hearth. As Matt Kramer explains, ". . . *bagna caôda* is a dish designed for the despair-inducing fogs that settle into Piedmont in late autumn and through the winter. Not only is it warming and nourishing to bone-chilled bodies, but its communal nature warms the spirit."

These days, of course, we can taste only the merest rumors of such things in our *bagna caôda*. But this is the season of half-remembered tales, of delicious whispers—the slow time of the colder months enticing these to quietly unfold upon the attentive tongue.

BAGNA CAÔDA DEL OMM BORGHESE
[Makes about 1 cup/serves 2 as a meal]

¼ teaspoon kosher salt
4 or 5 large garlic cloves
1 tablespoon butter or extra-virgin olive oil
1 cup half-and-half or light cream
1 3-ounce jar anchovy fillets in olive oil, contents drained, or
   5 or 6 whole salted anchovies, split into fillets and spines
   removed, then rinsed of salt and patted dry with paper
   towels
dash of hot pepper sauce (optional)
selection of food for dipping (see suggestions below)

Spread the salt in a little circle on a cutting board, place the garlic cloves on it, and flatten these with a sharp blow of a chef's knife or Chinese vegetable cleaver. Mince the salt and garlic together until the garlic takes on an almost pulpy texture.

Heat the butter or olive oil in a small saucepan over low heat. When the butter has melted, transfer the minced garlic to the pan and cook it gently, stirring occasionally, until it turns translucent. Be careful not to let it brown or, worse, burn. If either happens, discard everything in the saucepan and start again.

Meanwhile, pour about a third of the half-and-half (or cream) into a small bowl and add the anchovy fillets. Use a rubber cooking spatula or the back of a wooden spoon to dissolve these in the half-and-half. Then, when the garlic is ready, scrape the contents of the bowl into the saucepan and stir in the remaining half-and-half, with, if you wish, a generous dash of hot pepper sauce.

Cook this mixture over low heat until it begins to thicken and the flavor turns rich and mellow, which will take 15 to 20 minutes.

When the mixture is thick enough to coat the back of a wooden spoon, preheat whatever serving vessels you will be using (see *La Stufetta* on page 24) with boiling water. Quickly wipe these dry and share out the *bagna caôda* among them. Serve at once, with your chosen accompaniments. The Piedmontese traditionally drink Barbera with this dish. That or any similarly fresh, uncomplicated red will be perfect. If you don't own fondue forks, substitute small bamboo skewers or salad forks.

Cook's Note. Although many recipes for *bagna caôda* call for a small white truffle to be grated into the sauce, in most cases it is marked as optional and in a few cases admitted to be a waste of a rare delicacy. Unless you live in Piedmont, I say forget it. More appealing to me are the versions that call for the addition of a few tablespoons of finely chopped walnuts—a gesture to yet another local food.

BAGNA CAÔDA CON BISTECCA E PEPERONI
[Serves 2]

4 to 6 shallots (depending on size), peeled and halved
a 10- to 12-ounce strip steak or similarly tender cut of beef
2 or 3 red bell peppers
thick slices of toast, cut into croûtons
1 batch of *bagna caôda*

Impale the shallots on skewers, cut side facing down. Grill these, the steak, and the red peppers over charcoal until the steak is medium rare (or to taste), the peppers are black all over, and the shallots are soft and charred around the edges—removing each from the grill when done. Let the steak sit on a cutting board while the peppers cool in a brown paper bag. When these are cool enough to handle, peel away the burnt skin, remove the cores and seeds, and cut the pepper flesh into bite-size pieces, saving as much of the juice as possible. Divide the pepper pieces and their juices into two shallow bowls. Slice the steak thinly and divide this along with the grilled shallots onto two plates. Bring everything to table, including the croûtons. When all the roasted pepper pieces have been eaten, stir their juices into the remaining *bagna caôda*.

BAGNA CAÔDA CON FUNGHI E SCALOGNI
[Serves 2]

Bagna caôda *turns out to be an excitingly delicious match with grilled or sautéed mushrooms, especially wild ones—mushroom foragers take note.*

> 1 tablespoon extra-virgin olive oil
> 1 bunch (5 or 6) scallions, trimmed of roots and wilted ends
>   and cut into 1-inch lengths
> 1 pound assorted fresh mushrooms, such as portobello,
>   shiitake, oyster, etc., or portobello alone, sliced if
>   necessary into generous bite-size pieces
> thick slices of toast, cut into croûtons
> 1 batch of *bagna caôda*

Put a tablespoon of olive oil in a large nonstick skillet and quickly wilt the scallion pieces over medium-high heat, stirring constantly. They should be soft all through and their sharpness made dulcet. Divide the scallions onto two plates and put the mushrooms into the skillet at the same heat. Cook, stirring, until their moisture has cooked off and they have begun to brown at the edges. Portion these out on the same plates that hold the scallions and bring to table with the croûtons in their own separate bowl.

Variazioni. Once you have made and eaten *bagna caôda* a few times, all sorts of possibilities will propose themselves, including re-combinations of the above (red peppers, steak, and mushrooms, for instance, or mushrooms, shallots, and pan-fried potatoes). As already noted, artichokes make an excellent pairing (asparagus, unexpectedly, does not). Other possibilities: fennel, celeriac, cabbage, broccolini, Belgian endive, roasted beets, and—here, a bit of wild surmise—fried codfish balls. The important thing is that *bagna caôda* already knows what it wants to sauce—as I've said, all you have to do is listen to it.

I haven't found any evidence that the Piedmontese use *bagna caôda* as a pasta sauce, although the idea certainly appeals to me. However, they do use it as a simple dressing for roasted red peppers, in a dish that is often called

PEPERONI ALLA BAGNA CAÔDA
[Serves 4]

2 large red bell and 2 large yellow bell peppers, roasted, peeled, and cut into strips
3 large ripe tomatoes, peeled, seeded, and cut into strips (see note)
4 anchovy fillets, torn to bits
1 garlic clove, finely minced
1 batch of *bagna caôda*, kept warm

Preheat a large serving dish in a warm oven. Place the strips of roasted red and yellow pepper in the dish, and cover with the pieces of tomato. Scatter over the bits of anchovy fillet and the minced garlic. Finally, pour the warm *bagna caôda* over everything and serve.

Cook's Note. Tomatoes are quickly and easily peeled if you put them in a sieve and slowly pour a kettle of boiling water over them. The skins then slip right off.

LA STUFETTA

"Authentic" *bagna caôda* servers appear now and then in cooking catalogs (see surlatable.com) and are not especially expensive, usually costing somewhere between ten and twenty dollars. These are mostly standard trattoria ware, glazed earthenware units that incorporate both the warming dish and the heating stand, the latter having an opening in the side where a tea candle can be inserted to provide a source of heat.

Now, a tea candle, pushed to the limit, can just about melt a pat of butter. This means you'll have to cram as many candles into the base of the server as possible—making the whole business look a little too much like a chore, especially when you start thinking about cleaning up afterwards. As an alternative, you might consider one of those little electric hot plate–like coffee warmers; they're inconspicuous and would do the job just fine.

However, I wanted something more in the spirit of the original, so I tracked down a pair of ceramic butter warmers—ramekins held in wire racks over a tea candle—at amazon.com for about eight dollars the pair. Each ramekin holds a single serving—about half a cup of *bagna caôda*—and because of its small size (and especially if you preheat it with boiling water) a single tea candle keeps the contents nicely warm.

Acciughe sotto Sale

> The anchovies must be the beautiful red ones of Spain, aged for at least a year, that, once rinsed of their brine, become fresh and fragrant again.   —Giovanni Goria, *"La Bagna caôda"*

All preserved anchovies have been cured in salt; this is what gives them their distinctively pungent taste and—when their quality is good—their resilient texture. The difference is that those that come in cans or jars have been cleaned, filleted, and repacked in oil. The best of these anchovies are very close in taste and texture to those that remain packed in damp coarse salt.

Anchovy fanciers often prefer the salt-packed variety because the

minimal processing—only the head and some of the entrails are removed—means that the fish has been steeping in its own juices up to
the moment that you yourself remove it from the salt, tear it in half,
and pull the fillets, skin and all, away from the bony spine. The result
has a rough-edged, primitive taste that sweeps you back in time as far
as any mouthful of food has the power to do. With the oil-packed fillets, that edge has been entirely smoothed away, leaving behind on the
tongue a salty, fishy lusciousness that is equally if very differently pleasurable. The choice is yours.

What you should pay attention to, however, is where the anchovy
was caught and packed, because different parts of the world give the
same name to related but by no means identical—or identical-tasting—
fish. The anchovy of the Mediterranean and the warmer Atlantic waters
off Europe (*Engraulis encrasicolus*) comprises only about 10 percent of
the world's catch, the bulk of which comes from Chile and Peru. These
South American fish (*Engraulis ringens*) are primarily ground into fish-
meal but—despite their inferior taste and texture—are also sold in bulk
containers to restaurants and pizzerias at less than half the price of the
European ones. (This may help to account for the lowly reputation of
the anchovy pizza in this country.)

While working on this piece, I tasted several different brands of anchovies, some packed in olive oil, some in coarse salt, with points of
origin in Spain, Morocco, and Italy. The cheapest were those from Morocco (Granadaisa brand), at $1.29 a can. The most expensive were
from Spain (Ortiz), a 3.36-ounce jar that cost $5.99. In the middle
range—$3.29—were the anchovies imported from Italy (Scarfano).
These also came packed in a jar, the oil tinted toward the bottom an encouraging shade of pink (meaning that the fillets had been packed with
some of their original juice).

All versions I tried had the red color and the rich, no-holds-barred
flavor of the true anchovy, but the inexpensive Moroccan fillet had a
mushy texture and an aggressively salty taste. The hand-packed Spanish anchovies from the Cantabrian fishing ports on the Bay of Biscay,
on the other hand, had a firm, meaty texture and a taste that was a
nicely balanced intensity of fish and salt. The salt-packed anchovies
from Italy, which were almost as expensive as the Spanish oil-packed
ones, were chewier still, with a pronounced, almost gamey, taste—a little over the top for me if eaten plain, but delicious when melted into a

bagna caôda. The good news is that the middle-of-the-road Italian anchovies from the supermarket were quite decent—possessing the texture, if not quite the same degree of flavor, of the top-of-the-line Spanish variety. They are a perfectly acceptable alternative for those wanting to ease their way into this dish.

Salted anchovies are easy enough to find online—the problem is not paying through the nose for them. After some searching, I found the Pennsylvania Macaroni Company, in Pittsburgh, which charges about half what others do for the very reputable Agostino Recca brand. They carry both a 1-kilo can of salted anchovies as well as a 20-ounce jar of fillets preserved in olive oil from Stella del Mare. If you visit their site, browse around. They also have very good prices for Greek and Spanish extra-virgin olive oils, Giuseppe Cocco pastas, salame, and other good things. 2010-2012 Penn Avenue; Pittsburgh, PA 15222; (800) 223-5928; www.pennmac.com.

THE REVIEWER AND THE RECIPE

No one has ever stepped twice into the same river. But did anyone ever step twice into the same cookbook?
—with apologies to Marina Tsvetaeva

Sometime in early 1997 I got an e-mail from Russ Parsons, food editor of the *Los Angeles Times,* inviting me to participate with him in two panel discussions at a food and wine exposition being organized by Italian food authority Giuliano Bugialli that summer in Stowe, Vermont. I had never done this sort of thing before and initially had no intention of doing it then. But Russ was persuasive; there were going to be a lot of food people attending whom I had never met; and I was brought up with the stricture that you ought to try something once before ruling it out of your life.

In other words, I have no excuse whatsoever for the fact that I ended up saying yes. But I did, and a few months later I was unpacking my bags in the complimentary room provided me at a Swiss chalet–like inn. I was already feeling that I might have made a big mistake—and not only because I had been given a tiny room directly across from the checkout desk (i.e., noisy and not very private), with no air-conditioning (i.e., claustral and hot) and a single high casement window that opened onto the rubbish bins under the outside stairs (did I say "noisy, not very private, claustral, and hot"?).

No, it was because tomorrow and the day after I would be appearing in front of an audience of other food professionals (the *paying* participants, mostly physicians, would understandably be heading for the wine- and food-tasting events) in two discussions—one on the state of home cooking and the other on the art of cookbook reviewing—two subjects about which my opinions were, at best, very mixed.

Even though cooking is an integral part of my life, I've never felt that it ought to be treated as a defining characteristic of a happy home. In fact, I won't be in the least surprised if in the next decade the rising prices of gas and electricity and the ever-appreciating value of free time will see preparing the family meal go the same way as sewing its clothing or hammering together its furniture. Certainly, there's nothing creepier than those obviously unused showcase kitchens in upscale houses that have all the marble—and all the warmth—of a mausoleum.

As to the art of cookbook reviewing, I already knew the score. Russ and I had had a preliminary meeting to discuss topics that this panel might cover. The first thing he said to me was that in his view, before anything else, the most important part of cookbook reviewing was *testing the recipes*. He probably thought that this was a point on which he and I would certainly agree, thus establishing a collegial bond from the very beginning. Sure, we might quarrel about the value of this or that cookbook, but certainly not about the ethical foundation from which we issued our judgments.

A moment of awkward silence followed. Then: "Russ," I said, "I never test recipes." Furthermore, although I didn't say this, the very idea fills me with something close to revulsion. There are countless cookbooks from which I have never made a single dish but for which I have the highest regard and which I would recommend unreservedly to anyone. In fact, I would be hard put, if asked, to point to almost *any* cookbook—apart from Fannie Farmer, my point of reference when I was nineteen and just starting to cook on my own—whose recipes I have faithfully followed. They exist, but they're the exception that proves the rule.

It's hard for a conversation to recover once it has begun by running full tilt into a stone wall. Even so, the panel discussion, as I remember it, was a success. Much of it had to do with the difficulties of getting good but quiet cookbooks noticed in a world where trendiness and celebrity rules. However, when the panel opened up its discussion to the audience, the first person to stand up was Mimi Sheraton, author of several commendable cookbooks and, of course, the former *New York Times* restaurant reviewer, as formidable now as she was when restaurateurs trembled at the mention of her name. "I just want to say," she said, "that I think it is *essential* for a reviewer to test *at least* six or seven recipes if they're going to give an honest evaluation of a cookbook."

Beside me, I felt Russ quiver slightly, like a terrier who knows a rat is about to get a good shaking by the neck. He cast a glance in my direction but, bless him, spoke not a word. This allowed me—and to this day I feel no embarrassment about it (apart from having gotten myself into the situation in the first place)—to just sit there with my mouth shut. No one but Russ even noticed, because no one in the tent expected any disagreement. Sage nods all around, and the discussion continued. Like a Unitarian caught up in a gathering of Evangelicals, I felt argument was simply beside the point. They were coming from one place, and I from another, a universe away.

* * *

Of course, it's not in the least surprising to me that people believe that recipes ought to work and that if they don't something must be wrong. As a writer of recipes myself, I lay out their workings as clearly and completely as Matt can make me. (She's the one with the logical mind and the eye for the fine detail.) And it pleases us both very much when someone writes to tell us that one of our recipes has become a favorite of their own. But this is the decent, caring, parental side of my personality, and it is not the part of me that cooks.

I have written before—most specifically when recounting my wood-fired bread oven adventures—that I do not take instruction gladly. Push a book in my hand and tell me I just have to read it and chances are it will be a decade before I can bear to pick it up. If someone tells me that this is the way something must be done, I take no pleasure in doing it unless I can somehow prove them wrong. As a student, I sat at the back of the classroom writhing in the self-inflicted agony of bad attitude. Facts only interest me when they are pieces to a puzzle I have already decided to assemble, and then I would rather find them after hours of rooting around in a junkyard than have them handed to me on a plate.

Of course, there are many things I had to learn by being taught them—it's just that the more that teaching was required, the less likely I was to learn. I took to reading like a fish to water; I learned the

niceties of spelling and grammar—so far as I have—only by uncon-
sciously absorbing the way they work. The things that I had to learn by
concentrated application were mastered at first just sufficiently to get
by—multiplication—and later not at all. My final grade in a required
freshman college course that combined physics and calculus was 11 out
of a possible 100; my physics professor told me that I didn't even belong in college, and I never doubted he was right.

Cooking, though, was never like that, maybe because I grew up observing a practiced cook at work, day after day. Although she has always liked to eat, my mother's idea of a truly enjoyable meal was one
made for her at a good restaurant. Apart from baking, she only occasionally took an interest in cooking for its own sake, until all her children had grown up and moved away. (Even then, for the most part, she
was drawn to the new but preferred cooking the familiar. Like many,
she compulsively snipped recipes from everywhere and stuck them to
her refrigerator, until it resembled a bulletin board. Ninety-nine percent
of these quietly turned brown from age, never to be noticed again.)
When I was young, she treated cooking as what it actually was for
her—a major household chore.

However, she was also a person who gets pleasure from doing
chores well. She liked her sheets ironed and the bed made with them to
have tight corners. (A bed wasn't made right, she taught me, until the
bedclothes were pulled taut enough to bounce a quarter.) She cooked in
the same spirit, feeling genuine satisfaction when she sat down to a
meal that had turned out the way it ought.*

I was not an observant boy nor one who hung out much in the
kitchen. It was my mother's spirit that I absorbed, not her expertise.
When I moved into my first apartment, in a Lower East Side slum, I
spent the first night on my hands and knees rubbing paste wax into the
worn wood parquet floor and buffing it with one of my undershirts. I
did it because that was what you did when you moved into a new
place. That I didn't have a clue about how to do it properly was of no
real matter. If the result was, well, idiosyncratic, that was okay with
me. I had no notion of turning the apartment into a showplace; I just
wanted to make it feel like mine.

---

*I put this in the past tense because my mother now resides in an independent living commu-
nity, her apron pretty much permanently hung up on the back of the kitchen door.

Cooking, like many other things in life, can be a matter of confidence leading to competence, not the other way around. The first time I boiled an egg, sautéed an onion, broiled a piece of meat, I drew on nothing but the experience of my mother's rigorous self-assurance. It didn't even occur to me to think that I might be tackling something difficult. These were things a person just rolled up their sleeves and did.

Sum all this up and what you have is a very ambivalent relationship with cookbooks. As records of how somebody else does their cooking, I find them fascinating and rewarding of study. But the moment that I sense them turning into an instructional lecture on how I ought to do things in the kitchen, I slam the door in their face.

• • •

One of the biggest sources of miscommunication between Matt and myself occurs when I suddenly fall in love with a recipe. This is because Matt takes the recipe as being instructions for making a dish, where, as often as not, its nuts-and-bolts aspect (which some might say is its only aspect) rarely holds my attention. Instead, I see a dish wildly signaling to me on the other side, begging to be let out. If there's a problem here, it's that I sincerely believe that I have read and understood the recipe. And I couldn't be more wrong.

Let me give you a simple example. A few years ago I was captivated by the following recipe, which appeared on the back of a box of De Cecco fusilli.

FUSILLI WITH TOMATO AND GREEN OLIVE SAUCE
[Serves 4 to 6]

4 quarts salted pasta-cooking water
4 tablespoons extra-virgin olive oil
2 garlic cloves, minced
4 anchovy fillets
1 pound puréed tomatoes
½ cup green olives, pitted and finely chopped
1 tablespoon chopped capers

4 or 5 chopped fresh basil leaves
salt and pepper
1 pound De Cecco fusilli
pinch of dried oregano

Turn on the flame under the pot of salted pasta water. Meanwhile, heat the olive oil in a skillet. Add the minced garlic and sauté to a golden brown. Crush the anchovies with a fork and add them to the skillet. Then stir in the tomato purée and the olives, capers, and basil. Taste to check the seasoning.

When the pasta water comes to a brisk boil, add the fusilli and cook until al dente, about 12 minutes. Drain. Add the sauce and sprinkle with oregano. Toss and serve.

I haven't looked at this recipe since I tucked it away in my recipe file. Now that I do, I almost have to laugh. What was it that had called out to me? I have never like cooked tomatoes; the recipe requires a whole pound of them. I had then only just begun to tolerate green olives; the recipe calls for a solid half-cup of them. But this didn't matter to me, because I simply ignored these things, whisking them away like gaudy tissue paper concealing a present I was eager to open. Here, approximately,* is how the dish came out. Let's call it

GEMELLI WITH ONION, BELL PEPPER, BLACK OLIVES, AND TUNA

[Serves 2 or 3]

4 quarts salted pasta-cooking water
½ pound gemelli or similar short pasta
2 tablespoons extra-virgin olive oil
½ teaspoon hot powdered red chile
½ teaspoon kosher salt

---

*I say "approximately" because at the time I first made this we ate it on plain boiled rice rather than with any sort of pasta. These days, however, we're going through a gemelli phase (see, for instance, the zucchini recipe on page 268), and for this sort of dish—right now—nothing else will do.

½ teaspoon crumbled dried oregano leaf (see note)
1 or 2 garlic cloves, finely minced
2 tablespoons decent-quality balsamic vinegar
2 hefty celery stalks, cut into bite-size pieces, with any
    attached leaves finely minced
1 large red salad onion, cut into bite-size pieces
1 yellow bell pepper, cored, seeded, and cut into bite-size
    pieces
12 or so Niçoise olives, pitted and shredded
1 6-ounce can olive oil–packed tuna, drained
½ dozen fresh basil leaves, torn to bits (see note)
black pepper to taste

Heat the pasta water over a high flame. When it reaches a rolling boil, add the gemelli. Let the water come back to a boil and then stir the pasta to make sure the pieces aren't sticking to each other or to the bottom of the pot. Adjust the flame to maintain a steady boil.

Heat the olive oil in a skillet. Add the powdered chile, salt, crumbled oregano (if using), and minced garlic. Let this cook over medium-low heat until the garlic turns translucent, about 2 minutes. Then stir in the balsamic vinegar.

I cut up the vegetables while the pasta water is heating and add them to the skillet in the order in which they appear in the ingredient list. If you have everything prepped ahead of time, start about 10 minutes after the pasta water has been turned on. Let the celery cook alone for 3 or 4 minutes before adding the onion; then let this mixture cook for 3 or 4 more minutes before adding the bell pepper, giving everything a thorough stir each time a new ingredient is added.

Continue cooking, occasionally tasting the vegetables for doneness. Each of them should be tender, but still crisp and succulent. At this point, turn the heat down to low and stir in the olives, tuna, basil, and pepper, breaking the tuna apart with a fork. Cook, stirring gently, until everything is heated through. Finally, stir ½ cup of the pasta water into the sauce, drain the gemelli, toss it thoroughly into the sauce, and serve in warmed bowls.

Cook's Notes. Tuna: As far as I'm concerned, water-packed canned tuna tastes like laundered tuna, with all the flavor washed away. Most oil-packed canned tuna, on the other hand, is too mushy. We stick to an

Italian-style olive oil–packed solid light tuna—like Chicken of the Sea's Genova Tonno—which is firm in texture and full of flavor. Even better, if you can find (and afford) it, is the genuine article, imported from Italy and usually packed in jars.

Oregano/Basil: If I have lots of fresh basil at hand, I add a generous amount of it and omit the oregano entirely. Otherwise, I use a combination of both herbs or just the oregano by itself.

In some ways, it's not hard to see what happened when I appropriated this recipe: the red bell pepper replacing the abhorred tomatoes; the tuna subbing for the anchovies (where's the meat?!). However, to me, the most interesting factor is that, not so long before, I had done some extended experimenting with caponata, the Sicilian sweet-and-sour vegetable appetizer.* This not only explains where the extra ingredients— celery, onion, balsamic vinegar—came from, but it also points to why the De Cecco recipe drew me in the first place. We had, in fact, often used our caponata as a pasta sauce. But caponata is a little on the heavy side and it takes time to make; this dish was lighter and it could be prepared while the pasta cooked.

In other words, one recipe had functioned as a sort of fulcrum to shift my thinking about another one. The result was a dish that retained some connections with both but fell more directly in line with our taste. We're still eating it several years later and still finding it delicious.

Surely, an important aspect of any recipe is its use as a tool for understanding other recipes. The most familiar example of this, perhaps, is when one recipe is compared to another in a search for the "perfect" version of a dish. Ours is a competitive society, and in competition ranking is everything. Who would buy *The Place-and-Show Cookbook: Recipes That Almost Won a Blue Ribbon*? But to ask the question is to show the sterility of the approach: the greatest value recipes offer is their strange and wonderful display of diversity. *Iron Chef* to the contrary, cooking is not, at its best, a competitive sport. Some recipes are surely better than others—and without doubt some are more clearly explained than others—but beyond that what makes for perfection gets increasingly difficult to say.

---

*See the chapter entitled "Caponata Siciliana" in our book *Pot on the Fire*.

For example, Russ Parsons, in his *How to Read a French Fry*, says in the section on cooking eggs: "Even fried eggs should be cooked gently. Use medium heat rather than high to keep them from forming that tough, brown, frizzled bottom." But there are those for whom that brown, frizzled bottom is the whole point of a fried egg. "Place [the eggs] one by one in smoking hot oil," writes Robert Courtine in *La Vraie Cuisine française*. "Put a pinch of salt on each yolk and fold in the white, as it sets, with a spoon. Brown lightly, drain away the fat, and serve." Kitchen science may explain why eggs fried the one way or the other end up the way they do, but it takes no position on which we should prefer. In fact, knowing both schools of thought gives us a richer conception of what a fried egg is.

Recipe collectors tend to fall into two groups: those who save recipes for every dish that catches their fancy and those who essentially save the same recipe over and over again. Before I carted the bulk of my recipe clippings to the dump, you would have found a single file folder containing, say, twenty or thirty recipes for French onion soup. I didn't collect these because I thought that one day I'd hold a cook-off to discover which one was best. No, like a teenage boy who covers his bedroom wall with photographs of Christina Aguilera, I just couldn't have too many glimpses of the same desirable object.

A fundamental idea behind *Simple Cooking* is that one of the best ways to learn more about a dish is to get a bunch of recipes arguing with each other. But until I started wondering why I review cookbooks the way I do, I hadn't given any thought at all to how recipes for entirely different dishes might have something to say to each other, let alone profoundly influence my reaction to one I happened to spot on the back of a fusilli box.

If this is the case, and—especially after a lifetime of looking through cookbooks—I think that it surely is, it is likely that the new recipe that will interest me the most will be the one that I can use to give shape to some nebulous longing that is already alive and stirring within me. This might mean that the true test of a recipe lies somewhere else than in its making.

Back in the late eighties, I wrote a cookbook review column for *Book World*, the Sunday book review supplement of *The Washington Post*. They would ship me box after box packed with cookbooks, and I found less and less to say about any of them . . . except, "Hold!

Enough!" They didn't require that I test recipes, but they emphatically wanted me to focus my reviews on those cookbooks for which recipe testing was the only possible response—at least if the response was to be positive. So, instead, I decided to quit.

By then, however, I could usually learn everything there was to know about that sort of book by looking at its dust jacket. I knew it would be full of delicious recipes, because all cookbooks are full of delicious recipes these days. I knew almost all the recipes would work, because cookbook publishers spend lots of money to ensure that they do work, after their fashion. But the reason I didn't have to even open the book was because I knew that the recipes in these books were—in any meaningful way—pretty much all the same. "Wilted Mustard Greens with Shallots and Sherry Vinegar." "Chard Stalks Sautéed with Garlic, Parsley, Chives, and Thyme." Deborah Madison? Alice Waters? Molly O'Neill? Diana Shaw? Georgeanne Brennan? Sarah Schlesinger? Susan Sontag? Who cared?

Well, to be honest, a lot of cookbook buyers. These books sweep us off to a world where page-long ingredient lists have no connection to grocery bills, where what we make turns out just right and, most wondrously, makes everybody at the table happy. In this world, in other words, good food is what dinner is all about—whereas in real life, more often than not, it is little more than a fueling stop or the family jousting field. Like romance novels, cookbooks are powered by the fantasy of happy endings.

If you think I sound a little sour here, you're right. In fact, I used to believe the world conveyed in these books was all a sham. But that conviction has been beaten down by the sheer weight of the opposing view. Nowadays, I take a more conciliatory position. One definition of a pessimist is someone forced to spend too much time in the company of optimists. In the same way, I feel better the more I keep away from such books . . . and so that's just what I do.

Finding cookbooks that truly seize hold of my imagination is hard enough, but explaining why they do so is even harder, since each succeeds at this in its own individual and not always easily explicable way. Consequently, if I've never felt a whit of guilt recommending cookbooks without first testing their recipes, I'm wracked with it regarding those to which I haven't been able to find the time or inspiration to give their due—for instance, Ken Hom's *Easy Family Recipes from a Chinese-American Childhood*, Arthur Schwartz's *Naples at Table*,

David Lebovitz's *Room for Dessert*—as well as more deeply buried treasures like Richard Hosking's *A Dictionary of Japanese Food*, Larry Zuckerman's *The Potato*, and Irving Davis's *A Catalan Cookery Book*.

How to Read a French Fry is a case in point. It contains plenty of recipes, but for the most part I found myself skipping over them, appealing though they were, because I was so engrossed in the text itself. Time after time, Russ dives into the esoteric ocean of kitchen science and pops back up to the surface with another fascinating food fact alive and wriggling in his mouth: how the seasoning of cast-iron skillets works; why food doesn't fry as well in fresh oil as it does once the oil has been used a few times; why brining makes the best (and possibly the only really effective) tenderizing marinade; why custard sauces are made on top of the stove while custards themselves are baked in the oven. It's hard to imagine anyone spending time with this book and not making radical refinements in the way they ordinarily cook.

For me, it was, especially, the revelation that braising tough cuts of meat over high heat, if done properly, produces buttery tender chunks rather than the shreds associated with low-heat braising. Here is about as clear an example as you could want of a good food writer getting you interested in trying a recipe—even propelling you straight to the stove. And I went to mine, for once, sincerely expecting to stick to Russ's recipe. The method was new to me, the ingredients all appealed to me . . . what was to change? But as soon as I got down to his specific instructions, a familiar hand seized hold of the tiller and headed the ship off on a different course. Here is the recipe, with my divergences spelled out in italic print.

MUSHROOM POT ROAST
(Adapted from *How to Read a French Fry* by Russ Parsons)
[Serves 6 to 8]

1 3½-to-4-pound chuck roast
salt
1 750-milliliter bottle dry red wine
3 tablespoons olive oil
1 pound yellow onions, sliced
½ pound carrots, sliced
6 garlic cloves, smashed

1 celery stalk

1 bay leaf

stems from 1 bunch parsley, plus ¼ cup finely chopped fresh
   parsley

1 whole clove

½ cup red wine vinegar

2 tablespoons butter

1 pound button mushrooms, cleaned and quartered

freshly ground black pepper to taste

*When we went to the supermarket to buy the chuck roast, we found
whole Australian leg of lamb on sale. Russ has a recipe for whole leg of
lamb, too, but for various reasons it was more than I wanted to tackle.
So I boned our leg of lamb and cut three slabs of it—total weight
3½ pounds—to substitute for the beef, reserving the rest for other uses.*

Sprinkle the roast with salt on both sides and place in a 1-gallon ziplock plastic bag. Add the wine, seal the bag, and refrigerate for 8 hours,
or overnight, turning occasionally to make sure all the meat is covered
with wine.

*I started marinating the meat as soon as I had cut it up, which meant it
was in the wine for about 24 hours instead of 8. I also drank a glass of
it (quality check) before pouring the rest of the bottle over the meat.*

Preheat oven to 450°F. Heat the oil in a Dutch oven over medium-high
heat. Remove the roast from the bag, reserving the wine, and pat it dry
with paper towels. Place the roast in the Dutch oven and brown well on
both sides, 5 to 10 minutes per side.

*Instead of a cast-iron Dutch oven, I went with a Calphalon nonstick
5-quart casserole, since I knew that anything in which meat was
cooked for hours at high heat was going to be no joke to clean.*

Transfer the roast to a plate. Pour off all but 1 tablespoon of the rendered fat from the Dutch oven and reduce the heat to medium. Add the
onions, carrots, and 4 of the garlic cloves, and cook until the vegetables
are slightly softened, about 5 minutes.

As you will see, Russ plans to discard the vegetables, whereas we planned to eat them. (We like soft, mushy vegetables.) With that in mind, I doubled the amount of carrots and cut up everything in bite-size chunks instead of slices, including the celery. Also, since I had three pieces of meat to brown, I sautéed the vegetables separately in half the olive oil. When that was done, I started preheating the oven (about half an hour later than Russ).

Cut the celery in half. Tie both stalks together with the bay leaf and parsley stems using kitchen twine and insert the clove in a celery stalk, to make a bouquet garni. Add the bouquet garni and the reserved wine to the vegetables and simmer for 5 minutes.

As noted, I treated the celery—cut in chunks—as another vegetable. I left out the rest of the bouquet garni: no parsley stems, no bay leaf, no clove. After all, I had lamb on my hands, not beef. Instead, I added 1 teaspoon of powdered chile and a pinch of crumbled rosemary. As to the parsley—if I'd had some, I would have used it, but we rarely buy it, because 70 percent of it ends up rotting in the refrigerator.

Add the meat and vinegar and place a sheet of aluminum foil loosely over the meat. Cover the Dutch oven with a tight-fitting lid, place it in the oven, and cook until the meat is easily pierced with a sharp fork and is falling off the bone, 2 to 2½ hours. Every 30 minutes, turn the meat and stir the liquid and vegetables. If the level of the liquid gets too low, add up to 1 cup water, a little at a time, to prevent the meat and vegetables from scorching.

I left the pot untouched for the first hour and then began the stir-and-turn routine. As predicted, the lamb took 2½ hours. (Even though I had drunk some of the wine, there was plenty of liquid right to the end.) Also as predicted, the lamb was tender enough to eat with a spoon.

Transfer the meat to a plate and cover it with aluminum foil to keep warm. Pour the liquid and vegetables into a strainer over a bowl, pressing on the vegetables to get as much liquid as possible; discard the vegetables. Set the liquid aside until the fat floats to the top.

Discard the vegetables?! I'd almost as soon discard the meat! I did strain out the liquid, though, and I spooned off and discarded the fat.

Wash out the Dutch oven. Skim off the fat from the settled liquid and return the meat and liquid to the Dutch oven. Keep warm over low heat.

Melt the butter in a large skillet over medium-high heat. When the butter has foamed and subsided, add the mushrooms and the remaining 2 garlic cloves and cook, tossing, until the mushrooms are lightly browned, about 5 minutes.

I like mushrooms and had intended to add them as Russ directs. But after I tasted the dish, I decided it had plenty enough going on already, with its intense, mouth-puckering, full-flavored reduction of wine, vinegar, and meat juices. Of course, I also had all the undiscarded vegetables to serve along with the meat. So, at this point, I beached my craft and let Russ sail on alone.

Add the mushrooms to the pot roast and cook for 15 minutes over low heat to marry the flavors. Season to taste with salt and pepper, garnish with the chopped parsley, and serve.

We let everything rest in the refrigerator overnight and ate it the next day, serving it in large soup bowls (at the bottom of mine was a thickly buttered slice of sourdough toast).

Well, there you have it. Obviously, the dish that I prepared is, in spirit and—in large part—execution, Russ Parsons's. But he would not, I think, want to be held responsible for what ended up on our table, let alone have his book judged on the strength of it (at least if one sets aside the notion that "capacity to survive abuse" might be as good as any other way of judging a recipe). Also, Russ would probably tell me (and you) that I don't know what I missed by not trying it his way.

Who can argue with that? Not me. But then I didn't set out either to improve his recipe or to mess around with it; I just went and *made* it. Furthermore, if you happened to ask me whether you ought to try the recipe yourself, I'd answer quite honestly: "Yeah, you should. I did and I liked it a lot." And, most likely, I'd leave it at that. After all, you will be stepping into an entirely different cookbook.

MAXIMUM MARMALADE

> For a book on the history of marmalade, I am seeking informa-
> tion on how marmalade has developed in former British and other
> European colonies since it was first taken there.
> —C. Anne Wilson

When this query appeared in *Petits Propos Culinaires** back in 1984, I
had just acquired my first computer, a Systel II. Remembered by few
and missed by none, the Systel's selling point was that it was designed
to use an electric typewriter as both its keyboard and its printer, which
made it very affordable for anyone, like myself, who already owned
such a typewriter.

There were certain drawbacks to this arrangement, one of which I
discovered the first time I used it to print out the text of my food letter,
Simple Cooking. The typewriter had never before been subject to such
relentless use, since no mere human could type so fast for so long. Its
anguished clatter reverberated down the legs of the typing table to
pound a loud tattoo on the floor. My landlord lived directly beneath
me, and after half an hour of this he went storming out of the house,
slamming the door behind him. I didn't know which to expect first,
the self-destruction of the typewriter or the arrival of the eviction
notice.

However, the Systel II was ideal for tasks like copying out a bunch
of marmalade recipes from my old American cookbooks, because with

---

*An eccentric, scholarly publication about food and foodways that seldom treads the com-
mon path and often heads resolutely where angels dare not tread.

it they could easily be proofed, reorganized, and annotated without the mind-numbing tediousness of endless retyping. And, as it happened, I uncovered some truly odd variants, including one marmalade made from green tomatoes and pickled limes, another from rhubarb and figs, and another still from "oring roots," an ingredient Wilson would later identify not as orange tree roots (as I had wildly surmised) but as eringo, "a well-known aphrodisiac of Tudor and Stuart times."

As far as I was concerned, all this effort—I eventually sent off a couple dozen recipes—had nothing to do with cooking and everything to do with getting a pat on the head from a culinary historian whose *Food and Drink in Britain* had greatly impressed me. I was fond of marmalade, it is true, but I was even fonder of marmalade's mystique. My grandmother's kitchen shelves were filled with stoneware crocks, both large and small, in which James Keiller & Son Dundee Marmalade was then sold. Even when empty, they possessed a majestic solidity that not only made them impossible to discard but suggested a fierce loyalty to secret receipts, uncompromising standards, and eccentric production methods. Marmalade wasn't something you *made*; it was something you went to a fancy grocer in Boston to *select*.

And what a choice there was. It ranged from the relatively ordinary—Chivers Olde English, Robertson's Golden Shred, the above-mentioned James Keiller & Son Dundee—to the increasingly singular, such as Frank Cooper's Coarse Cut Vintage Oxford or Wilkin & Sons Tiptree 'Tawny' Orange. Still, no matter how they sliced it—coarse cut, thin cut, chip cut, silver shred—or how long they aged it, every serious British producer agreed on one fundamental rule: to be authentic, it must be made with the impossible-to-find-in-America, famously bitter Seville orange. As the British food historian, writer, and rather prodigious marmalade maker Alan Davidson states unequivocally in *The Oxford Companion to Food*: "Only bitter oranges can be used to make proper marmalade, which depends not only on their bitterness but also on the aromatic rind, which is quite different from that of the sweet orange."

Although this sentence appeared in print decades after the time about which I write, the unspoken sentiment, like some irrefutable first cause, cast a disheartening pall over the idea of making marmalade— real orange marmalade—in these United States. "No Seville oranges, dear chap? Don't waste your time."

The worst of the thing is that there's more than a little truth to this. It lies in that phrase "proper marmalade," which can roughly be translated as "marmalade as we Brits know and love it." Once you've tasted the stuff, you don't forget it, especially if you're susceptible to its dour charm. It is, after all, the only fruit preserve with an attitude problem. Where the others are all lambs, this one is a lion. Ordinarily, sugar works as a calmative, soothing everything into unctuous fruitiness. With marmalade, it plays the lion tamer, which with whip and chair just manages to keep its bitterness at bay.

Traditional marmalade makers have gotten so good at maintaining this fine edge of control that they have gradually learned how to persuade the Seville orange to balance itself on beach balls and jump through flaming hoops. Read, for instance, this description of how Wilkin & Sons Tiptree 'Tawny' Orange is made:

> This rich dark marmalade is made from Seville oranges that are cooked with sugar and nothing else. The dark colour and spicy flavour come from oranges that have been cooked whole, then cooked with sugar, left to cool overnight and cooked a third time to caramelise the sugar—a quite unique product that is well worth the extra effort in the making.

"Unique," for once, seems almost an understatement.

There have been many efforts to put a finger on what distinguishes marmalade from other preserves—it is made only from citrus fruits, it contains chunks of peel, it has no added pectin—but what makes it special is its potent mixture of the noble and the uncouth. It is, in other words, the Rob Roy of fruit jams—an analogy that is all the more apt when one learns that it was the Scots who first ate marmalade for breakfast . . . and what it was that marmalade replaced.

• • •

> [At breakfast] there is always, besides butter and toasted bread, honey and jelly of . . . preserved orange peel.
> —Bishop Pococke, *Tours of Scotland* (1760)

It was the Scottish habit, well into the eighteenth century, to start the day with a neat dram of Scotch whiskey. It warmed the body (which was more than the smoldering chunks of peat in the fireplace could do), provided the system with a salutary slap, and boosted the spirits sufficiently to face another gray and drizzling day. And, whatever you might think of the habit, to try it once is to know that it is far from hedonistic—but rather on a par with a cold bath or a dose of cod-liver oil. And this analeptic aspect was underscored still further when the whiskey had been transformed, as it often was, into a tonic by the addition of medicinal herbs and spices, following a formula in which bitter-orange peel usually played an important role.

After the dram came breakfast itself, which for most Scots was one or another variation of oatmeal mush, either poured into a bowl or fried into a cake and eaten with butter and cream. Those who could afford to might also eat some smoked fish or a slice cut from a mutton ham or a singed sheep's head. The very wealthy had all of the above. Everything was washed down with buttermilk or—more popularly among the menfolk—a jug of ale.

However, at just this time the rising popularity in tea drinking touched off a sea change in Scottish breakfast habits. Tea by itself might never have been able to bring this about, but its adoption coincided with a drop in the price of sugar. Who wanted hot mush and ale when with the teapot, creamer, and sugar bowl came barley bannocks, wheaten scones, oatcakes, and toast, served with preserves made of black currants, raspberries, and strawberries, along with the now everpresent bitter-orange marmalade?

The morning dram proved not nearly so easy to abandon as the ale. Dr. Johnson encountered both the dram and the newfangled Scottish breakfast during his tour of Scotland and the Hebrides and made a point of mentioning the universality (among males) of the former, even as he waxed poetic about the latter.

> A man of the Hebrides, for of the women's diet I can give no account, as soon as he appears in the morning, swallows a glass of whisky; yet they are not a drunken race, at least I never was present at much intemperance; but no man is so abstemious as to refuse the morning dram, which they call a skalk . . .
>
> Not long after the dram, may be expected the break-fast, a meal in which the Scots, whether of the lowlands or mountains, must be confessed to excel us. The tea and coffee are accompanied not only with butter but with honey, conserves, and marmalades.

> If an epicure could remove by a wish, in quest of sensual gratifica-
> tions, wherever he had supped he would breakfast in Scotland.

Still, the ritual of the skalk was doomed to fall from the favor of all but
rural diehards. Caffeine and alcohol are uneasy companions, especially
in the morning, because they propel the drinker in contrary directions.
Alcohol prepares you to face hard physical work in the cold outside; a
dose of tea or coffee, the rigors of indoor occupations where intellectual alertness is the primary concern. The morning snort, whatever its
restitutive benefits, aided not a whit in this.

To the Scot who cherished not the alcohol itself but the austere
cathartic it embodied, the disappearance of the dram threatened to reduce the breakfast table to nothing more than a simpering synecdoche
of self-indulgence. Casting about for something—anything!—among all
this feminine frippery that might offer an echo of that manly physic, he
found it in the pot of marmalade. There, in profuse quantity, was the
same bitterly astringent peel that had for centuries been prescribed to
revivify the heart, calm the stomach, and cure rheums, coughs, and
colds.

This link between marmalade and the virile tonic that preceded
it is quite possibly the reason why the former managed to sustain its
refractory nature over the centuries: it was abetted by a substantial
constituency who possessed the same qualities themselves. To put it
another way, marmalade, at least the tough-love variety, is preemi-
nently a guy thing, and not only in terms of consumption. As Alan
Davidson notes in his entry on marmalade in *The Oxford Companion
to Food*, "A minor but interesting facet of this British attainment is
that, among all the numerous culinary operations carried out in British
kitchens, marmalade-making is one which is quite often performed by
men."

I was a pipe smoker during the same period I was developing my
taste for this sort of marmalade. Both of these are hallmark pursuits of
the English male, and it was impossible not to notice the uncanny resemblance of the language of the English marmalade maker to that of
the English tobacconist. Not only do they share such terms as "coarse
cut," "fine shred," "vintage," "tawny," and the like—to the point where
in some instances it is hard to tell by name alone which is which
(MacBaren's Golden Ambrosia, Stute's Thick Cut, Thomas Radford's

Old Scotch)—but both emphasize the rough-and-tumble physicality so appealing to the masculine temperament.

Since the pipe smoker can be sent out of the house or at least into the study when he craves this kind of pleasure, pipe tobacco has it all over marmalade when it comes to macho noxiousness. However, the comparison prompts us to shove aside the genteel, even aristocratic, pretension with which British firms wrap their products. The truth is that any touch of genuine nobility about marmalade comes not from the English kings and queens who have lent it their patent but from the Scottish laird who sought out a decoction to break his fast that was as rebarbative as himself.

· · ·

> The imported English and Scottish marmalades also have a role, often as a small food-gift. Although these marmalades are widely purchased, they tend not to go into everyday use, but to sit for long periods on the refrigerator shelf before a suitable occasion can be found to broach them. It is probably true to say that interest in Seville orange marmalade [in the United States] . . . is now at a low ebb.
>
> —C. Anne Wilson, *The Book of Marmalade*

What we are talking about is how a foodstuff can come to resonate with a meaning that words can only approximately capture and certainly never hope to define. Other citrus marmalades, such as lime, grapefruit, and lemon—however delicious, however bitter, however similarly produced—will never have the same plangency for those able to pick up the wavelength of the original.

The British are dubious, I suspect, that most Americans possess the equipment to detect it, and mostly, I think, they are right. American men aren't entirely indifferent to the hairy Harris tweed model of masculinity, but they don't pursue it with anything like the same fervor. I certainly know guys who are aggressive marmalade fanatics. But they are more the exception than the rule, and I don't think that even they know of the existence of such ultra-puissant versions as Tiptree 'Tawny' Orange.

If you don't pick up on that resonance, bitter-orange marmalade becomes just another choice on the upscale market's preserve shelf. And to the extent that we have become indifferent to it, it isn't because we fail to appreciate its special qualities but because those qualities have become less special. With fruit-laden, high-end American products like Stonewall Kitchen's Peach Pomegranate Jam, American Spoon Foods' Sour Cherry Preserves and Wild Thimbleberry Jam, and Clearbrook Farm's Oregon Boysenberry Preserves to choose from, who's going to reach for the dusty jar of British marmalade? Genuine enthusiasts, without doubt, but apparently not me. Because, without my really noticing it, once preserves like these entered my life, my interest in buying and eating marmalade quietly faded away.

Even so, I continued to *think* about it . . . and that brings me back to C. Anne Wilson's query and my immersion in that horde of old American cookbooks. If you have made marmalade before, you will be generally familiar with the process. For orange marmalade, you are essentially directed to clean and cut up the fruit, cover it generously—sometimes very generously—with water, and boil it for about half an hour. Then you add sugar and cook the mixture down until it sets. However, I soon noticed that recipes written before the Depression often directed that the marmalade be *made without adding any water at all*.

If I had been paying more attention—after all, I wasn't thinking of following any of these recipes—I would have noticed that, prepared as directed, these marmalades would have been too thick to spread. And, in fact, this is the way the preserve was made before commercial producers discovered that adding water greatly reduced the amount of fruit required, while the resulting "spreadability" persuaded the public to buy it regardless. (Previously, if softening was required, it was done at the table—perchance as Margaret Dods suggested in *The Cook and Housewife's Manual*—by liquifying the paste "ex tempore with a little tea.")

This misreading, though, was a fortunate thing, because what came to me in a flash was that there was no reason except economy in contemporary recipes for that liquid to be water. Economy, of course, is a potent persuader, especially in hard times. But these days it shouldn't cost all that much more to replace the water with the fruit's own juice. Wouldn't that produce a marmalade as equally fruit-intensive as any carriage-trade preserve?

What got me to finally put this notion to the test was the introduction several years later of half-gallon cartons of not-from-concentrate orange and grapefruit juice. It embarrasses me to think that the reason I procrastinated was a reluctance to squeeze the juice from all that additional fruit . . . but the evidence certainly could be read that way. In any case, I began my experimenting by replacing the water in a standard grapefruit marmalade recipe with not-from-concentrate ruby red grapefruit juice.

The thick, tawny-colored result was noticeably different from ordinary grapefruit marmalade in its density of flavor and the tightness of balance between bitter and sour and sweet. Instead of the usual sourball pucker, that edge of medicinal bitterness gave the marmalade a three-dimensional quality that lifted it to a new level. It was, in the complicated response it demanded, a very adult preserve.

The name I gave to the outcome of this method was "maximum marmalade," and that this was no exaggeration became all the more evident when Matt and I repeated the experiment with organic lemons. There, the result was so mouth-fillingly intense that it was almost masochistic. It was impossible to be sure whether the yelp from my taste buds was one of pleasure or panic. It wasn't a matter of the marmalade being too bitter, too sour, or too sweet, but too much of all three at once. However, the most that this demanded of the preserve maker was some effort to control and shape the results. When we tackled Key limes soon afterwards, we got it exactly right.

Even when the fruit wasn't especially sour, the intensification of flavor brought the marmalade to life. The one we prepared from Florida navel oranges, which would otherwise have been pathetically sweet and bland, proved instead to be innocently refreshing—a maximum marmalade that, for once, children could love. And a small step up in acidity and brightness of flavor meant that a marmalade we made from Temple oranges was revelatory in its easy accessibility combined with a wealth of citrusy flavor notes. Kids would love this one, too, if grownups let them anywhere near it.

By then, I thought I had this marmalade business in the bag, but there was one final twist to the story still to come. Our pal and subscriber Ed Ivy has corresponded with us over the years. At one point we learned that he owned some land in Florida with wild orange trees growing on it and begged him to send us some of the fruit.

These wild trees are a source of entertainment for native Floridians. Tourists, seeing a citrus bonanza for the taking, often pull their cars over to the side of the road and pick armfuls of the wild oranges before they think to bite into one, only to discover that they are as sour as lemons. All sweet oranges in Florida grow on trees grafted to sour orange rootstock—which often takes over the whole tree once an orchard is abandoned. Pick a wild orange and chances are the fruit will be inedible, at least for eating out of hand.

The likelihood that these same trees will be bearing genuine Seville oranges is, of course, rather negligible. That fruit is also a cultivated variety, selectively bred for the perfume of its peel. In fact, Seville oranges were once widely grown in Florida, and—though very hard to find—some are still. But even if all you can get hold of are the wild native sort, they are close enough kin to the Seville to make excellent British-style marmalade . . . as we were about to discover for ourselves.

When Ed's shipment arrived and we cut open the box, what met our eyes was as motley a crew as can be imagined. As with most wild fruit, there was clear visual evidence of a lack of pampering. The color of the peel was dull and dingy; its texture was as rough and blotchy as the back of a toad. A casual glance was also enough to know that they would not be bursting with juice. But a fingernail pressed into the peel released a pungent citrus aroma with hints of tangerine (something also present in its deeply bitter taste). We opened our copy of *Jane Grigson's Fruit Book* to the recipe for whole orange marmalade ("the simplest, easiest, and best flavoured") and set to work.

Again, however, I adapted the recipe, replacing the water called for with orange juice, and not that squeezed from the remaining sour oranges but from sweet Florida juice oranges. Although the former had it all over the latter when it came to potency, to citric punch, the sweet orange won hands down in terms of brightness and clarity of flavor. Maybe it was time for the two of them to get together and pool their resources, instead of duking it out for the title of Marmalade King.

The result, after all the soaking, cutting, and boiling, was, to put it simply, the best orange marmalade I've ever eaten in my life. And I wasn't the only one who thought this—we gave some of our very limited supply to marmalade fiends of our acquaintance who said exactly the same thing. Who begged us for more. This is because the stuff brought you back to the first time your taste buds encountered real British marmalade and shouted, "Wow!" And here they were, shouting it all over again.

This, in short, was a marmalade to make a Scotsman sit up and take notice . . . and, for an American marmalade maker, if that isn't a triumph, I don't know what is.

IMPORTANT NOTES ABOUT MARMALADE-MAKING

Choosing the Fruit. Select fruit that has smooth, firm skin and feels heavy for its size. Smaller fruits generally have more flavor than their larger siblings. Organic citrus is best (no pesticide residues); don't be put off if the peel has greenish patches—outside color is no indicator of inside flavor.

Boiling the Peel. Marmalade recipes universally direct you to boil the peel to soften it. Don't worry if the result seems mushy—once you cook the peel with sugar to make the marmalade, it will become resilient and chewy again. The only citrus fruit I've encountered that didn't require preboiling is the Meyer lemon. Otherwise, if you like your peel chewy, boil it less; if you like it soft, boil it more. Here, experience will prove the best guide.

Batch Size. The recipes that follow—apart from the first of them (which dealt with our boxload of sour oranges)—are for small, sometimes very small, batches of marmalade. These not only are easier on the cook but make the best marmalade, since longer cooking emphasizes the taste of the increasingly caramelized sugar over that of the fruit. This approach makes even more sense when—as it is for us—preserve-making is not a way of dealing with a bumper crop but motivated by, say, the appearance of little bags of Key limes at the supermarket. If you decide to make more marmalade than you can conveniently store in your refrigerator, you should seek out and follow the instructions in any contemporary preserving manual for giving the sealed jars a final water bath before storing them away on a closet shelf.

The Preserving Pot. The essential thing to remember about preserve-making is that what you are doing is cooking down sugar syrup, and that sugar syrup must be treated with the utmost respect. It can give you a terrible burn; it can boil up and over a pot in a matter of seconds, making a mess you'll never forget. I let this happen once, and years later Matt and I were still cleaning the results from hidden crannies in our stove. The rule of thumb is that the sugar-fruit-water mixture should *at most* fill the pot halfway up. So select something large—at least six- to eight-quart capacity (for the amounts in the recipes that follow). Ideally, the pot should be as wide as (or wider than) it is tall, to allow for maximum evaporation, so our own choice is a large Dutch oven (for example, the six-quart Calphalon "Every Day" nonstick model). However, a stockpot can also be used, if you'd prefer to trade surface evaporation for more boil-over control.

Testing for Doneness. This is, at least psychically, the hardest part of making marmalade, because if you wait for *definitive* evidence that the batch will jell, it may cool to the consistency of latex. The trick is to catch it right at the cusp, and there may be as many solutions to this as there are cooks: the drip-off-the-spoon method, the ripples-when-blown-upon method, the candy thermometer. I dithered among these until Matt came up with the plate-in-the-freezer method. This requires putting a dinner plate (the thicker, the better) into the freezer before starting. Then, when the time comes to start testing, you drop a half-teaspoon of the boiling liquid close to the rim of the plate, return it to the freezer, and, after a minute, take it out again and prod it with your finger. If it has jelled enough to hold its new (prodded) shape for at least a moment (it shouldn't be solid), the marmalade is ready. If, as is likely, it doesn't jell, try the test again in ten minutes, working clockwise around the plate. I suggest stopping the cooking the moment the jelling occurs, since marmalade will continue to cook during the time it takes to ladle it into jars. And it should be a little loose—cooking jam to a rigid set is like grilling a steak until well done.

MAXIMUM ORANGE MARMALADE
(Based on a recipe from *Jane Grigson's Fruit Book*)
[Makes about 4 pints]

3 pounds Seville or wild sour oranges (see note)
12 cups pure cane sugar
12 cups (3 quarts) freshly squeezed or packaged
    not-from-concentrate orange juice

Using a vegetable brush or plastic scrubber, clean the surface of the oranges. Put them into a large pot with 3 quarts of water. Bring this up to a simmer and cook for an hour and a half. At this point, the skin of the oranges will be quite tender and easily pierced. Set the oranges out to cool and pour off and discard the water.

Preheat oven to warm (170°F). Pour the sugar into a pan or oven-proof bowl and set it in the oven to heat. (This step is optional, but it will speed up the marmalade-making.) Put a thick china plate into the freezer compartment. Also, fill a medium-size pot half full of water and start it boiling. Use this to sterilize the preserving jars and their lids while the marmalade cooks, setting them out on a cooling rack to dry as you remove them from the pot.

When the oranges are cool enough to handle, cut them in half and remove the pips. Gather these together and tie them up in a small piece of cheesecloth. These will provide some additional pectin to help the marmalade jell. Using a very sharp knife, slice the orange halves in half again and then cut these, peel and pulp together, into thin strips.

In the chosen preserving pot, put the cut-up oranges, the bag of pips, the orange juice, and the warmed sugar. Bring to a roiling boil over high heat and then reduce the heat some, but keep the contents boiling steadily. Use a ladle or skimmer to remove any persistent scum. After 20 minutes, deposit half a teaspoon of the contents of the pot onto the chilled plate and return it to the freezer. In a minute or so, prod it with a finger, to see if the marmalade has started jelling (see "Testing for Doneness," above). If not, repeat this step every 10 minutes, until the marmalade has jelled enough to be clearly semifirm.

Turn off the heat. Discard the bag of pips, stir the marmalade to evenly distribute the peel, and ladle it into the waiting jars, using a preserving funnel to keep the hot marmalade from landing on your fingers. Fill each jar to within ½ inch of the top, then seal tightly with the screw-on lids. Set the jars back on the cooling rack to cool overnight. Then refrigerate and let mellow for at least two weeks before broaching.

Cook's Note. If you don't have a friend or relative in the citrus-growing states to send you wild sour oranges (or if you simply want to use the real thing), you can order genuine Seville oranges in season from Rising C Ranches, which specializes in hard-to-find citrus fruits, many of them (Eustis limequats, Chinotto sour oranges, Rangpur limes) perfect for marmalade. 5800 S. Buttonwillow Avenue; Reedley, CA 93654; (559) 626-7917; www.ripetoyou.com.

TEMPLE ORANGE MARMALADE
(Based on a recipe from *Preserving Today* by Jeanne Lesem)
[Makes about 2 cups]

"[Temple oranges] make an exceptional marmalade," writes Helen Witty in Fancy Pantry, *and her enthusiasm for this cross between an orange and a tangerine got us interested in trying it ourselves. We had already been experimenting with Jeanne Lesem's single-piece-of-fruit lemon marmalade recipe and found it worked equally well with Temple oranges. In contrast with the marmalade recipe above, this one and the variations that follow produce a notably clear preserve packed with fresh fruit taste. Slicing the fruit before cooking makes it possible to cut the rind very thinly, creating tender, thread-like slivers that marry perfectly with this gentler—but still full-flavored—marmalade.*

> about 6 to 8 Temple oranges
> pure cane sugar

Choose the nicest orange from the bunch and use a vegetable brush or plastic scrubber to clean its surface. Trim off the very top and bottom. Then slice the fruit in half from stem to blossom end and cut these halves in half again the same way. Using a very sharp knife, slice each of these quarters, rind and pulp together, as thinly as possible, discarding any seeds. This should yield about ¾ cup. Squeeze enough of the other Temple oranges to amply cover the sliced fruit with juice (we used about 2 cups). Cover and let sit at room temperature for about 24 hours.

Transfer everything to a saucepan, bring to a boil, uncovered, then boil gently 15 to 20 minutes, or until the peel is tender and translucent (see note about boiling the peel, above). Measure the contents of the saucepan, pour this into the preserving pot, and stir in three-quarters of that measure of sugar. (For example, we had approximately 2 cups of orange juice, peel, and pulp after boiling, and so added 1½ cups of sugar.)

Put a thick china plate into the freezer and fill another pot with enough water to sterilize the preserving jars. Bring the sugar and fruit mixture to a roiling boil over high heat and then reduce the heat some, but keep the contents boiling steadily. Use a ladle or skimmer to remove any persistent scum. Meanwhile, sterilize the preserving jars and their lids.

After 15 minutes, deposit half a teaspoon of the contents of the pot onto the chilled plate and return it to the freezer. In a minute or so, prod it with a finger, to see if the marmalade has started jelling (see "Testing for Doneness," above). If not, repeat this step every 10 minutes, until the marmalade has jelled enough to be clearly semifirm.

At this point, turn off the heat, stir the marmalade to evenly distribute the peel, and ladle it into the waiting jars, using a preserving funnel to keep hot preserves from landing on your fingers. Fill each jar to within ½ inch of the top, then seal tightly with the screw-on lids. Set the jars on a cooling rack to cool overnight. Then refrigerate and let mellow for a few days before broaching.

Variations

The following are examples of how we used the above recipe to make a series of small-batch marmalades, adapting it as necessary to the needs and virtues of each particular fruit. Given variations in size and weight, directions cannot be—and should not be treated as—ironclad. The formula, however, is simple: Cut up the fruit, cover it generously with juice, boil it to soften the peel, measure it, add approximately three-quarters that amount of sugar (sour fruit like lemons or limes will require more), and cook it until it jells.

Florida Navel Orange Marmalade. (If substituting California navels, choose plump, firm oranges with smooth, tight skins.) Prepare 1 orange following the directions for Temple marmalade above, but cut each navel orange half into thirds rather than halves. Depending on yield, squeeze enough additional oranges to cover the sliced orange amply with juice. (We got 1⅓ cups of peel and pulp from our largish orange and covered this with 3 cups of juice—which required 8 more navels.) After the initial boiling, the pulp/juice measurement was 3⅓ cups; to this we added three-quarters this measure of sugar, or about 2½ cups. The yield was about 3 cups. Note: Navels vary widely in vivacity of flavor; taste the contents of the pot after all the sugar has been dissolved. If the flavor is insipid, perk it up by adding 1 tablespoon of fresh lemon juice for each cup of pulp and juice that went into the pot before you added the sugar.

Meyer Lemon Marmalade. A friend in California sent us a small box of these, and we immediately made a lovely marmalade from them. Meyer lemons have a more flowery aroma and sweeter flavor than ordinary lemons; they make a choice marmalade. Also, their peel is so thin and tender that it shouldn't require a preliminary boiling. One lemon, trimmed, quartered, and sliced very thinly, produced about ⅔ cup of sliced peel, to which we added ¾ cup each of lemon juice and water. After a day of soaking, we added an equal (instead of three-quarters) measure of sugar and prepared the marmalade following the master recipe, with a yield of approximately 2 cups. Note: To make a marmalade of ordinary lemons, choose especially firm fruit with smooth, tight skins. Follow the instructions and proportions for Temple orange marmalade, but as above use a half-and-half mixture of lemon juice and water and use an equal measure of sugar.

Key Lime Marmalade. We bought a mesh bag of Key limes (a little over a pound) at the supermarket and selected half a dozen of the nicest looking, which together weighed about as much as a plump lemon. We scrubbed these, halved them from stem to blossom end, and sliced them as thinly as we could (easiest to do when the cut side faces down), discarding the tiny seeds. This resulted in about ⅔ cup of sliced peel and pulp. Then we juiced the rest of the limes, getting a total of ½ cup. To this we added 1 cup of water. We poured this over the lime slices and let everything sit at room temperature for 24 hours. After the initial boiling, the pulp/juice measurement was close to 2 cups. As with the Meyer lemon marmalade, we added an equal measure of sugar, then proceeded as directed in the master recipe. This set very quickly—in about 20 minutes—and produced 2 cups of marmalade. Note: We also made this marmalade using Persian (common green) limes. It was perfectly fine, but not as good as this.

PINEAPPLE LEMON MARMALADE
(Adapted from *Fine Preserving* by Catherine Plagemann)
[Makes about 2 pints]

Wait to make this until you spot a noticeably fragrant pineapple signaling its ripeness with an exterior that is all yellow/orange/pink instead of green. The reason for making the sugar syrup is to shorten the cooking

time of the marmalade itself and so capture the bright pineapple taste,
which would otherwise be muted. Prepare the syrup in a deep pot and
watch it carefully to keep it from boiling over.

> 1 ripe pineapple
> juice of 2 lemons and the zest from one of them
> 4 cups pure cane sugar
> 1½ cups canned unsweetened pineapple juice

Slice the top and bottom off the pineapple, cut away the peel, and remove the eyes. Cut the fruit in half and cut each half lengthwise into
quarters, to make eight segments in all. Trim away the tough core section from each of these, then slice the flesh with a very sharp knife as
thinly as you can (or feed it, 2 or 3 segments at a time, through the slicing disk of a food processor). Reserve any juices as well. The yield will
be approximately 3 cups. Pour the lemon juice over this.

Slice the lemon zest into thread-like strips. Put it in a small pot with
½ cup of water, bring this to a boil, reduce it to a simmer, and cook the
lemon strips for 15 minutes, adding more water if necessary to keep
them from boiling dry. Add the peel (and any remaining water) to the
sliced pineapple.

In a large pot, dissolve the sugar in the pineapple juice and bring
this mixture to a boil over medium-high heat, watching it all the while
to prevent it from boiling over. Lower the heat as soon as it starts to
bubble, but keep it boiling rapidly for 5 minutes, skimming away any
persistent scum.

Put a thick china plate into the freezer and fill another pot with
enough water to sterilize the preserving jars and their lids.

Add the pineapple, zest, and accumulated liquid to the large pot.
Bring this to a roiling boil over high heat and then reduce the heat
some, but keep the contents boiling steadily. Use a ladle or skimmer to
remove any persistent scum. After 15 minutes, deposit half a teaspoon
of the contents of the pot onto the chilled plate and return it to the
freezer. In a minute or so, prod it with a finger, to see if the marmalade
has started jelling (see "Testing for Doneness," above). If not, repeat
this step every 10 minutes, until the marmalade has jelled enough to be
clearly semifirm.

At this point, turn off the heat, stir the marmalade to evenly distribute the peel, and ladle it into the waiting jars, using a preserving funnel to keep the hot marmalade off your fingers. Fill each jar to within ½ inch of the top, then seal tightly with the screw-on lids. Set the jars back on the rack to cool overnight and then refrigerate.

Further Reading

Marmalade is surely one of very few preserves that are worthy of serious study, and C. Anne Wilson's short, pithy, and rewarding *The Book of Marmalade* gives the subject full justice, enlivening the tale with flashes of dry wit, vintage photographs, and a concluding section of historical and contemporary recipes. Anyone interested in Scottish foodways should seek out a secondhand copy of Catherine Brown's scholarly and quietly passionate *Broths to Bannocks: Cooking in Scotland, 1690 to the Present Day*, which has unconscionably been allowed to fall out of print. Brown is as much at home before a crofter's fireplace as she is in an Edinburgh tavern (circa 1786) or a Glasgow slum (circa 1945): a book rich with historical insight, Scottish lore, and many, many recipes. Equally rewarding in their own way are two excellent books by F. Marian McNeill—*The Scots Kitchen* and, especially (as regards this essay), *The Book of Breakfasts*. The subject is the British breakfast in general, but the book's heart is in the Highlands.

COD & POTATOES

Eaten with butter and potatoes, cod forms a basic ration on which man could thrive indefinitely.
—Evelene Spencer and John Cobb, *Fish Cookery*

When, twenty years back, I wrote a pamphlet on chowder,* I thought I had said all I would ever have to say on the subject of cod and potatoes. Not that I thought I'd summed the matter up—it was just that the other great dish that combined the two, fish and chips, fell outside my purview. Gerald Priestland produced an entire book on the subject—*Frying Tonight: The Saga of Fish and Chips*—and while he devotes a whole chapter to the evolution of fish fryers and another to paper wrappings, he provides not a single recipe. That's because, like you and me, Priestland goes to a fish fry place for them, which is as it should be. There's no satisfactory way of making fish and chips at home without owning two deep-fat fryers—and most of us, these days, don't own even one. Consequently, while the dish makes an excellent subject for a journalist—especially a British journalist, which Priestland is—it is only of limited interest to a cook.

So, there it is: chowder on the one side and fish and chips on the other, and in the middle . . . plain old cod and potatoes. What is there to say about that? Matt and I make it, we eat it, we like it very much. But this is such simple eating that it would be hard to work up a recipe

---

Downeast Chowder (Boston: Jackdaw Press, 1982). An expanded and revised version of this work appears in our book *Serious Pig*.

for it, let alone an essay; there just isn't anything there to write about. Or so thought I—or would have, had I ever bothered to think about it at all.

Still, stick to a trade long enough and second chances come along, even third and fourth ones. Mine came when I read a surprisingly affecting passage in Mark Kurlansky's introduction to his *Cod: A Biography of the Fish That Changed the World*. There, he describes his trip out to the cod banks off Newfoundland in a small fishing boat. The purpose of the trip was catching cod, but only to tag and release them. The cod stock has been dangerously depleted, and the Canadian government has halted commercial fishing until the fish rebound, something that these fishermen were monitoring. Unlike most fish, cod can take the rough handling necessary to tag them, but occasionally one does die and it then becomes the fishermen's supper.

> Bernard kneels over a portable Sterno stove at the stern. He uses his thick fishing knife to dice fatback and salt beef and peel and slice potatoes. He soaks pieces of hardtack and sautés it all in the pork fat with some sliced onion. Then he fillets the cod in four knife strokes per side, skins the fillets with two more, and before throwing the carcass over, opens it up, sees it is a female, and removes the roe. Holding it by a gill over the gunwale, he makes two quick cuts and rips out the throat piece, "the cod tongue," before dropping the body in the sea . . .
>
> Bernard dumps the food on a big baking sheet, which they put on a plank across one of the holds, and they stand in the hold where the catch should have been and with plastic forks start eating toward the center. The dish, called Fishermen's Brewis, is monochromatic, with off-white pork fat and off-white potatoes and occasional darker pieces of salt beef. What stands out is the stark whiteness of the thick flakes of fresh cod. This is the meal they grew up on.

Perhaps it's my Yankee upbringing, but reading this passage moved me even as it made me hungry. Fishermen's brewis or, more often, just fish and brewis, is to Newfoundland what fish chowder is to New England. The word "brewis" (pronounced "brooze"—hence the old joke about the new parson who, offered fish and brewis for breakfast, replied that he would be happy to have the fish, and perhaps just one brew) is very old indeed.

However, in its classic form, it is not nearly as richly worked out—let alone as delicious—as the dish that Bernard prepared. "Brewis" shares the same roots as "broth," and it refers to a dish of dried bread softened with drippings or water. In Newfoundland, the bread in question is hardtack, and a traditional recipe goes something like this:

FISH AND BREWIS

hardtack as required
salt cod as required
salt pork as required

The Night Before: Break the hardtack into pieces, allowing 1 piece per person. Place in a large saucepan well covered with water. Soak overnight. Put the salt cod in a shallow bowl and cover with water. Soak this overnight as well, changing the water first thing in the morning.

To Prepare the Meal: Cut a few slices of salt pork into tiny cubes and fry these until golden. (These are called "scrunchions.") Heat the hardtack in its soaking water almost to the boiling point but do not let it boil. Drain immediately and discard the water. Keep hot. Meanwhile, simmer the soaked salt cod in fresh water for about 20 minutes or until the flesh easily flakes. Drain, pick away any skin and bones, and combine the cod with the sopped hardtack. Serve with the scrunchions sprinkled over.

Think of Bernard's version as a twentieth-century riff on this and you can see three centuries of Newfoundland cooking flash by your eyes: salt pork and salt beef (presumably a form of corned beef) and hardtack and potatoes. But the real luxury, the single ingredient that pulls everything else into perspective, is that incredibly fresh piece of cod.

Fish and brewis and New England fish chowder have followed a very similar evolutionary path, the latter being properly made today with salt pork and butter and milk and crackers and potatoes. Except, when we think about chowder, the traditional dish we have in mind is made with fresh, not salt, cod. However, "traditional" dishes change through time like everything else. It's been so long since salt cod played a major role in Yankee cooking, chowder-making included, that it has

pretty much fallen off the charts—apart from a lingering taste for codfish cakes and salt cod hash.

On the other hand, Newfoundland continued to be a major producer of salt cod right through the last century, and dishes there that
call for it still retain their currency—at least in traditional recipe collec-
tions. This is what makes the fresh fish in Bernard's version so conspicuously luxurious.

•   •   •

Salt cod is made by soaking eviscerated but otherwise whole cod in salt
brine for several hours, then hanging it up in the sun for several days
until it is dry and hard as a board. New Englanders made a fortune
making it and selling it, but they weren't especially partial to eating it
themselves. They might serve it occasionally as a display of Yankee fru-
gality, but they felt pity for anyone forced to consume it regularly. Salt
cod was poverty food.

That good things can be done with salt cod will get no argument
from me, but taken strictly as a piece of fish, it is no special treat. And
how could it be? I don't think there's a soul who would deny that while
you can get both pleasure and nourishment from a piece of jerky you
cannot reconstitute it back to anything with the taste and texture of a
cut of beef. This is doubly true with something as evanescently flavored
and delicately tender as a piece of fresh fish.

Certainly in New England, by the middle of the nineteenth century,
the poor were happily giving up salted fish in favor of fresh, as that became more affordable. This little affected the salt cod industry, which
was able to sell abroad the bulk of what it produced. In 1874 alone, the
fishing town of Gloucester produced fifty-three *million* pounds of salt
cod, exporting the premium cuts to Portugal and Spain, the worst of it
to feed workers on plantations in the West Indies (where it would be
made into such dishes as Jamaica's stamp-and-go).

However, as the poor began eating fresh fish, wealthier New Englanders became all the more convinced of the virtues of eating meat. In
this, of course, they were in step with the rest of the country: meat, not
fish, was considered the proper fare of true Americans. In *Saltwater
Foodways*, her superlative history of New Englanders and what they
ate, Sandra Oliver devotes two long, fascinating chapters to their rela-

tionship with fish. As she points out, "Fish-eating was associated with
poverty and Roman Catholicism. Fish were undomesticated at a time
when wild food was not preferred fare. Fish was eaten and produced by
people with whom many nineteenth-century Yankees did not wish to
identify."

Her unraveling of these prejudices is too complex a matter to expli-
cate here, but for our purposes her argument can be summed up in two
words: "Fish stinks." The stink was associated with the people who
caught it, the people who ate it, and the food itself. It was only as the
stock of individual items—oysters, lobsters, clams, and, eventually,
haddock and cod—became depleted that they began to creep up in culinary esteem.

Even so, the distance fish has yet to travel to catch up with meat,
even in these health-conscious, omega-3 fatty acid–obsessed days, can
be seen by comparing the meaning of "meaty" versus "fishy." For while
the one has overtones of something substantial, worth sinking your
teeth into, the other conveys something with a bad smell, morally as
well as physically. In this regard, it is even worse than "garlicky" as a
term of opprobrium—whereas the latter merely means that you reek of
low-class foreign food, the former implies hidden spoilage, rot, decay.

Why has this prejudice come about? Perhaps it is because with meat
there are many days and many leagues between the death of the animal
and the meal; with seafood it can be a matter of seconds and inches, as
anyone who has eaten a raw oyster will know very well. For a fish-
loving culture, this intimacy is the relish that whets the appetite, a savor
to be pursued to the full. Conversely, in a meat-oriented culture such as
ours, where there is no such sense of urgency, where game is hung and
meat is aged, seafood, by the time we get around to eating it, has lost
the edge of freshness that makes it so captivating.

In Norway, where fish is consumed spanking fresh, every morsel
that can be winkled from its carcass is treated as an epicurean delight.
In his chapter on that country in *The Cooking of Scandinavia*, Dale
Brown writes:

> From long association with the cod, the Norwegians have learned
> not only how to cook it well, but how to eat it in its entirety. They
> claim that the best part of all is the head—the meat on the back of
> the neck and around the jaws. The dimple of flesh on top of the

skull is much appreciated by them. The inch-long tongue is also considered a delicacy, and wherever cod are caught in quantity, the tongues will be amassed and sold. They may be boiled or sautéed and served with lightly browned butter . . . Yet another delicacy is the pink roe, which is boiled, sliced and used as a garnish to the fish itself, or when floured and sautéed in butter, as a topping for sandwiches. Even the liver is savored; when not boiled with the fish, it will be cooked in only a little salted water to which, at the last moment, both vinegar and pepper are added. Curiously, it does not taste like cod-liver oil.

Now, little of this would be news to Bernard, but it is almost unimaginable to you and me. It has taken me almost a lifetime to escape from the feeling that eating fish is a form of penance. I could never understand why, when our family would go out to expensive restaurants, my father always had broiled haddock or cod, never the prime rib, roast leg of lamb, veal chops, or grilled lobster inevitably ordered by his offspring.

At the time I thought that the source of my father's ritual was a chastening fear of extravagant consumption he had learned as an orphan during the Depression . . . but the truth may be that he actually loved the stuff. Recently, my mother and I had dinner at Le Garage, a restaurant in Wiscasset, Maine, where the two of them used to stop on their way back from shopping trips down the coast. I ordered finnan haddie, a dish that I adore but almost never have a chance to eat. My mother remarked in surprise, "You know, your father always ordered that here," and I felt a sudden pang of sadness and regret—another connection between us discovered too late.

• • •

A few days afterwards, I would find myself ordering codfish cakes at Moody's Diner . . . not only getting in touch with my Yankee roots, it seemed, but eating my way up the evolutionary chain of New England seafood processing. How soon would it be before I was ordering the fresh fish special myself? Earlier, it turned out, than I would ever have thought. This is because Matt, who actually looks at the recipes when she reads a cookbook, kept noticing how often an author would declare that his favorite fish dish was a combination of cod and potatoes.

Cod and potatoes, of course, make up a famous culinary marriage. Where cod goes, potatoes almost always come along, hand in hand. "Two in One and One in Two," as Gerald Priestland put it, "not a takeover but a marriage, not a conquest but a companionship." There are certain pleasures in food as in life that are so quiet that only through long familiarity can you fully learn to appreciate them. And, in truth, the deliciousness that comes from combining potatoes and cod is a surprisingly delicate thing.

Like the potato, cod has a distinctively light and tender flesh, because the fish's rich oil accumulates in its liver—rather than, as with bluefish or salmon, permeating its flesh. Consequently, good as cod and potatoes are alone, they are lifted up to heaven with the judicious addition of fat. One is protein, the other carbohydrate—but fry them up and serve them together, hot, crispy, and slightly greasy, and they become the two halves of a single perfect whole.

Fortunately, it isn't the frying per se but the melding touch of richness that makes this so—although surely the special appeal of fish and chips comes from rigging out identical twins in identical outfits, thus producing a surfeit of culinary charm. The following dishes do not possess quite that surfeit—perhaps the writers' emphasis on how good they are anticipated the reader's likely failure to even notice a recipe that called for ingredients as ordinary as these. But I suspect the truth is a little closer to home—that the writers themselves are surprised each time they eat them how delicious cod and potatoes can really be.

Ingredient Notes

Fish: Cod—really, no substitutes, although haddock will certainly serve. Marian Morash, in *The Victory Garden Fish and Vegetable Cookbook*, writes that whenever she serves her husband, Russ, any other fish, no matter how deliciously prepared, he is likely to say, "Well, it's nice, but not as good as a piece of fresh cod." My father would have wholeheartedly concurred.

Potatoes: We recommend Yukon Gold, Red Nordland, Red Pontiac, or White Rose, in no particular order.

ROAST COD ON OVEN-FRIED POTATOES

There are many fish-and-potato recipes, but this, despite its simplicity—or because of it—is the ultimate.

—Mark Bittman, *Fish: The Complete Guide*
to Buying and Cooking

[Serves 4]

Simplicity is certainly the watchword in a recipe with only five ingredients, and we rate it as highly as Mark does. However, while he slices his potatoes into thin disks, we cut ours into matchsticks. The amount of potatoes called for may seem excessive, but when you eat them you will wish you had prepared even more.

6 tablespoons unsalted butter
2½ pounds potatoes, peeled and cut into matchsticks
2 teaspoons kosher salt
3 or 4 8- to 12-ounce cod fillets
black pepper to taste

Preheat oven to 425°F. Melt 4 tablespoons of the butter over medium heat in a large nonstick skillet with an ovenproof handle. When it begins to foam, add the potatoes and 1 teaspoon of the salt. Stir to coat the pieces with butter, and put them in the oven. Remove the skillet every 10 minutes to give them another stir, until they are all colored a deep gold. This will take 40 to 45 minutes.

Meanwhile, unwrap the cod and season it with the remaining teaspoon of salt and plenty of black pepper. Top the fillets with slivers of the remaining 2 tablespoons of butter, set them on top of the golden potatoes and slip the skillet back into the oven.

Roast the cod until the fish begins to separate into flakes. Check for doneness by inserting a table knife into the thickest part of the fillet—the fish is done as soon as the flesh is opaque throughout. This will take 8 to 10 minutes, depending on the thickness. Be careful not to let the cod overcook or it will dry out. Serve with a simple salad or vegetable dish.

COD BAKED WITH OLIVE OIL, GARLIC, AND POTATOES
[Serves 4]

"One of the best recipes in the book," states the British food writer Lynda Brown in The Cook's Garden *about the following recipe. It is certainly very good, but what interests us almost as much is that if you added some minced parsley and wedges of hard-boiled egg, you would have the spitting image of that Portuguese classic* Bacalhau à Gomes de Sá—*compare what follows with the recipe for this dish as given in Jean Anderson's* The Food of Portugal—*except, of course, that there it is made with salt cod and here with fresh fish. Our version of the recipe, while it (naturally) uses fresh cod, pushes things a bit closer to the Portuguese.*

4 tablespoons extra-virgin olive oil, plus a little extra
3 or 4 onions, thinly sliced
3 or 4 large garlic cloves, finely minced
2 pounds waxy potatoes
3 or 4 8- to 12-ounce cod fillets
salt and black pepper to taste
8 or so brine-cured black olives, pitted and chopped

Heat the olive oil in a large skillet over low heat. Add the onion rings, spreading them out to fill the pan. Cover the skillet and cook, stirring occasionally, until they are reduced to a soft, golden mass. Don't rush this; it should take 25 to 30 minutes. During the last 10 minutes, stir in the minced garlic.

Meanwhile, boil the potatoes in their skins until they are cooked through, about 30 minutes. Drain, let cool, slip off their skins, and slice into ½-inch disks.

Preheat oven to 375°F. Select a shallow casserole or other ovenproof dish large enough to hold the fish in a single layer. Grease the dish lightly with olive oil. Then layer the bottom with potatoes, reserving about one-quarter of them. Spread about a third of the onion-garlic mixture over these and set the fish onto this. Season with salt and pepper. Fit the remaining potato slices between the fish and the sides of the dish. Spread the remaining two-thirds of the onion-garlic mixture on

top, scraping in any remaining olive oil, and dot this all over with olive
bits.

Slip the dish into the oven and bake for about 30 minutes, or until
the onions have begun to brown around the edges and the flesh of the
fish flakes easily and is an opaque white throughout. Serve with a plain
green salad, some good bread, and, if you like, a small pitcher of olive
oil to allow diners to dribble a little more over the fish at the table.

DUTCH COD AND POTATO BAKE
[Serves 4]

*This recipe from the Netherlands can be seen as a northern European
response to the Iberian-inspired one above: "You say garlic, we say
sour cream; you say olives, we say bread crumbs." It is worthy competition.*

> 4 tablespoons butter, plus a little extra
> 2 or 3 yellow onions, chopped
> 2 slices good white bread
> 2 pounds waxy potatoes
> salt and black pepper to taste
> 3 or 4 8- to 12-ounce cod fillets
> 2 eggs
> 1 cup sour cream
> ¼ cup chopped parsley

Melt 2 tablespoons of the butter in a medium skillet and sauté the
onions until they are translucent and tawny-colored but not browned.
Tear the bread, including the crusts, into bits. In a small skillet, melt the
other 2 tablespoons of butter and gently toast the crumbs to a golden
brown. Boil the potatoes for 30 minutes, or until cooked through.
Drain, let cool, slip off their skins, and slice into ½-inch disks.

Preheat oven to 375°F. Select a shallow casserole or other ovenproof
dish large enough to hold the fish in a single layer. Grease the dish
lightly with butter and line the bottom with most of the potato slices.
Season them with salt and pepper and set the fish on top. Spread the
sautéed onions over the fish, seasoning these as well. Tuck in the rest of

the potatoes around the edges. Beat the eggs, then blend in the sour cream and a pinch of salt. Pour this mixture over the fish. Sprinkle with the toasted bread crumbs and the minced parsley. Bake for 25 to 30 minutes, until the flesh of the fish flakes easily and is an opaque white throughout. Serve at once.

EL NAZALLI BEL BATATA
[Serves 4]

"Fish baked on a bed of thinly sliced potatoes," writes Manuel Vázquez Montalbán in his L'Art del menjar a Catalunya *(Peninsula, 1977), "and seasoned with aromatic herbs, chopped onion and tomato, garlic, parsley, and lemon offers a trip to paradise without LSD." A slight exaggeration, perhaps, but as Colman Andrews notes in* Catalan Cuisine *(whence comes the quote), "the results are marvelous." We found versions of the dish not only in that book but in* ¡Delicioso! The Regional Cooking of Spain *by Penelope Casas and in* Mediterranean Harvest *by Paola Scaravelli and Jon Cohen. What follows is based mostly on theirs, which comes from Morocco, with bits and pieces taken from the others.*

> 4 tablespoons extra-virgin olive oil, plus a little extra
> 1 tablespoon imported sweet paprika
> ½ teaspoon black pepper
> ¼ teaspoon cayenne pepper
> 1 teaspoon ground cumin
> 2 garlic cloves, finely minced
> ¼ cup each chopped fresh parsley and cilantro
> 1 teaspoon kosher salt, plus more to taste
> ½ cup dry white wine
> 3 or 4 8- to 12-ounce cod fillets
> 2 pounds waxy potatoes
> 1 medium yellow onion, thinly sliced
> 2 large ripe tomatoes
> ½ lemon

In a mixing bowl, blend half the olive oil with the paprika, pepper, cayenne, cumin, garlic, parsley, cilantro, salt, and 2 tablespoons of the wine. Coat the pieces of fish with the resulting paste and marinate at room temperature for 1 hour. After about 45 minutes, preheat oven to 375°F.

Meanwhile, boil the potatoes in their skins until they are cooked through, about 30 minutes. Remove them to a dish and when they are cool enough to handle, slip off their skins and slice them into ½-inch disks.

Put the onion slices and the remaining 2 tablespoons of olive oil in a skillet and sauté them gently until they are soft and golden. Don't let them brown.

Slice the tomatoes into rounds about ¼-inch thick. Use a very sharp knife or mandoline to cut the half lemon into paper-thin slices or, alternately, cut away the peel entirely and slice the flesh into rounds. Either way, discard the seeds and the lemon end. Finally, select a baking dish or casserole large enough to hold the fish in a single layer and grease the dish lightly.

When the hour is up, spread first the potatoes and then the sautéed onions in the baking dish. Season this with a pinch or so of salt. Lay the pieces of fish, being careful not to dislodge the herbal coating, on top of the vegetables. Lay the tomato and lemon slices over and around the fish. Lastly, swirl the remaining wine in the marinade dish and dribble the result over the fish. Bake for 25 minutes, or until the flesh of the fish flakes easily and is an opaque white throughout. Serve at once.

Further Reading

If you'd like to check out other interesting variations on this theme, see Gary Rhodes's spectacular recipe for Roast Cod on Potatoes with Fried Anchovies in *More Rhodes Around Britain,* Jane Grigson's Gratin of Cod in *Fish Cookery,* Marian Morash's Baked Creamy Cod with Leeks and Potatoes in *The Victory Garden Fish and Vegetable Cookbook,* and Nancy Harmon Jenkins's Fish Packets from Istanbul's Pandeli Restaurant in *The Mediterranean Diet Cookbook.*

TWO WITH THE FLU

A fever of 103 degrees, night shivers, a dry harsh cough, aching muscles, stuffy nose, giddy head . . . and then, just as I managed to stagger onto the road to recovery, Matt succumbed to the same virus herself. As I lay in bed, sweaty, querulous, bored by and stiff from my confinement there but with no inclination to get up, I began to think about what we might have for supper. Neither of us had much appetite, but, even so, we both hungered for something soothing and warm that would slide effortlessly down our gullets, stroking our taste buds, comforting the rawness in our throats, and calming our queasy stomachs as it went.

I mentally pawed through the contents of our cupboards, searching for something with sufficient potency to lure me out from under the covers. Not that I was in the mood to attempt anything in the way of creative cookery. In fact, what I really wanted was chicken noodle soup . . . but without the tedium of downing spoonful after spoonful of broth. In other words, I craved chicken noodle soup without the soup. Let's call it . . . noodle chicken.

As an intellectual exercise, concocting the ideal restorative is no simple matter. But instinct, given free rein, can make it seem that way. I had recently bought, on pure speculation, a package of the thin Japanese wheat noodles called *somen*. I was drawn to them not because I had any idea of how I would use them but because they were divided—within the cellophane packaging itself—into neat little bundles, each bound with a blue ribbon. Now the residue of my fever made the thought of these silky strands slithering down my throat so compelling that it began to pull everything else together along behind it.

Despite my state of convalescence, I wanted potency, not bland-ness—but potency sheathed in a velvet glove. The noodles, being Japanese, naturally suggested soy sauce, minced ginger and garlic, slivered scallions. I also wanted an intensely flavored chicken broth and tender chunks of chicken meat—which, thanks to our cook-ahead method (see below), I already had on hand. This seemed a good starting point, quite sufficient in itself . . . and yet I still wasn't out of bed. That, it seemed, required something de luxe, a simple but persuasive touch of pampering—on the order of poached quail eggs or miniature shiitake mushroom caps, neither of which, of course, were lying around, or tender little dumplings, which would require too much effort. But there was a bright red pepper. If I could only face the task of peeling it . . .

Surprisingly, I could. In fact, I was already shuffling in the direction of the kitchen, a gleam in my eye.

• • •

The result was something so delicious that it has been a regular presence at our table ever since. I say this not to boast but to express a feeling only a little short of astonishment. I almost never work up a recipe out of whole cloth—such cooking talents as I have are usually directed at coming up with a special understanding of a familiar and typically very ordinary dish. I do occasionally whip up something to eat from whatever happens to be in the kitchen, but the whole point of such hunger-driven cooking lies in its unabashed immediacy—me hungry, me eat—which all but rules out any notion of reproducibility.

In this instance, however, hunger had little to do with what was going on. I was sick a lot when I was a child; in fact, for several years I had made a deal with God. When things got too much for me, I would tell Him so in my prayers that night—and the next morning I would wake up with a fever. My memories of the resulting times in bed are not of being lovingly cosseted but of total immersion in comforting solitude. For me, being sick was a way of securing the right to be left alone. The comforter's task, then, was not so much to soothe what hurt as to tempt me back into everyday life.

Until a tonsillectomy permanently exorcised this ability, my mother found the best way to treat these mysterious bouts of fever was to let boredom work the cure—a remedy that remains effective for most things that ail me today. But if tedium is the stick, the carrot has never been as easy to find. Consequently, this stratagem of my own inner comforter—to lure me into the kitchen and then succeed in making me supremely happy there—seems all the more impressive. I'd be the last one to know if these dishes have any true medicinal qualities; what I can testify to is their powers of enticement—for cook and eater alike.

INTRODUCTION

As you will see, the following two recipes are identical in spirit and all but identical in their ingredients. I have chosen to present them separately because neither is a variation of the other but is rather a separate orchestration of the same inspirational force. Each requires two easily obtained and inexpensive items—a cooking thermometer that can be immersed in simmering water and a quart-size microwavable ziplock bag (a Ziploc "double zipper" bag by preference), which we use for poaching meat. The method described below has three unique advantages: (1) the meat's juices and flavor are neither diluted nor lost during the cooking process; (2) the scum produced in the cooking clings to the sides of the bag, eliminating the need for skimming; and (3) the meat can be cooked in a small amount of liquid with no worry that it will overcook or dry out. This method also makes it possible to cook two or three cuts of meat simultaneuosly in the same pot—removing each bag at the end of its ideal cooking time. The meat, removed from its bag and refrigerated in its own juices, keeps for several days until needed. Note that the addition of water—called for in the following instructions—is necessary only when additional meat broth is wanted.

MEAT-COOKING METHOD

Fill a large pot about half full of hot tap water and set it on the stove. Turn the flame to high. Meanwhile, put the pieces of meat into a quart-size microwavable ziplock bag. Dissolve 1 teaspoon of kosher salt in 1 cup of water. Pour this over the meat. Tie the bag shut after forcing out as much air as possible. Lower this into the water on the stove.

Insert a thermometer into the water (we use an instant-read and hold it in place with the pot's cover). Bring the temperature up to 170°F and then adjust the heat to keep it there (a 5°F fluctuation in either direction is of no concern). Once this temperature has been reached, if you are preparing chicken, cook it for 3 hours; if beef, cook it for 8 hours.

When the meat is ready, grasp the knot of the bag with a pair of kitchen tongs. Lift the bag out and set it into a shallow bowl. Gingerly untie the knot and open the bag. Let its contents cool for 20 minutes. Remove the meat and shred it, discarding any bone, pieces of fat, or cartilage. Put the shredded meat into a bowl. Fold the top of the cooking bag over until it reaches about halfway down the bag's side. Now close one hand tightly around the top of the bag and hold the bottom firmly with the other. Invert it over the bowl of meat and loosen your fingers enough to allow the broth to stream into the bowl, closing off the flow when it reaches the fat. Reserve about a tablespoon of the fat separately (if desired) and discard the rest. Refrigerate the bowl of meat and broth and cover when cool. As noted above, this can be done a couple of days before proceeding with the rest of the recipe.

NOODLE CHICKEN
[Serves 2 with the flu]

kosher salt
1 tablespoon each chicken fat and peanut oil or
    2 tablespoons peanut oil
1 tablespoon soy sauce
½ tablespoon sugar (optional)
6 large leaves Napa or Chinese cabbage
6 scallions, including green tops, trimmed
1 large garlic clove, minced
1 large red bell pepper, cored, seeded, and peeled (see note)
4 chicken thighs, cooked and shredded as directed above,
    with accompanying broth (see note)
1-inch chunk ginger, peeled and grated or minced (see note)
1 teaspoon fresh chile paste (see note) or hot sauce to taste
½ pound Japanese somen noodles (see note)

Fill a pasta pot with 4 quarts of water and bring this to a boil. Stir in 1 to 2 tablespoons of salt. Put into a separate medium-size pot the chicken fat and/or peanut oil, 1 teaspoon of salt, the soy sauce, and the sugar (if using) and begin to heat this over a medium-low flame.

Cut the thick white stems of the cabbage into ½-inch strips. When you reach the green leaves, cut these in half from top to bottom, then cut these into ½-inch strips also. Keep the stems and leaves separate.

Slice the scallions into 2-inch lengths, then cut these in half vertically (all but the narrowest green ends, which can be used whole). When the oil in the pot is hot and the soy sauce has begun to release its odor, add the cabbage stem pieces, the scallion strips, and the minced clove of garlic. Stir all this occasionally for several minutes, until the scallions are wilted and soft and the cabbage stem pieces tender.

Cut the peeled red bell pepper pieces into ½-inch strips. When the scallions and cabbage stems have softened, add the pepper pieces and the strips of cabbage leaf to the pot. Mix well and cook another 2 or 3 minutes, stirring occasionally, until the leaves have wilted. Then add the chicken meat and the jellied broth. Turn the heat up to medium.

When the chicken jelly has melted, stir in the minced ginger and the fresh chile paste. Continue cooking until the chicken meat is heated through. Taste the broth for seasoning, adjusting as necessary.

Strew the noodles into the roiling salted water in the other pot. Cook until tender—about 3 minutes—and pour out into a colander or large sieve. Shake out any excess water and divide the noodles between two large soup bowls. Then ladle over the contents of the medium pot and serve at once. Chopsticks are optional.

Cook's Notes. Bell Pepper: Use a vegetable peeler or very sharp paring knife to remove the skin from the pepper. (Doing this makes a real difference to the finished dish, so don't skip this step.)

Chicken Thighs: Matt and I both prefer dark meat to light. We suspect that a chicken breast would be an acceptable replacement, but we've never been able to bring ourselves to find out.

Ginger: I almost never use a garlic press to crush garlic, but crushing ginger in one makes sense, since gingerroot is full of coarse fibers that add nothing to a dish. Cutting the peeled ginger into garlic-size chunks and squeezing them through a garlic press produces a flavor-intensive purée. Otherwise, use a porcelain ginger grater or mince the ginger with a cleaver.

Fresh Chile Paste: Sometimes called *sambal oelek*, this can be found in Asian grocery stores and some supermarkets. Look for the gold label with a red rooster on it and a simple list of ingredients—fresh chile paste, vinegar, salt, and preservatives. To temper the fire, we sieve out all the seeds when we start a new jar.

Somen Noodles: These thin white noodles, made of wheat, are related to udon noodles but are noticeably thinner—a delicate wisp of a noodle that still manages to retain a distinct texture and delicious taste. Most of the packages available at our Asian grocery come from Korea, where the noodle is called *somyun* and is also very popular. Typically, the Japanese eat somen cold and the Koreans eat them hot, tossed in fiery sauces. These noodles cook very quickly; don't let them get mushy.

NOODLE BEEF
[Serves 2 with the flu]

kosher salt
2 tablespoons peanut oil
1 tablespoon soy sauce
½ tablespoon sugar (optional)
2 medium to large carrots, peeled
1 small to medium head bok choy
6 scallions, including green tops, trimmed
1 garlic clove, minced
1 pound boneless beef short ribs, cooked and shredded as
    directed on page 72, with accompaning broth (see note)
1-inch chunk ginger, peeled and grated or minced (see above)
1 teaspoon fresh chile paste (see above) or hot sauce to taste
½ pound Japanese somen noodles (see above)

Fill a pasta pot with 4 quarts of water and bring this to a boil. Stir in 1 to 2 tablespoons of salt. Into a separate medium-size pot put the peanut oil, 1 teaspoon of salt, the soy sauce, and the sugar (if using) and begin to heat this over a medium-low flame.

Cut the carrots into thirds. Turn the resulting cylinders on end and slice each vertically into wide thin strips. Add these together to the pot with the hot oil and flavorings, tossing the mixture with a spatula

as you do. Cook these for 5 minutes before adding any other ingredients.

Cut both the thick white stems and the green leaves of the bok choy
into ½-inch strips but keep them separate. Slice the scallions into 2-inch
lengths, then cut these in half vertically (all but the narrowest green
ends, which can be used whole).

Stir the bok choy stem pieces, the scallion strips, and the minced
clove of garlic in with the carrot slices. Cook, stirring occasionally, for
several minutes, until the scallions are wilted and soft and the cabbage
stem pieces are tender. Taste a piece of carrot—at this point it should be
soft but still slightly crisp. If so, add the shredded beef and its jellied
broth. Turn the heat up to medium.

When the beef jelly has melted, stir in the minced ginger and the
fresh chile paste. Continue cooking until the beef is heated through.
Taste the broth for seasoning, adjusting as necessary.

Strew the noodles into the roiling salted water in the other pot.
Cook until tender—about 3 minutes—and pour out into a colander or
large sieve. Shake out any excess water and divide the noodles between
two large soup bowls. Then ladle over the contents of the medium pot
and serve at once. Chopsticks are optional.

Variations. A good handful of fresh bean sprouts or snow peas
makes a delicious addition to either version of this dish.

Cook's Note. Beef: Boneless beef short ribs are our particular favorite for this dish. If these are only available with the bone in, buy
about 1½ pounds to account for the waste. Thick-cut blade steak is a
good second choice.

Further Reading: *A Soothing Broth*

Treating food as if it were a subspecies of medicine is depressingly common these days, and those who embrace that notion as an answer to
all their health concerns must have a hard time organizing the daily
menus, with this to be eaten to strengthen the immune system, that to
ward off cancer, the other to keep the arteries flowing cleanly, the bones
from crumbling, the brain's synapses firing smoothly, and unwanted fat
cells on the run. "Regimen" is the word for this sort of disciplined eating, where pleasure is always subsumed to the needs of the rigorously
healthy life.

There is, however, another, very different tradition of food-as-medicine writing, directed to those who find that the consequences of their not-so-ordered lives have put them in need of a restorative or calmative or analeptic—something, in other words, that will gently coax back to terra firma what excess has driven up into a tree.

This is the subject of a valuable and very appealing little volume by Pat Willard called *A Soothing Broth*, an extended meditation on the role of the cook as comforter, with a widely gathered collection of "tonics, custards, soups, and other cure-alls for colds, coughs, upset tummies, and out-of-sort days." Most such books are directed to the fellow sufferer, a sharing of what the author has found palliative when under the weather. But for Willard, it is the role of soother, not sufferer, that strikes a chord of deep emotional resonance, and that makes her book all the richer: its subject is really the act of feeding as a form of reconnection to those we care about as well as for.

Illness and other acute forms of bodily discomfort shove the sufferer off into a separate world of pain. The bowl of steaming broth or the shimmering spoonful of custard is a rescue line tossed across that abyss; any tug at the other end means a diminution of feelings of helplessness and isolation at both ends of the rope. And this is equally true when the patient needing succor lies within ourselves.

Willard's writing, consequently, is always as suggestive about and sensitive to the needs of the caregiver as it is to those of the cared-for, a balance that carries over into the collection of old-fashioned recipes and remedies (often, of course, the two are the same) that she has gathered from amateur and professional comforters alike. (Tending the sick at home was, until very recently, almost as regular—and as exhausting—a task as doing the weekly laundry.)

She includes concoctions for specific ailments—apple soup for constipation; velvet cream for insomnia; *lait de poule* (hen's milk, a frothy mixture of orange flower water, sugar, and egg yolks, blended into boiling water) for a sore throat—as well as those that are universally solace-giving, like junket eggnog and stewed macaroni (about which she writes: "The macaroni is melting soft, surrounded by a thin sauce of milk; it has the effect of making your stomach feel as if it is wrapped up in a comforting quilt").

I also enjoyed her recipes for various restoratives and invigorating tonics, some repellent (the family fled the house when her grandmother set about preparing her seaweed-based winter tonic), others quite inviting (who could refuse a morning dose of "good quality" bourbon infused with sage blossoms and lemon peel?). *A Soothing Broth* is, in short, a treat as well as a treatment—and a replacement for half the stuff in your medicine cabinet.

PEPPER POT HOT

All hot! All hot!
Pepper pot! Pepper pot!
Makes backs strong,
Makes lives long,
All hot! Pepper pot!
　　　　—traditional Philadelphia street cry

To tell this story properly, I have to take you back about thirty years to the time when, just out of college, I spent a while teaching at a tiny progressive private school near Stockbridge, Massachusetts. The faculty there was a motley crew of the very young and the very old—either just starting their careers as teachers or at the very end of the line . . . and in either case not in a position to be too choosy about who hired them. I was one of the young ones; the math teacher, Steve Stephens, was one of the old ones, in years if not in spirit. Scrappy and full of contrarian opinions, Steve had led an adventurously checkered life during which he had made and lost a couple of fortunes, and was very enjoyable company.

Unlike most of the faculty, Steve lived off campus, in a house that while not of his own devising had certainly been adapted to his tastes. When, for instance, he decided to put a glass-surrounded fireplace in the center of his living room, he designed it himself using window safety glass from junked automobiles, thus saving thousands of dollars. He was also a gourmet cook, and on one of the occasions he had some of us other faculty over to dinner, he served his version of Philadelphia pepper pot, which I found so delicious I couldn't get it out of my mind.

Thirty years ago, recipes for Philadelphia pepper pot were still relatively common in American cookbooks, often including the various bits
of lore as to why it is attached to Philadelphia—some of it spurious,*
some of it interesting and perhaps even true.† Of these recipes, the one
that most appealed to me appears in Sarah Tyson Rorer's *Mrs. Rorer's
Philadelphia Cook Book*, which was first published in 1886.

PHILADELPHIA PEPPER POT

1 knuckle of veal
1 pound of plain tripe
1 pound of honey-comb tripe
bunch of pot-herbs‡
1 onion
¼ pound of suet
2 medium-sized potatoes
1 bay leaf
3 quarts of cold water
2 tablespoonfuls of butter
2 tablespoonfuls of flour
salt and cayenne pepper to taste

---

*That it was created by George Washington's cook at Valley Forge, who found he had only
some tripe and peppercorns at hand one evening and was forced to improvise, concocting a
dish that won him—and his hometown—instant acclaim. If true, he was a lucky chef to have
any peppercorns in his larder, let alone a sufficient supply to season enough soup for an army.
In any case, I have yet to find a reference to the dish connecting it to Philadelphia that dates
back further than the late nineteenth century . . . which makes the whole story sound more
like fakelore than folklore to me.

†That into the last century black women sold it out of pushcarts in the streets of Philadelphia.
The food historian Karen Hess told me that West Indian blacks made up a large part of the
catering trade in that city, and there's little doubt regarding the African origins of the dish, as
the versions in early American cookbooks make clear. In fact, Sarah Rutledge's recipe for
"Pepper Pot" in *The Carolina Housewife* (1847) is at least kissing cousin to contemporary Jamaican recipes for the same dish. The Philadelphia version, however, substitutes black peppercorns for the hot bird peppers, Northern root vegetables for the yams and plantains, and,
perhaps most significantly, tripe for the traditional mélange of salt meats.

‡Mrs. Rorer does not explain what these might be, but from the recipe it seems they include
fresh thyme, parsley, and a hot red pepper. I would add some minced celery leaves as well.

Wash the tripe well in cold water. Put it in a kettle, cover it with cold water and boil eight hours; this should be cooked the day before you want the soup. Wipe the knuckle with a damp towel, put it in a soup kettle, cover with the water, place it on the fire and bring slowly to a simmer, carefully skimming off the scum. Simmer gently for three hours, then strain and return soup to the kettle. Wash the pot-herbs, chop the parsley, rub off the thyme leaves, and cut only half the red pepper (they usually put a whole one in each bunch). Cut the potatoes into dice; add all these and the bay leaf to the soup. Cut the tripe into pieces one-inch square. Cut the meat from the knuckle into small pieces; add these also to the soup; place it on the fire and, when at boiling point, season with the salt and cayenne. Rub the butter and flour together and stir into the boiling soup, and then fifty small dumplings made as follows. Chop the suet fine, measure it, and take double the quantity of flour, one-quarter of teaspoonful of salt, mix well together, moisten with ice water (about a quarter of a cup). Form into tiny dumplings about the size of a marble, throw into the soup, simmer for fifteen minutes and serve.

This is a recipe for a hearty soup, to be sure, but, to my mind, one better titled "Tripe Soup with Suet Dumplings" than "Pepper Pot." You don't merely season a pepper pot with a pinch of cayenne; the pepper has to be an integral part of the conception of the thing. Steve's version was nothing like this. It was suavely smooth and rich, its creamy broth speckled with lots of black pepper, and there was plenty of green bell pepper cooked with the tripe. The closest recipe I've ever seen to what I tasted that night is the one in *Dine at Home with Rector: A Book on What Men Like, Why They Like It, and How to Cook It.* (This cookbook, published in 1937, is so much on Steve's wavelength that I can easily believe he owned it.)

> You start by dicing up a couple of slices of bacon a good quarter-inch thick and frying them golden brown. An onion and a green pepper, both chopped fine, are cooked with the bacon for five minutes. Then you introduce three pints of good veal or chicken stock and three quarters of a pound of honeycomb tripe, washed and drastically shredded. Here the mixture gets seasoned with a bay leaf well crumbled, a pinch of thyme, say half a teaspoon of salt and a teaspoon of whole black pepper well crushed. Bring it

to a boil and put in a cupful of diced potatoes, then simmer it
gently for about an hour. Thicken it with two tablespoons each of
butter and flour well creamed together and just before serving,
add a half cup of cream.

Unfortunately, I didn't come across this recipe until I was writing this
piece—helpful for it but only incidentally to me. Because before I had a
chance to wheedle the recipe out of Steve, he was killed in a head-on
automobile collision late one night in the middle of a blizzard (he was
never one to do things by half measures), and years of subsequent
searching failed to come up with anything like his recipe. I was entirely
on my own—which meant, practically speaking, that for decades nothing happened at all.*

This lack of initiative is partially explained by the fact that, offal-
lover though I am, tripe is something I have always been more willing
to eat than to cook. You would think that someone who handles brains
and kidneys without qualm would have little problem dealing with
stomach lining, but there it is. Raw tripe—rubbery, webby, squeaky—
reminds me less of an animal organ than something sliced from an old
Playtex girdle; it just doesn't whet my appetite.

Of course, the prepared version is not all that different, except in
one important way. Cooking tripe makes it deliciously succulent. If
you've never eaten the stuff, it's hard to explain what it's like. Fried oysters come to mind, but they're too soft. A tender piece of gristle is
closer still—but most people don't eat gristle, however toothsome, and
would consider anyone who attached the phrase "deliciously succulent"
to it to be a barefaced liar. Don't even get me started on cow hoof.

In any case, it isn't the texture that many people find off-putting
about tripe, it's the taste, and, to an even greater extent, the smell. In
raw tripe, especially, this can quickly turn my stomach . . . although it's
not easy to explain why. The phrase that most immediately comes to
mind is "cow breath." It isn't exactly a bad odor, but there's something
oppressively intimate about it, a sense of getting a little too close to a
very large animal's maw.

---

*Of course, the Rector volume had been sitting in plain view on the shelf for years—ever since
Matt moved in and brought her cookbooks with her. But the book has no index, the recipes
are all in prose, and, perversely, the chapter on soup is second to last in the book. It's a miracle that I ever stumbled upon the recipe at all.

However, once tripe is cooked, that aspect pretty much fades away. What is left tastes like gristle seasoned with a spritz of stomach acid—chewy, tasty, and with the vaguest whisper of the abattoir. There's nothing quite like it for provoking a visceral response. Probably the line that separates those who love tripe from those who hate it has to do with the strength of that reaction . . . or how our particular psychology deals with it—just the way a loud explosion outside on the street sends some of us straight under the bed and others bursting out the door with camcorders already rolling.

As long as I wouldn't cook tripe, my only dependable fix came when I would go back to Maine (about twice a year) and get the chance to order fried tripe at Moody's Diner. It's always on the menu, and it's almost always very good—a crispy, deep-fried coating wrapped around chunks of tangy chewy juiciness. Apart from that, my only other recourse—and a not very satisfactory one—was to reach for a can of *menudo*, the classic Mexican tripe soup. When we lived in Maine, I had to persuade my pal Bill Bridges to send me some from Texas, but here in central Massachusetts I can find it for myself. That there might be a canned version of pepper pot, however, never even crossed my mind.

• • •

Then, a few months ago, wandering past the Campbell's soup section in an aisle of the local supermarket, there one was, flagging me down from the top shelf—just above eye level, where grocers put items that rarely generate impulse sales, since shoppers don't tend to see them unless they're intentionally looking for them. At our supermarket, all the canned soups with gourmet pretensions are up there in one long row.

There are a good number of Campbell's soups—tomato, chicken noodle, cream of mushroom—that can be found without fail in any supermarket, whatever its size, but there are other varieties that appear only because of local interest or a whim of the grocery buyer. In one store, it might be oyster stew or cream of onion, in another Scotch broth or shrimp bisque. Strangely, a supermarket we frequented in Maine was partial to chicken wonton (I was so astonished to see it, I bought some. It was awful). But here at Easthampton's Big E, by gum, was Campbell's pepper pot.

I took down a can and examined it. The ingredient list was promising, despite the fact that three of the first four ingredients were actually three different ways of saying water. It began as so—

> *Ingredients:* beef tripe stock, water, cooked beef tripe, beef stock, potatoes, enriched macaroni product, carrots, flour, tomato paste, salt, lard, vegetable oil, sweet red peppers, green peppers, etc.

—with "etc." marking the point where such things as "beef fat spice" (yes, that's just a single ingredient) begin to make their appearance. Still, your heart has to warm to a canned soup these days with a touch of lard in the formula. This perhaps can be explained by another encouraging sign: this Campbell's variety is made in Canada, a country that still takes humble, hearty soups very seriously. (Appropriately enough, they produce Campbell's Scotch broth as well.) I bought two cans of pepper pot, a container of milk, and headed for home.

Let me say straight off that this stuff is wicked good, even more so if you dilute the contents of the can with milk instead of water and stir in a generous dose of Tabasco as you heat it up. (Astute readers may have already noticed the mystifying absence of peppercorns *or* hot peppers from the list of ingredients.) There's only a minimal amount of tripe, but it makes its presence felt; the soup's flavor has just enough animal edge to balance off the blandness of the potatoes, carrots, and tiny plump tubes of macaroni. This is one of those dishes that work not by harmonious agreement (think chicken noodle soup) but because of the attraction of opposites—neither of which the soup whisperer at Campbell's allows to get the upper hand.

A can of Campbell's pepper pot became a regular midnight snack for me, even an occasional breakfast. And there things would have remained quite happily if it were not for one aspect that kept sticking in my craw: the price. A dollar seventy-nine seemed just too damned much to pay for a can of condensed soup. (Campbell's Scotch broth costs $2.49 a can; you can imagine how often I buy *that*.)

This is one of the unexpected pains of growing old: your sense of what things *ought* to cost gets more and more out of whack with what things *do* cost. For decades you keep your equilibrium as prices creep up and up; then, for some reason, you just lose it. A few weeks ago I went to our local newspaper stand to see if they had a special issue of a computer magazine devoted to the new Macintosh operating system,

OS X. I was sure that (a) I wouldn't find it and (b) it would be priced at something ridiculous, like $7.95. Well, they did have it, and it cost $12.95.

I was not only incredulous but angry . . . no, *mortified*—all but imagining that the help was snickering at me as I slunk out of the store. It isn't as though I can't afford that much money or that, looking back on it, the amount seems all that outrageous. No, what it's like is going down a flight of stairs and discovering too late that the last step is a few inches deeper than the ones that came before. The shock is out of all proportion to the physical jolt. You feel at once stupid and betrayed.

I relate this not because I imagine it to be all that fascinating but because it illustrates something intriguing: the complex strands of motivation that make us decide when and what to cook. I can leaf through cookbooks all day, engrossed by the recipes and the color photographs of the finished dishes . . . and then put them down and go open a can of soup, a can of soup that reminds me of a dish I ate once decades ago and that I can now only vaguely remember. Then, because that can of soup costs fifty cents more than I think it ought to, I plunge into unknown waters, setting out to prepare a dish from a piece of offal that, in its raw state, I have so far in my life pretty much managed to avoid having any contact with at all. How do you figure that?

Furthermore—remember I have yet to see George Rector's recipe—I immediately begin to compose a version of pepper pot that, mostly by dint of creative misremembering, is almost entirely my own. First, I confuse the macaroni for barley. I seem to recall the Campbell's version containing corn and grab a can of Niblets. Finally, I decide to replace the potatoes with something with a little more presence—a can of hominy. By the time I throw in a can of beef stock, I've already spent at least the price of a can of pepper pot, and this before I've even factored in the tripe.

By now, this just doesn't matter. Appetite has commandeered the steering wheel and told me to sit back and enjoy the ride. Culinary correctness is also left in the dust. Because what I'm setting out to replicate came out of a can, half of what I've assembled in my cart is also canned, even though such goods rarely intrude into my serious cooking efforts. Here's what came out of all this.

PEPPER POT NOT
[Serves 4 to 6]

1 pound beef tripe, honeycomb by preference
1 carrot
1 onion
1 celery stalk
2 or 3 tablespoons unsalted butter
1 teaspoon hot pepper sauce, or to taste
1 or 2 large garlic cloves, minced
1 tablespoon tomato paste
scant ¼ cup barley
1 14½-ounce can low-sodium beef or chicken broth
1 15-ounce can white or yellow hominy
1 15¼-ounce can whole kernel corn
1 cup half-and-half (or milk, if preferred)
salt and black pepper to taste
minced parsley for garnish

Rinse the tripe under cold running water and pat dry with a paper towel. Use a sharp knife to cut it into bite-size pieces.

Chop the carrot, onion, and celery into medium dice. Melt the butter in a large soup pot over medium heat. When it is bubbling season it with the hot pepper sauce, then add the chopped vegetables and the minced garlic. Cook, stirring, until the onions are translucent. Add the cut-up tripe and the tomato paste. Stir some more, letting the tripe absorb a little of the color and flavor of the seasonings.

Mix in the barley, the can of broth, and the entire contents (including the liquid) of the cans of hominy and whole kernel corn. Bring up to a gentle simmer, cover, and let cook until the tripe is tender but still chewy, about an hour to an hour and a half.

Finally, mix in the half-and-half. Let this heat up while you season the soup to taste with salt and grindings of black pepper. Serve garnished with minced parsley.

It is one of the clichés of cooking that homemade soups are better than canned soups, but this is not always true. Yes, a really good homemade soup is usually better than a canned one, and, conversely, even a pretty bad homemade soup can outmatch certain canned varieties—beef noodle, for instance—if only by default. However, Campbell's black bean soup, modestly enhanced with a tablespoon of sherry, is about as good as a soup can get. And since I already thought pretty highly of their pepper pot, I wasn't all that confident that my own efforts would produce something any better.

But it was better. My version took everything I liked about the canned soup and stroked it until it purred. The barley had more flavor and more texture than the macaroni; the hominy outclassed the potatoes; the corn kernels added a gentle sweetness; the quantity of tripe gave the soup more savor, more punch, more chew. It reminded me of the day I replaced my portable monophonic record player with a real stereo system and put one of my favorite recordings on the turntable. It was the same music, sure, but now the sound had gained palpable richness and depth.

• • •

> *Pozole*, like the beloved, hearty tripe soup *menudo*, really is something special: a beautiful one-bowl meal to serve when a crowd comes, a rustic specialty to eat from the street stands at night or, in the case of *menudo*, the morning after. But of the two, *pozole*—in any of the national colors [of Mexico] (white, red, or green)—is my favorite. It offers more of the contrasting textures—soft-cooked and crunchy-raw—and each guest gets to doctor it up *al gusto*, as the Spanish saying goes.
> —Rick Bayless, *Authentic Mexican*

I had posted a photograph and a description of my pepper pot in the "John's Midnight Snack" section of our website and got back a message from a visitor there telling me that what I had come up with was a variation of her favorite Mexican soup, *pozole*. I e-mailed her back in confusion. What do you mean, soup? I asked. *Posole* is the Spanish word for hominy. No, she replied. It's the name of a soup. It's made with hominy, and that's what the recipes call for: h-o-m-i-n-y. At this point, with tempers getting a little frayed, I thought I had better check to see if I knew what I was talking about. And what do you know, we were both right—except she was a bit more so than I.

For a brief time back in the early nineties, Matt and I toyed with the idea of moving to New Mexico, and I plunged into a preliminary exploration of that area's indigenous foods. That none of the dishes I prepared stayed for long in our repertoire is mostly explained by the fact that it was one too many Maine winters that fueled this notion rather than any true yearning for a radical change in landscape—certainly not if it meant exchanging one set of limited culinary possibilities for another.

However, I did learn some things, including that in New Mexico the word for hominy—i.e., whole kernels of corn treated with slaked lime, which can be encountered fresh, frozen, canned, or dried—is "posole." This, at the time, I thought to be, plain and simple, the Spanish term for it. Not so. In Spain hominy seems to be unknown; in Mexico it is called *nixtamal*, the word used by the native Nahuatl, who discovered it.

As it turns out, it was also called *nixtamal* in New Mexico until well into the last century, and the soup made from it was called, again as it is in Mexico, *pozole de nixtamal*. It was only as the traditional ways faded that the one word, with the *z* anglicized to an *s*, has come to mean both the stew and its featured ingredient.

Pozole comes from the Nahuatl word *posolli*,* which means "foam" and originally referred to a thick, fermented nutritious cornmush beverage. This, as the Spanish conquistadors recorded when they first encountered the Nahuatl, or, as they called them, the Aztecs, provided the basic sustenance of the poor. As Sophie Coe explains in *America's First Cuisines*, Nahuatl dishes that made their way into Mexican cooking gradually became Ladino-ized by the addition of pork, a process that over the centuries transformed *posolli* into *pozole*—which gives the dish a very venerable history indeed.†

Perhaps because of this fact, *pozole* (as we will now call the soup, restricting "posole" to mean the New Mexican dried kernels of

---

*Among the words besides posole that the Nahuatl contributed to the English language are avocado, cacao, chile, chocolate, coyote, guacamole, mesquite, peyote, tamale, and tomato. *Menudo*, which sounds as though it ought to be one of them, is actually a Spanish word that means something along the lines of inconsequential remnants, small change. The plural, *menudos*, means offal; the diminutive plural, *menudillos*, chicken gizzards.

†In Mexican folklore, the creation myth of *pozole* is quite different. As Jeffrey Pilcher tells the story in *¡Que vivan los tamales!* this happened in eighteenth-century Chilapa, where the women, preparing for a visit by the Archbishop of Puebla, realized that they had too much corn to grind. So, instead of making tortillas, they simply cooked the *nixtamal* with pork to make a stew.

hominy, since that is what they call them, and using *nixtamal* is only going to cause even more confusion) evokes the same sort of heartfelt response from Mexicans (and Mexican-Americans) that a bowl of grits can provoke in Southerners, the sense that with the right food you can sure taste your roots, no matter how far away you are from home . . . or however much home seems to be changing out of all recognition, right beneath your feet.

As with *menudo*, *pozole* also comes in three different styles (which, as Rick Bayless points out, match the three colors of the Mexican flag): *verde*, made with pumpkin seeds and tomatillos; *rojo*, made with assorted dried red chiles; and *blanco*, made with pork and hominy and not much else. My version, given below, started out as almost identical to my pepper pot, with pork replacing the tripe. But as I got drawn further into these dishes I started to get my act together, replacing the canned hominy with dried posole, adding Mexican oregano and New Mexican powdered chile, and, of course, leaving out the barley. But the corn I kept. It is not, it turns out, untraditional, and it helps to underline the dish's special brightness.

POZOLE ROJO
[Serves 4 to 6]

Note that the dried posole requires an overnight soaking.

> 1 cup dried posole (see note), presoaked and parboiled
>   as directed on page 96
> 1 tablespoon melted pork fat or corn oil
> 2 medium yellow onions, chopped
> 2 garlic cloves, minced
> 1 15¼-ounce can whole kernel corn, including liquid
> 1½ pounds pork shoulder or butt, trimmed of excess fat,
>   or 4 to 6 boneless chicken thighs
> 1 large ripe tomato, cut into chunks
> 1 red and 1 green poblano chile, roasted, peeled, seeded, and
>   chopped (see pages 96–97)
> 1 red and 1 green jalapeño chile, cored, seeded, and minced
> ½ teaspoon Mexican oregano

1 teaspoon New Mexican (or other semi-hot, richly flavored)
   powdered red chile
salt and black pepper to taste

FOR GARNISHING:
minced scallions, avocado chunks, hot red pepper flakes, lime
   wedges, fresh cilantro, and tortilla chips

Starting the night before, prepare the dried posole.

Heat the fat in a large pot. Add the onions and garlic and sauté until both are translucent. Meanwhile, measure the liquid from the parboiled hominy and the can of corn into a large bowl and, if necessary, add enough water to make 1 quart. When the onions and garlic are ready, add this liquid and all the other ingredients except the garnishes. Bring the pot to a low boil, cover it, and cook for 2 hours at a gentle simmer.

Remove the meat and shred it with two forks. Return the meat to the pot and cook it for an additional 15 minutes. Adjust the seasoning if necessary and serve in large shallow bowls with the garnishes set out separately.

Additions and Subtractions. The addition of a split pig's foot to the stew is traditional and will add a silky quality to the broth. To substitute canned hominy, use the white variety, skip the overnight soaking, and include all the liquid in the can when you add it to the stew.

As it happens, *pozole* and *menudo* are treated like identical twins. Writers on Mexican food mention them in the same breath and print their recipes side by side. This is because they are made the same way, served the same way, and eaten with the same heightened appreciation. Once I started cooking tripe and preparing dried posole it was inevitable that I would turn my hand to the making of *menudo*.

• • •

[*Menudo*] is undoubtedly the one dish most Mexican-Americans identify as their own . . . When I asked why it was so universally popular, the answer was "If you like *menudo*, you are a true Mexican" or "It's ours. Everyone else eats our tacos and salsas, but you won't find *menudo* at Taco Bell."

—Marilyn Tausend, *Cocina de la Familia*

One of the problems with attaching your cultural identity to a particular food is that the moment you do so outsiders start forming lines to get a taste of it. I remember back in the fifties when the ability to consume chile peppers, especially really, really hot chile peppers, was the pluperfect instance of *auténtico macho mexicano*. Stories abounded of gringos fleeing from cantinas in humiliating panic, their throats on fire and their eyes filled with tears.

However, there's nothing like a tough-guy persona connected to a particular food—garlic, chiles, maguey worms, blue corn fungus—to whet the . . . well, maybe not the appetite, exactly, but certainly the competitiveness of a certain type of American male. Consequently, these days Mexicans are lucky to find any hot peppers in their local market at all, so many are sucked north of the border to fill the bottles of an endless number of boutique sauces, each one fierier than the next.

Menudo, containing as it does both tripe and lots of hot chile—and, in Mexico, it isn't *menudo* unless it burns its way down the gullet—has all the requisite qualities to rebuff the outsider while warming the heart (and stomach) of the native enthusiast. With *menudo*—as with the prickly pear or, for that matter, the armadillo—it's only a matter of penetrating the rebarbative exterior to feast on the deliciousness within.

In Mexico, *menudo* is credited with potent restorative powers that, in English-language narratives, tend to be restricted to its reputation as a cure for what Mexicans refer to as *la cruda*—a brain-grater of a hangover. Rick Bayless suggests it is because of the high vitamin B content in the dish. My own suspicion is that the soup's strong, spicy aroma gently galvanizes the prostrate nervous system long before the first mouthful reaches the stomach.

The ritual of the Sunday morning bowl of *menudo* has made its way over the border, wherever Mexican-Americans settle in. As a reader wrote, "Where we lived in California, the Mexican market only made it on Sunday, and the line formed at 6 a.m. You had to bring your own pot—typically Mexican graniteware, speckled blue and gray." I can easily imagine taking my own little pot, sitting down on the curb, and, brain reeling, hands shaking, and stomach quivering, lowering my face to within a few millimeters from its steaming contents and quietly, deeply inhaling its vapors until the storm within subsides.

• • •

Although there is no doubt that *menudo* has been finding more and more fans on this side of the border—every year sees an increasing number of *menudo* cook-offs being held at county fairs and local celebrations (and not just to mark Cinco de Mayo)—among Anglos it remains pretty much a guy thing and, thus, far more likely to be served up at the local firehouse than at the family supper table. Mexican-Americans must find this a tad strange. For them, the analeptic powers of a bowl of *menudo* are seen as a special enhancement to an everyday dish rather than merely a morning-after treatment for a night on the town. As Himilce Novas and Rosemary Silva tell it in *Latin American Cooking Across the U.S.A.*:

> [*Menudo*] . . . is welcomed at table anytime, but especially for breakfast on Sundays. In fact, many churches with congregations of Mexican immigrants cook up enormous batches of *menudo* to serve along with tacos and tamales after early morning Mass. (Second-generation Mexican-Americans tend to opt for coffee and doughnuts instead.)

It may be that everyone in the congregation is suffering a hangover, but I imagine instead that for them a steaming bowl of *menudo* is the perfect way to freshen their spirits for a pleasant day of rest . . . while it primes their system for another demanding week of work.

Even so, even so . . . this is not to say that the Anglo take on *menudo* is entirely wrong. When, earlier in this essay, I referred to *pozole* and *menudo* as identical twins, I did not mean to imply that they have identical personalities. On the contrary. Mexicans, I think, would agree that, of the two, *pozole* is the light child and *menudo* the dark child. *Pozole* is what you eat to celebrate Christmas and your birthday; *menudo* is what you eat to bring yourself back from the dead.

In this regard, *menudo* reminds me of onion soup in the old days at Les Halles, the former central wholesale food district in Paris. There, as dawn crept over the horizon, sleepy late-night revelers shared tables with equally sleepy carters, porters, and butchers, the one group downing a big bowl of onion soup to ease their way into dreamland, the other doing exactly the same thing to ease their way out of it. Robert Courtine could just as easily have been writing about *menudo* when he penned these words in *The Hundred Glories of French Cooking*:

In her presence all castes dissolve. Rich and poor are equals in appetite. And from the subtle depths of all past ages the scent of the
gratinée is the incense of haves and have-nots together in the dark,
together because of the dark. The early-to-bed know nothing of
her. They are the sons of error and she is certainty itself.

• • •

Most north-of-the-border cookbooks reduce *menudo* to the sum of its
formula:

tripe + hominy + chiles + garlic

but in Mexico, where cooking from books is still a somewhat heretical
notion, that formula is simply an outline to be fleshed out by local
tradition and the inclinations of the cook. So, for instance, Elisabeth
Lambert Ortiz, in *The Complete Book of Mexican Cooking*, offers a
recipe for Sonoran-style *menudo* (*menudo estilo sonora*) that calls for
scallions, cilantro, and corn cut from six cobs, whereas the recipe for
the same dish in Diana Kennedy's *The Art of Mexican Cooking* contains none of these things (although it does suggest cilantro as a garnish).

Furthermore, neither Ortiz nor Kennedy puts chile into the soup itself, instead allowing eaters to crumble in fiery dried *pequín* to their
taste at the table—a style known as *menudo blanco*. But James W. Peyton, in *El Norte: The Cuisine of Northern Mexico* (an area that embraces Sonora), adds his chile directly to the broth, in the manner of
menudo roso, which is supposedly *not* the way they do it there.

So, shall we declare the recipe of one or the other of these authors
inauthentic? You won't get me to touch that question with a ten-foot
pole. The point is that the more Mexican cookbooks the *menudo* enthusiast looks at, the more the true nature of the dish becomes apparent, even though one pays the price of learning that a *menudo
completamente auténtico* may require more of an effort than most of us
are willing to make.

For example, even if you choose to set aside rumors that the *real*
stuff is cooked inside a length of the animal's intestine, it's not difficult
to find Mexican recipes that call for a beef hoof. Long cooking trans-

forms this into a gelatinous mass that gives that soup's broth a silky smoothness, a perfect backdrop to the fiery burn of the chile and the upfront gaminess of the tripe (and analogous to the role that milk or cream plays in pepper pot).

In Mexico, local abattoirs are still common enough, as is the appetite for every edible part of the animal from snout to hoof. A calf's foot is merely a pricier equivalent, but try finding one of those in an American meat market nowadays—at least outside of large ethnic neighborhoods. Most likely, you'll have to make do with a pig's foot—which is exactly what Mexican-Americans do.

And this is fine, except that such tears and subsequent makeshift patches can only weaken the web of connections that define the soul of the dish. Unlike the hoof, the pig's foot looks out of place in a beef tripe dish. It becomes optional. It vanishes entirely (as it does in Park Kerr's otherwise carefully crafted recipe in *The El Paso Chile Company's Texas Border Cookbook*, replaced by the quarter cup of olive oil—an ingredient that is a stranger to Mexican cooking in general and to *menudo* in particular). Regular oregano replaces the Mexican version, which in truth is a very different herb, a member of the lemon verbena family. And so it goes . . .

• • •

> *Menudo* is cooked best by the little old ladies and their daughters who pull picnic tables out into the dirt streets in front of their houses in dusty little Mexican working towns. Under the light of a gas lantern, they feed the local workmen a great bowl of Menudo and a pile of tortillas for a few pesos. The competition between these good ladies is fierce, and that keeps the Menudo good.   —Bruce C. Moffitt

I first sampled *menudo* back in the seventies, when my brother Peter took me to La Casita, a Mexican restaurant in Washington, DC. I had it as my first course, and it was so good that it completely blotted out the memory of everything else I ate that night (which was quite a lot). Afterwards . . . well, *menudo* is not all that easy to find in New England, even in Mexican restaurants (although that has been changing in recent years). Instead, as already reported, I ate it out of cans.

It goes without saying that canned *menudo* is to the version served at La Casita what a postcard of Paris is to actually being in that city.

Still, you can't help picking up that postcard occasionally, even if it's only to weep. In fact, the general awfulness of canned *menudo* has sent me in the opposite direction of the course described in my pepper pot adventures, forcing me to find for myself the missing pieces of the puzzle, the absence of which reduced what I was eating to a thin, coarse-edged, acidic caricature of what a fuzzy, fading memory still remembered as pungent, rich, and good.

As pepper pot led me onward to *pozole*, the connections between it and *menudo* became more and more apparent . . . and had all the power of a revelation. The unctuousness added by the pig's foot, the depth provided by the meaty beef bones, the bonus in flavor and texture that came from combining the flesh of roasted fresh chiles with the concentrated presence of the chile powder: here lay the key to the *menudo* of my dreams.

Even so, the re-creation of a gustatory memory, however skillful, can have no claims to authenticity. The respect and interest are there, but not the experience. Unlike Bruce Moffitt, but probably like the majority of my readers, I have not benefited from the instruction of the old ladies of Sonora. But in cooking, as in life, we can only try to improve on what we have.

NOT-SO-PSEUDO *MENUDO*
[Serves up to 6]

Truth in Recipe Writing: As already explained, menudo, *like chili con carne, has a firm yet fluid identity, allowing the cook an amazing amount of freedom so long as the results remain true to the essence of the dish. Consequently, what follows has been tweaked to my own taste, at the heart of which lies the following equation:*

tripe + beef gristle = superior *menudo*

If your reaction is yeah! *proceed full steam ahead. If, instead, it's* huh? *you will just have to tweak the recipe some more. My feelings won't be hurt. However, I do think that home-cooked posole, good beef broth, and plenty of roasted fresh chiles are essential to a top-drawer result, and I urge you to give the dish the extra effort these things need. They make all the difference.*

Note that the dried posole requires an overnight soaking.

FOR THE POSOLE:
1 cup dried posole (see source note)
2 quarts water

Briefly rinse the posole under cold running water and place it in a bowl. Cover it with 1 quart of the water and let it soak overnight. The next day, discard the soaking water and put the posole in a pot with the remaining quart of water. Bring it up to a simmer, skimming off and discarding any scum that rises to the surface. Lower the heat, cover, and gently simmer for 3 hours, ignoring any cooking instructions that might be on the package.

THE BROTH:
3 pounds meaty beef ribs or 1½ pounds bone-in short ribs
½ tablespoon kosher salt
1 quart water

Dust the beef with the salt and put it in a large pot with the water. Bring to a gentle simmer, skim off any scum that rises to the surface, and cook gently for 2 to 3 hours, or until the broth has a nice beefy taste and the meat and gristle peel easily off the bones. If using the beef ribs, chop the strips of meat and gristle into bite-size chunks, discarding the pieces of fat. If using the bone-in short ribs, shred the meat, chop up the gristle, and, again, toss the fat. Also, skim off and discard most of the beef fat floating on top of the stock, reserving 2 tablespoons.

TO ROAST THE FRESH CHILES:
3 each green and red poblano or Anaheim chiles

I find chile peppers perfect candidates for roasting on top of the stove if you have a gas range. Turn the flame up to medium and, using tongs, place the peppers, two or three to a burner, directly over the flame. They blacken quickly and make very little mess. If you have an outdoor grill, this is another excellent option. If all else fails, roast them under the oven broiler. In any case, turn the peppers so that the skin blackens on all sides.

Once each is completely blackened, remove it to a large piece of aluminum foil. When all are done, fold over the foil to make a package and let the peppers cool until they are comfortable to handle. The time in the foil allows the residual internal heat in the chiles to steam the blackened skin loose, making this relatively easy to peel away. When this is done, pull away and discard the stem, the central core with the seeds, and the veins. Use the edge of a spoon to scrape away any remaining seeds. Chop the flesh into small pieces and reserve this and any remaining juices held by the foil.

FOR THE *MENUDO* ITSELF:

1 to 1½ pounds fresh beef tripe
1 pig's foot, split down the center, or 1 pound fresh (not smoked) pork hocks
2 tablespoons reserved beef fat (see broth recipe above) or butter or corn oil
4 to 6 medium yellow onions, chopped
3 or 4 large garlic cloves, minced
2 tablespoons hot powdered red chile
½ tablespoon Mexican oregano (see source note)
the beef meat and gristle plus broth, partially cooked posole, and roasted chile pepper flesh (as described above)
salt and black pepper to taste

FOR GARNISHING:

minced scallions, hot red pepper flakes, lime wedges, chopped fresh cilantro, and plenty of tostadas or tortilla chips

Rinse the tripe under cold running water and pat somewhat dry with paper towels. Using care and a very sharp knife, cut the tripe into small bite-size pieces. Rinse the pig's foot and set aside.

Meanwhile, heat the fat in a large heavy pot. Add the onions and garlic and sauté, stirring occasionally, until the onions begin to brown. Then stir in the powdered chile and, once this has blended in, the pieces of tripe. Keep stirring until all the tripe has been colored by the chile.

Stir in the Mexican oregano, the beef meat and gristle plus broth, the pig's foot, the partially cooked posole, and the roasted chile pepper flesh. Bring the *menudo* to a gentle simmer and cook over low heat for 1½ to 2 hours, or until both the tripe and the posole are tender.

Serve in wide shallow bowls with some or all of the garnishes. The pig's foot can be divided among the bowls, served separately to an aficionado, or discarded.

Mildly Deleterious Shortcuts/Alterations. To substitute canned hominy, add a 15-ounce can of the white variety (liquid included) to the *menudo* at the same time the partially cooked dried posole would be added. A mixture of 3 each green and red jalapeño or serrano chiles can be used instead of the roasted poblanos: just core, seed, and chop them up, stirring them in at the same time that you add the onion and garlic. If the idea of the gristle doesn't appeal to you, simply choose the bone-in beef short ribs option and discard the gristle along with the bones and fat when you make the stock. Or close your eyes and use canned beef broth instead. Some purists will object to the presence of tostadas or tortilla chips here, instead of corn or flour tortillas. Fair enough—but having had *menudo* with all three, I much prefer the crispy chips to crumble into the soup.

One of the rarely discussed pleasures that cooking has to offer is just what we have done here—throwing ourselves into the water and letting it sweep us away . . . until it eventually deposits us, shivering but exhilarated, on a strange stretch of riverbank. Of course, we have to be prepared to swim like hell if we need to, but the real joy comes from surrendering to the flow.

> The spicy scent of toasting chiles—*anchos* and *poblanos*—reached my nostrils, along with that of the soup itself, with its onion, garlic, peppercorns, and tripe, simmering uncovered over the fire. The quartered calf's foot bubbled along with them, softening and blending its rich flavor with the other ingredients. Later Spy would strip the meat from the bones and knuckles, chop it into chunks, and toss it back into the mix. Spy always added some hot chiles to his *menudo*, what he called *cuaresmeños*. He'd brought the seeds north with him from the Mexican state of Jalapa during his scalp-hunting days and grew them with great devotion in our backyard garden in Santa Fe. "My *menudo* can raise the dead," was his boast. He'd discovered it during his drinking days and found it a sure cure for the anguish of his hangovers.
>
> —Robert F. Jones, *Deadville*

Sources

Los Chileros de Nuevo Mexico offers a range of New Mexican food-stuffs, including dried posole, Mexican oregano, salsas, and various forms of dried green and red chile at very reasonable prices. It is a favorite source of ours. P.O. Box 6215; Santa Fe, NM 87502; (505) 471-6967; www.888eatchile.com.

THE LAUGHING NUT

It is very known that satisfying pistachio eaten by braking tightened shells between front tooth is very hard. Generally, and also it is a fact that these kind of fancies which work fingers and teeth in a serial mode as parts of a machine, calms psychologically and keeps people from distress.

—Turkish website

I can almost remember the first time I ate a pistachio nut, with "almost" meaning that I can evoke the experience without being able to pinpoint the time or the place. I was certainly young enough for the nut to be an unknown quantity to me and old enough to be tempted to risk a nickel for a fistful from one of those old-fashioned sidewalk dispensers. You slipped in the coin, turned the crank, and down the chute came a rather parsimonious rattling of bright red pistachios. "Bright red" isn't exactly right—I guess the adjective comes to mind because they were so obviously dyed. "Tawdry red" gets it better, a term that pushes the meaning more toward "carny" than toward "appetizing."

However, there was nothing faux about the nuts themselves. They were delicious, so much so that they left behind an indelible impression. I didn't mean that to be a pun, but it is: my hands were stained pink-red by the dye, annoying to a little boy's sense of amour propre. Yuck, it might as well be lipstick. Years later, the California Pistachio Board would circulate the rumor that foreign pistachios were dyed like that to hide flaws that American nuts simply didn't possess.

This was a lie, but it was a clever one, and like many good lies it touched on an impolitic truth. Pistachios are dyed red because tarting them up in that manner is thought to make them more festive . . . just like the bright, garish pink of cotton candy, which persuades you to shell out coinage for a raspy bite of air.

Of course, wherever there's a hint of the carny in the air, there's an equal suggestion of the rube. And as I grew older I caught on to the fact that red-stained fingers were the badge of one. I have always lacked the self-confidence to not mind making a conspicuous fool of myself. To this day, I steer clear of dyed pistachio nuts and, in fact, thought that they had long been put to rest. But then I noticed a whole shelf of them at the local supermarket—and from a California grower, no less— beckoning to purchasers who want to recapture their youth, perhaps, or are just ready for a good old low-class hot time.

In any case, pistachio nuts played no other role in my early life; if anyone in my family had a taste for them, they kept it to themselves. My mother had tried putting out salted mixed nuts during the holiday season, but they vanished so quickly that you would have thought our Electrolux had a secret hankering for them. So they were replaced by a big bowl of unshelled nuts and a progression of increasingly ingenious nutcrackers. Those and the Spanish peanuts reserved for bridge parties pretty much summed it up.

●　●　●

Meanwhile, unbeknownst to me, the pistachio was beginning to establish a presence in California. This had actually started back in 1929, when an American plant scientist, William E. Whitehouse, convinced that the state was ideally suited for growing that nut, spent six months gathering seed stock from all over Persia. He started the journey back to the United States with a twenty-pound sack of the best pistachios he could find but unfortunately ate every one on the long and boring passage home—swearing each time he grabbed another handful that this would be absolutely, absolutely, the last he would take.

Just joking. Whitehouse was clearly made of sterner stuff than I. In fact, he planted those nuts when he got back to California, and so began the long job of turning pistachios into a commercial reality—long, in part, because it takes a new tree seven years to produce its first crop. It wasn't until 1950 that a really stand-out tree could be selected, one with noticeably larger and plumper nuts. It was named "Kerman" after the famous carpet-making city near where the nut had been collected. Branches from this tree were grafted onto heartier rootstock, and the foundation of the California pistachio industry was at hand . . . or would be after twenty-five more years. The first commercial crop didn't appear until the mid-seventies. When it did, I was waiting for it.

Iranians call the pistachio *khandan*, or "laughing nut," because of its appearance once the ripening process has sprung open the shell. You can see what they mean, but in my experience the best most Middle Eastern pistachios can do is smirk. American pistachios, on the other hand, gape so wide that you would think they were flirting with their dental hygienist. If we were in the habit of giving nicknames to our nuts, this one would be Mr. Chortlehead.

In truth, Mr. Chortlehead has plenty to guffaw about. You may not know this—I certainly didn't—but on the tree the nuts are encased in a bright- to pale-green fruit, looking a little like miniature olives. When these begin to shrivel and turn yellow, they are harvested and, in the Middle East, spread out in the shade to dry, where the husk withers and falls off. In the process two things happen: the shell is stained a mottled shade of brown, and the nutmeat develops a deeper, more complex flavor.

California growers, however, invented a method that removed this coating the moment the nut was picked, long before it had a chance to stain the shell. The result is a pistachio with a pure ivory-colored exterior enclosing a clean, fresh-tasting, delicately but brightly green nut. Whether it tasted better than the Middle Eastern pistachio hardly seemed relevant, since it was so purely Californian: so big, so clean, so perfect. Put the one next to the other and there was no doubt as to which looked foreign, something that the California growers played upon by circulating that canard about imperfections. (In this regard, consider the "perfect" California black olive.)

No matter. For me, then, the California pistachio was a gastronomic wonder—all the more so because it was so expensive and, in the beginning, so hard to find. The first time I tasted one, the rest of the nuts faded so far into the background that they might as well have been wallpaper. Sure, I knew they still existed, but who cared? For me, the pistachio was not only in a class by itself, it was first in a field of one. In short, I became a pistachaholic, and it took decades before the addiction showed any sides of subsiding—and then, perhaps, because I no longer had the stamina to support the intensity of the craving.

I estimate that over the past twenty-five years I have eaten my way through as many as a thousand pounds of pistachio nuts (although since these were in the shell, the actual nut meat weight would be about half that), at an expenditure of from four to five thousand dollars. It makes you think.

Not, as it happens, about wasted time and wasted money—what else are time and money for? I think it was La Rochefoucauld who said that we commit the sins of our youth to have something to meditate on in our old age. And that's just what I'm doing here—if, admittedly, jumping the gun a bit. But I have a lot of sins to mull over, so I might as well get started.

•   •   •

Casting back to the start of my serious pistachio-eating period—which began the moment they first appeared in specialty food markets—what comes to mind, strangely, is my bottom bureau drawer. Because it was there, buried under the sweaters and folded pairs of jeans, that I hid my stash. And for good reason—at the time I was teaching at a small private school, living in a large, seedy mansion in which were combined the school's offices, its meeting hall, a girls' dormitory, and a scattering of faculty apartments. Students were constantly in and out of mine, whether I was there or not, and, when I wasn't, helping themselves to the snacks in the cupboard, the Brie hidden in the back of the refrigerator, the tequila bottle buried in the freezer. The better the stuff was, the more they liked it. There was no distracting them by leaving a bag of potato chips out on the counter; they would just take that, too.

The pistachios, I vowed, they would not get. This was especially important because they were nearly impossible to come by. I had to depend on my friend Ken's occasional forays to Zabar's in New York. Among his booty would always be a one-pound sack of the nuts for me, to be squirreled away until late Saturday night—a time when the students, I well knew, would be engaged in various forms of self-abuse which they would have no interest in sharing with me.

For maximum effect, these evenings also required a superior spy novel—Desmond Bagley, Derek Marlowe, Adam Hall. At the height of my powers, I could devour a whole pound of pistachios and a three-hundred-page thriller between eleven in the evening and two-thirty the next morning. I would then switch off my bedside lamp with a sigh and fall off to sleep to the gentle rattle of the pistachio shells settling in their plastic bag beside me. Bliss, this was thy very name.

Now, what was the important thing here? The addictive flavor of the nuts? Their rarity and expense? The fact that I had them all to myself? Well, yes, all those things. And, if you had asked me then, that's where I would have ended the list. But in hindsight I see that the most important thing of all—the defining factor—was what you might call the "drip-feed effect."

All too often, if I settle down to watch a movie with a bag of popcorn in my lap, the snack is relegated to the same place as the soundtrack—a pleasurable background blur. It's only when I find my hand groping around in an empty bag that I realize I've finished off a "family-size" portion in the first half-hour of the film. The same is true when I'm reading a thriller. Unlike that sack of popcorn or a can of Poppycock, pistachios have a built-in self-regulating mechanism. It isn't at all annoying, because you, the eater, determine the tempo; but neither can you circumvent it.*

Well, not true, you can . . . but you do so at your peril. Once, Ken showed up with a bag of *shelled* pistachio nuts. The idea of them thrilled me, but that feeling ended the moment I started eating them. Outside of their shell, they seemed somehow anemic, caponized—still good, yes, but in an ordinary, salted-nut kind of way. Some people get the same pleasure with a nutcracker and a bowl of walnuts, but, believe me, they're not reading in bed. I think that Turkish website gets it just right: ". . . these kind of fancies which work fingers and teeth in a serial mode as parts of a machine, calms psychologically and keeps people from distress."

That's the secret of the pistachio: the small effort you have to make to get at them, with its series of tiny delights—the satisfying crack as the shell splits apart, the texture of the dry, crinkly skin of the nut itself,

---

*Over the years I've found only one serious competitor to the pistachio in this regard: salted-in-the-shell peanuts. They demand the same start-and-stop rhythm—indeed, rather more so. Unfortunately, while they're nearly as good, they're also incredibly messy, and the shells are so intensely salty that about halfway through the (twelve-ounce) bag—if you are opening them with your teeth, which you have to do if you are also holding a book—your tongue shrivels up and threatens to die.

the salty residue that clings to your fingertips. Add to these the sporadic little shocks—the nut that can't be split, the sharp, sour taste of the occasional spoiled one—and what you have is a bobbing in and out of semiconsciousness that keeps pleasure from sinking into a polymorphous blur. This holds satiety at arm's length for a good long time . . . say, three-quarters of the way through a thriller.

• • •

That, of course, was then. Today I no longer read a thriller in one evening—and certainly not in bed. If I tried, my joints would complain about it for the rest of the night. And I can't remember the last time I ate a pound of pistachios at one sitting; wretched excess these days is half that, at best. In fact, until recently they were only a very occasional presence on my snack shelf—all that gorging of yesteryear appeared to have worn my interest out.

Then one day I noticed a supermarket bin heaped with bags of Turkish pistachio nuts. Old memories stirred; my curiosity was piqued. I brought home a sack and gave them a try. They puzzled me, and at first I thought I simply didn't like them. They were too salty and too small, and not a few tasted . . . not spoiled, exactly, but a little too much like pencil shavings. The sack, with those that remained, worked its way to the back of the shelf—ignored, but not, as it turned out, forgotten.

My mind wouldn't quite let them go. Okay, they were seriously salty and a bit of a pain to get out of their shells (a short session with them left my thumbnails wrecked). But these Turkish pistachios also had a kind of stubborn realness, a taste that suggested that there might be more to the nut than plump perfection. It came to me that these might be the barrel scrapings of something better, and that maybe it would be worth the effort to find out if this was so.

A decade ago, pursuing this notion would not have been easy, since the small grocery stores found in end-of-book source lists had often gone out of business by the time the cookbook went to press. But nowadays . . . an hour of Web searching brought me to Abdurrahman Ildeniz at www.turkishtaste.com, which sells premium Turkish pistachios from the two places in that country most famous for them, Antep and Siirt.

They proved to be a revelation. The ones from Siirt had a delicately mottled, cream-colored shell that had the length of their California cousins but nothing like their plumpness. No matter. Barely salted, they were the first pistachio I've had that tasted a bit like their near relative, the cashew, but with a slightly sharper, more resinous bite. And the flavor lingers in the mouth.

The Antep pistachios were much darker and slightly smaller than the Siirts, but with the same mottled shell. In contrast to the California nut's gaping guffaw, these had barely broken into a smile, but they were not particularly difficult to open. And their taste more than made up for any shortcomings as to size: suavely salted just enough to point up their rich, resin-touched flavor—tasting not unlike a pine nut, but with more staying power and without the soapy aftertaste. Try a California pistachio after one of these and you might as well be eating a macadamia. I was totally won over.

However, the interesting thing is how much they turn out to be in sync with an older nut fiend's needs and prejudices (and, let's face it, at seven dollars a pound plus shipping, financial wherewithal). My younger self would have loved their taste but been driven to distraction by the patience required to extract them. And, at least I now think, they are just too good to eat while reading. This is a nut that in every way demands your full attention.

So here I am, back in love with an old flame. We have both matured a lot since our last affair, which adds a whole new dimension to the attraction. But, at bottom, really, it is still the business of it, that serial working of the fingers and the teeth that enchants me most. It is why the pistachio remains, for me, quite simply, *the* nut.

• • •

Afterthought

When this essay originally appeared in *Simple Cooking*, I was given some chaff for saying nothing about the best way to *open* a pistachio nut. To be honest, I hadn't given the matter thought, because in my experience there was only one way: to insert the split shell between one of your upper front teeth and twist. This may not be the smartest way to go about it—I now have a fissure line running from top to bottom on the tooth I use for this—but it's about the only way to get the job done if you're holding a book in the other hand.

However, it isn't perfect. If you take out of the arena those pistachios that have refused to open at all (and which I just discard, having
never found a good way to deal with them), you are still left with those
that have just split enough to offer a hairline crack. Teeth are useless in
dealing with these, and so in my experience are screwdrivers and sharp
little knives. My own solution involved taping a dime to a steel plate
(so it wouldn't bounce around) and pounding one edge of it with a
hammer, flattening it until it was nearly as sharp as a knife. This gives
you something to insert, something to twist, and it never fails. The
problem with it, as you might guess, is that eventually, unwittingly, you
spend it.

Enter Carolyn Wynne, who wrote me about a pocket screwdriver
sold by Lee Valley Tools (www.leevalley.com) that resembles a plump-
ish but sharp-edged one-inch-wide steel washer. What makes it special
is that it's "ramped" so that the edge gradually increases in thickness
from 0.030 to 0.090 inch. This allows it to handle a wide range of
screwheads and, more to the point, pop open almost any pistachio. You
won't spend it, you'll find it useful for other tasks, and since you can
only buy it by the dozen ($7.95, at the time of writing), you'll pass
them out to grateful friends.

Sources: Turkish Taste

My search for pistachios brought me to Turkish Taste, but that is far
from the only reason to visit it. The site caters mostly to fellow countrymen, which means that the prices are modest and the selection generally uncontaminated by the need to bow to ignorant tastes.

I was delighted with the breakfast section, which offers such treats
as Marmara *birlik*, black olives, Tahsildaroglu aged feta cheese, *Kayseri
pastirma* (air-dried cured beef), and Turkish butter. Those with a sweet
tooth will find separate sections featuring preserves and honey (including quince and fig jam and comb honey), helva (the Turkish take on
halvah) and sweetmeats (many unknown entities here), and another
reserved for Turkish delight. Elsewhere, you'll find Turkish sodas (including the notorious *Uludağ gazoz*), bottles of turnip juice, teas and
Turkish coffee, filo dough, very inexpensive extra-virgin olive oil, nuts,
seeds, dried fruit . . . and on and on. And if that isn't enough, there are
also toiletries (olive oil soap, rose water, lemon cologne), kitchenware

(tea glasses, handsome Turkish coffee pots—both brass and stainless steel), and lots of gift items. In short, a treasure chest just waiting to be explored. Be warned, though, that this is a very small business, and service, especially when a response is required, can be slow. However, orders are shipped promptly and I have always been treated with the greatest of courtesy. Besides the website address, you can reach Turkish Taste by mail: P.O. Box 825; Greenland, NH 03840; (603) 661-5460; e-mail: sales@turkishtaste.com.

SIGNOR MINESTRONE

There are . . . dozens of versions of minestrone, which is a really solid soup thick with vegetables and cheese and rice or pasta and intended, with bread and wine, to constitute the entire midday meal of hungry working people.
—*The London Sunday Times* (March 29, 1959)

In America, "minestrone" is just a fancy name for vegetable soup. We buy it in cans. We find it offered as the soup of the day in coffee shops . . . Around here, it isn't a dish, it's a cliché. In Italy, on the other hand, and especially in Liguria [the region that stretches along the Italian coast from the French border to Tuscany—its capital is Genoa], it's not just a dish but an eagerly appreciated one—a celebration of the season.
—Colman Andrews, *Flavors of the Riviera*

When my mother moved to a retirement community on the coast of Maine, I stayed a bit afterwards to help her settle in. There, each member was required to eat dinner regularly in the common dining room, and one of my major tasks was to accompany her the first time she went. So, I went to the main building to pick up a copy of the menu for the week.

My mother had heard that the place was known for the quality of its meals, and, on the menu at least, several seemed quite inviting to me—except, of course, the one being served the night we would be eating there. On that evening, diners were offered a choice between moussaka and *pasta alla puttanesca*. As it happens, I like both these dishes, but it seemed to me rather unlikely that the chef at a Maine retirement community would manage simultaneously to cater to the cautious palates of the diners and imbue these dishes with enough gusto to bring them to life.

It is beyond my powers to convey the full experience of the meal, starting with our entry into the huge dining hall. It proved to be nearly empty, except for two or three large tables occupied by various cliques of very elderly folk (my mother, at eighty-one, seemed positively young in comparison), who obviously dined there every night. They were being served by a two-person waitstaff, one male, one female, both of whom were in their teens.

I had imagined a room full of lively chatter, but this place, despite the bright lights, was crepuscular, even slightly creepy. We had been told to expect to join—to even be welcomed by—another couple at a table for four, and not being gifted at small talk I had rehearsed a few conversational gambits. A waste of time: there were no such couples, and we were led to an empty table for two, with no one making any attempt to intercept us.

My mother did try to strike up a conversation with a solitary woman waiting for the rest of her party at a nearby table, who not only responded pleasantly but offered to lead us to the closet where we were meant to hang our coats—an offer that we gratefully accepted. Moreover, this exchange gained a certain poignancy when she repeated the offer three more times before her companions arrived—as well as reintroducing herself and asking our names again each time she did so.

Meanwhile, Tiffany, our waitperson, had begun to bring our food. What appeared to be blueberry scones turned out instead to be full of bits of olive and onion—tasty enough for me to later ask for a second round. As a starter, my mother had ordered the "toss salad." I, less trustingly, had chosen the minestrone. (We both ordered the moussaka.) In the salad, my mother made the better bet; although drenched in dressing, the salad was composed of mixed baby greens, with no iceberg in sight. On the other hand, the minestrone was, well, minestrone . . . which, in my experience, might be defined by the absence of anything you really like in a soup, with the remaining lackluster ingredients boiled down to mush.

As it turned out, attendance at dinner that evening was unusually low (abetting my suspicion that those who ate there by choice knew what was coming and opted out). My mother has been back since in other company, and her spirits have been considerably lifted from where they were when we made our way back to her cottage. But I found that I couldn't get the taste of that minestrone out of my mouth. It was, if anything, as good as any version I had sampled before, but that was pretty small praise. What was it about this soup that I don't get? Or, to put it another way, was there an authentic way of making it that I might actually like?

• • •

You might think that life is too short to spend much time trying to find appealing versions of dishes you don't especially like—and, if you do, you'll get no argument from me. However, quite apart from my suspicions regarding the salad, I had ordered the minestrone that night because the soup was already on my mind. In the past several years, Matt and I have grown very attached to certain Italian bean dishes (see, for instance, the essay "Beans in a Flask" in our last book, *Pot on the Fire*), and minestrone was, in my mind, rightly or wrongly, one of the classic Italian bean soups. I had meant to pursue that impression, but without this negative prodding I might never have done so. Off to the bookshelves I went . . . and, as is often the case, returned more perplexed than before.

Roughly translated, *minestrone* becomes "big soup," which some food writers take to mean that it has lots of ingredients, while others interpret it as signifying that the soup is meant to be a meal in itself. Italy is a country of hearty soups, so neither distinction takes us very far. Depending on where you look, you can find support for either camp; this quote from Waverley Root, which appears in *The Cooking of Italy*, is unique in putting the lie to both at once.

> The next dish was the Genoese variety of minestrone with pesto. When pesto is served with minestrone, it is added at the last moment, floated on a soup the Genoese prefer to be thick. The minestrone I had at Da Mario [a popular Genoese restaurant] contained peas, potatoes, oil, garlic, a little onion and a few herbs.

Not only was his minestrone conspicuously restrained in the number of ingredients, it was far from providing a meal. Before it, Root enjoyed an appetizer of *bianchetti* (fried baby anchovies) and, after it, feasted on *cappon magro* (a rather overwhelming composed dish of seafood and vegetables), plus dessert.

When push comes to shove, "minestrone" is—as Anne Bianchi honestly admits in *From the Tables of Tuscan Women*—"a rather nebulous term . . ." Or, put another way, it is one of any number of dishes that Italians know when they see . . . cook . . . eat them, and are content to leave it at that. If anything, the word suggests something special—a soup raised by some culinary magic to a higher power. As Colman Andrews writes in *Flavors of the Riviera*:

> In Genoa and vicinity, a particularly well-made minestrone, with an abundance of ingredients—the kind one might make to honor a guest, for instance—is sometimes called "Signor Minestrone," or, in Genoese dialect, *Scignore Menestron*. In local slang, a *menestron* is also a gourmet or connoisseur.

This means that the foreign cook who wants to master the art of minestrone in its largest form will first have to learn the secrets of many different regional cooks, since each part of Italy goes about preparing it in its own signature way. This was obviously beyond my scope, and, truth to tell, my ambition, so I decided to exit the fray waving a white flag, and content myself with finding a few minestrone recipes that (a) were to my taste, (b) had a manageable list of ingredients, and (c) offered a range of perspectives on what makes a soup a minestrone.

With this in mind, I turned first to Pellegrino Artusi's great classic of Italian cooking, *Science in the Kitchen and the Art of Eating Well*, first published in 1891. Artusi concludes the introduction to his minestrone recipe by stating that he had spent some time polishing it to perfection, and his recipe is lengthy enough to give some idea how he did so.*

---

*I worked out my version of his recipe using (but greatly augmenting) the differing versions in the recent English editions of Artusi's book—one by Kyle M. Phillips III and the other by Murtha Baca and Stephen Sartarelli—as well as consulting the original Italian text from the 1891 edition, which can be downloaded without charge at www.pellegrinoartusi.it/la_cucina_artusiana.htm.

MINESTRONE
[Serves 6]

2 ounces (a heaping ½ cup) dried white beans, preferably
cannellini or *caponi di sartocchio* (see page 123), rinsed
well and soaked in water overnight
2 quarts homemade beef or chicken broth
2 tablespoons extra-virgin olive oil
2 tablespoons chopped pancetta or fatty prosciutto
1 large garlic clove, minced
several large sprigs flat-leaf parsley, stemmed and chopped
1 celery stalk, 2 peeled carrots, 2 small or 1 medium
zucchini, 2 peeled potatoes, and 1 peeled onion, all cut
into bite-size pieces
½ head Savoy cabbage, 1 bunch Swiss chard, and 1 bunch
(or 12-ounce bag) spinach, all rinsed carefully
¼ cup tomato sauce or 1 tablespoon tomato paste
a thick slice of pancetta (optional)
salt and black pepper to taste
1 cup arborio rice
freshly grated Parmigiano-Reggiano

Three Hours Before Preparing the Minestrone: Add the beans and the
meat broth to a large soup pot and bring to a boil. Cook at a gentle
boil for about 10 minutes, skimming away and discarding any scum.
Then cover the pot, reduce the heat so its contents remain at a simmer,
and cook the beans until they are tender but still firm. Taste them occasionally, since cooking time will depend on the type of bean and their
age. Then use a slotted spoon to remove the beans from the pot. If
preparing the rest of the soup directly, leave the broth at a simmer; otherwise, bring it back to one when you continue.

When It Is Time to Make the Soup: Heat the olive oil in a large skillet. When it is hot, add the pancetta, garlic, and parsley. Sauté until
the garlic is translucent, then turn the contents of the skillet into the
broth, along with the chopped celery, carrots, zucchini, potatoes, and
onion.

While this cooks, slice the Savoy cabbage, Swiss chard, and spinach
leaves into shreds and finely chop the chard and spinach stems. Add all

this to a thick-bottomed stockpot, cover, and set over high heat just long enough for the leaves to wilt and release most of their liquid. Turn out the contents into a large sieve, pressing with the back of a wooden spoon to squeeze them as dry as possible. Add this mass to the broth as well, along with the reserved beans and the tomato sauce. (Artusi observes that here some cooks add a piece of cured or salt pork to enhance the minestrone's body and flavor. If you wish to do this yourself, slip in the optional piece of pancetta.)

Season to taste with salt and pepper, undersalting a little since the soup needs less than it might immediately seem. Stir in the arborio rice (making sure it all gets down into the broth) and simmer until the rice is tender. Finally, remove the pot from the heat and let the soup sit uncovered for at least 15 minutes before serving—minestrone should never be eaten piping hot. Put the grated Parmesan in a small bowl on the table so that each eater can stir it in to taste.

Cook's Notes. Made just as detailed above, this soup is wonderful. Still, surrendering to my own instincts, I adapted it as follows: I used a quart of homemade chicken broth and made up the other quart with the bean-soaking water (2 cups) and the liquid squeezed from the greens (2 cups). I also sautéed the chopped onion along with the garlic in the olive oil. Finally, I added the chopped cabbage directly to the skillet, wilting only the other two greens and waiting to add these until the last 10 minutes of cooking.

Usually, when I like a soup it is because it has an intensity or depth of flavor that belies its diluted nature. A well-made crab bisque is an example of what I mean by intensity: so much of the flavor of that crustacean lies in parts of it that are difficult or impossible to eat but that a soup can extract and, it often seems, heighten. A good minestrone falls in the other category: soups with unusual depth. Even before we sat down to table I had a hint of this when, at the stove, I tasted it for salt. For once, I couldn't tell if it needed salt or not (true, a little had been used to make the stock, but no more than a teaspoon). I did add some, another teaspoon to the whole pot, and all during the meal was never sure if I hadn't added too much. In the ordinary course of events, I have to *really* oversalt a dish to be bothered by this.

Also, when Matt and I began to eat the minestrone, we kept wondering what the spinach, the zucchini, the parsley, the potato, et cetera, did for the dish; perhaps some of these components could be left out. But gradually we came to understand that each did do something, even if we couldn't easily put our finger on it. What follows is my best attempt at explaining this.

Imagine a bright spring morning. There are birds chirping, insects buzzing, leaves rustling, children shouting at a distant playground. The scent of new vegetation is in the air, slightly astringent rather than flowery, but very pleasing, nonetheless.

If you were preoccupied, you might hardly notice any of this except maybe the warmth of the sun, that it was a "nice day." But pause and pay attention and a quiet pleasure unfolds, one that has a depth to which you were previously oblivious, a harmony composed of many now identifiable parts. Few of these could be said to be essential, many could be replaced by something else much like them, but each adds to the totality in its own unique way.

This is exactly how a minestrone works. Each aspect of it is rather delicate, and the main goal of the cook is to let all the parts shine through. At first I noticed only how delicious the soup's broth was, a sort of essence of vegetableness, thickened lightly with bean pulp, potato, and rice. Then I realized how good the different vegetables were, that piece of cabbage or carrot, that slip of chard or spinach. Each was itself but carried with it some of its conversation with all the others. This is why Artusi can encourage his readers to "feel completely free to adapt this recipe to the tastes of your own part of Italy, using whatever vegetables are at hand."

Like the components of our imaginary spring day, the possibilities of any particular minestrone always exceed what we finally decide to put in it—even, with tact, things that don't immediately seem to belong. Just as a flurry of snowflakes is not unknown in May, so can some winter squash find its way into a minestrone made mostly of fresh spring vegetables. The important thing here is to attend to Nika Hazelton's injunction in *The Regional Italian Kitchen*: Contrary to common American belief, a minestrone is not just a catchall for every available vegetable but a mixture of judiciously balanced ones.

Another important characteristic of minestrone is that, because the soup is built around no special ingredient—beef, say, or chicken or meatballs or shrimp—no spoonful is to be treasured more than another. When I finally sat down to the real thing, I found myself facing goodness that didn't urge me to gobble it right down. Instead, I ate slowly, happily, and with great satisfaction, all the way to the bottom of the bowl.

MINESTRONE MYTH NO. 1

All versions of minestrone have one thing in common: they have to simmer for two hours at the very least, and preferably three.

This method dates back to when soup was made in fired clay pots that had to be used over a gentle flame. This isn't an easy technique to master in today's kitchen, whether here or in Italy. Far better to add the vegetables so that when the soup is done each has reached its own sort of tenderness—the zucchini and the shredded greens mouth-meltingly soft but still in coherent pieces, the green beans and the cabbage yielding but with something left to chew.

Ligurian minestrone is always finished with a spoonful of pesto stirred in just before it is served. As always, the pesto is never heated, and the pesto used in soup is traditionally made without either *pinoli* or walnuts. This is real old-fashioned Genoese soup, the kind eaten by dock workers in the harbor.
—Fred Plotkin, *Recipes from Paradise*

As I write these words, a memory suddenly bubbles up from the depths. I can almost name the day back in 1971 when I first had *pesto alla Genovese*; it was an encounter that shook my world. I thought this thick green amalgam of fresh basil, olive oil, pine nuts, and cheese was one of the most delicious things I had ever tasted. Alas, this was a time when nobody grew basil and nobody, except in large Italian neighborhoods, sold it. I treasured every sprig I could lay my hands on and, meanwhile, read everything I could on the subject.

Thirty years ago, not a lot was written about dishes utilizing pesto, but one that could be found—thanks to books like Jean-Noël Escudier and Peta Fuller's *The Wonderful Food of Provence*—was *soupe au pistou*, the just-north-of-the-border sister version of *minestrone alla Ge-*

novese. This might have been my first encounter with a truly memorable minestrone, if it weren't for one thing.* The thought of wasting something as delicious as pesto by stirring it into some sort of vegetable soup absolutely appalled me. You might as well shave a fresh truffle into a big pot of Irish stew.†

That was then, when I would be lucky to eat pesto tossed in pasta three times in a whole summer—and dreamt of having enough to slather on English muffins every morning for breakfast. Nowadays, of course, pesto has become so ridiculously ordinary that fresh basil is available in supermarkets year round—if anyone still bothers to make it themselves, given how many upmarket saucemakers are eager to do it for you.

Now, amusingly, my concern was just the opposite—that the pesto would prove to be that "special ingredient" the presence of which would override the delicate balance that makes minestrone work. But, obviously, the Genoese don't think so, and, besides, Waverley Root's description of the *minestrone alla Genovese* at Da Mario had piqued my interest. Pesto works well with both potatoes and peas, and a dish that included all three seemed particularly inviting. Needless to say, Root neglected to get the recipe. But I was pleased to find some relatively uncluttered versions of *minestrone alla Genovese* that contained those ingredients. Here's how we worked it out ourselves.

MINESTRONE ALLA GENOVESE
[Serves 4 to 6]

"A Ligurian minestrone, as opposed to a Lombardian one, should contain no broth, no soffritto (sautéed onion and garlic), not a trace of

---

*Which was not that Escudier or Fuller (his American translator) called for making the *pistou* with Gruyère or Edam cheese. Horrible idea? Well, Colman Andrews writes in *Flavors of the Riviera* that the chef at Nice's La Merenda, a tiny place famous for its preparation of local dishes, confided that "the secret of his particularly creamy version was shredded Emmenthaler."

†My second bit of food writing, after a pamphlet on onion soup, was one called *Aglio, Oglio, Basilico*, at heart a paean to pesto, published in 1981. By then, after ten years of making it, I considered myself quite the expert. Did I even mention *pistou* or *minestrone alla Genovese* anywhere within? Yes. I gave the subject one grudging line.

pancetta or meat, and no elaborate seasonings," Anya von Bremzen tells us, something confirmed by the thoughtful recipes from Colman Andrews and Fred Plotkin. Another distinction is the absence of tomato, although this is more a preference than a rule.

> 1 cup dried white beans, preferably cannellini or *caponi di sartocchio* (see page 123), rinsed and soaked in water overnight
>
> 1 quart water (use the water in which the beans have been cooked, supplemented as necessary)
>
> 2 garlic cloves, minced
>
> 2 large leeks, trimmed of their roots and the thick, dark green part of their tops and cut into bite-size pieces
>
> 2 medium potatoes, cut into bite-size cubes
>
> ¾ ounce dried porcini, soaked 20 minutes in warm water, then drained (but see note)
>
> ¼ cup fruity extra-virgin olive oil
>
> 2 tablespoons freshly grated Parmigiano-Reggiano
>
> ½ teaspoon hot red pepper flakes
>
> 1 medium or 2 small zucchini, cut into small pieces
>
> 1 bunch spinach or Swiss chard plus 1 small head of Savoy cabbage, washed carefully and cut into shreds
>
> 2 cups fresh green peas
>
> 2 teaspoons kosher salt
>
> ½ teaspoon black pepper
>
> 8 ounces uncooked linguine, broken into 1-inch pieces, or any suitable small pasta shape
>
> ½ cup *pesto alla Genovese* (see note)

Three Hours Before Preparing the Minestrone: Put the beans and their soaking liquid in a soup pot, if necessary adding enough additional wa-ter to cover the beans by ½ inch. Bring to a full boil, reduce the heat until the water gently bubbles, and cook for 10 minutes, skimming away and discarding any scum that rises to the surface. Then cover the pot and simmer the beans until they are tender but still firm. Taste them occasionally, since cooking time will depend on the type of bean and their age. When done, remove from the heat and pour off the liquid, re-serving it and the beans both.

When It Is Time to Make the Soup: Measure the bean-cooking liquid, adding more water if necessary to make a full quart. Return the liquid to the soup pot and bring to a boil. Add the garlic, leeks, potatoes, and reconstituted porcini (and, optionally, most of their soaking liquid), bringing everything up to a simmer. Cook uncovered, gently simmering all the while, for ½ hour.

Then add the olive oil, grated Parmesan, and dried hot red pepper flakes. When all this has been stirred in and the cheese has dissolved, add the zucchini, then the shredded greens, handful by handful. When the last handful has wilted enough so that the soup liquid covers everything, bring it back to a simmer and cook for another ½ hour.

Now stir in the peas and the broken pasta pieces. This time, keep the heat high enough that the soup cooks at a slow boil. Cook for 10 minutes, then add the beans. Bring back to a boil and let simmer 5 minutes, or until the pasta is al dente and the beans have a chance to heat through.

Remove the pot from the heat and let sit 15 minutes, or until the soup is cool enough to eat. Note that it is also delicious at room temperature. Put the pesto in a small bowl with a spoon and let each eater add some to taste.

Cook's Notes. Dried Porcini: The reason for discarding the mushroom-soaking liquid is to get rid of any grit. However, using care you can dribble most of this flavorful stuff into the soup, leaving the silt at the bottom undisturbed. (You can even go so far as to taste it for any gritty residue.) Note, though, that this little trick is not risk-free.

Pesto alla Genovese: Depending on the strictness of your moral standards, you can whip up a nut-free batch especially for this dish, or you can join the slackers (who exist even among the Genoese) and use a good nut-redolent version. Colman Andrews observes that "various authorities maintain that pesto destined to be used in soup should not contain pine nuts, or cheese, or even oil." Plainly, the road to authenticity for such is paved by discarding all the tasty stuff. Why not go all the way and discard the garlic and the basil as well? Then you would have a *pesto alla Genovese* of irreproachable *autenticità*. Recipes also differ as to whether the cook should stir it into the minestrone before it is served or whether eaters should be allowed to do this themselves. In any case, a heaping tablespoon per person is considered by most to be a generous portion.

Because quite decent already-made pesto is readily available these days, I haven't provided a recipe. However, anyone wishing to make it from scratch should turn to Fred Plotkin's *Recipes from Paradise: Life and Food on the Italian Riviera*, which contains a veritable treatise on the subject, running to a dozen pages, and, elsewhere, an elaborate version of *minestrone alla Genovese*.

MINESTRONE MYTH NO. 2

There is one inviolate ingredient: Parmigiano-Reggiano rind.

This wretched bit of Italian parsimony came about because (a) the rind does, after long simmering, eventually dissolve and (b) there's nothing else you can do with it (except the one thing you *should* do—throw it away). With Parmesan, the closer to the rind you get, the less flavor there is. As anyone who has gnawed on one will know, the rind is nearly tasteless and does nothing for the soup that a generous grating of the actual cheese can't do better.

• • •

Abundance of vegetables—piles of white and green fennel, like celery, and great sheaves of young, purplish, sea-dust-coloured artichokes, nodding their buds, piles of big radishes, scarlet and bluey purple, carrots, long strings of dried figs, mountains of big oranges, scarlet large peppers, a last slice of pumpkin, a great mass of colours and vegetable freshnesses. How the dark, greasy, night-stricken street seems to beam with these vegetables, all this fresh delicate flesh of luminous vegetables piled there in the air, and in the recesses of the windowless little caverns of the shops, and gleaming forth on the dark air, under the lamps.
—D. H. Lawrence, *Sea and Sardinia* (1921)

It is time to admit that I was wrong in considering minestrone a "bean soup." The beans are almost always there, it's true, but this is because, I think, they are meant to stand in for the meat that, except to give depth to the stock, isn't ever present. Maybe the best way to sum up minestrone is as the quintessential vegetable soup. Or, to hone it down even further—the quintessential vegetable gardener's soup. Italians are as famously obsessed with how their vegetables are grown as they are with how they are prepared (see, in this regard, Faith Willinger's *Red, White, & Greens*), and it is the dovetailing of these passions that produces a truly five-star minestrone.

A corollary of this, however, is that Italian vegetables have more flavor than ours, since they are grown for taste rather than for visual appeal or, worse, longevity. True, Italy, like France, increasingly suffers from the deprivations wrought by convenience and a bureaucracy heavily tilted to corporate interests. But motivated cooks there can still find local market gardeners who offer the traditional varieties grown with love and care. This explains a soup like *minestrone alla Genovese* that resolutely shrugs off the usual enhancements that attend the making of a vegetable soup: stock, a *soffritto* of chopped aromatics lightly sautéed in olive oil, a piece of preserved pork.

The addition of the pesto at the end does provide a variation to this theme, but in a distinctly minor way. Such a small amount is used that if the vegetables haven't already pulled more than their fair share of the weight, the resulting soup tastes primarily of diluted pesto—the very opposite of the desired effect. Alas, this was just what happened to me when I first made the soup following the general rule, which—at least given the amount of flavor in the vegetables I had—called for simply too much water. Cutting the amount in half, plus some other tinkering (all included in the recipe), produced a much better soup, and one that continued to improve as we ate it.

This experiment encouraged my natural inclination when making soups to add as little water as possible—unless the ingredients demand dilution. But could one do this and produce something that could still be called minestrone? The answer was waiting for me in Nika Hazelton's *Regional Italian Kitchen*. Hazelton, who grew up in Italy, writes of the summer Tuscan minestrone made by Isolina, their family cook. Because she used fresh shell beans, she added no water at all; in adapting the recipe, I used (from necessity) precooked dried beans and included their flavorful cooking liquid in the soup as well. Even so, the essential part of the method has been preserved: the soup is not diluted with water. It is also astonishingly good.

MINESTRONE ESTIVO
[Serves 4 to 6]

8 ounces dried Pescadero (see sources) or other variety of
   cranberry bean, borlotti,* or pinto beans, rinsed and
   soaked in water overnight
¼ to ½ cup olive oil
2 garlic cloves, minced
2 large tomatoes (about 1 pound), halved and sliced
½ pound green beans, French-cut and sliced into 1-inch
   lengths
2 medium yellow onions, cut into thin rings
2 large or 4 small summer squash or zucchini, sliced
1 medium-size head escarole, rinsed well and shredded
6 sprigs flat-leaf parsley, minced
2 sprigs basil, minced
salt and black pepper to taste
freshly grated Parmigiano-Reggiano

Three Hours Before Preparing the Minestrone: Put the beans and their
soaking liquid in a soup pot, if necessary adding enough water to cover
the beans by ½ inch. Bring to a full boil, reduce the heat until the water
gently bubbles, and cook for 10 minutes, skimming away and discarding any scum that rises to the surface. Then cover and simmer the beans
until they are tender but still firm. Taste them occasionally, since cooking time will depend on the type of bean and their age. When done,
pour off the liquid, reserving it and the beans both.

When It Is Time to Make the Soup: Cover the bottom of a deep pot
with half the olive oil and sprinkle with the minced garlic. Layer the
sliced tomatoes over this, then, in exact order, the green beans, the
onion rings, the summer squash, and the shredded escarole. Sprinkle
this with the minced parsley and basil and pour over the bean-cooking
liquid and the rest of the olive oil.

Cover the pot and put it over a medium flame. Cook for 10 minutes,
until the escarole has wilted and it and the rest of the vegetables have

---

*According to the USDA, Italian borlotti beans are identical to the American cranberry bean.
Furthermore, a large percentage of the borlotti beans sold in Italy are actually cranberry beans
imported from the United States.

begun to release their liquid. Then turn the heat to low, add the reserved beans, stir everything well, and season to taste with salt and pepper. Put the cover back on and simmer until the green beans and squash are tender. This should take somewhere between 15 and 20 minutes. Then let the minestrone cool for at least 15 minutes before serving (it is also delicious at room temperature). Put a small bowl containing freshly grated Parmesan on the table for each eater to add to taste.

Place a bowl of this soup next to the one I ate at the beginning of this story in the retirement community dining hall, and, at first glance, they would seem very much the same. There would be the two sorts of bean, the various assortment of vegetables, the greens, the familiar taste of tomato. But taste the two and their profound difference becomes immediately apparent. The one tastes only of soup, the other of something more—perhaps the presence of the gardener, certainly the care and attention of the cook. It is this and nothing else that makes a minestrone not only good . . . but true to itself.

Or, as they say on the street: Hey—to you, that's *Mister* Minestrone.

Sources: Beautiful Beans

A culinary resource that has long been familiar to Californians is Corti Brothers, of Sacramento, a store famous for its highly sophisticated selection of specialty foods and beverages. One thing that can be found there and nowhere else are shell beans grown by Reno Dinelli in Pescadero, south of San Francisco on the California coast. The area—the soil deep, the climate cool—is ideal for beans, and Dinelli makes the most of this, raising two varieties in particular that are wholly out of the ordinary.

One of these is *caponi di sartocchio*, brought from Tuscany to California in 1912 by Dinelli's father. A heritage variety of *Phaseolus coccineus*, it is a large but quick-cooking white bean with a smooth texture, a soft skin, and a subtly delicious flavor. These would be ideal for making minestrone if they weren't all but impossible to find in this country. The usual choice, cannellini beans (in fact a variety of *Phaseolus vulgarus*), while very good, pales in comparison. If you're a lover of the latter, when you sample *caponi di sartocchio*, you'll think you've died and gone to heaven.

The other bean—also quick-cooking and possessing the same luscious texture and tender skin but a more robust (pinto-bean-like) flavor—is Dinelli's cranberry, or borlotti. These beans have a lovely mottled color until cooked, when they turn a pinkish beige. Corti Brothers buys up the entire crop of both and sells them for (at the time of writing) $4.95 a pound. There is a website—www.cortibros.biz—which, though limited, gives a good sense of the store's wide-ranging interests, and where back issues of their always interesting quarterly newsletter can be read. Corti Brothers; P.O. Box 191358; Sacramento, CA 95819; (800) 509-3663.

Further Reading, Further Cooking

At first glance, Anne Bianchi's *Zuppa! Soups from the Italian Countryside* seems to be made up of nothing *but* minestrone recipes, for its subject is hearty, vegetable-intensive *zuppe*. But, in fact, there are some specific minestrone recipes as well, including versions made with farro, chestnuts, fennel fronds, and lentils and tomatoes.

In *The Fine Art of Italian Cooking*, Giuliano Bugialli provides meticulously detailed recipes for Tuscan versions of *minestrone di riso* and *minestrone alla contadina*, which is served on top of thick slices of Tuscan bread. Following these is a recipe for *ribollita*, or "reboiled" minestrone, which is made by reheating leftover minestrone with stale bread so it becomes a kind of bread soup.

Elizabeth David's seminal *Italian Food* offers five minestrone recipes, including two from Italian cookbooks, one of them G. A. Sala's *The Thorough Good Cook* (1895). She also makes this observation: "In the making of minestrone . . . wine is not generally employed, although it would often be an improvement."

Lynne Rossetto Kasper, in *The Italian Country Table*, offers two minestrone recipes—one for *minestrone estivo* (but with five cups of broth) and the other for *minestrone della famiglia*, which relates not only how her Tuscan grandmother made it but how her grandfather and aunt dressed it to their taste at the table. She then provides a kind of primer for improvising your own minestrone, with lots of tricks for adding depth of flavor to the broth, rescuing bland versions, and seasoning the soup before serving it.

CONFLICTED ABOUT CASSEROLES

> The French name "casserole" has a certain amount of terror for
> the American housewife. The foreign word startles her and awak-
> ens visions of cooking as done by a Parisian *chef*, or by one who
> has made the culinary art his profession. She, a plain, everyday
> housekeeper, would not dare aspire to the use of a casserole. And
> yet the casserole itself is no more appalling than a saucepan. It is
> simply a covered dish, made of fireproof pottery, which will stand
> the heat of the oven or the top of the range. And the dainty
> cooked in this dish is "casserole" of chicken, rice, etc., as the case
> may be. Like many another object of dread this, when once
> known, is converted into a friend.
> —*Marion Harland's Complete Cook Book* (1903)

How things change. I thought of Marion Harland and this passage
when, exactly one hundred years later, I was asked to write a blurb for
a new cookbook by Jim Villas, *Crazy for Casseroles: 275 All-American
Hot-Dish Classics.** Housewives have now so much lost their fear of
the casserole that the word rarely if ever "awakens visions of cooking
as done by a Parisian *chef*." Quite the contrary. This treasure trove of
old familiars—tuna noodle casserole, shrimp Creole, cheese strata,
Johnny Marzetti, Chicken Divan, frozen chopped spinach casserole†—

---

*My quote appears on the back jacket of the hardcover edition.
†The only truly surprising absence—and it may be, *must* be, in there somewhere—is Green
Bean Bake, made with a can of cream of mushroom soup, a dash of soy sauce, milk, and a can
of Durkee's French-fried onions. I remember practically swooning when I first tasted this at a
supper party back in 1969.

summons up the image of a cozy kitchen with steamed windows, the clatter of the table being set, and the soothing aroma of a family favorite emerging hot and bubbling from the oven.

One of the genuine pleasures of *Crazy for Casseroles* is the impression it gives that all Villas had to do was appear at a neighbor's back door around dinnertime to glean another choice recipe for his collection. Think what you might of casseroles, it's hard to imagine any other aspect of our national cooking that would reward the compiler with such rich helpings from family and friends: Three-Soup Chicken and Almond Casserole Scarborough, Lizzie's Low Country Chicken Bog, Hootie's Hot Seafood Shroup, Flossie's Butternut Squash Orange Bake, and Shrimp Royal ("Royal" rather than "Royale," Villas explains, because the first is, in fact, his sister's married name).

The term "casserole," of course, embraces a wide range of American dishes, some of them very old indeed, and many of them containing nothing at which any cook, however fussy, need turn up their nose. Villas includes plenty of these in *Crazy for Casseroles*, but they do not lie at the heart of this book, and they are not the dishes that prompted fellow blurber Jeremiah Tower to paraphrase St. Augustine—"God grant me strength to be chaste, just not yet." This statement, and others like it, signals to the casserole aficionado that Villas is not one to flinch when called on to dive straight into the deep end of the pool.

"If I had to pinpoint the one casserole," he writes, "that the women in my Southern family—mother, sister, aunt, or niece—prepare at least once a month for all sorts of informal occasions, it would have to be Poppy Seed Chicken," which, if you don't know the dish, is made with a can of Campbell's condensed cream of chicken soup, a cup of sour cream, a stick of butter or margarine, and half a pound of Ritz crackers.

This doesn't mean that Villas believes that, when it comes to such dishes, anything goes:

> To maintain the distinctive character of the American casserole, I by no means have any objections to the use of such traditional components as leftover cooked foods, canned broths, soups, and tomatoes, packaged bread stuffings, certain frozen vegetables, plain dried noodles, pimentos, and supermarket natural aged cheeses. On the other hand, nowhere in this book will you find canned meats and vegetables, frozen chives or dried parsley flakes, processed cheeses, liquid smoke, MSG, bouillon cubes, crushed potato chips, or, heaven forbid, canned fruit cocktail.

Unfortunately, such distinctions don't survive long under serious scrutiny—as is usually the case when one attempts to keep a foot planted firmly in each of two warring camps. In this instance, one camp is our unselfconscious vernacular cooks, who simply don't bother to make such distinctions at all; the other is the small minority of cooks who wouldn't be caught dead making *anything* with three different kinds of canned soup. Villas is gamely proposing that there is a happy middle ground between the boobs and the snobs, a place where reasonable folks—him, you, me—can stand tall.

It's a nice enough sentiment, sure, but it seems to me to lure the reader out onto awfully thin ice. It's like saying that beanbag furniture and lava lamps are okay, but not, heaven forbid, plaster gnomes and fake pine paneling. For example, the recipes in *Crazy for Casseroles* seem to call for enough Parmesan to absorb every ounce produced in Emilia-Romagna, at least until you decode that interesting phrase "supermarket natural aged cheeses." As it happens, a diligent searcher can find jars of the familiar dry and powdery "Parmesan" that declare themselves "all natural" and aged for any number of months. If these are okay, why not processed American cheese?

Similarly, if packaged stuffings are in, why diss crushed potato chips? Those, after all, are usually made from nothing more than potatoes, oil, and salt, whereas the former usually sport an ingredient list that requires an advanced degree in food-processing chemistry to decipher. And what's wrong with frozen chives if you're happily throwing frozen spinach into every casserole in sight? There are distinctions to be made here, to be sure, but this is not the way to do it.

• • •

Today the word casserole is applied to any deepish pot in which cooking actually goes on, or even to pots more rightly called sauteuses or deep skillets.
—Irma Rombauer, *The Joy of Cooking* (1951)

Those who browse old cookbooks will be aware that the casserole as we Americans know and love it is a recent creation, and one that only vaguely resembles the European dishes that were devised to make the most of what was originally a fragile clay cooking dish. Indeed, as Russ Parsons perceptively observed in a piece on casseroles that appeared several years ago in the *Los Angeles Times*, American manufacturers have so radically "improved"—i.e., changed the composition and qualities of—the cooking dish itself that it, too, has little connection with the Old World original.

What Villas has in mind by the phrase "all-American hot-dish classics" is, as best as I can work out, the product of two distinct moments in the history of our national cooking. The first was the craze for chafing dishes that swept the country in the early 1900s, when it became fashionable to invite guests home for a light late-night meal after an evening at the theater, to be made by the hostess herself at tableside (the servants, of course, having long ago gone to bed).* (Tableside cooking as a mode of casual entertaining replayed itself in the fifties with the arrival of the electric skillet—although the dishes prepared with that were not nearly as fine . . . remember sukiyaki parties?)

Of course, what the chafing dish did was put the finishing touches on a dish that was prepped and often partially cooked earlier in the day. The following recipe—which appears in an extremely short (four-page) chapter called "With the Casserole" in *Marion Harland's Complete Cook Book*—exhibits just how.

CREAMED CHICKEN AND MACARONI

Cut cold boiled or roast chicken into small dice of uniform size, and into half-inch lengths half the quantity of cold, cooked macaroni. Make a good white sauce, season highly with paprika, salt and a suspicion of onion juice. Beat two eggs light and stir into them four tablespoonfuls of cream, heated, with a pinch of soda. Mix well with the chicken and spaghetti; put over the fire in a frying-pan, or broad saucepan, and stir and toss until smoking hot. Serve in a deep dish.

Notice that, unless you count the serving dish, there is no "casserole" in use here at all. However, if Harland's final step had been to combine the sauce, chicken, and spaghetti in an ovenproof dish and put that into

---

*If there were any servants to speak of. One of the unspoken advantages of the chafing dish was that it allowed young couples to entertain with style but without the trappings and expense of formal dinner parties.

a moderate oven until "smoking hot," you would have something amazingly anticipatory of tuna casserole. (Canned tuna was still an imported novelty at the time, but food writers were even then noting how closely it resembled chicken.)

What is important here, however, is that Harland has set the scene for the appearance of our American casserole by completely disregarding any thought that the cooking vessel itself might have something to impart to the dish. Instead, it is the idea of the entrée and main starch of the meal melded in a creamy sauce and brought to table in a single serving dish that becomes the casserole: a simplication that still manages to retain the genteel suggestion of sauceboat and serving platter.

This sense of amalgamation—as opposed to the simpler cooked-together oneness of, say, a beef stew—is a defining quality of this kind of casserole, and it is shared by the many dishes from that era that are made to this day (and, in fact, can be found in *Crazy for Casseroles*). These include Turkey Tetrazzini (1912), Shrimps de Jonghe (1900), Lobster Newburg (1895), and Chicken Divan (circa 1900).

Many of these also share something else: a pleasant confusion between the richness of the ingredients—eggs, butter, cream—and of those who first ate them. These dishes were often given names that implied an association with the rich and famous—or at least with the places where those people ate—which put that fare on the same footing, almost, as a rib roast. And, to an impartial palate, they merited that equal billing. For example, Shrimps de Jonghe (the name of a Dutch family who made this the signature dish of their Chicago hotel restaurant in the early 1900s) deservedly appears in Junior League spiral-bounds to this day. It is easily made and quite delicious.

SHRIMPS DE JONGHE

[Serves up to 4 as a main course, 6 or more as an appetizer]

½ cup (1 stick) unsalted butter
1 garlic clove, minced
½ cup bread crumbs
¼ cup finely chopped fresh parsley
¼ cup dry sherry
salt and black pepper to taste

a dash of hot pepper sauce
2 pounds shrimp, cleaned, cooked, and peeled

Preheat oven to 400°F. Cream together the butter and the minced clove of garlic. Blend in the bread crumbs and parsley and moisten the mixture with the sherry. Season to taste with salt, a grinding of black pepper, and a dash of hot pepper sauce, blending this in well. Spread the shrimp in a shallow baking dish and dot with the butter mixture. Bake for 25 minutes and serve hot.

Cook's Note. There has been much fiddling with this recipe over the years. Perhaps the best notion I've come across is to add some chopped onion and celery tops, peppercorns, a bay leaf, and a large pinch of salt to the water the shrimp are boiled in, to pep up their flavor.

Jean Anderson, in her *American Century Cookbook*—one of the best books there is on the unfolding of our vernacular cooking during the last century—points to a 1916 Campbell's booklet, *Helps for the Hostess*, as the moment when that company first put forth its products as the easy alternative to "long-winded sauces," thus launching the classic American casserole. This is true enough—except that while Campbell's may have had the idea, they lacked, and would lack for some time, the right soup to bring it to fruition.

In *Helps for the Hostess*, cooks were instructed to thicken their soup of choice with a roux of flour and butter, thus plunging them back into the very long-windedness they were supposedly escaping. In fact, none of the Campbell's soups of that era—oxtail, mock turtle, tomato-okra, mulligatawny, chicken gumbo—had the starch-thickened base necessary to become an instant sauce.

It took the company almost thirty years to follow its own idea to its logical end and introduce the first in a line of thickened soups that would be used primarily as sauces: cream of mushroom soup, in 1934. Cream of chicken soup didn't appear until 1947, over a decade later. And that was the one that really lit the fire—Campbell's wouldn't introduce a soup that met with such instant success until the launch of cream of broccoli in 1990.

Today, their bestsellers are, in order of preference, chicken noodle, cream of mushroom, tomato, cream of chicken, and cream of broccoli, with purchasers using one of every three cans as a recipe ingredient;

with cream of mushroom soup, that figure jumps to 80 percent. (In my opinion, this last is a very conservative estimate. Eaten straight . . . well, if your taste in soup runs to mushroom-flavored pancake batter, it can't be beat.)

Even so, it is hard to credit corporate machinations for the adoption of convenience foods as a casserole mainstay, when the evidence can just as easily point in the opposite direction—not only Campbell's own painfully slow stumbling toward the light, but the decades that Birds Eye Frosted Foods had to wait after introducing frozen spinach in the 1930s before anyone noticed how terrific the nasty stuff was in Green Rice Casserole, No-Nonsense Spinach Casserole, and Shrimp Florentine.

• • •

> At one time a badge of shame, hallmark of the lazy lady and the careless wife, today the can opener is fast becoming a magic wand . . . We want you to believe just as we do that in this miraculous age it is quite possible—and it's fun—to be a "chef" even before you can really cook.
> —Poppy Cannon, *The Can-Opener Cookbook* (Crowell, 1952)

This shift in attitude toward convenience foods, rendering them an accepted, even welcomed, component of American home cooking was the second of the two defining moments in the creation of today's casserole. It made its debut as an amalgamation of rich ingredients; now it was streamlined—some might say dumbed down—through the use of canned soups and their like.

The compelling question, of course, is why kitchen-proud homemakers so quickly and radically revised their perception of these foods. One possible answer would begin by noting that the rise in popularity in these dishes coincided with an unprecedented surge in home ownership. Housing developments began springing up all around the country in the fifties—an astonishing 25 percent of all American homes in 1960 had been built within the span of the last ten years.

As it happens, my parents were a part of this phenomenon. In 1957, they bought our first house, a three-bedroom garrison in a small development. (A garrison had a second floor that protruded a few inches in the front to give it a "colonial" look.) It was the newest house I had ever been in, which made it exciting, but it wasn't an excitement that would last. My grandparents' home, which was not all that far away and in which I had spent the first five years of my life, was an extremely complex organism—wheezing, stubborn, and surprisingly delicate. The electric wiring dated back half a century; fuses blew at a sneeze. The steam heat rumbled up from a massive furnace in the basement to hiss at you from cast-iron claw-footed radiators. In the fall, heavy glass storm windows went up; in the spring, these were replaced with freshly painted wooden screens. It was a house that today would be considered a homeowner's nightmare, but my grandfather took it all in stride. For a child, it was a place of endless mystery and delight—much of these feelings I conveyed in my book *Home Body*—and, fifty-five years later, it remains for me the template of what a home should be.

The new house . . . well, it was like replacing a friendly old dog with a stuffed toy—comfortable, unthreatening, endlessly embraceable, but really, nothing at all like the original. This was not merely a matter of newness. The same construction techniques that made these houses easier to afford also meant that more corners could be cut in their manufacture. Ceilings in the new house were lower; windows had shrunk; walls and doors were hollow where before they had been solid. The overall experience was one of compression. You couldn't call the house cramped, exactly, but its space never quite made it to spaciousness.

The builders were well aware of this. They took those things and sold them as advantages. Home buyers, it proved, would overlook the fact that a house was cheaply built if it was also cheap to heat and cheap to maintain. In my grandfather's time, a house required continuous care, and owning one meant mastering all sorts of knowledge and performing a never-ending round of upkeep, both indoors and out (or paying someone else to do these things for you).

The houses of the fifties and afterward demanded no such commitment. Curiously, the result was something you might call responsibility deprivation. Here were houses that asked for little care in a culture still primed with an ethos of devoting time and money to keeping them up. Homeowners felt vaguely immoral doing nothing—and, with nothing much to do, threw themselves into home improvement to fill the void.

At first glance, it might seem that there was as little to improve as there was to fix. All the houses in our development came with a garage, a breezeway, and a fully equipped kitchen with turquoise-colored appliances and, something quite à la mode, a dishwasher and a waist-high oven built into the wall. In fact, there were so many things to like about the place that it would be hard to enumerate them all—from the shiny wood floors to the clean, tight basement with its convenient bulkhead doors. What more could anyone want?

Well, as it turns out, lots of things. The breezeway quickly revealed itself as being a bit too breezy; after a year or two, it got turned into a sunroom. Fiberglass insulation was unrolled in the attic; an exhaust fan was installed in the kitchen; a downstairs closet became a very small guest bathroom. Half the basement was upgraded into a cheery family room, turning the living room into a showcase for company. Garages were expanded; backyards got swimming pools and privacy fences; front yards got flower gardens and statuary.

This new definition of "house-proud," I think, helps us make sense of the sea change that made respectable the recipes that *Crazy for Casseroles* celebrates. Like the homeowner, the home cook need no longer shoulder a wearying responsibility—in this instance, the one incurred by dishes made from scratch. Like tract houses, dishes incorporating convenience foods—canned soups, crackers, frozen vegetables—as their foundation were affordable, easy to maintain (they always turned out well), and, with a handful of almonds or water chestnuts tossed in, easily made fancy.

Today, all this is taken for granted. Fifty years is quite long enough for a way of cooking to become a tradition and for the dishes that come out of it to be considered classics. The fact that these even now still manage to teeter at the edge of questionable taste testifies as much to their power of attraction as to the lowering of our standards ("Campbell's soups have done more to debase the cooking of Americans—and their palates—than any other factor," said an unnamed source quoted approvingly by John and Karen Hess in *The Taste of America* well over a quarter century ago).

In truth, we're not talking about good taste and bad taste here; we're talking about the fact that things change and that we change with them, whether we are aware of it or not. That makes the issue of goodness a very slippery one, and it's a mistake to trust anything like a quick response to it. Reading an early draft of this essay, Matt recalled a favorite dinner party casserole of her mother's. Shirley herself had gotten it from Jean, a savvy but down-to-earth professor's wife, and it proved so popular that whenever Shirley served it, she, too, was besieged by requests for the recipe.

JEAN'S TWO MEAT TWO RICE CASSEROLE
[Serves 8]

6 tablespoons butter
1 pound each lean pork and veal, cut into 1-inch cubes
2 onions, chopped
1½ to 2 pounds mushrooms, sliced
2 cans cream of mushroom soup
1 soup can water
⅓ cup soy sauce
1 cup each uncooked white rice and wild rice
4 cups sliced celery

Preheat oven to 325°F. Melt half the butter in a large skillet and sauté the meat cubes over medium heat until browned on all sides. Turn these into a large casserole. Add the remaining butter to the skillet and sauté the onions and mushrooms until both have just started to brown. Blend the soup, water, and soy sauce together until smooth. Wash the rices in two changes of water and add to the meat with the celery and the soup mixture. Stir well. Cover and bake for 2 hours. Serve with a tossed salad and garlic bread.

For the late fifties, the presence of the wild rice, the two kinds of meat, the quantity of fresh mushrooms,* the soy sauce, all gave the casserole an air of sophistication. At the same time, the can of cream of mushroom soup immediately assured the hostess that she could approach the recipe without fear. Similarly, it signaled to the other women at the table that this was not the sort of competitive cooking meant to put them on their mettle. Their enjoyment eating it could only be enhanced by the appreciative awareness that, once given the recipe, any one of

---

*In our vernacular cooking, mushrooms are almost always seen as a refinement rather than as a basic component of a dish the way, say, celery or carrots are. This isn't because mushrooms are expensive but because enough people regard them with suspicion for them to be deemed an acquired—and, to that extent, an enlightened—taste.

them could make it just as well . . . which, of course, is exactly why so many asked for it.

In other words, the pleasures inherent in this kind of cooking are essentially, emphatically, social. One need only compare the open-handed communality of the cooks in *Crazy for Casseroles* with, say, Madame X in *The Cooking of South-West France*, who agreed to teach Paula Wolfert about the local cuisine while refusing—through distraction and, if that failed, outright deception—to reveal any of her hard-won cooking secrets. Madame X's cabbage and dumpling soup may or may not taste better than Jean's casserole, but the reason one was not shared while the other was—over and over again—had nothing to do with goodness. One of the unalloyed benefits of the nonthreatening, noncompetitive nature of convenience-food cookery is that it radiates a contagious sense of companionship and good cheer.

It was this, I realize now, that captivated me when I first leafed through *Crazy for Casseroles*. I had been completely absorbed by the image of other people happily making and eating this food—something very different from thinking I might want to make it myself. This isn't to say that I wouldn't gladly gobble it up as a dinner guest, which has happened more than once—remember my response to green bean casserole. I might even, in that flush of pleasure, ask, like all the others, for the recipe. But, in the end, I would never use it. These dishes are not what makes me want to cook.

*   *   *

> Casserole: a porous dish of clay or earthenware, much used in French cooking. The heat penetrates it slowly and all the juices and flavors of the meats, etc., are retained.
> —Artemas Ward, *The Grocer's Encyclopedia*

Artemas Ward's description reminds me—perhaps it is that word "porous"—of my grandfather's house. Maybe it is just that, having used such casseroles, I know that they are an example of form determining function: too fragile to handle high heat on top of the stove or within it, they require the low, sustained heat that, it turns out, retains the juices and flavor of the dish. An old house likewise demands an alertness that shapes our experience of it and, for good or ill, our personality. This can, at times, be annoying, but its reality is such that its absence can make another, newer house feel strangely empty, even sterile.

This must be how I feel about the now ubiquitous, nonporous, high-heat-fired CorningWare casserole dishes—which can be (some of them, anyway) used on top of the stove as well as in it, and which can take as hot an oven as you care to put them in—because I don't own any . . . whereas we have several of the old-fashioned clay kind.* What these lack in cold perfection they make up for in resonance—if I can use that word to convey how an inanimate object can compel your attention and reward it with accretions of experience.

This same term can be usefully applied to a certain sort of recipe as well. Jean's casserole called to mind *baeckeoffe*, a traditional casserole from Alsace, which might not be considered a dinner party dish on its native turf, but could certainly fill that role here. Made with three kinds of meat, marinated and then baked in wine, and brought to table in the cooking vessel, where its seal of flour paste is broken to release a cloud of delicious aromas, it has all the necessary class, enhanced with a touch of drama. It is also rather easy to make.

BAECKEOFFE
[Serves 8]

1 pound boneless stewing pork
1 pound boneless shoulder of lamb
1 pound boneless stewing beef
2 pig's feet, split in half (optional—see note)

FOR THE MARINADE:
1 tablespoon kosher salt
½ tablespoon black peppercorns
1 sprig fresh or 1 teaspoon dried thyme
2 bay leaves

---

*Dutch ovens are another matter. That familiar, weighty covered pot (usually made of cast iron, either plain or coated with porcelain) is the master of many tasks, cosseting casseroles being just one of them. And these also acquire their own personality as the years pass.

2 or 3 garlic cloves, minced
1 or 2 sprigs fresh celery leaves, chopped
several sprigs fresh flat-leaf parsley, chopped
½ bottle dry white wine (preferably an Alsatian riesling)

FOR THE CASSEROLE:
butter or lard for greasing
3 pounds waxy potatoes, peeled and sliced
2 onions, chopped
2 leeks, trimmed and sliced
4 carrots, peeled and cut into bite-size pieces

FOR THE LUTING (SEALING) PASTE:
1 scant cup flour
5 tablespoons water
1 tablespoon cooking oil

The Day Before: Cut the meats into bite-size pieces and put them in a large nonreactive container with the pig's feet (if using). Toss with the salt, pepper, thyme, bay leaves, garlic, celery leaves, and parsley. Moisten with the wine. Cover and refrigerate overnight.

Assembling and Cooking: Preheat oven to 400°F. Select a large ovenproof casserole with a lid. Grease the bottom and sides with the butter. Lay the pig's feet on the bottom and cover with half the potatoes, onions, leeks, and carrots. Remove the meat from the marinade and add, covering it with the remaining vegetables, ending with the potatoes. Strain the marinade through a sieve and pour the liquid over the contents of the pot. If necessary, add some extra wine or water to bring the liquid barely to the top of the vegetables.

Work the sealing paste ingredients into a dough and roll this out into a rope long enough to wrap around the casserole. Put the lid on the casserole and press the sealing paste firmly against the join all around the pot. Put the sealed pot into the oven and cook for 1 hour. At this point, reduce the heat to 350°F and continue cooking for 1½ hours more.

For the most dramatic presentation, bring the casserole to the table, set it on a trivet, and break away the seal with the edge of a table knife. Otherwise, of course, this can be done in the kitchen and servings of the *baeckeoffe* brought to table in shallow bowls. Serve with a green salad, a loaf of crusty bread, and some of the same wine used for making the marinade.

Cook's Notes. The pig's feet provide a gelatinous cast to the *baeckeoffe*'s juices. Oxtail is another traditional option, as is nothing at all.

The luting paste is meant as much to keep the wine's vaporous aromas from escaping as it is to keep the cooking liquid from evaporating. A band of heavy aluminum foil will work almost as well.

Readers may smile at my describing this dish as easy to make, especially in contrast to Jean's casserole, with its single short paragraph of instruction. And they are probably right to do so, even though in Alsace *baeckeoffe* is considered the next step up from convenience food. The name means "baker's oven," and the dish is traditionally made on Mondays, the casserole being dropped off in the morning at the local bakery, to slowly cook in a corner of the bread oven while the housewife concentrates on getting the laundry done. This means that the prep work is all done early on and that no special bother need be spared to make it.

What it does require—and this goes a long way toward explaining the difference in recipe length—is that the cook take responsibility for the dish. The recipe only points the way. It has been shaped by many, many years of spirited input from a countless number of Alsatian cooks. They disagree about the kinds (and cuts) of meat—*Le Baeckeoffe d'Alsace*, a Strasbourg restaurant, offers several variations, including one made with duck, another with ox cheeks and calves' feet. Some add carrots to the marinade; others, cloves.* Some insist that a tablespoon of red wine vinegar pulls the flavors of the dish together; most don't mention it. An Alsatian riesling is the wine most often used in the dish, but recipes can be found calling for gewürtztraminer, sylvaner, or pinot blanc (or even Alsatian beer). Some cooks use shallots instead of onions (small ones, peeled but left whole); others use only leeks. The addition of other vegetables apart from the leeks and potatoes is a mat-

---

*Anyone wanting to push the envelope further still should turn to *Saveur Cooks Authentic French* (San Francisco: Chronicle Books, 1999), which gives a recipe for *Baeckeoffe de Foie Gras*, a creation of Émile Jung of the three-star Au Crocodile, also in Strasbourg, with its lobe of fresh duck foie gras and black truffles.

ter of taste; some add none but most add something—carrots, celeriac, tiny turnips.

Over the years, Anne Willan has given us at least three recipes for *baeckeoffe*, in *French Regional Cooking*, *La France Gastronomique*, and *Château Cuisine*, each quarreling amicably with the others. Interestingly, the last, most recent recipe of the three is by far the simplest, as if suggesting that time eventually pares things down to the essentials: the meat, the potatoes, the wine, the onions, the garlic, the bouquet garni.

If you make the dish, you will ponder on these things yourself. In fact, if you make it more than once, that may well be because you want to resolve some questions that came up the first time around. Those who ate it might have found it simply delicious, but you want to know if it would taste better if you sautéed the leeks in a little lard or butter before adding them to the casserole; whether veal might go better with pork and lamb than stewing beef.

Such issues and their resolution continually sharpen its focus. Keep at it and the dish will eventually attain the melodic tautness of a well-tuned guitar. It will ring true, and that, to a cook, is an astonishingly satisfying thing. This explains why we collect so many recipes but end up making, over and over, the same familiar dishes. The other night, listening to the Be Good Tanyas singing "Oh Susanna," I thought how hard it was to wear out a good tune. You just keep making it new. Surely the same is true with recipes, dishes; it's why I like so much to cook.

• • •

> Being lazy and liking to cook and to entertain, we struggled futilely for a long time over how to combine these features pleasantly. Finally the thing came to us—that thing being a casserole. Stews and other wrongly demeaned dishes take on a dash of simplicity and sophistication when prepared in a casserole.
> —Marian Tracy, *Casserole Cookery*

Since there could be no better characterization of me than as a lazy person in love with cooking, perhaps the reason that Marian Tracy and other casserole makers go one way and I the other can be found in the word "entertaining." This is something I rarely do—I'd much rather get together with friends and family at a restaurant, where we can all walk away from the dirty dishes together. I do understand, though, that entertaining must make a lot of people nervous, there being so many, many reassuring books on the subject.

Even so, earlier in my life I was innocent enough to often have people over, in couples and in groups, and it never occurred to me that they might turn up their noses at a good Irish stew (let alone *baeckeoffe*, had I known about it then). Nor have I ever read a food writer who argued to the contrary. Where then does the fear come from that such things are "not good enough for company"—or, more to the point, that guests might secretly sneer at their hostess for serving them? Could it be that Marian Tracy—who would go on to publish at least two further books on convenience food–based casserole cookery (Poppy Cannon was no slouch in that department either)—was less reading the mind of her public than planting in that mind a germinating seed of doubt?

Just as the invention of the personal deodorant transformed body odor, until then a mere fact of life, into a universal embarrassment, so could casserole cookery, which impressed cooks with its unthreatening easiness, make the uncertain work of preparing something pleasing from scratch seem rife with potential discomfiture.

Convenience-food cookery frees the cook of responsibility for the dish, and freedom from responsibility is such a delicious experience that it becomes part of the deliciousness of the dish itself—just as it is part of the deliciousness of living in a tract house. The vinyl siding doesn't so much fool the eye as persuade it that what it sees is surely good enough if this means never having to scrape and paint the outside of a house again.

A bargain with the devil, this, albeit one that's easy enough to ignore. (That's what's so nice about deals struck with Old Scratch.) But, nonetheless . . . it used to be that old houses, like old people, aged into increasingly fragile, complex collations of successes, failures, and compromises—which is to say surviving the consequences of what seemed like good ideas at the time. Today's houses, locked in a lackluster permanence, gather no such patina. The passage of time merely makes them increasingly boring.

And so it is with tuna noodle or poppy seed chicken or Jean's casserole. They will never again be as good as the first time you tasted them, however slowly the experience rolls downhill. In fact, Shirley can't remember the last time she made that casserole; she was as astonished as we were to find the recipe card, stained and brown with age, still in her file.

When Matt first entertained, she served it to company herself. But the recipe card brought back less a rush of nostalgia than one of surprise. She remembered the casserole as being distinctly cosmopolitan for its time, which may indeed be true. Her astonishment, though, came from the fact that two key ingredients—the can of condensed soup, the slug of soy sauce—had completely vanished from her memory. As soon as she saw them, the recipe lost its sheen . . . and any interest she might have had in making it again.

We get tired, too, of dishes that demand more from us than to be just thrown together. But, most always, that says something more about us than about them. We've made them too often; we and they both need a rest. But if we return to them, even decades later, they can spring instantly back to life. They need to be freshly tuned, it's true—the amount of butter cut back; the garlic actually added to the dish, not merely rubbed around the inside of the pot. They won't taste the same as they did back then, but, with luck, they'll taste just as good. They might even taste better—after all, you have learned a few things since, some tricks that, it turns out, this old dish is eager to learn. That, after all, is what keeps it—and us—feeling young.

Addendum

BAECKEOFFE WITH MUNSTER CHEESE
[Serves up to 4 as an entrée, 6 or more as a side dish]

While researching baeckeoffe, *I occasionally came across this version— very unlike the traditional version and very much like an American casserole. In the same high-calorie spirit, it is generally offered as a side dish to roast beef or leg of lamb; I would instead suggest it as an entrée, served with a green salad on the side.*

1 tablespoon unsalted butter
4 shallots, finely diced

¼ cup heavy cream
½ teaspoon kosher salt
½ teaspoon black pepper
1 pound potatoes, peeled, boiled, and thinly sliced
12 ounces Alsatian Munster, sliced thin
½ bottle Alsatian riesling wine

Preheat oven to 375°F. Melt all but a sliver of the butter in a small skillet and sauté the minced shallots until they turn translucent. Don't let them brown. Remove the skillet from the heat and gently stir in the cream, salt, and black pepper.

Use the other bit of butter to grease the bottom and sides of a casserole. Cover the bottom with a layer of the sliced potatoes, use a spatula to spread over this a portion of the shallots and cream, then top this with the Munster. Repeat this until all the potatoes have been used, ending with a layer of Munster on top. Pour the wine over.

Put the casserole, uncovered, in the oven and bake for 45 minutes, until everything is bubbling hot and the cheese on top has become a golden brown crust.

REAL ITALIANS

They are sold fresh, made right in front of the customer, a bit like
sushi. I am told that at Amato's it takes six months to train someone to make an Italian properly.
                              —Charles Swett (personal correspondence)

The year was 1971 or 1972, and I was spending what would prove to
be one of my last summers at the family cottage on Long Island in
Maine's Casco Bay. This was also the first year ever that I had some real
spending money. Not a lot of it, but, as anyone who has been in that
position will know, there's a big difference between having none and
just enough to have a little fun.

My idea of that was to take the island steamer into Portland and
wander around the city, checking out the paperback racks at the news-
stand, poking around the one downtown supermarket for various items
that couldn't be found at Clarke's, the island grocery, and maybe taking
in a matinee—although that would mean a long wait for the five
o'clock boat to get back home. But, wherever my wanderings would
take me, I always made sure that there was enough time to get to 71 India Street—Amato's—home of the "original" Italian sandwich.

I put "original" in quotes because it's the sort of claim that, under
scrutiny, becomes as insubstantial as mist. What can be said with confidence is that at the turn of the last century Giovanni Amato opened a
bakery and had the idea to sell his bread from a pushcart to fellow Italian immigrants laying stones and working on the Portland docks.
Sometimes the workers wanted cheese, so he started bringing cheese.
Then they asked for salami. It was only a matter of time before he put

it all together, layering on top of the meat and cheese an assortment of vegetables. He sold the resulting extravaganza, dressed with salt, pepper, and salad oil, for what has always been a very reasonable price.

By the time I began going there, an Amato's Italian cost twenty-five cents (these days they're still a terrific bargain at two dollars and change). At two bits apiece, I could afford to buy a sackful and live off them for the next few days. The first one, though, I always ate at the Casco Bay Line wharf, while waiting for the three o'clock sailing.

At this point I should confess that I have never been fond of most commercial cold cuts in a sandwich, and those offered by Amato's proved no exception.* Fortunately, I soon discovered that I could order a "veggie"—made with cheese but no meat. This had an additional advantage: order a regular Italian and the counterman just takes one from a waiting row and finishes it up with a drizzle of oil and some salt and pepper. With a veggie, he calls the order over to the sandwich maker, who makes the whole thing from scratch.

Amato's bakes its own bread, and the loaves in size and shape pretty much resemble the usual hoagie or hero roll. They are delicately crusty but also soft enough so that the sandwich maker can slice one almost all the way through and then fold it open like a book. He or she then begins to generously layer the bread with the following ingredients, listed in order (ordinarily, of course, it would have Italian cold cuts or ham layered on first):

> provolone or American cheese
> a scattering of chopped onion
> thin slices of green pepper
> thin slices of sour pickle
> thick slices of ripe tomato
> a few pieces of imported black olive

The counterman takes the result, seasons it as described above, cuts it in half, wraps it up, still open-face, in waxed paper, and pops it into a sack.

---

*In the New Orleans French Market many years ago, I ordered that famous local specialty, a muffaletta—a Frisbee-like loaf crammed with various cold cuts and provolone and dressed with olive salad—at Central Grocery. I took a few bites and then relegated the rest—enough to feed a high school football team—into a trash bin. This is not meant as a put-down of muffalettas (muffalette?). But it is an extremely *dry*, meat-and-cheese-crammed sandwich that demands a mouthwatering response to comfortably eat. And a thick wad of cold cuts just doesn't do that for me.

There on the dock, the results of my shopping stacked beside me on the bench, I would carefully undo all this, watching out especially not to let a cascade of salad oil spill onto my lap. There is no graceful way to eat this sandwich; its very generosity almost ensures that something will escape your grasp, usually at the worst possible moment. The seagulls knew this and gathered around expectantly, heads cocked, following my progress with cynical beady eyes.

No matter. The first bite tosses all such pernickety fussing aside, transporting you to an immediate state of bliss. The fact that the tomatoes are genuinely ripe and hand-sliced directly onto the sandwich gives it an immediate succulence—all that tomato juice mingling with the salad oil. This, however, is just the booster rocket that gets you into orbit. What keeps you there, floating effortlessly miles above earth, is the sandwich's perfect marriage of flavor and texture. When the tomato taste reaches its limit, the blast from the green pepper kicks in; the onion growls softly but continuously in the background; the bits of black olive keep the palate paying attention; and, at the outermost rim, the cheese and bread provide a comforting insulation, not to mention the promise of ultimate fullness. They don't dilute all that vegetable sharpness; they balance it out. For me, a sandwich without that equilibrium, that carefully crafted euphony, is barely worth the effort required to consume it, but this one has it in spades.

However, to my surprise—and it affects me the same way every time—the focal point, the still center in all this raucous commotion, is the sour pickle. I think I've spent more time contemplating this pickle and its effect on the sandwich than I have any other single ingredient in a lifetime of eating. It is so simple, it works so well, and yet there is something about it that mysteriously eludes comprehension. After all, it's not unlike the green pepper—which, while the sandwich would surely suffer from its absence, is in the end just another team player.

That pickle, though . . . well, the word that keeps coming back to me is "succulence." The sour pickle is not only juicy, in the way the tomato is juicy, but it actually makes your mouth water (as, say, a lemon does). And the black olive and the green pepper, both of them with their own kind of piquancy, spread that sourness across your palate, mellowing it out as they do.

Now, I make no claims for Amato's as the culinary destination of a lifetime. In fact, if I had to choose between a veggie and a toasted bun heaped with fried clams, I guess that the clams would occasionally win out. Still, an Italian sandwich, Amato's style, gives an unusual amount of pleasure and, perhaps more important, offers a kind of perfection that rarely comes one's way.

The nice thing about all this is that if you're not in a position to go there yourself, you can make a very close approximation at home. The only problem will be finding the right bread. The best solution would be to go to your local Italian bakery and get their hero/submarine/hoagie roll hot from the oven. As our pal Charles Swett, who lives right around the corner from Amato's, told us: "The key to the Italian sandwich is one thing: bread, bread, bread. Fresh every day."

If you're ever in Portland, you can also pick up a bottle of their "special" olive- and soybean-oil blend, which is, it must be said, good stuff. Even so, a lot of Maine eateries offer real maple syrup for your pancakes at a small surcharge, and if I ever have the ear of Dominic Reali, Amato's current owner, I'll tell him I'd gladly shell out the same for a shot of extra-virgin olive oil on my sandwich. That's the only thing holding it back from claiming the title of not only the original Italian but the absolute best of them all.

. . . AND OTHERS

> When I lived on the Italian Riviera the common snack consisted of a crusty roll split and filled with sliced tomato, salt, olive oil, and a few leaves of fresh basil—no butter, of course—just squashed to make the oil and juice impregnate the bread.
> —Tom Stobart, *The Cook's Encyclopedia*

The vegetable-intensive sandwich that Giovanni Amato invented is, of course, firmly rooted in Italian foodways, where bread and tomatoes have been worked into every imaginable combination, from soup (*pappa al pomodoro*) and salad (*panzanella*) to all sorts of pizza, especially *Sardinaira* and *scacciata*. But the idea of the vegetable—and especially tomato—laden sandwich is hardly restricted to Italy. We've discussed some of these in the past—*pan bagnat*, *panafla*, and *pan Bologna* in *Simple Cooking*, and Catalan's *pa amb tomàquet* and Malta's *hobz iz zejt* (shared by Maurice Frechette) in *Pot on the Fire*. Here we range further afield, turning up some new and worthy additions to the canon.

MARINATED ZUCCHINI AND
RED PEPPER SANDWICH
(Adapted from Susan Hermann Loomis's *Italian Farmhouse Cookbook*)
[Serves 4]

This unusual and rather dramatic sandwich is based on a dish that Susan Hermann Loomis sampled at Da Mino, a small restaurant in the center of Robbio, a farming town in Lombardy. The chef, Enrica Abatte, calls it a carpaccio vegetale *(vegetable carpaccio) and serves it as a layered salad. What made me think of using it—adapted as follows—as a sandwich topping was its unique pickle-like crispness combined with an unexpected succulence—not something that comes directly to mind with raw zucchini, red pepper, and a green such as watercress. (Abatte makes it with arugula, but to my palate the cress, although equally sharp, is more in balance with the other ingredients.) Quite simply, it's a knockout.*

    4 medium zucchini, trimmed and sliced paper-thin
    2 red bell peppers, stemmed, seeded, and sliced paper-thin
    6 ounces of a sharp green such as watercress or arugula,
       rinsed, patted dry, and stemmed
    ¼ cup extra-virgin olive oil
    2 tablespoons decent balsamic vinegar
    1 teaspoon kosher salt, or to taste
    ½ teaspoon hot red pepper flakes, or to taste
    1 long loaf of French bread, cut in quarters and split
    2 ounces Parmigiano-Reggiano, shaved paper-thin (see note)

The Day Before: Put the sliced vegetables and watercress in a large bowl. Whisk together the olive oil and balsamic vinegar to make a dressing, seasoning it to taste—but generously—with the salt and hot red pepper flakes. Toss the contents of the bowl with this, making sure that none of the zucchini rounds have clumped together. Cover with plastic wrap and refrigerate overnight.

The Following Day: Remove the marinating vegetables from the refrigerator about an hour before making the sandwiches. Then retoss the salad and divide it among the sandwiches, including all the juices. Layer each with a fair share of the shaved cheese. Serve open-face.

Cook's Note. The simplest way to get paper-thin shavings of Parmesan is to use a vegetable peeler.

ROASTED PEPPER AND EGGPLANT SANDWICH
[Serves 4]

> 3 or 4 tablespoons extra-virgin olive oil
> 2 garlic cloves, minced
> ½ teaspoon dried Greek oregano
> 1 teaspoon kosher salt, or to taste
> ½ teaspoon hot red pepper flakes
> 2 small tubular eggplants, trimmed and cut (unpeeled) into
>   ¼-inch rounds
> 2 red bell peppers, chopped
> 3 portobello mushroom caps, sliced thick
> 4 scallions, trimmed and cut into 2-inch lengths
> 1 tablespoon decent balsamic vinegar
> 1 loaf Italian bread

Preheat oven to 450°F. Add the olive oil, garlic, oregano, salt, and hot red pepper flakes to a 12-inch ovenproof skillet. (I use a 12-inch, durable-nonstick wok, which works perfectly for this recipe.) Stir well and then add the eggplants, peppers, mushrooms, and scallions, tossing them gently until they are all coated with the seasoned oil. Make sure that the eggplant slices don't clump together.

Put the pan in the preheated oven and roast the vegetables for 30 minutes, removing the pan and tossing them gently every 5 minutes. At the end of this time, taste the eggplant and peppers for tenderness, especially the skin. When ready, turn into a large bowl, dress with the balsamic vinegar, and let cool for 30 minutes. (At this point, the salad can be refrigerated and kept until later. If so, let it return to room temperature before serving.)

Meanwhile, cut the bread lengthwise and grill under the broiler, crumb side facing the flame, until toasted. Cut each length in half, and top each segment with its fair share of the vegetable mixture. Press this down firmly with a spatula and let sit for 10 minutes before serving.

Variation. For added oomph, first spread the bread with the garlic and olive oil emulsion described in the French-fry sandwich recipe on page 151.

SANDVIÇ FASULYE PIYAZI
[Serves 4]

Fasulye piyazi is a popular Turkish bean salad that street vendors have transformed into a sandwich by serving it in pita bread. This recipe calls for canned beans, but obviously, if you prefer, they can be prepared from scratch. The canned beans are briefly heated because they then better absorb the flavors of the other ingredients.

¼ cup extra-virgin olive oil
1 garlic clove, peeled and very finely minced
¼ teaspoon kosher salt
pinch of hot red pepper flakes
1 19-ounce can cannellini beans
1 red salad onion, sliced paper-thin
1 small green pepper, cored, seeded, and sliced paper-thin
2 medium pita rounds, cut into 4 pockets

FOR GARNISHING:
imported black olives, pitted and quartered; lemon wedges;
   minced flat-leaf parsley
extra-virgin olive oil

Pour the olive oil into a small bowl. Add the minced garlic, salt, and pinch of hot red pepper flakes. Stir gently until the salt is dissolved.

Heat the beans briefly in their own liquid until they are nice and hot. Strain and add to a bowl with the thin-sliced salad onion and green pepper. Gently toss in the seasoned olive oil. Let this sit for an hour.

Spoon the salad into the pita pockets, dressing each sandwich with bits of olive, the juice from a lemon wedge, a generous scattering of parsley, and a final drizzle of olive oil.

SALADE BLANKIT
[Serves 4]

This popular Tunisian sandwich—blankit is the term for a long loaf of French bread—clearly shows the influence of Provence's pan bagnat. But it is its own self nonetheless, and there are many variations to be found on the streets of Tunis. Usually, the sandwich is made with flaked canned tuna (see note), but Kitty Morse, in The Vegetarian Table: North Africa, *found this delicious vegetarian version at Patisserie Ben Yedder.*

Properly, the tomato, bell pepper, and onion should be grilled, then peeled, and everything chopped together to make a salad. Frankly, I find grilling onions and tomatoes tedious and the results unimpressive, so I devised the following skillet method instead, using roasted red peppers from our supermarket's olive bar. (I also skip the separate preparation of harissa, the Tunisian garlic–hot pepper sauce, incorporating its ingredients into the filling itself.) Appalled? Well, you can find more authentic versions in, among others, Kitty Morse's book and Anissa Helou's Mediterranean Street Food.

½ teaspoon caraway seeds
¼ cup extra-virgin olive oil, plus extra for garnishing
2 garlic cloves, finely minced
2 medium onions, coarsely chopped
½ teaspoon Tabasco or other hot sauce
4 each green and imported black olives, pitted and chopped
2 tablespoons capers, chopped
juice squeezed from 1 lemon
2 roasted red peppers, cut into small pieces
3 or 4 tomatoes, cut into chunks
2 waxy potatoes, boiled, peeled, and cubed
salt to taste
1 long loaf of French bread or 4 crusty oblong French rolls
2 hard-boiled eggs, chopped
1 Kirby (pickling) cucumber, peeled and chopped

Heat a small skillet over a medium flame. When it is hot, put in the caraway seeds and gently toss until they are lightly toasted. Quickly turn them into a mortar or food processor fitted with its steel blade and pulverize into a coarse powder.

Put the olive oil in a large skillet and gently heat. Add the garlic, onions, and ground toasted caraway seeds. Cook over medium heat until the onion begins to brown at the edges, 6 to 7 minutes.

Turn off the heat and add the hot sauce, chopped olives, capers, and about half the lemon juice. Stir well. Toss in the chunks of roasted red pepper, tomato, and potato, so that everything is covered with the garlic-onion sauce. Taste and add salt and enough of the remaining lemon juice to achieve a pleasing balance of flavor.

Slice the bread (quartered) or the rolls in half lengthwise. Pull out some of the crumb so that the filling will fit without spilling out. Heap the bottom half with the salad and then top with the chopped egg and cucumber. Put a cruet of olive oil on the table for eaters to dribble over their sandwiches to taste.

Variation. For the standard version of this sandwich, add a 6-ounce can of olive oil–packed tuna, drained and flaked, to the sandwich mixture at the same time you toss in the pieces of roasted red pepper and tomato.

LEBANESE FRIED POTATO SANDWICH
[Serves 4]

Anissa Helou sampled this French-fry roll-up in Lebanon. I can't imagine making my own fries to have it, not with Burger King, Wendy's, and McDonald's a short walk away. Take the fixings with you and wow 'em at your local burger palace (especially when you exhale).

> 5 large garlic cloves, peeled
> 1 teaspoon kosher salt, or to taste
> ½ cup extra-virgin olive oil
> 3 or 4 tablespoons strained yogurt (optional—see note)
> 2 medium pita rounds
> 1 king-size order of fries
> lemon wedges

Using a mortar and pestle or food processor fitted with its steel blade, work the garlic and salt into a very fine paste. Then drizzle in the olive oil very slowly, whisking constantly (as if making mayonnaise). Temper the results, if you wish, with the strained yogurt.

Split the pita rounds at the edges to make four flat disks. Spread the inner (coarse) side with garlic sauce to taste. Divide the fries evenly among them, sprinkle these with lemon juice, and roll them up tightly. Wrap each in a paper napkin and eat at once.

Cook's Note. To make strained yogurt, put ordinary yogurt in a fine-meshed sieve and let as much moisture as possible drip out.

Further Reading: Mediterranean Street Food

Rummaging through our cookbook collection in preparation for this essay, I was reminded again how small a role street food plays in many otherwise meticulous investigations into foreign foodways. There are, I understand—having written on the subject myself—pragmatic reasons for avoiding it. Sometimes the snack requires daily practice to pull it off; other times it calls for tedious preparation—fine when you're buying from a stand, but silly for a quick snack to make at home.

Other times still, it can be considered, either by author or editor, just too weird or off-putting. *The New York Times* reported in 2003 that Turks were agitating to save *kokoreç*, a greasy concoction of toasted bread and fried lamb intestines, from being banned once Turkey joins the EU (which had prohibited the sale of some kinds of sheep offal during the mad cow disease epidemic in the 1990s). Although *kokoreç* is Turkey's signature fast-food delight, not one of our several Turkish cookbooks offers a recipe for it.

There have been a few honorable exceptions to this rule,* but none have had the range, charm, or just plain usefulness of Anissa Helou's recipe-packed *Mediterranean Street Food*, a book that I would rate as a "must-have" purchase for both the street-food enthusiast and anyone interested in little-explored corners of that area's cooking.

I have to admit, however, that I approached the book with more than a touch of skepticism. "Here we go again," I muttered to myself. "Pizza, pissaladière, socca, focaccia, shish kebab, shawarma, falafel—another round-up of the usual suspects."

---

*Examples that come immediately to mind are Vatcharin Bhumichitr's *Vatch's Thai Street Food*, Rose Grant's *Street Food*, Rohani Jelani's *Malaysian Hawker Favourites*, James Mayson's *Street Food from Around the World*, and Keith Ruskin Miller's *Indonesian Street Food Secrets. Eating Alfresco: The Best Street Food in the World* deserves special mention for both Nelli Sheffer's stunning color photographs and Israel Aharoni's evocative text. Sadly, though, the recipe section at the end of the book seems mostly an afterthought.

I was wrong. The author was born in Lebanon and grew up in Beirut's golden years—the late fifties and early sixties—when it was considered the Switzerland of the Middle East: prosperous, peaceful, and friendly. There, as a little girl on regular strolls with her uncle, she fell in love with the rich assortment of street food sold along the Corniche, Beirut's oceanside promenade: "sesame galettes that looked like handbags, grilled corn, mountains of seeds and nuts spooned into cones made out of old newspapers, luscious sweets and candies, ice cream, and refreshing drinks."

This fascination never dimmed—in fact, once she was old enough to escape her parents' watchful eyes, it flowered. She dragged her friends for late-night bowls of hot, milky *salep* (a thick drink flavored with powdered orchid tuber); for lunch she often stopped for some *manaqish* (a crispy flatbread topped with thyme, sumac, and sweet onion). This book—illustrated with the author's own black-and-white photographs—not only takes us on a tour of this world but also shares her rich fund of knowledge about this food and her own experiences eating it.

So, for instance, in her discussion of Moroccan snail soup (the broth is a revivifying mix of, among other things, hot chile, anise seeds, mint, green tea leaves, licorice root, and orange peel), she describes the general Mediterranean love of snails and how different cuisines purge them of their slime. Elsewhere, in her discussion of *slada matecha*, the omnipresent Moroccan tomato and onion salad served as a side whenever you order grilled offal, meat, or fish, she tells of being served some with an order of fried fish in the southern part of that country. The fishmonger then surprised her by producing a bottle of argan oil from under his counter and dressed her salad with it. This oil, with its delicate nutty taste, is produced in a rather unusual way. Nimble-footed goats leap up into the argan trees to eat the fruit. Villagers then gather the pits after they have worked their way through the animals' digestive tracts, extract the kernels from them, and press these for the oil. One has a hunch that olives don't grow in that region and, here again, necessity has been forced to become the mother of invention.

Helou makes the interesting observation in the opening pages of her book that the Middle Eastern and African edges of the Mediterranean offer a far richer street food experience than does the European part. This is because the latter has traditionally offered so many alternatives in the form of humble eating places, take-out shops, and, especially, taverns (imagine Spain without tapas—which, after all, are a highly evolved form of bar food). Only after you pass from Greece into Turkey does street food really come alive.

An unexpected corollary to this fact will occur to you once you begin exploring the rest of the book. Because of the absence of inexpensive sit-down eateries, a lot of this street food is what we would consider "restaurant food." But here it is sold and eaten alfresco. Of course, it can also be taken home and eaten there. But how much easier—and more fun!—it is to wander from stall to stall, having your first course here, your main course there, your dessert and tea or coffee somewhere else . . . each prepared by an expert in that one thing.

If I've stressed some of the odder fare so far, this isn't to say that the book isn't full of immediately appealing and often simply prepared food. It is, and these cover the entire range from soups to desserts, with chapters as well on snacks, salads, and dips (pilaf-stuffed mussels, fava bean salad, chili shrimp); pizzas, breads, and pastries (potato boreks, onion pie, Moroccan doughnuts); sandwiches; barbecues; one-pot meals (pork and cannellini bean stew, chicken tagine with potatoes and peas); sweets; and drinks. No recipe, though, for that Turkish *kokoreç*—and maybe just as well. As a Turkish customer said to the reporter from the *Times*, "If I tried to cook this in my home, it would leave an awful smell."

WOK FRAGRANT

My grandfather was the one who introduced me to the world of Chinese restaurants, at least as they were in the 1950s, beguilingly ersatz palaces spun of velvet and gold. As a teenager, I spent my summers with him, working at odd jobs at his apartment house in the daytime and otherwise generally hanging around with him when I wasn't off somewhere by myself.

Grampa was drawn to Chinese restaurants for all the usual reasons: here was food that, while piquantly exotic, hit all the right notes so far as price, quantity, and greasy goodness were concerned. But the selling point that clinched the deal was that in Boston's Chinatown they not only stayed open past midnight but were actually bustling then. If there's just you and a waiter in an otherwise empty place, it's hard to ward off inner tremors of self-pity. But if the joint is jumping, you feel instead like a welcomed initiate to a secret club.

So it was that, whenever the *Jack Paar Show* started to bore him, Grampa would launch himself from his prone position on the couch and come drag me out of my bedroom and away from my science fiction tale. He would rev up the '52 Cadillac Series Sixty and we would head off to downtown Boston. Once we turned onto Harrison Avenue, I started eagerly inhaling that ineffable—for a sixteen-year-old, at least—after-midnight aroma of the louche.

Our destination was China Pearl at 9 Tyler Street, and my grandfather always ordered *ho yu gai pu*, a dish of crisp, batter-coated pieces of fried chicken. (I remember this because every visit he had to work out with the waiter which of the many chicken dishes on the menu it was.) For me, the high points of the meal were the appetizers— spareribs and egg rolls—and the pork fried rice.

It would only take five more years for me to learn enough about Chinese food to become embarrassed at how touristy my taste was then, especially my fondness for the fried rice. This new awareness certainly affected how I ordered and ate in Chinese restaurants, as well as immediately dispelling any fondness I might have had for italicizing whatever was set before me with the cruet of soy sauce.

However, I would also be a liar if I said that I never ordered red-glazed pork ribs or fried rice again. On the contrary. Like many people who reach this point, my tastes simply bifurcated. The lover of real Chinese food—clams with black bean sauce, mu-shu pork, fragrant crispy duck, *chiao-tzu*—went his own way, not entirely disowning but hardly ever mentioning his slightly furtive shadow, the lover of sham Chinese food.

For years in the early eighties, I worked in an office building that sat right at the corner of Boston's Chinatown, and I did a lot of happy culinary exploring there, in places like Henry's, Tai Tung, Moon Villa. Even so, one year when the assistant director of my department offered to treat me to a birthday lunch—anywhere and anything I wanted—I opted for spareribs and pork fried rice . . . and not from any of my Chinatown finds but from a take-out joint in the downtown shopping district. (Although the place itself was blatantly lacking in authenticity, their sparerib portions blew away the competition's.)

There was an element here, no doubt, of that rarely discussed inclination to just eat bad food—which has more in common with taking a fistful of uppers, drinking moonshine whiskey, or smoking vile cheroots than it does with the pleasures of eating. But in this instance something else was also at work.

Restaurants in Chinatown that were frequented by actual Chinese diners had two menus with corresponding attitudes toward those who ordered from each. I had spent a lot of time getting recognized in such places as that unusual (and, in my own mind, highly estimable) *gwai lo* who wanted to eat the real thing. All it would have taken was three words—"pork fried rice"—to permanently erase everything I had so far managed to accomplish. In fact, by then I'd come to believe that fried rice, like chop suey, had no true roots in China at all, but was a phantasm created to please American eaters.*

The truth, however, turns out to be more complex. Ken Hom, in his affecting and delightful cookbook-as-autobiography, *Easy Family Recipes from a Chinese-American Childhood*, tells how the workers at his uncle's restaurant used to joke about the abandon with which non-Chinese customers added soy sauce to everything in sight. His explanation for this—that Americans "prefer foods on the salty side"—seems an odd accusation, coming from a culture that relishes so many salt-laden sauces, condiments, preserved vegetables, bean pastes . . . (the list is endless, actually). Overuse of soy sauce may be ignorant, but it isn't perverse.

I also think he is a bit misleading when he goes on to say that "never would soy sauce be . . . used in fried rice, especially when one wants the clean, mild taste of rice made subtly smoky as it is stir-fried in the wok."

Point of fact: American customers have never had the opportunity to become familiar with real fried rice, because the ersatz stuff is way too profitable. Take yesterday's leftover white rice, thoroughly dampen it with soy sauce, toss in bits of barbecued pork and various vegetables, leave it in a vat on the steam table all day, and listen to that mental cash register ring every time another order goes out. The result, if not the method, isn't all that different from the so-called rice pilafs that many restaurants offer as an alternative to baked or fried potatoes. So, let's call the stuff "Chinese pork–flavored rice pilaf" and be done with it.†
But hold on to that phrase "subtly smoky," because, as we shall now see, those two words encapsulate the heart of true fried rice.

---

*Although many Chinese writers have said this about chop suey (from Chinese—Cantonese dialect—*tsaâp suì* "mixed bits"), they are wrong—or, rather, didn't come from the right part of China. Li Shu-Fan, in his 1964 autobiography, *Hong Kong Surgeon*, remembers eating chop suey in a restaurant in Toishan (China) in 1894 and speculates that the dish was brought to America by the people of that region, who were among the earliest immigrants to the United States.
†This shouldn't be confused with what might better be called "rice-tossed" dishes. In these, cooked rice is stirred into a mélange of wok-cooked ingredients and served directly after the rice is heated and has absorbed the small amount of cooking liquid. These are part of the repertoire of Chinese home cooking and are very good. But while they, too, can be called "fried rice," they aren't our subject here.

• • •

Back in 1979 I was an exchange student at the Chinese University of Hong Kong. My college's cafeteria had a few regular items on the menu, one of which was a plate of fried rice topped with an over-easy fried egg or two, which I would break up and mix into the rice. The rice was very lightly fried with some scallions, a dried chile, and a bit of minced meat, probably pork.
— R. W. Lucky (personal correspondence)

It was a prewar account of a long train journey in China that shook my mind free of Chinese restaurant fried rice—and it is, alas, all too symptomatic of my reading habits that I can't recall the book. I'm rather good at remembering bits and pieces from my reading but terrible at remembering where it was that I actually read them. So, although what follows is to a certain extent confirmed in Buwei Yang Chao's *How to Cook and Eat in Chinese,* it is extrapolated from memory and inked in by imagination.

When you wanted something to eat on a long train trip in China in the 1930s, what you got, most likely, was fried rice. The ingredients—cooked rice, eggs, scallion, seasonings—were easy to store, and the dish required only a few moments to make. Cooking oil was heated to smoking in a large wok. The rice and bits of scallion were tossed in, resulting in a burst of sizzling, as the damp surface of the rice vaporized. The cook tossed this around for a moment until all the rice was lightly seared in this manner. Then he pushed this up the wok's sides and poured a beaten egg onto the freed-up surface. With a few rapid twists of his spatula, this mass was first scrambled and then broken into pieces, which were quickly mixed into the rice. Finally, he dribbled over some soy sauce, rice wine, and toasted sesame oil and, with one quick motion, scooped everything, smoking hot, into an eating bowl . . . and was ready to start on the next order.

What enchanted me—enchants me still—about all this is a near-magical economy—of fuel, of ingredients, of effort, of equipment, of space—that produces—out of nothing! in seconds!—something filling and truly delicious to eat. Once perceived, this image prevented me from ever looking at fried rice the same way again. Afterwards, whenever and wherever I came across that dish, I looked hopefully for some sign of this magic, even though I never found it.

There's a Chinese phrase for this sort of instantaneous, high-heat cooking, where even slivers of food retain their inner moisture and fresh taste beneath a crisply seared exterior: *wok hai* or, roughly, "wok breath" or "wok fragrance."* Until the publication of Grace Young's *The Breath of a Wok*, I'd never seen this discussed in Chinese cookbooks, perhaps because it is generally considered the province of restaurant cooking, requiring as it does a well-honed deftness and the ability to endure furnace-like working conditions.

However, with the advent of the home-kitchen restaurant stove and, more to the point, the much cheaper wok-friendly outdoor propane burner, now aspiring home cooks can also achieve *wok-hai* creations. I've cast more than one longing glance at the Eastman Outdoors "Big Kahuna" burner, which retails for around fifty dollars, has a rating of 65,000 BTUs (ten times the average burner on a gas stove), and can handle a twenty-two-inch wok with élan.

However, such a unit isn't necessary to make wok-fragrant fried rice. Because cooked rice is light and particulate, it doesn't cool down a hot wok the way heavier, wetter ingredients can. This means it can be sear-fried pretty quickly, even when made on an ordinary home range.

WOK-FRAGRANT FRIED RICE

Caveat. Be aware that this is one of those seemingly simple dishes where every word—including "and" and "but"—is the subject of fierce contention. Some cooks heat the wok before adding the oil. Some cook the eggs in the wok before adding the rice; others wait until the very end, then push the finished rice up the sides of the wok and scramble the eggs in the hollow in the center. Still others stir the beaten eggs directly into the rice and stir-fry until set. Seasonings are various and optional—both Barbara Tropp and Ken Hom make a point of using nothing but salt. This is how I make mine, at least right now.

The Rice. The Qing Dynasty poet and essayist Yuan Mei (1716–

---

*It is also sometimes called *wok chi*, which means, again loosely, "wok energy" or "wok spirit"—*chi* being a hard word to pin down. Almost always the word "elusive" is appended to the phrase, since *wok chi* is considered something nearly mystical—hard to obtain and easily dissipated. Its presence is an indication that the chef is working at the very top of his form.

1798) wrote of savoring the "juices" of rice, which is only possible, he said, if the rice is properly cooked in just the right amount of water. Ideal fried rice enhances this further by encapsulating the moistness within a crusty coating. (This is why the rice must be boiled in advance; during the resting time it absorbs the moisture clinging to its surface, which makes it less sticky and keeps it from sopping up all the oil.) A super-hot wok can achieve this with tender long-grain rice, but if you're preparing it on a kitchen range, you're much better off selecting a plump short-grain rice (but not the super-sticky sweet rice). My favorite for wok-fragrant fried rice is Chinese Royal rice (see page 165), but, perversely, instant rice, which takes only five minutes to cook, works amazingly well, and has the advantage of not needing to be kept overnight to dry out.* If this is too outré for your tastes, a good short-grain (not sticky!) rice such as Lundberg organic short-grain sushi rice is just fine.

The Wok. To do this properly, you'll need a standard cold rolled–steel wok. These are the inexpensive, metal-colored woks sold at Asian groceries. One with a flat bottom is fine—and necessary on an electric burner. If you're buying such a wok new, know that it may have been coated with machine oil to keep it from rusting and needs to be thoroughly cleaned, then seasoned with peanut oil. To do this, heat a tablespoon or so until the oil is almost at the smoking point, swirl it around the inside of the wok, let it cool down, wipe it clean with a paper towel, then repeat that process two or three more times. Once seasoned, the wok should not be washed but wiped out, scouring away any stubborn bits with coarse salt.

The Thing Itself. Wok-fragrant fried rice is as hard to describe as it is good to eat, and the best way to tell when you've achieved it is by taste. Don't bring any expectations to the cooking. The rice won't be visibly crusty, and it shouldn't be burnt or scorched. But if you take a bite now and then as you cook it, you'll find you can't miss the transformation. It really is that noticeable . . . and that delicious.

---

*Stuart Chang Berman, in his adventurous *Potsticker Chronicles* (Wiley, 2004), dismisses instant rice, preferring Uncle Ben's enriched rice for this purpose. He didn't win me over. The enriched rice has slightly more texture but an odd taste and, following his directions, takes about half an hour to cook and another hour or so to dry. I see no advantage here.

PLAIN BOILED RICE
[Serves 1]

1 cup uncooked short-grain rice
1⅔ cups water

At Least Four Hours in Advance (skip this step if you have cooked rice on hand or are using instant rice): Put the rice in a large bowl and rinse it in two changes of cold water. Meanwhile, bring the measured water to a boil in a small (1½-quart) saucepan. Stir in the strained rice. Reduce the heat to the lowest flame possible, cover the rice, and cook for 15 minutes. Then uncover the rice until most of the steam has evaporated. Turn off the heat, place a folded napkin over the rice, replace the cover, and let the pot sit off the heat for another 15 minutes. Finally, turn the cooked rice into a large bowl, breaking up any clumps. Let cool, then cover it with plastic wrap and, depending on how soon you plan to make the fried rice, either put the bowl in the refrigerator or leave it on the counter. Jim Lee, in *Jim Lee's Chinese Cookbook*, says that even in summer you can leave it out for a day or two. I certainly do overnight.

Cook's Note. The Chinese prepare boiled rice without adding salt. When making fried rice, this adds to the "sweetness" of the kernels and thus emphasizes the contrast with the savory seasonings. By the way, this amount of rice is twice as much as needed for the recipe below. Save half for the next batch.

MAKING THE FRIED RICE

about 1½ cups day-old cooked rice (or "instant rice"), at room temperature
2 scallions, trimmed and cut into slivers
1 garlic clove, minced
1 tablespoon minced fresh ginger
½ Chinese sausage, cut into shreds (see note), or 1 tablespoon coarsely chopped prosciutto or country ham
1 or 2 eggs, beaten
pinch of salt

     toasted sesame oil
     1 to 2 teaspoons Chinese rice wine or dry sherry
     2 tablespoons good fresh lard or peanut oil
     light (ordinary) soy sauce (see note)
     hot red pepper flakes or coarse-ground black pepper

Use a spatula or your fingers to break up any clumps in the rice. Put the scallion slivers, minced garlic, minced ginger, and shredded Chinese sausage in a small bowl.

Season the beaten eggs with a pinch of salt, a drizzle of the toasted sesame oil, and the Chinese rice wine/sherry. Lightly wipe a 9-inch non-stick skillet with about a teaspoon of the lard and put it over medium heat. When it is hot, pour in the eggs. When they have set at the bottom, tilt the pan slightly and use a spatula to lift this layer, allowing the uncooked egg on top to run underneath. Continue doing this until all the egg is set. Remove from the heat and cut into small pieces with a spatula.

Put the remaining lard into a wok. Turn up the flame beneath it as high as it will go. Let it heat until the fat starts to haze—i.e., just before it starts to smoke. Swirl it gently to coat the lower sides of the wok, then turn in the scallions, garlic, ginger, and meat. Notice how, immediately, your kitchen smells like a Chinese restaurant. Stir a few times with a spatula and add the cooked rice. Toss with the spatula to thoroughly coat it with the oil and to mix the rice and the seasonings together.

Keep turning the mixture over. After a minute, dribble in some soy sauce and more Chinese rice wine/sherry with one hand, while still turning the mixture with the other. If you want to measure this, use no more than ½ tablespoon of each. When this has been absorbed, toss in a pinch of red pepper flakes.

Continue tossing the rice over high heat until the surface of the grains becomes slightly translucent and toasted-looking. This will take about 4 or 5 minutes. At this point remove the wok from the heat. Stir in the chopped egg and, if you wish, a little more sesame oil. Serve at once.

Cook's Notes. Ingredients: The brand of soy sauce I use is Pearl River Bridge Superior Light; sesame oil, Kadoya pure; Chinese sausage, Sun Ming Jan (the one with gin in it). I should note that cookbooks tell you to poach Chinese sausage before using it in a stir-fry. My own feeling is that by shredding it and cooking it over this kind of high heat, there's no danger, and I love the densely chewy result. As to rice wine, food writers universally condemn Chinese rice cooking wines as grossly inferior, which they doubtlessly are. However, in the world of bad choices, I think I prefer it over the usual substitute, dry sherry, with which it really has nothing in common apart from some flavor notes. Rice wine is not, in the true sense, a wine at all, but a grain-based brew like sake or barley wine. In any case, when Matt and I were pondering the three or four versions of cooking wine at our Asian market, a Chinese woman, pleased by our interest in her country's cooking, struck up a halting conversation with us. We asked her about rice wine, and without hesitation she plucked Yu Yee Brand Chinese Shao Shing Cooking Wine from the shelf. No lectures, no sad sighs. Instead, she proffered the selected bottle with a smile. "This one is the best, I think," she said.

Variations: with fried eggs—use these instead of the usual scrambled eggs (as described by R. W. Lucky on page 158); with shrimp—substitute 6 to 8 shelled and coarsely chopped raw shrimp for the ham; with cooked green peas or edamame (tender green soybeans)—add ½ cup with the scallions, garlic, and ginger.

After I had made this one or two times, I realized that I could never eat pork fried rice in a Chinese restaurant again; I would only burst into tears. I haven't been eating many glossy red spareribs either, having discovered crispy-skin roast pork belly, which blows the ribs out of the water. But the *gwai-lo* factor still comes into play. When I go into a Chinese BBQ store to order some, the cashier confers with the cook, then comes back to ask, "You sure you not want sparerib?"

Despite my happiness with my own wok-fragrant fried rice, I still like to imagine that in every Chinatown in America, there's an unmarked four-table joint where Chinese can sneak off to order fried rice—the real stuff, served smoking from the kitchen. But I know I'll never find it. And if I do, they probably won't let me in.

A Note on Chinese Rice

In Tibet, a dumping ground for China's worst commodities and its worst food products, the rice was tasteless, stubby-grained ker-

nels, speckled white spheres that were devoid of flavor and character. Indeed, for all the rice consumed in China, much of it is
undistinguished, is of such shadowy and shallow flavor that it is
seen as the food of peasants; at banquets in fancy restaurants rice
is almost never served.
      —Edward Gargan, *The River's Tale: A Year on the Mekong*

The Chinese grow 90 percent of the world's rice crop and eat most of
what they raise—the average Chinese eats almost 200 pounds of it a
year (a lot, but nowhere near the record; that goes to Myanmar, where
the per-person average is 441 pounds! To put all this in perspective, the
average American eats about 20 pounds a year). The Chinese have such
a profound relationship with it that their word for cooked rice is syn-
onymous with "meal." I've read more than one account where, facing
an American (riceless) dinner, Chinese guests would make plans to seek
real sustenance before or afterwards. As her friend Huan confessed to
Emily Hahn, in *China to Me* (Doubleday, 1944), "When I have my
meal here, I go first to Jimmy's Kitchen and eat something. Or I go over
afterwards to Sun Ya and have noodles. Without rice, we Chinese go
hungry."

Still, one wonders, is there ever anything special about this rice? Although Chinese cookbooks can be highly opinionated on how to cook
it, I've yet to read a Chinese-born food writer waxing nostalgic about
the wonderful rice grown in the paddies along the Li River in Guangxi
or on the astonishingly lovely mountainside terraces of Yuan Yang in
southern Yunnan.

The reason for this, I suspect, is that until very recently most Chinese had never tasted the best that their country can produce. As
H. Frederick Gale explains in a June 2003 article in *Amber Waves*, a
publication of the USDA, on the growing Chinese consumer revolution,

> Until the 1990s, urban Chinese consumers purchased generic rice
> at set prices from government-run grain shops. Rice was usually
> procured by government authorities from local farmers, who
> tended to offer the government their lowest quality product. Rice
> was often broken and unpolished, and stones and other foreign
> material were often mixed in with the grain.

As the new and ever-growing class of consumers showed a willingness
to purchase the more expensive imported Thai *Hom Mali* (jasmine)

rice instead of the native inferior product, Chinese entrepreneurs started getting the message. Today, Gale continues, "China's rice industry is highly competitive, and rice is no longer a generic commodity. Consumers can choose among numerous brands differentiated by type, quality, and origin, and prices reflect rice attributes and quality."

These higher-quality, regionally grown Chinese rices have already started appearing in the United States. One that I found at our local market was labeled "Royal Rice," a short-grain variety grown in Xiaozhan, Tianjin, and supposedly the favorite food of the Emperor Qianlong (1711–1799). It is conspicuously nubby, off-white in color, and nearly opaque, with a deep "toasted-rice" aroma. When cooked, the grains are almost tubular, nearly as dry as long-grain rice, and possess a pleasingly chewy texture and lots of flavor. The English text on the back of the bag describes it as "the ideal ingredient in making fried rice," and I found that to be true, since the grains were plump enough to hold their moisture and relatively unsticky.

Another interesting thing that I learned during my research is that this same consumer population is turning away from rice entirely as the defining element of a meal, just as they also see switching from drinking tea to coffee as a sign of affluence and more sophisticated taste. It reminds me, in a way, of the diffidence toward ordinary bread that developed during my lifetime, when au courant consumers turned first to dinner rolls, then to artisanal loaves, and now, thanks to the low-carb craze, entirely away from breadstuffs altogether. Inferior quality was often given as the reason for this turn away from rice, which certainly makes sense. But, although rarely discussed, it was equally the case that affluence allowed treating what had only recently been a necessary part of the meal as, first, an accessory to it, then as something entirely dispensable.

Even so, you cannot understand China if you don't understand the meaning of rice. In *The Attic*, a memoir by Guanlong Cao of his childhood as the son of a "class enemy" (which is to say a former peasant farmer), he tells how his family was forced to live in a cramped attic over a button factory and scrape out a living however they could, all the while subjected to endless humiliations. They were always hungry, and so food becomes one of the book's major themes. Some of the passages are revoltingly cruel, others are humorous, still others profoundly sad.

Among the latter is Cao's account of the behavior of his brother,

Bao, on his return from serving two years in prison on suspicion of making antirevolutionary remarks. (He was never actually charged or brought to trial.) Before, Cao writes, he "ate like a fireman," finishing off his food before the rest of the family had a chance to settle in. Now, he ate slowly, taking tiny bites of rice and chewing them forever, all the while keeping one arm raised and curved around the bowl as if to ward off attack until he had eaten it all. Then, Cao continues,

> although Mother never allowed us to leave a grain of rice in our bowls, she never permitted us to lick the bowls, either. But in front of all our eyes, Bao gracefully polished his bowl with his tongue. The bowl, covering his face, revolved slowly. The tip of his tongue flicked over the rim, like a snake peeking from behind a boulder. After licking, he put his bowl down on the table and, blankly, looked at Mother as she wept. For a long time after he got out of jail, he didn't allow anybody to wash his bowl. It didn't look as if it needed washing, anyway.

THE COOK PREPARES
HIS BREAKFAST

Matt goes off to her job at the library early in the morning, so I usually breakfast alone. Breakfast for me, as for most people, is usually a conservative meal—who wants to get all chefly first thing in the morning? On the other hand, impulse is harder to restrain when you're just up and you know that nobody's looking. My usual breakfast in winter is steel-cut oatmeal or boiled stone-ground grits, and the rest of the year it's a single Wasa sesame crispbread spread with chunky peanut butter mixed with half a teaspoon of cinnamon (which supposedly helps lower my triglycerides, but the two flavors work well together, too), everything topped with slices of banana. Easy, quick, filling, and tasty. But then, on other days, whimsy strikes. Here is a selection of entries from my online breakfast diary—the good, the bad, and the ugly.

BEEF KIDNEY

I bought this because beef kidney is something that I almost never see at our local supermarket. It was now or never, and I knew it would have to be eaten at breakfast, which is to say, alone. Indeed, I had to wait until Matt was entirely out of the house before I unwrapped it, and who can blame her? The aroma lies heavy on the nostrils as I write this, about an hour after eating it. And worse, the taste still coats the mouth, outlasting the cup of coffee I thought would flush it into oblivion. Make no mistake: a beef kidney is potent stuff.

The thing about buying a beef kidney is that, like most offal, it doesn't improve with age. You have to deal with it quickly and entirely—you can't whack off a piece and stick the rest back into the fridge until you're in the mood again. This urgency is unwelcome in breakfast food, and the fact that cooking one is a bit of a chore does nothing to improve the situation.

To start with, how *do* you cook a beef kidney? I hadn't a clue and, this early in the morning, I wasn't in any mood to go rooting around in cookbooks. So I muttered, "To hell with it," and just cut out the tough vascular tubing in the middle. (This I then sautéed in butter and ate as a little snack while I got the onions ready for frying—not bad, very chewy, with a taste of fried suet—I assume you wanted to know that, right?)

Here's how the cooking went. I fried up a bunch of onions with a little minced garlic stirred in. I seasoned this with a dash of hot sauce and lots of black pepper. Meanwhile, I cut up Mr. Stinky into bite-size chunks and tossed them in a slug of cheap French syrah from the half-empty bottle in the refrigerator.

When the onions had browned, I added the kidney chunks, wine and all, sprinkled over a generous pinch of salt, stirred everything a bit over high heat to get things cooking, then lowered the heat, covered the pan, and simmered the contents for about ten minutes, while I brewed the coffee and made some toast. This I tore into pieces and laid them on the bottom of a shallow bowl. The contents of the skillet went on top of this—yep, the whole big pile. Honestly, it was quite good, just not really *breakfast*. Would someone please pass the breath mints?

BREAD-CUP EGGS

Last week I bought a baguette to make some pepper-and-egg sandwiches, and to keep the proper ratio of bread to eggs, cut off its ends. It seemed a shame to just toss them into the garbage, but what would I do with them? They would be stale the next day. I already had a sackful of bread crumbs.

Then inspiration struck. I hollowed them out, using a small sharp knife to cut through the crumb as closely as I dared to the crust, pulled out this plug with my fingers, sliced enough off the very tip of each "bread cup" so that it would stand on its end, and put them both into a plastic storage bag. Next morning, I made this tasty breakfast.

The oven was preheated to 350°F. Meanwhile, I spread a little butter at the bottom of each hollow, broke an egg into it, set both in a buttered ovenproof dish, and put this in the oven. I baked the eggs until the whites were set and the yolks still runny, somewhere between twenty and twenty-five minutes. Not only were these things cute as a button but the bread became very crunchy during the baking. Delicious little meal.

If you become attached to this dish or want to serve it to more than one person, you could just cut a baguette into four-inch lengths (an egg needs more space than you might think) and hollow each one out from one end, leaving about half an inch to serve as a bottom. That should work as well as using just the heels. Still, it is especially pleasant to rescue something headed for the garbage and work a little bit of magic with it . . . even if the only person delighted with the trick is yourself.

SCRAMBLED EGGS WITH CHUNKS OF AVOCADO

One of the unexpected perks of being a food writer is that folks send me food. Not often, but every now and then a parcel will arrive at our door (or more usually at our post office box), full of jars of pickles, fresh-picked Meyer lemons, barbecued brisket (only once, alas), or—in this instance—avocados from a reader's backyard, stems still attached.

My habit, when I buy avocados, is to let them ripen, peel and stone them, slice them, and eat them on buttered toast or English muffins, seasoned with a judicious dash of hot sauce. When this bonanza arrived I thought I might do something different, something wild, like make guacamole with them. I even went out and bought a bag of tortilla chips. But when push came to shove, Matt and I both found that we just wanted to slice them and eat them on toast, so that's what we did.

However, I felt I wouldn't be living up to the gift if I didn't do *something* different, so this morning I made scrambled eggs with chunks from the very last one. Before I poured in the beaten eggs, I sautéed some fresh minced garlic in the hot butter. I added the avocado, stirred it quickly about, then turned in the eggs. The avocado melded with these, even while remaining intact, and its vegetative-tasting smoothness was a neat match to the curds of scrambled egg. It was very good and I'm glad I did it.

THE SENSATION

After I posted an account of a breakfast of chopped chicken liver spread on toast online, Alan Wenokur sent me an e-mail about a now-defunct restaurant in Detroit that had served a sandwich called a "Sensation"—chopped liver on challah, dipped in egg and pan-fried.

Always unwilling to leave well enough alone, I decided to make this with slices cut from a sourdough rosemary bread produced locally by Jonathan Stevens and Cheryl Maffei at the Hungry Ghost Bakery. Then I proceeded just as you would imagine. I beat up an egg, seasoned it with salt and lots of black pepper, spread this mixture on a plate, dipped in the bread (one side only), spread the non-egged side with cooked chopped chicken liver, and browned the resulting sandwich on both sides in butter. The result was as delicious as Alan promised, and, as I had suspected, chicken liver and rosemary make a super match.

EGGS BAKED IN CREAM

These came about because I had some heavy cream left over in the refrigerator, and had no special plans for it. So I fried up two eggs in butter in a small nonstick skillet until they were just cooked on the bottom. At that point, I poured some cream over them (I didn't measure it, but it wasn't much, maybe a quarter of a cup), seasoned already with a dash of hot sauce and a pinch of salt. Then I stuck the pan into a preheated 350°F oven for four or five minutes until the whites were set but the yolks still runny. A little on the decadent side, even for me, but that didn't keep me from adding some crumbled bacon to the dish when it came out of the oven. Mellow, rich, and tasty.

The container of cream wasn't empty, so I decided to make the eggs again. When I ate them the first time, I thought I'd like the dish even better if the cream had had more of the consistency of a pouring custard. So, this time around, I beat one egg into the quarter-cup of heavy cream, seasoning it again with a dash of hot sauce and a pinch of salt. I then proceeded exactly as above, except this time I heated the cream-egg mixture in a little pot, stirring it frequently, and starting it a few minutes before I began frying the eggs. The mixture had just begun to thicken when I poured it over the eggs in the skillet and put everything into the 350°F preheated oven. The result was less like a custard than fried eggs dressed with very rich, very molten scrambled eggs, which is weird, to be sure, but also insanely good.

RICE BROWNS

Digging around in the refrigerator I came across a small bowl of left-over rice, a wedge of yellow pepper, and a piece of onion. I minced up the vegetables plus half a clove of garlic, melted a chunk of butter in the skillet, and turned everything in, including the cooked rice. I let all this cook, turning it over with a spatula, until the rice was coated with the butter. The rest was just having the patience to let things take their course. When the rice was beginning to brown, I divided it in half and flattened out the first half into a large pancake shape. I put a slice of cheese on this and scooped the other half of the hot rice onto this, spreading it out to cover the cheese. I didn't dare flip it over—there was nothing to hold the thing together. So when I judged that the rice on the bottom was a nice crispy brown, I just turned it upside-down onto a plate. It was savory, crunchy, and tasty, and a shot of habanero hot sauce kicked it up something fine. I'd surely make it again.

CANNED BEEF TAMALES: Q&A

Q. Rumor has it that you buy your canned beef tamales at an odd-lot surplus store.
A. Yes, that's true. To be specific, Big Lots, where markdown items go to die (see page 298). Of course, much of the stuff there never had a chance to get marked down, because it was born down. Still, where else can you find a simple, white twenty-ounce soup mug for 49¢? This af-ternoon I walked past our local Starbucks and someone sitting at one of the outside tables had emptied their coffee *venti* into one of those mugs. I felt a thrill of secret recognition. You go, girl.
Q. Did you go into Big Lots hoping to find canned tamales or did you just happen upon them?
A. I went in looking for a cheap outdoor extension cord for my Little Chief electric smoker. I didn't even imagine that they would have a food

department . . . let alone how fascinating it would be. For example, I found lots and lots of obscure brands of lonely guy food—little pop-top cans of potted meat product and Vienna sausage; cans of chili and beef stew; those rectangular tins of corned beef and pressed pork loaf; and, obviously, canned tamales, at 99¢ each. This is half the price of the ones at the supermarket. I came home with a sackful.

Q. What do you see when you open the lid?

A. The first time you open one, you see a *huge* orange blob of congealed fat. After that, you learn to turn the can upside down, so the blob will be at the bottom when you open it and you can scrape out only as much as you want.

Q. And how much do *you* scrape out?

A. All of it. No, no, just joking. I prefer getting my caloric buzz by tossing on some shredded Mexican-style cheese just before serving. Anyway, inside the can you find six tamales wrapped in waxed paper, surrounded with a thin red chile sauce. Here's how to tell if you're a canned tamale addict: you lick the waxed paper after you remove the tamale.

Q. Yuck. You don't do that, do you?

A. Of course I don't—at least not after I discovered that it got stains all over my T-shirt. Now I wipe the sauce off the waxed paper and into the pot with my fingers. Anyway, the recipe is simple: heat and eat.

Q. I don't think so. You never leave well enough alone. Confess.

A. Well, okay, I admit to a little adjusting. I already mentioned the grated cheese. But my secret—I'm sort of embarrassed to say this, because it's little over the top . . .

Q. So unlike you. Go on, we'll never tell.

A. I added a splash of that very pricey Austrian pumpkin seed oil. It has a dark color that looks green in the bottle but pours out a deep maroon. It's viscous stuff, thicker than olive oil, and intensely flavored of pumpkin seeds. The problem is that it's *so* intensely flavored I've had a hard time finding a use for it.

Q. Then canned tamales came along and all became clear.

A. You could put it that way. The point is that a lot of Mexican dishes have pumpkin seeds in them, and I thought, why not? I tried it and it made an amazing difference.

Q. They suddenly tasted good?

A. Well, they tasted good before. Now, they tasted even better. However, the miracle was that for the first time I didn't get a wicked attack of indigestion after eating them. There's a moral there, somewhere.

EGGS FLORENTINE

I have an occasional weakness for creamed spinach, and when our local Stop & Shop had a sale on the new deluxe concoction (made with real cream, butter, onions, etc.) put out by Birds Eye, I bought a box. Any comparison of what I actually experienced with the product shown in the photo on the box will only make you weep, so let's just say that the "real cream sauce" wasn't all that bad.

I thought I might improve the situation by using it to make eggs Florentine, which meant doing it a few times to get it right. I found that I could speed things up by removing the tub of spinach from its box and leaving it in the fridge overnight to let the contents defrost. In the morning, I gently peeled back the plastic covering, made two large holes in the spinach mixture, and broke an egg into each, re-covering everything with the plastic film. I took a small skillet, poured in water until it was about two-thirds up the sides of the container, and set this on the stove. I brought the water up to a solid simmer, set the timer for fifteen minutes, and went about my morning business.

When the timer went off, I added more water (if the skillet boils dry, things get woofy *really* fast) and reset the timer for fifteen minutes. When it rang again, the eggs were done. The little plastic container is easy to lift onto a plate. Remove the cover, salt, pepper, stir a little, and eat. Then go back to the store and get a few more boxes before the sale ends.

One note, though: if you want your yolks to be runny all through, slip them into a little bowl, then add them fifteen minutes later to the partially set whites.

FRIED-CORN-AND-ONION OMELET

Recently I've been doing something that I can hardly believe originated with me, but which I haven't encountered before—frying onions (and sometimes other things, like chopped bell pepper) in the omelet pan before adding the eggs. This adds another, welcome dimension to the omelet-making and -eating experience. It can also be varied to take advantage of special situations. I'm writing this in August, when we had an ear of corn left over from a Sunday corn-on-the-cob feast.

After supper, I cut off all the kernels. The next morning I sautéed these and some chopped onion in butter—seasoning them with salt and black and red (hot!) pepper—until the corn had slightly caramelized and the onions were tinged with brown. Once I had it the way I wanted it, in went the eggs (beaten with a tablespoon of water and a pinch of salt). When it came to the moment of flipping over, I quickly set in some slices of ham and cheese. The result had an appetizing nubbly look and went down very easily. Let's do it again.

RETURN TO HALLOUMI

Halloumi is a brine-cured sheep's milk cheese from Cyprus. Raw, it has a rubbery, squeaky texture and a mild-salty, feta-like flavor. But the thing that makes Halloumi special is that it can be grilled over coals or fried in an ungreased nonstick skillet without melting—an act which also distinctly improves it. Fried Halloumi is firm (it holds together even if you lift it up by one end) but not rubbery—no "telephone lines" stretch out when you pull it apart, and the taste becomes more distinct. In Turkey and Cyprus, Halloumi is often flavored with mint, but this import wasn't—which, as far as I'm concerned, was all for the best.

The first time I reported on this, I received an e-mail from Tom Weir, who lives in Dromahair, Ireland, and who also eats Halloumi for breakfast. He suggested that I marinate the cheese in lemon juice and dust it with dried oregano and black pepper before tossing it into the skillet. Always one to gild the lily, I also sprinkled the slices with some Turkish Marash red pepper flakes and torn bits of Greek olives. Finally, I rubbed some bread slices with olive oil and grilled them, to serve on the side.

Everything turned out very good. Next time, though, I'll leave out the olives (too much salt) and maybe add some capers (also salty, but I can use far fewer of them). All I needed was a pot of Turkish coffee and I would have been swept off to some island on the Aegean Sea . . . or, for that matter, to Dromahair. Thanks, Tom—have a piece of toast.

FIVE-MONTH-OLD CROISSANT

When I helped my mother move into her new home in a retirement community, I carried the microwave oven that the previous owners had left out to the storage shelves in the garage, because she wanted to use her own. On my next visit, thinking I might want to take it home with me, I went out to the garage to check it out, opened the door and found a croissant inside. Now, I call this a five-month-old croissant because I know it's *at least* that old. But since the place was empty for about a year before she moved in, it's very probable that the croissant was there all that time. Puzzling that out was all well and good, but the real question was: "Could I eat it?" This might sound like desperation: "Wasn't your mother feeding you?!" Of course she was. But for some reason the idea of eating it *interested* me. Naturally, surviving eating it also interested me . . . but whom could I ask for advice whose response wouldn't be, "Are you *crazy?*"

There was no one, of course, so I had to work it out for myself. Being entombed, so to speak, in a metal box had kept it protected from rodents and the like, but had not prevented its moisture from quietly leaching away. So, while it might be stale, it wasn't moldy or infested with insects. And, more important, it might be *good* . . . i.e., entirely transformed into a buttery shattery crust. So I bit off and ate one end. Hey! It was!—like a palmier, but not so hard and not covered with sugar. So I bit off and ate the other end. And so it went.

THE RUMINATIVE COOK

FALAFEL

In the narrow, exciting streets [of Jerusalem in 1881] there were
little cookshops that sold kebab—bits of meat, tomato, and onion
broiled on spikes. In the early spring bunches of green chickpeas,
roasted in the bread ovens, were sold. These foods were sold to
the peasants who came into the city to work, and our nurses liked
them, and we liked them too.

> —Bertha Spafford Vester, *Our Jerusalem*

Falafel: sharp peppers and fried dried pea balls sandwiched in a
flat roll called a pitah. Falafel is a standard meal around some urban and most interurban bus stops, where one spends a good part
of one's life.

> —*Commentary*, 1951

Falafel—the national street food of Israel—has yet to make an indelible
impression on the American appetite.* True, you can find mixes for it
in supermarkets (usually just one brand), and vegetarians, at least,
know what it is. But if you want to get it freshly made in a fast-food
setting (something Israelis take for granted), you have to seek out one
of the little eateries that make a specialty of it, in Middle Eastern and
especially Jewish neighborhoods. There, the proprietor, often a recent
immigrant himself, deep-fries the delectably crunchy nuggets of ground
chickpeas and spicy seasonings to order, passing them to another fam-

---

*Sometimes *felafel*. The English language versions of both Israeli newspapers that I consulted
on the Internet while researching this essay allow either spelling, and both appear with approximately the same frequency.

ily member, who arranges them in a pita, douses them with tahini sauce, then smothers them in add-ons that can range from chopped salad to pickled vegetables to (if he believes you can take it) a generous dose of the fiery Yemenite condiment called *zhug*.

When I ate falafel for the first time in my life—about a decade ago at an Israeli-run place called Rami's in Coolidge Corner, Brookline, just outside of Boston—I was taken aback by the amount of silage they heaped on. It was all delicious and it left me happy and full, but also a bit confused. To a habitual carnivore like myself, a falafel sandwich can provoke a feeling of cognitive dissonance—the gustatory equivalent of being forced, after a lifetime of doing the opposite, to read from right to left.

Although falafel is regularly described as "the Israeli hot dog," that comparison can be taken only so far. True, like the hot dog, falafel is ideally suited for a street vendor to prepare and a strolling diner to consume. Each comes wrapped in its own kind of bun; each allows the addition of a range of condiments to substantially enhance the experience of eating it. At this point, however, the two radically diverge—as can be seen by the very different nature of those eater-applied additions.*

What the hot dog is about is meaty succulence; in fact, it is so meaty and so succulent that only the most intensely flavored condiments can hope to improve on it—hence, the hot dog vendor's standard offerings of mustard, relish, ketchup, chili, and sauerkraut, sometimes, even, bacon and cheese. The falafel, however—and I say this intending no disrespect—is a meatball made without the meat. Nutritious, yes. Delicious, yes. It possesses both those qualities in spades. But when it comes to succulence, meaty or otherwise, the falafel is simply a nonstarter.

This is why an order of falafel topped with, say, a ladle of hot chili is as hard to imagine as a hot dog served in a bed of salad greens. Appetite coheres around the two in almost entirely opposite ways. To those of us used to having a piece of meat as the focal center of a fast-

---

*An add-on of a sort that the hot dog and the falafel sandwich *do* share is the French fry. In Israel, it is not uncommon to get a serving of fries (by no means always hot) dumped into the pita with your falafel; the Hebrew for this variation is *falafel im cheeps*. While I've never seen a hot dog stand serving fries this way (hard to get them into the bun), I find nothing wrong with the idea. This is because the French fry is *sort of* succulent. It meets the hot dog in the doorway leading out and the falafel in the doorway leading in, providing a mediating presence to both.

food meal, the falafel vendor seems suspiciously like someone trying to sell us the crust while withholding the fried chicken, while to his regular customer, the crunchy falafel balls are less the focal point of the meal than its signal treat—the plums in the plum pudding.*

More accurately still, they are equivalent to the bowl of toasted croûtons at the salad bar. In fact, if you replace the salad bowl itself with a round of pita, what you have is so much like a falafel sandwich as to make little difference—the mix of fresh and pickled salad ingredients (onion, tomato, lettuce, cucumber, corn relish, three-bean salad, marinated mushrooms), the creamy soak of dressing, and, scattered throughout, those big, greasy, garlicky, Parmesan-and-herb-sprinkled crusts.

However, a pita stuffed full of croûtons, no matter the amount of dressing you poured over them, would not be especially—or even perversely—satisfying as a meal. This is because it is not the salad ingredients that serve the croûtons, but the reverse. And so it also is with falafel—they come into their own as the *foundation* of a sandwich. And this is why, in every narrative about them, it is ultimately the "salad" that turns out to be the most interesting aspect of the story.

• • •

> Many years ago, my mother-in-law opened a falafel café in Givatayim. She made falafel every day by grinding soaked chickpeas with fresh garlic and spices. After frying the falafel balls in vegetable oil, she served them the favorite Israeli way: inside a split, very fresh pita with several spoonfuls of diced cucumbers, tomatoes, onions and parsley. For those who wanted, she added shredded green or red cabbage, hot sauce, pickles and tahini.
> —Faye Levy, *The Jerusalem Post*

Given the age and simplicity of falafel, its exact origins are necessarily somewhat obscure. The Egyptians, and particularly the Coptic Christian Egyptians, claim it as their own, making it with dried white fava

---

*Israeli street vendors, as it happens, have a simple solution to salve an attack of falafel-engendered meat deprivation anxiety: *steak im pita*. As described in the Israel section of *The World Atlas of Food*, this is made by stuffing thin slices of charcoal-broiled steak into a pita and then topping it up with crunchy raw vegetables, tahini sauce, and a dash of chile sauce. In other words, *steak im pita* takes the falafel paradigm and flips it right side up again.

beans (*ful nabed*) and calling it *ta'amia*. Claudia Roden, in her *Book of Middle Eastern Food*, writes that during Lent, when they are forbidden meat, Copts make large amounts every day, giving away what they don't eat themselves as a form of penance. Bean croquettes have also long been familiar food in Lebanon and Syria—again, made as often with *ful* as with chickpeas—and they are said to have been brought to Israel by the Yemenite Jews, who played an important part in shaping the Middle Eastern flavor of that nation's cuisine.*

In fact, falafel vendors were present at Israel's very first Independence Day celebration, on May 14, 1948—as evidenced by this excerpt from an Israeli newspaper article written at the time:

> Entire Sephardi families arrived at Zion Square and the other major squares, set themselves up with their kids and their food right there on the ground, and spent most of the day there among the other celebrants. Many peddlers showed up and sold sandwiches, crackers, cakes, falafel, peanuts, candy, gum, and more.

Such scenes caused the government to consider banning falafel vendors as lowering the tone of this important patriotic event. Instead, falafel became the food associated with that holiday. And why not? European immigrants to Israel took to falafel for the same reasons that settlers here fastened onto corn on the cob as a celebration of national identity: it was tasty, inexpensive, and about as easy to assimilate as anything in this brave new world.

Jews have other reasons to be drawn to falafel. Because of its vegetarian composition, it is classified as pareve under Jewish dietary laws, meaning that it can be eaten with either a meat or a dairy meal and—equally important—before or after either, a welcome quality in a snack. (Although meat can be eaten soon after most dairy meals, observant Jews may wait as long as six hours after eating meat before allowing themselves any dairy products.)

Another reason for falafel's popularity is that in combination with the toppings that are served with it, a single order provides a filling and nutritious meal at very little cost. This means that in a country much given to socializing in public places, it is possible to sit down with a friend for a leisurely bite without any pain to the pocketbook. It also

---

*The word itself is said to come from the Arabic phrase *umm al-falafel*, meaning "mother of peppers," which, if true, suggests where the star power of the dish actually resides.

means that teenagers, in Israel as everywhere always famished and foot-loose, are able to gorge themselves to their hearts' content. Indeed, they have transformed that gorging into a display of adolescent cool, as Gloria Kaufer Greene explains in *The New Jewish Holiday Cookbook* (Times Books, 1999):

> Israeli teens are masters at skillfully stuffing so much into their pita sandwiches that the doughy pocket seems on the verge of bursting. They push in the salad with a vengeance, until the falafel balls themselves are a mere pittance, squashed almost into oblivion. These teens then eat these meal-size sandwiches while walking and chatting, losing nary a lettuce leaf in the process. Tourists, on the other hand, sparsely fill their own loaves, but still leave behind a telltale trail of chopped vegetables and dressing.

The acquisition of the mastery necessary to adroitly devour an over-stuffed falafel sandwich has certainly done its part in creating a shared sense of identity among Israelis. As Robert Rosenberg writes nostalgically in an essay on the demise of the *hatzi-mana* ("half-portion"—i.e., a half instead of a whole pita, with fewer falafel):*

> It was the most appropriate thing to eat while sitting on the iron bars of sidewalk railings. This posture, which required an adolescent agility and balance, was mastered by whole generations whose financial resources were limited to a weekly movie, the bus ride back and forth, and the *hatzi-mana* that could only be eaten without spoiling clothes by adopting that same posture.

Perhaps because I am part of such a generation myself, that phrase "eaten without spoiling clothes," with its wealth of connotations (good clothes were next to priceless and had to be carefully protected, without displaying any appearance of doing so), conjures up a lost universe of white sport coats, Saturday evening dates, hot summer nights, snack bars with sliding-screen service windows and yellow outdoor bug lights, and hot dogs consumed at a casual but meticulously calculated forward tilt that kept the mustard, the catsup, the fried onions from falling on your one dress shirt.

Hot dogs, packed as they are with protein and fat, possess an ag-

---

* *An Arithmetic of the Soul in an Uncivil War—From Yom Kippur 1987 to Independence Day 1988 through the Intifada,* www.ariga.com/visions/tlvtlv/pqtlv.shtml.

gressive potency, a carnivore's swagger; for a pittance, they let you nosh at the top of the food chain. Falafel doesn't do that, but it shares with hot dogs the show-off agility that comes from deftly devouring a potential mess. There's also that fiery chile heat, until recently something unimaginable to an American teen. How different the means, how very similar the ultimate destination—full of food and full of beans.

• • •

> The falafel-makers at Shuk Bezalel off King George Street and just behind the bargain clothing stands have announced that they will no longer sell the *hatzi-mana*. "People come down here, fill up half a pita with every salad they can, and eat a whole meal for less than a shekel [about twenty-five cents]," one kiosk owner complained.
>
> —Robert Rosenberg

The earliest photograph of a falafel vendor I could find (circa 1960) suggests that originally the day's supply was cooked at home and simply served from a heap at the stand—an easy and much less expensive arrangement that may have also produced a better product, since oil stales quickly when kept hot all day. In a fuel-challenged culture, hot fried food is an unaccustomed luxury. Its adoption by Israeli falafel vendors may well reflect the creeping influence of European culinary taste. For whatever reason, as prosperity has grown and competition quickened, falafel is now almost always sold hot from the fryer and there are special machines that form the balls and fry them on command.

As Matt and I began our recipe research, we quickly discovered that there were some distinctly different schools of thought regarding falafel-making, starting with the original and purest form, where raw chickpeas are soaked until tender, then pounded or ground to a coarse consistency with onion, garlic, and a mixture of herbs and spices. The result, when properly made, is nutty-tasting, with a tender but chewy texture also reminiscent of baked nutmeats; frying renders the strong legume flavor of the raw ground paste all but mute.

The more recent the recipe, however, the more likely it is to call for cooked chickpeas instead of raw ones, and for a portion of these—up to half—to be replaced with bulgur or bread crumbs. Certainly, this is the case with all the falafel mixes I have examined. The result when cooked is a puffy fritter that is more delicately textured on the inside and somewhat crisper and quite a bit greasier on the outside—sort of the falafel version of "extra crispy" Kentucky Fried Chicken. To my taste, these falafel proved all first impression and not much else—predictably, those made from a mix had that bitter aftertaste which comes in equal part from granulated garlic and stale spices.

As much as I was drawn to the honest, rough-hewn character of the original version, I quickly discovered that I lacked the equally rough-hewn stamina of the cooks who once prepared it by hand using a mortar and pestle. We do happen to own a large stone mortar, and after I easily pulverized a single chickpea, I confidently poured in the whole bunch of them. It only took a few minutes of steady pounding before I threw in the towel; my arm was already hurting and I could tell I had at least a half hour more to go.

Every cloud has its silver lining, though, since I used this experience as an excuse to purchase a powerful electric meat grinder, which ground the falafel to the texture of very coarse damp cornmeal. A food processor fitted with the steel blade can do the same, but the bowl will need constant scraping down, since the paste has a tendency to cling to its upper sides.

As we experimented with the recipes we had turned up in our research, we did a small amount of fine-tuning to adapt them to our taste. The most notable example of this is our omission of parsley and cilantro—one or the other or both of which almost always appear in traditional versions. We did this not because we don't like those herbs but because we thought they worked best as an addition to the tahini sauce. Then, to give our falafel the requisite flecks of green, we replaced the usual onion with some scallions. Here is the result.

SLIGHTLY UNORTHODOX FALAFEL
[Makes about 32 falafel]

In our experience, eight falafel are enough for a sandwich, and one sandwich, with the necessary additions, makes a meal. So calculated, the recipe below will feed four.

> 6 ounces (a generous ¾ cup) chickpeas
> 1 teaspoon cumin seeds
> ½ teaspoon coriander seeds

1 teaspoon kosher salt
½ teaspoon powdered chile
½ teaspoon freshly ground black pepper
½ teaspoon double-acting baking powder (see note)
3 scallions, trimmed of any wilted ends and minced
1 or 2 large garlic cloves, coarsely chopped
vegetable oil for frying
assorted toppings (see recipes below)
4 loaves fresh pita bread (see note)

The Day Before: Pick through the chickpeas, removing any pebbles, dirt clods, or other detritus. Rinse them and put them in a bowl. Cover with plenty of cold water and let them soak until needed the next day. (If they soak for more than 36 hours, they may sprout.)

To Make the Falafel: Put the cumin and coriander seeds in a small ungreased skillet and set this over a medium flame. Gently shaking the pan to keep the seeds from scorching, heat them until they release their scent and just begin to brown. Turn them into a mortar or small sturdy bowl and grind them to a soft powder with a pestle or the tip of a spoon. Stir in the salt, powdered chile, black pepper, and baking powder.

Remove the chickpeas from the soaking liquid, reserving ½ cup. In a medium bowl, toss the chickpeas, minced scallions, and chopped garlic together until well mixed. Then either grind this mixture into a coarse paste in a meat grinder fitted with the cutting disk with the smallest holes or pulse-grind it in a food processor fitted with the steel cutting blade.

Blend in the reserved soaking liquid, bit by bit, until the paste has the consistency of moist cornmeal—just damp enough to hold its shape when formed into a ball. Thoroughly mix in the ground seasonings. To make traditionally shaped falafel (see note), use dampened hands to shape small pieces of the paste into tablets about 1 inch in diameter and ½-inch thick. As each is made, set it on a piece of waxed paper. When all are formed, let them rest in the refrigerator for half an hour.

Heat the frying oil in a deep-fat fryer to 350°F (or, if you have an electric fryer that doesn't show temperatures, turn it to medium high). Set the oven temperature to warm and put a heatproof platter or a cookie sheet on the rack. Fry the falafel in batches of 8 for about 4 minutes, or until they are colored a rich but not dark brown. Use a pair of tongs to remove the cooked falafel to the platter, returning this to the oven while the next batch cooks.

Meanwhile, slit the top edge of each pita so that it opens up like a purse. Although this is not traditional, we like to put about a third of the toppings into the pita before adding the falafel—otherwise, half the sandwich has no falafel and the other half has nothing but. In any case, serve at once and let the eaters fill their sandwiches as they wish.

Cook's Notes. Seasoning: This varies widely, especially regarding the amount and proportions of cumin and coriander. Feel free to adjust these to your own taste.

Shaping and Frying: Falafel can also be formed into hamburger-like patties and pan-fried in shallow oil, turning them once so that they brown on both sides.

Baking Powder: This is optional and does not appear in the earliest recipes. However, it lightens the falafel a little without affecting their taste.

Pita: In our opinion, pita bread loses a bit of character and charm every minute it is out of the oven—i.e., we don't buy it unless we can get it fresh at a Middle Eastern bakery. We prefer to take a good crusty Italian loaf, cut it in half, hollow out the center, and eat our falafel in that.

I'LL HAVE THAT WITH . . .

Prefer a falafel stand that offers you a free selection of pickles and vegetables that you can add as you eat.

—israeliculture.about.com

Falafel, as we now understand, exists to be dressed . . . hence, in the competitive world of Israeli falafel sellers, to be overdressed. What follows is provided simply to indicate something of the range of possibilities; only the most dedicated falafel enthusiast will want to duplicate at home the multiplicity of offerings available at a good falafel stand. The minimal requirement is tahini sauce, along with some Israeli salad, onion-sumac relish, and perhaps a dousing of your favorite hot sauce.

Even so, if you are one of those who are never happy unless they have a real challenge to engage them, let me point you to *amba*, which Phyllis Glazer, writing in *The Jerusalem Post* (April 2, 1998), describes as "an orange-colored sauce made from unripe mango, turmeric, and fenugreek. It is used for flavoring and thickening and usually is served in places selling shwarma or falafel." If you find a jar of it, you will learn, as I did, that lightning can indeed strike twice in the same mouth.

TAHINI SAUCE
[Makes about 1 cup]

Tahini is a runny paste of finely ground unroasted sesame seeds. The flavor is gentler than the Chinese version made with roasted seeds, but it still has a rich sesame taste. Tahini is available at most supermarkets and natural food stores. As a dressing for falafel, dilute it to the thickness of a creamy salad dressing, and, since density can vary from brand to brand, you may need to adapt the following proportions to achieve this consistency.

> ½ cup tahini paste
> juice of ½ lemon
> 1 garlic clove, very finely minced
> ¼ cup minced cilantro, flat-leaf parsley, or a mix of both
> ¼ teaspoon kosher salt
> ½ cup water or yogurt

Put the tahini in a small pitcher. Stir in the lemon juice, minced garlic and cilantro, and salt. Stir in the water or yogurt until the sauce has an easily pourable consistency. If done ahead of the meal, stir again briefly before using.

ISRAELI SALAD

> In the kibbutz dining room, a colorful selection of whole salad vegetables [is] placed for kibbutzniks to cut up and dress as they choose. The ability to chop vegetables to the smallest, most perfect dice for this salad is considered a mark of status among many kibbutz cooks.
>
> —Gloria Greene, *The New Jewish Holiday Cookbook*

[Serves 4]

In Israel, this Middle Eastern salad of chopped garden vegetables is a favorite addition to every meal, sometimes eaten separately, other times added to a pita sandwich of falafel or shwarma. (By "every meal" I definitely also mean breakfast—Israelis take that meal very seriously, and salat yisraeli *is a featured component.) In an article in* The Jerusalem Post, *Faye Levy notes that while everyone knows the necessity of good ripe tomatoes in this salad, good cucumbers are equally important.*

In the United States, if you get into a discussion of cucumbers with Israelis, they become passionate. "American cucumbers are inedible," they say. Their favorite type is what gardening catalogs call Middle Eastern cucumbers. I too prefer these small, thin cucumbers because they are crisp and delicately sweet and have tender skins with no trace of bitterness. Because of their fragility, this type of cucumber is not available in supermarkets, but you may be able to find them at your local farmers' market, and you can certainly grow them yourself.* Otherwise, use plump, tight-skinned, unblemished Kirby (pickling) cucumbers.

4 or 5 medium garden-ripe tomatoes
4 or 5 Kirby (pickling) cucumbers, peeled if desired
3 whole scallions, ends trimmed and any tough or wilted
    green tops discarded (see note)
1 large half-sour kosher pickle
several sprigs flat-leaf parsley or cilantro (optional)
1 red or green bell pepper, cored and seeded
1 tablespoon extra-virgin olive oil
1 tablespoon freshly squeezed lemon juice
salt and freshly ground black pepper to taste

Finely dice all the vegetables and put them together into a salad bowl. Toss with just enough olive oil to make the vegetables glisten. There

---

*Most specialty seed companies sell these Beit Alpha–type cucumbers under their own proprietary names (in italics below), but all are a very shiny medium green, with entirely edible thin and tender skins and remarkably crisp and juicy flesh. *Amira*—The Cook's Garden; P.O. Box 5010; Hodges, SC 29653; (800) 457-9703; certified organic Mideast prolific cucumber—Seeds of Change; P.O. Box 15700; Santa Fe, NM 87506; (888) 762-7333; *Tamara*—Shepherd's Garden Seeds; 30 Irene Street; Torrington, CT 06790; (860) 482-3638.

should be no puddle of oil at the bottom of the bowl. Then toss with the lemon juice and season to taste with salt and pepper. This salad tastes best if served directly after being made.

Cook's Note. Seasoning: A small salad onion often replaces the scallions. Individual Israelis might add some lettuce; substitute radish, cabbage, carrot, or another garden vegetable for the bell pepper; or add some garlic, hot pickled pepper, or green olive bits to provide extra savor. However, such additional ingredients should not be allowed to overcomplicate what is essentially a very simple salad.

ONION-SUMAC RELISH
[Makes enough for 4 to 6 servings of falafel]

Powdered sumac has a deep burgundy color and a pleasantly sour taste with slightly citrus-y overtones—not unlike lemon juice without the lemon taste (in fact, sumac-ade became a popular summer drink in the United States during the Depression, when a lemon was a rare treat). Sumac is widely used in Middle Eastern cooking, often combined with thyme and toasted sesame seeds to make za'atar, which is used as a garnish and, mixed into a paste with olive oil, spread on top of pita before it is baked. In this relish, sumac tempers the harshness of the raw onions and adds a piquant, not-quite-placeable sour note. Any leftovers will make a welcome addition to a bagel spread with cream cheese. Mandatory with shashlik or steak im pita.

> 1 medium Bermuda onion, sliced into rings
> ½ tablespoon powdered sumac (see note)
> ½ tablespoon good olive oil
> ½ teaspoon kosher salt
> sprinkling of cayenne pepper

Place the onion rings in a medium-size bowl. Add the rest of the ingredients and mix thoroughly. Let everything marinate together for 3 hours, stirring occasionally. The onion rings will lose about half their original volume. Drain and serve.

Cook's Note. Powdered sumac can be purchased at any Middle Eastern grocery or from The Spice House; 1031 N. Old World Third

Street; Milwaukee, WI 53203; (414) 272-0977; www.thespicehouse .com.

ZHUG (YEMENITE GREEN CHILE PASTE)
[Makes about ½ cup]

Another popular Israeli food introduced by Yemenite Jews, this pico de gallo–like condiment is often served by itself with bread and puréed raw tomatoes as an appetizer or snack, or as an accompaniment to broiled fish, meat, and poultry. Zhug has no set formula*—feel free, for instance, to substitute flat-leaf parsley for half the cilantro leaves, and cumin seed for the caraway.

> 4 or 5 green or red serrano or jalapeño peppers, stemmed
> and seeded (see note)
> a small bunch cilantro, stemmed
> 6 garlic cloves
> ½ teaspoon black peppercorns
> 1 teaspoon each coriander and caraway seeds
> 6 green cardamom seeds (see note)
> 1 tablespoon freshly squeezed lemon juice

With a food processor, use the steel blade to pulverize all the ingredients until they form a well-blended but still coarsely textured mass. If using a mortar and pestle, separately mince the chile peppers, cilantro leaves, and garlic cloves; pulverize the peppercorns and the coriander, caraway, and green cardamom seeds; then put all the ingredients into the mortar and pound them into a rough paste. Thin the result with a little water until the mixture has the moist consistency of a salsa.

Cook's Notes. Chiles: Authentic *zhug* is reputedly fiery stuff. If you like the heat, go with the serranos; otherwise, use jalapeños.

Cardamom: Apart from its use in Scandinavian pastries, cardamom is little known in this country, but it is one of the most ancient of spices and also one of the most expensive, third after saffron and vanilla. In

---

*Nor does it have any set spelling. I've come across *zhoug, z'hug, schoug, z'chug, zehoug,* and *zug.*

India it is used as a component of curry powders, an ice cream flavoring, a breath freshener (said to be especially effective on garlic), and a digestive aid. The Bedouin flavor their coffee with it. Consequently, there is a thriving market in seeds that provide a passable imitation of the flavor of cardamom at a cheaper price—all of which, unfortunately, have an unpleasant mentholated aftertaste. The real thing is labeled "fancy green" and is available at The Spice House (see note above), a superlative source for any spice.

The Falafel Maker

> In making falafel, a special tool ('aleb falafel) is used to give shape to the puréed beans. This also has a lever which when released causes the falafel to pop out into the hot oil.
> —*The Oxford Companion to Food*

These gadgets have been around in Israel for some time—I found a reference to one in Lilian Cornfeld's *Israeli Cookery*, the earliest Israeli cookbook I own. But I had almost given up hope of being able to purchase the device myself, until I came across the Internet site of a gift shop in Jerusalem, offering one (plus a packet of Israeli falafel mix) for a reasonable sum. I bought one out of curiosity but ended up putting it to serious use—it's not only an incredible time-saver, but the falafel it produces are neat, cute as a button, and all the same size, which makes them easier to fry. And the device itself, made of brass and cast aluminum, reeks of retro charm. It can be ordered from, among others: Jerusalem Depot; P.O. Box 10010; Jerusalem, 93503; Israel; (866) 854-1684; www.jerusalemdepot.com, which sells the standard tool at a very decent price; or from Jerusalem Shoppe; 5 Otniel Street; Jerusalem, 93503; Israel; www.jerusalemshoppe.com, where you can purchase the basic model or a master set of four, each a different size, which should cover all your falafel needs.

Special thanks to Elisheva Urbas, former editor and continuing friend, for much assistance with this essay, tempered with a certain amusement at our efforts. As she wrote to us in one e-mail, Israelis would consider the whole enterprise of making falafel at home "kind of weird and not worth the trouble." But then, living as she does on New York's Upper West Side, she has a falafel joint just around the corner.

Further Reading

Readers seeking works that embrace Jewish cooking in its various manifestations should begin with Claudia Roden's groundbreaking *Book of Jewish Food: An Odyssey from Samarkand to New York*, which intertwines an adventure of personal discovery with much historical research (including a selection of archival photographs), traditional tales and ·stories, and 800 carefully chosen recipes, many of· which have never appeared before. There are informative sidebars on everything from knishes to *kobea* (rice dumplings with meat fillings) to *kaimak* (clotted cream made from buffalo milk) and instructions for preparing everything from an eggplant to a quince. Roden also explains Jewish dietary laws, relates what the ancient Hebrews ate, and describes the various holidays and festivals on the Jewish calendar. This splendid volume should have pride of place in any serious cookbook collection—certainly in any devoted specifically to Jewish cooking.

Gil Marks's *The World of Jewish Cooking* covers much the same ground as Roden's book and, if not quite in the same class, is well worth exploring. Of particular interest are the chapters on pasta and dumplings (with recipes for *kubba kari*, a spicy rice dumpling from Calcutta stuffed with lamb or chicken, and *manty*, a Chinese-style dumpling from Uzbekistan); and breads (with recipes for *miloach*, a Yemenite flaky flat bread, *maali*, a Romanian cornbread made with eggs and cheese, and *yutangza*, a buttery, cilantro-flavored steamed bun from Bukhara).

Until recently, cookbooks that specialized in Israeli cuisine were harder to track down, perhaps because of the general perception that there is no such thing. This may have been an accurate assessment during the early years of independence when the country was at war with many of its neighbors, a time when money was tight and all but the most basic of foods relatively scarce. But things have changed considerably since then, and Israelis in general have become much more interested in their evolving national cuisine.

Indeed, Israeli cooking has much in common with American cooking—since it, too, is the product of an amalgamation of several immigrant cuisines and of the gradual adaptation of specific dishes to a new climate and different foodstuffs. A sense of the resulting ferment can be found in three Israeli cookbooks written by—and to some extent for—American Jews who had migrated to Israel as part of the Aliyah

Movement and brought with them our own peculiar let's-gather-that-into-a-cookbook sensibility. All of these books are out of print but are usually easy to find.

Sybil Zimmerman's *Israeli Cooking on a Budget* is the one most specifically directed at Jewish-American cooks who found themselves at sea in a world without supermarkets. (Zimmerman had already written a fat tome entitled *Coming Home: A Practical Planning Guide for Living in Israel.*) However, because of its rigorous practicality—including an enthusiastic endorsement of a patent fuel-efficient cooking unit—her cookbook is mainly of historical (and, to those who lived in Israel then, of great nostalgic) interest.

Lilian Cornfeld's *Israeli Cookery* is quite another story. Although it looks, walks, and quacks like a home economics textbook—which is no surprise, since Cornfeld was a professional nutritionist—her genuine curiosity about the culinary life unfolding around her is apparent in the first recipes of the book, which were collected from the Yemenite Jews and include one for *zhug*, "a paste sharp enough to raise the roof of your mouth, but certainly appetizing and disinfecting [!] in a hot climate." The nutritionist bent is never quite put aside—many of her recipes were collected in institutional kitchens (especially old-age homes—the elderly being very fussy about authenticity)—but the book provides a kaleidoscopic view of the early years of Israeli cooking (with plenty of photographs) and some quite interesting recipes.

However, if you want to add just one vintage volume on this subject to your cookbook collection, my hands-down choice would be *The Israeli Cook Book*, by Molly Lyons Bar-David. One of the pleasures of writing about unfamiliar cuisines is the chance encounter with a treasure such as this, written by an intelligent and indefatigably curious food writer. Three of the four acknowledgment pages thank hundreds of individual cooks for their contributions, and the book itself is packed with them, often prefaced with helpful introductions. These range from the truly odd—a recipe for cow udder, "the only meat that Jews eat with dairy . . . since it cannot possibly contravene the humane merciful law of 'thou shalt not cook the kid in its mother's milk' "—to the truly delicious: an Ethiopian recipe for potatoes deep-fried with bay leaves, a four-page collection of herring salads (French, Russian, Lithuanian, Italian, Dutch, German, etc.), a recipe for roasting a chicken with its interior coated with lemon marmalade.

In short, this is a delightful book from the first recipe—for falafel!—
to its concluding pages, which treat at length the newfound passion for
coffee (introduced to a previously tea-drinking nation by German Jews)
and offer this fascinating little peek into Israeli army life:

> And in the army camps a new ritual has begun: instant coffee is
> put in cups and water is added, drop by drop; all the while a
> spoon is beaten against the side of the cup, until the drink is total
> froth and creamy. You can almost locate an army camp in the
> dark by the sound of the rhythmic beating of spoons against cups,
> like some ancient drummed message echoing from hill to hill.

PASTA WITH ANCHOVIES

So much depends on the fine points for [pasta with anchovies] to be right . . . It's not nearly as foolproof as *aglio-olio*, with which it competes in popularity in Campania, because there's an extra ingredient to showcase and balance. In the province of Salerno, where anchovies are still preserved under salt or salt water in crockery, everyone understands these fine points, although, of course, not everyone agrees on what they are.

—Arthur Schwartz, *Naples at Table*

The ruminative cook and your ordinary dog have at least this much in common—both have the most fun when let off the leash. Fastened to it, the dog knows from the start that he'll begin at point A and end at point E (or wherever), getting yanked back whenever he attempts to vary the route by a detour through a tempting rosebush. The owner here is the one who feels real contentment . . . unless, of course, the dog manages to slip its leash.

Set loose on his own in the backyard, however, there's no nonsense about a walk, a route—just some scampering here, some nosing about there, a lot of jumping marks at the base of the tree, and a couple piles of dirt produced by some futile but enthusiastic burrowing. What the dog gets from all this he keeps to himself, but there's no doubt at all about his satisfaction.

The same is true for us ruminative cooks, which makes our excursions so hard to write about—they're often instructive to no one but ourselves . . . which is to say, not very instructive at all. But perhaps this very lack of instruction itself is worth writing about, if we can look at the subject as really concerning the relationship between a particular cook and a particular dish. In this instance, the first is me and the second a dish I've been messing about with for the last several months: pasta with anchovies.

Italy, of course, has any number of pasta dishes that incorporate anchovies, but the simple dish most often associated with that name is generally attributed to Calabria, the toe (and some of the instep) of Italy's boot. The province has a landscape very much like Corsica's—a wild and untrammeled place of mountains, gorges, and ravines, and the occasional lonely hill town, with a reputation for delicious but frugal cookery that still holds on tightly to its traditional roots. The following recipe conveys all of this, and more.

PASTA AMMUDDICATA
(Adapted from *Italian Regional Cooking* by Ada Boni)
[Serves 4]

fillets from 6 anchovies (see note)
¾ cup olive oil
2 cups homemade dried bread crumbs (see page 206)
¼ teaspoon hot red pepper flakes
salt as needed
1 pound spaghetti

Preheat oven to 175°F. Bring a large pot of salted water to a rolling boil. As the water heats, cut the anchovies into small pieces. Heat half the olive oil in a skillet, add the anchovies, and cook them until dissolved into a paste. Put aside but keep hot. Heat the remaining oil in another pan and sauté the bread crumbs until golden. Sprinkle them with the hot red pepper flakes, put them in a bowl, and set this in the warmed oven.

When the water comes to a full boil, add the pasta. Stir it well as soon as it softens—to keep any of the strands from clumping together—and cook it until tender but still firm. Drain and dress it with the anchovy sauce, tasting for salt as you do. Serve at once, bringing the seasoned bread crumbs to table for eaters to add as they like.

Cook's Note. Anchovies: In this and the following recipes, either

whole salted anchovies that are still in salt brine or fillets of salted anchovies packed in olive oil can be used. However, bear in mind that a
whole salted anchovy yields two fillets.

"Economical" is certainly the watchword here, all the more so when
you consider the meaning of the dialect word *ammuddicata*, which is
bread crumbs. These were the equivalent of the fistful of grated cheese,
the treat that made the dish something to look forward to.* In southern
Italy, especially in the old days, bread crumbs sopped with olive oil and
toasted a golden brown were an affordable and delicious way to elevate
many a humble dish to a higher gastronomic level. Certainly, the anchovies played their role, too—it's just that in such households, they
didn't designate a feast.

Nowadays, of course, they are the special thing: imported, expensive, ordered by mail. For us, "pasta with bread crumbs" lacks resonance, while "pasta with anchovies" commands immediate (if not
always respectful) attention. So they, not bread crumbs, now give the
recipe its name (and, in consequence, the amount of the latter is usually
greatly decreased).

Brutal simplicity in cooking is a powerful force that can attract and
repel in equal measure. For example, our Calabrian version is hardly as
simple as pasta with anchovies gets. In *The Fine Art of Italian Cooking*,
Giuliano Bugialli's formula is refined down to three ingredients (with
the option of adding salt, if necessary):

> 5 whole anchovies in salt or fillets from 10 anchovies in oil
> 1 cup olive oil
> black pepper

The hair-shirt severity of this has its own effect on the cook's imagination—more so, I suspect, than Bugialli intended. Take the common

---

*This analogy between toasted bread crumbs and grated cheese helps explain why knowl-
edgeable food writers insist that the latter simply doesn't belong in this dish (e.g., Arthur
Schwartz, in *Naples at Table*: "Cheese is totally inappropriate"). If toasted bread crumbs are,
essentially, standing in for the grated cheese, it's an affront to add both. Some argue that anchovies and Parmesan are simply incompatible flavors, but it isn't hard to find Italian recipes
that combine them. No, this aesthetic springs from an intimacy with poverty that is increasingly alien to most of us.

addition of garlic. Why, the ascetic might ask, gild the lily, when anchovies are the very epitome of pungency? The answer, of course, is that garlic expands pungency's flavor spectrum. In other words, the hair shirt calls out for the bed of nails. And that in turn provokes a desire for the lashings delivered by some fiery chile pepper, the astringent bite of parsley. "Anchovies?" replies our inner eremite right back to Brother Giuliano. "I'll give you anchovies . . ."

• • •

It was Matt who first had the desire for pasta with anchovies and cobbled together a potential recipe after consulting several of our Italian cookbooks. In essence, it's the same recipe we use today, despite my endless tinkering. That's because, although I truly do want to improve it, the real goal of ruminative cooking is to keep working out tiny new twists and turns to keep the dish alive and interesting to me, no matter how many times I make it.

Now, if you're one of the multitude who don't care much for anchovies, you've probably already left our little group. But if you're still with us, now may be the time to abandon ship. One of the ruminative pleasures of this dish is the intimacy it establishes between the fish and the cook. Food writers argue that whole anchovies preserved in salt have more flavor and are actually less salty than single fillets put up in olive oil. And this, against all reason, does seem to be true.*

However, perhaps the best reason to use whole salted anchovies is the rebarbatively primitive experience of dealing with them. A preserved anchovy is essentially a fish with its head yanked off. When that goes, so do most—but by no means all—of its entrails. The cook must decide how much of what remains is edible, and that is decided mostly by appetite duking it out with disgust.

To start, there's the decision whether to rinse the fish in cold water when you remove them from their briny sludge. Some do, but I don't— I just wipe away the excess salt and any loose scales with my fingers. The tail, I suspect, no one eats, and it's the first thing I pull off and discard. But what about that bloody, sodden mass at the other end, some-

---

*It may be that the fillets are removed and kept in salt brine before they are put up in olive oil, and so absorb more salt than those that are left inside the fish.

times with fins still hanging out of it? Work it through a sieve? Or just quickly get it out of sight?

Now I pull the fillets away from the spine. Most people throw that away, too—that it's the spitting image of a centipede may have something to do with that. But anchovy spines are loaded with flavor, and fanatics from Catalonia to Japan fry them in oil until they're tender and crispy, then enjoy them as a snack. Once again I toy with the notion of cooking them for a few minutes in the olive oil before discarding them, to further punch up the anchovy intensity. Once again, though, I don't. Some other time.

Lastly, I mince the fillets with a cleaver before adding them to the pan. This isn't necessary if using fillets preserved in olive oil, which simply melt when heated. But the fillets from whole salted anchovies can have bones that don't dissolve, little needles that eventually lodge between the teeth or impale themselves into the palate. Chopped up, they're barely noticeable.

After a while most of these things are done by rote, but there's always the exception that nudges you to try something different. And, more important, there's the simple fact that doing all this takes enough time to allow observation, reaction, reverie. By this last word I don't mean daydreaming—the mind wandering away from the job at hand—but a kind of free-floating attentiveness that opens you to suggestion, the occasional impulsive diversion away from the charted course.

Usually, this impulse comes from the sometimes irresistible temptation to add something—the pulpy sweetness, say, of minced onion, the piquant fleshiness of some chopped black olives—that might smooth out, just a little, the rough edges of all those aggressive flavorings. (Interestingly enough, such additions lend their own note of sharpness to the dish, even as they temper it.) Here is a seductive example in the manner of a recipe from Umbria, utilizing both olives and capers.

SPAGHETTINI AROMATICI
[Serves 4]

1 pound thin spaghetti
½ cup olive oil

    fillets from 2 or 3 salted anchovies, chopped
    2 garlic cloves, minced
    1 teaspoon dried oregano, crumbled
    4 sprigs flat-leaf parsley, stemmed and finely chopped
    1 tablespoon capers, chopped
    12 imported black olives, pitted and chopped

Bring a large pot of salted water to a rolling boil. Add the pasta. Stir it well as soon as it softens to keep any of the strands from clumping together and cook it until tender but still firm. Drain well.

Meanwhile, heat the olive oil in a skillet. Add the anchovies and the minced garlic. Cook these together over medium heat until they dissolve into a paste. Then turn the flame down low and stir in the oregano, parsley, capers, and chopped black olives, mixing everything well.

Toss the pasta and sauce together in a large preheated bowl and serve at once.

If you try this recipe, I think you'll find it to be very good. But you may also agree with my own feeling that adding other ingredients in this way transforms rather than improves the dish. "Pasta with anchovies" has an identity that, in part, depends on there being no confusion as to what, exactly, defines the dish. Whatever I was looking for, it wasn't another ingredient. No, it was more like another . . . presence.

Standing over the sink, scraping off the scales and excess salt with my fingers, wondering whether the red-black thread of fish intestine would be tasty or terrible, my mind idly toyed with this idea. It's one thing to add a new character to a narrative and another to give the one already present a top hat or a dressing gown to cover his pajamas. These by analogy were the sorts of things I ended up considering: Cognac, balsamic vinegar, Cajun hot pepper sauce . . . presences.

Of these, the one that came closest was the balsamic vinegar, but when I used enough to add a mellifluent undercoating, the resulting sauce was too acidic. However, it did lead me to the solution, which had been staring me in the face the whole time—the bottle of wine waiting on the shelf for supper. About two tablespoons did the trick. The wine was there but not there, rounding edges without dulling them, soothing the flavors without smoothing them out. For the mo-

ment, at least, I had pasta with anchovies just where I wanted it . . . at
least until I get around to sautéing those spines.

SPAGHETTINI CON ACCIUGHE UBRIACHE
[Serves 4]

*A large (14-inch) wok is ideal for preparing the sauce and tossing it
with the pasta, but if you don't own one, use a skillet for the one and a
large, preheated bowl for the other. The amount of parsley may seem
excessive, but we've found that it balances things out just to our taste.*

> fillets from 6 salted anchovies, chopped
> ½ cup olive oil, with 1 tablespoon held apart
> 1 teaspoon crushed hot red pepper flakes (see note)
> 2 or 3 garlic cloves, minced
> 2 tablespoons red wine
> 1 cup loosely packed flat-leaf parsley leaves, coarsely
>   chopped
> ½ cup homemade dried bread crumbs (see page 206)
> 1 pound thin spaghetti
> salt as needed
> plenty of black pepper

Bring a large pot of salted water to a rolling boil.

As the water heats, cut the anchovies into small pieces. Heat the
olive oil in a skillet (or wok), add the anchovies, hot red pepper flakes,
and garlic, and cook over medium-low heat, stir-pressing with a heatproof flexible spatula to encourage them to dissolve. After 5 minutes,
add the wine and parsley. Stir well.

Once the anchovy sauce is under way, heat the remaining oil in a
small skillet. Mix the bread crumbs into the hot oil, stirring them until
they are uniformly saturated with it. Then, continuing to stir occasionally, sauté the bread crumbs until golden over low heat. Turn into a
small bowl.

When the water comes to a full boil, add the pasta. Stir it well as
soon as it softens to keep any of the strands from clumping together.
Cook it until tender but still firm. At this point, scoop ¼ cup of the wa-

ter from the pasta pot and add it to the sauce. Now, drain the pasta and toss it with the anchovy sauce. Add more salt if necessary and black pepper to taste. Serve at once, with the bread crumbs in a separate bowl for eaters to add as they like.

Cook's Note. Hot Pepper Flakes: These should be seedless and not too coarse—about the size of sesame seeds.

These ruminations on pasta with anchovies have influenced my thinking about other dishes we eat, including pasta with clam sauce (still evolving) and the following version of pasta with cauliflower.

GEMELLI WITH CAULIFLOWER
[Serves 4]

> 1 small to medium head cauliflower
> fillets from 1 salted anchovy, chopped
> ½ cup olive oil, with 1 tablespoon held apart
> ½ cup homemade dried bread crumbs (see page 206)
> 1 teaspoon crushed hot red pepper flakes (see note
>   above)
> 2 or 3 garlic cloves, minced
> 2 tablespoons red wine
> 1 tablespoon balsamic vinegar
> 1 cup loosely packed flat-leaf parsley leaves, coarsely
>   chopped
> salt as needed
> 1 pound gemelli
> plenty of black pepper

Bring a large pot of salted water to a rolling boil.

Trim the cauliflower and cut it into bite-size pieces, if necessary halving the florets and chopping up the stem part. Add these to a large pot of boiling salted water and cook until just al dente, or about 3 minutes. Use a slotted ladle or sieve to transfer the cauliflower to a bowl. Then add and cook the gemelli.

Follow the directions in the recipe above, adding the balsamic vinegar at the same time as the wine. Stir the cauliflower into the sauce for the last few minutes of the pasta cooking time. Finish and serve the same way.

Last Word. Since this essay was written, Matt and I decided that we actually liked pasta with anchovies better without the bread crumbs, delicious as they are. We came to this realization separately and were both hesitant to bring it up, so sure were we that the other adored the bread crumbs. Now we eat the dish without them. The last word? There is no last word.

A Note on Bread Crumbs

Since good bread crumbs make such a difference in dishes that use them, readers might be interested in knowing our method for making them. First, you need a loaf of artisanal-style coarse-textured white bread. It should be made with nothing but flour, water, salt, and either sourdough starter or yeast. (We keep an eye out for these on the day-old-bread shelf of the various bakeries in town for just this purpose.)

When you find one, slice it, then spread the slices out on wire cooling racks in an out-of-the-way place. Cover them loosely with brown kraft (or some similar large-sheeted) paper until they are completely dried out. This takes longer than you might think—usually about four days.

When the bread is ready to be turned into crumbs, get out your biggest mixing bowl and line it with an old, clean dish towel. Put the rusks into this, breaking each one into three or four pieces as you do. Gather the corners of the dish towel, twist them together to form a compact bundle, and set this onto the kitchen counter.

Take a rolling pin or other wieldable object in one hand and, holding tightly with the other onto the twisted ends of the bundle, pound the rusks vigorously but carefully until they have been reduced to the consistency of building rubble.

If you have a food processor, reverse the blade so that its dull side faces in the direction of the spin. Process the crumbled rusks into crumbs, sifting them into the bowl through a sieve or colander. When all the pieces have been processed, empty the crumbs that haven't filtered through into the processor and give these another whir. (Then, either discard those that don't make it through the second time or let them have their little victory and just add them to the other crumbs.)

If you *don't* have a food processor—well, you've guessed what to do. Continue pounding and sifting until you've got the whole batch through the sieve or colander or have had enough of the whole business.

Put the crumbs into a ziplock plastic bag and keep them in the freezer until needed. They'll stay fresh that way for a few months.

SUSSING OUT SATAY

The satay can be made of pork or chicken, but turtle remains the favourite of the Balinese of Den Pasar.
— Miguel Covarrubias, *Island of Bali* (1937)

The Malays crouch over their portable stoves, fanning the embers below sticks of spicy broiled goat known as satay.
— Patrick Anderson, *Snake Wine* (1955)

Every spring, when I free our barbecue grill from its protective wrappings and end its hibernation, I vow that this will be the year that I begin grilling satay. But when autumn rolls in and I stow it away again, there are no charred remnants of spicy chicken or beef drippings to feed the grill's winter sleep. The reason, although it took me a long time to grasp this, is my love-hate relationship with this particular grill food. More accurately, I am always stopped short by the invisible barrier that deflects my attention from dishes that I really like but that always seem to be doled out with a grudging hand.

The Chinese claim satay as their own, on the strength of the fact that in Cantonese the words *sah tay* mean "three pieces." Actually, food historians believe that satay was introduced to Southeast Asia by Arab traders, but it surely could be argued that Chinese restaurateurs use this semantic false friend as justification for rigorous portion control—sometimes to their own detriment.

A few decades back, when I lived near Boston, a satay place appeared one day in that city's Chinatown. The satay was very good, but an order consisted of four skewers, each with a single flattened strip of meat, and cost as much as the far more generous entrées served at any of the nearby Chinese restaurants. The second and last time I was there, gnawing away at my minuscule repast, the proprietor was counting the day's take with an impassive expression that somehow managed to fill the small dining room with gloom. I wanted to go over, seize him by both shoulders, and say with emphatic firmness: "Try doubling the portion size." I didn't, of course, and I found the place closed for good the next time I came by.

Surely this aura of stinginess was what prevented me from plunging wholeheartedly into satay-making—as distinct, that is, from satay-eating. I never had any trouble devouring it, but preparing it seemed altogether too complicated a business for what was essentially a snack. Over the years, I had accumulated a pile of recipes for the dish, but none of them dealt with the problem of how to transform this finger food into a satisfying meal.

So, this spring, I laid my hand on my grill and swore I would sidestep the recipe pile and head off to the library to learn all I could about satay as it is made and eaten on its own turf. After all, what good were the recipes to me if I didn't ever seem to want to make them? I was missing something important . . . and I hoped that immersion in some amateur culinary ethnography would provide a clue as to what that something was.

Happily, I found a raft of books on Southeast Asia, some dating back to the beginning of the last century, and bits of prose here and there—sometimes a phrase, sometimes a paragraph—that helped me find my way to the heart of traditional satay. Of course, what this also meant is that what I discovered was, except in the most isolated parts of Southeast Asia, completely out of date. That part of the world is in a state of rapid change, which has profoundly affected even the lowly outdoor seller of snacks.

Singapore, once famous for its satay street vendors, has, for reasons of sanitation, relocated almost all of them to indoor food courts, thus relegating the vitality and variety of that world to the realm of memory. In the same vein, I learned that satay vendors in Jakarta no longer bother to marinate their meat now that they can buy it fresh several times a day.

However, perhaps the most telling signs of change are there in full view in our local Asian market: sagging shelves loaded with bottled Southeast Asian dips and marinades—even cellophane-wrapped blocks of ground peanuts seasoned with chile, garlic, onions, and spices for making instant peanut sauce. And these products are all strictly home-grown, quite distinct from the Bali H'ai–type stuff you find in American supermarkets.

This means that my quest to touch the soul of satay has inevitably been a quixotic one. But doesn't that adjective characterize the experience of all travelers, not only those who wander abroad through the dusty pages of old books? Without the romance of the unfamiliar, why would anyone ever leave home at all?

> When the sun goes down, tiny outdoor *saté* stalls open for business along busy thoroughfares, their flickering candles and gas lanterns inviting passers-by to sit down for an inexpensive treat. In any town the itinerant *saté* vendor, ringing his bell and shuffling through the streets with all his ingredients and his charcoal brazier slung from the ends of a pole across his shoulder, seems to stay up long after everyone else has gone to sleep . . . Throughout most of this predominantly Muslim area, beef, goat, and chicken are the most common *saté* meats, but carabao [water buffalo] *saté* appears in Makasar, shrimp *saté* turns up wherever shellfish are available, and in Chinese areas one can find *saté* made from tender chunks of pork. The Balinese produce a *saté* from a paste of chopped-up turtle meat mixed with coconut milk and spices. The mixture, kneaded onto the end of a stick for grilling, comes off the coals as one of the most heavenly concoctions I have ever tasted.
>
> —Rafael Steinberg, *Pacific and Southeast Asian Cooking*

Satay* in one form or another has made itself at home in almost every country in Southeast Asia. And while the number of different foodstuffs grilled on skewers there is nearly beyond count, no one would have a problem recognizing them as satay. Indeed, if simple cooking can be loosely defined as those dishes whose form is almost entirely shaped by function, satay is about as good an example as one could hope to find. It is a dish whose rigorous simplicity has been honed by the persistent ingenuity of appetite overcoming the immovable solidity of poverty.

---

*Also spelled *saté*, and sometimes *satai*. Here, for the sake of consistency, *satay* is used throughout.

This is all the more impressive because it is usually made solely of a very luxurious ingredient: richly seasoned meat.

How has this happened? Traveler after traveler to the region, if he mentions satay at all, begins by describing its intoxicating aroma, one that can seek out and seize hold of your attention through all the cacophony of the market street. The aroma of satay is essentially the same as that which drives the neighbors to distraction when the steaks hit the barbecue grill: meat juices vaporizing on glowing charcoal . . . but here this knee-jerk response is amplified by the additional nuances of caramelized palm sugar, soy sauce or some cousin of it, citrus, and spice.

It's hard to imagine a better way to attract a customer. You don't need signage or even a strong pair of lungs to cry out the enticing particulars of your offerings. You just squat there on the roadside and let the cooking smells reel in your clientele. On a busy street, you might have two dozen skewers on the grill. In places where business is slower, you might have just one.

When a buyer stops, you pass him the first skewer. While he nibbles at that you put another on the flames, and so it goes until he is full and you reckon the bill by counting up the used skewers. There are no plates or bowls or eating utensils to deal with; the cooking implement is the eating implement and, after that, the bill . . . perhaps even the complimentary toothpick. Best of all, these skewers are made from the ribs of palm leaves that have been gathered for free by your children.

Obviously, grilling small bits and pieces of meat on a skewer is an ideal way to get maximum mileage from any kind of carcass. As an anonymous satay seller—the account of whose typical day appeared in *The Jakarta Post* on October 15, 2000—explains:

> At 8 a.m. I go to Tanah Abang market [in Central Jakarta] to buy three or four live young chickens and other needs. They cost me about Rp 200,000 [$17.45]. I clean the chickens and make the satay myself. Almost all of the chicken parts can be used for the satay; I can even sell the heads and bones for Rp 700 [6¢] per chicken to a mie ayam [chicken noodle] vendor who will chop them up and cook them.

Even so, since he charges customers only about twenty-five cents per skewer, he can afford to leave no part of what he does to chance. The same marinade that provides the satay with its depth of flavor also keeps the meat from spoiling as it sits all day in a large recycled tin container by the vendor's side. The marinade tenderizes the meat, which—in days past, at least—came from tough, cheap cuts of goat, water buffalo, and stringy old fowl, while the homemade peanut sauce that accompanies the dish—made by the vendor's wife—provides the unctuous savor that, in more expensive meat, is supplied by the animal's own fat.

In sum, satay as made on its own turf is a dish with no rough edges, and it was a lack of such carefully considered fine-tuning that made my own satay-making so frustrating. Gradually, as I pored over pictures in various travel books and read such accounts of satay-making as I could find, I began to feel the peculiar satisfaction that comes when problems at last fall into focus and solutions start to slot themselves into place.

The art of satay-making may be fueled by necessity, but it rules by ingenuity, with the added enticements of smoke and spice. Joan and David Peterson's *Eat Smart in Indonesia*, a guide to that country's food, lists two dozen different versions, among them:

satay ampla—chicken gizzards grilled on skewers

satay asam—chunks of lamb or goat in sweet-sour sauce grilled on thin bamboo skewers

satay Bali kebelet—a paste of liver covered by a paste of chopped meat, spices, and coconut milk, rolled around thick skewers and grilled

satay Bali limbat—a paste of chopped meat, spices, and grated coconut rolled around thick skewers and grilled

satay buntel—balls of minced lamb and onion wrapped in caul and grilled on skewers

satay empal ikan—fish balls grilled on skewers

satay kelinci—rabbit meat grilled on skewers

satay kerang—clams grilled on bamboo skewers

satay lilit ayam—spices and chicken meat pounded to a paste and wrapped around thick skewers and grilled

satay Padang—pieces of marinated offal grilled on skewers

satay pentul—balls of minced pork wrapped like drumsticks around skewers and grilled

satay penyu—pieces of turtle meat grilled on skewers

The Satay Grill

The vernacular satay grill is simplicity itself—a narrow, rectangular rolled-steel box with a grill rack on top with bars that run the length of the unit. Unlike home grills, this one has no air vent at the bottom. Consequently, between orders, only a minimal amount of oxygen reaches the coals—just enough to keep them smoldering. The only barbecue grill available in the United States that even approaches this design is our old friend the Japanese hibachi, which, with its wobbly grills and minuscule cooking area, has confounded American outdoor cooks since its introduction back in the early sixties. However, most units made in this country pose equally serious problems for satay grilling. Kettle grills, with their curved sides, make it difficult to get the meat close to the charcoal. Gas grills don't generate enough heat to caramelize the exterior without at the same time cooking the interior to the consistency of beef jerky.

Fortunately, there was an obvious solution to all this. I headed down to the local discount warehouse and bought the cheapest grill in the store. Made in China, it was no more than a metal box with four little legs screwed onto the base, a grill rack, and a cover. True, the sides sloped down to the bottom, but they were so short that it was easy to heap the charcoal up them. The grill was flimsy, even junky—but for satay-making, it felt just right.

The Skewers

One of the things you notice immediately in photographs of satay vendors is that the skewers they use are substantially longer than the ubiquitous eight-inch bamboo ones sold at most supermarkets. But because the latter were the very things on which I had eaten satay in Chinese restaurants, I had assumed that they were what one wanted for the job. And they are, if the job is that of serving up appetizers—or perhaps even cooking them, when that means searing them on the surface of a restaurant grill. This is why the meat on such skewers is often flat as a board; the chef has only to give it a quick sear on both sides and send it out. But over charcoal, the length of the harder-to-find ten-inch skewers (or the even harder-to-find twelve-inch ones) gives you both a necessary safety margin and leverage, making the satays easier to manipulate as they cook.

The next decision is between metal and bamboo. Metal skewers heat up, cooking the interior of the meat and providing another threat to the fingers. I also like the way the slight texture of the wood helps keep the skewered meat from slipping loose, which is not always true of metal skewers, even those that are square rather than round.

The main problem with bamboo skewers, of course, is that they burn. It doesn't much matter if the tips flare up, but even insignificant charring at the butt end can cause the skewer to give way and send the meat tumbling onto the grill. To prevent this, cookbooks advise you to presoak the skewers for anything from half an hour to half a day. However, even if it works (which I doubt), I have come across no evidence that satay sellers do this. They have an even simpler secret: they don't expose the skewers to the flame. Satay grills have a metal lip on both their front and back edges. This protects the exposed wood of the skewer at both ends, while fully exposing the meat to the flame. Such a lip is easy enough to improvise on your own grill with pieces of scrap metal or a folded strip of aluminum foil.

The Fuel and the Fan

Satays are traditionally cooked over the intense heat provided by the vigorous use of a palm-leaf fan to transform the smoldering charcoal into a fiercely glowing mass—not an easy job if you have to do it all day long. As the Jakarta satay vendor attests:

> I found that dealing with this job was quite difficult in the begin-
> ning, especially when I had to manually fan the satay during the
> cooking process, which made my arms stiff and sore. I know that
> other vendors use electric fans instead, but I don't do this because
> it affects the taste.

Chunks of real charcoal are ideal for cooking satay because they generate so much heat, especially when you fan them to keep them constantly aglow. The last time I saw a palm fan was when I bicycled past a funeral procession in New Orleans about twenty years ago; you may still be able to buy them today, but where? In any case, I'm not sure they're such a good idea with an ordinary grill—their indiscriminate blast will send charcoal ashes flying everywhere. A "personal" battery-powered fan would do the trick, but so will a small, stiff piece of card-board.

The Sauce and the Starch

Many see the dipping sauces as the whole point of satay—especially peanut dipping sauce, which often combines the opulent richness of both peanut paste and coconut milk with the palate-tingling scorch of Southeast Asian chiles. However, if the meat is tender, flavorful, and juicy, such a sauce can easily take away as much pleasure as it gives, since it drowns out the taste of the flame-seared marinade, and sometimes even that of the meat. In fact, I was seriously tempted to dispense with it altogether, the way I have with sauce when eating my own barbecue.

Fortunately, before I put peanut sauce on permanent hold, I discovered two important things. The first is simply that a little of it goes a long way—the trick is to dip, not dunk, each bite of meat, and to vary the effect by alternating between that sauce and a different, more purely astringent one, such as the tangy lime sauce given on page 227.

The second was bound up in a larger problem—what starch to have with this meal. This, it turns out, was the missing part of the satay equation, the secret to transforming a snack food into a meal. Barbecue has its side of Wonder Bread; fajitas have their flour tortillas; jerked chicken has its grilled breadfruit slices; and satay has . . . what? If you only know it, as I did, in appetizer mode, the question will bring you up short. But in Southeast Asia, satays are commonly sold with *ketupat*—a cake of tightly compressed cold boiled rice.

R. Talbot Kelly, in *Burma Painted and Described*, gives a nice description of how this was traditionally made, at least at the outdoor market in the Burmese town of Taungdwingyi:

> In all corners of the bazaar are stalls for the sale of food. In one sausages and rice cakes simmer over a little charcoal fire, while from the next is wafted the delicious smell of sandalwood. There, roast meat, cut into small strips, is spitted on bamboo skewers, which are stuck all round the rim of a basket containing what appear to be candles of unusual size. These, however, prove to be "sticks" of rice prepared in a curious way. A special kind of rice called "*kowknyin*" is placed in a [length of] green bamboo, to-

gether with a little water, the bamboo then being closed with a plug and put into the fire; by the time the bamboo is dried and commences to burn the rice is cooked. The bamboo is then split, and the rice, beautifully cooked, is extracted.

Today, in rural Indonesia, roadside vendors still sell *ketupat* wrapped in square woven coconut-leaf bundles. They must be a neat sight. Several Southeast Asian cookbooks tell you how to make the dish more simply—you put fully cooked short-grain rice into a greased pan, press it flat, cover it with banana leaves (if you have any) or foil (if you don't), let it cool, then serve it cut into brownie-size squares. This is an especially appealing idea if the satay is to be part of a picnic. Skewer the meat, snipping off the pointed ends with kitchen shears, and seal these skewers and the marinade in a ziplock plastic bag. Put that and your rice squares in the cooler and you're ready to travel.

Even so, there are other alternatives, including toast—our old breakfast pal being enthusiastically embraced by the Thai for just this purpose. Nancie McDermott, in *Real Vegetarian Thai*, says that this West-meets-East touch can be found in upcountry Thailand, where toast is offered alongside meat kebabs as a means of soaking up every last bit of scrumptious sauce.

However, Matt and I prefer to cook up either a batch of boiled rice or a package of rice-stick noodles and portion one or the other into shallow soup bowls, serving the grilled satays directly on top. By the time you've finished eating those, the rice or rice noodles will be delicately flavored by the smoky juices of the meat. Stir it up with the remaining peanut sauce, the last of the cucumber wedges, and any other leftover vegetables. There you have it: two of my favorite Asian snacks—a brace of satay, a particularly delicious version of rice or noodles tossed with peanut sauce . . . and a made meal.

THE INGREDIENTS

Dark Soy Sauce. A thicker, more potent, and sometimes somewhat sweeter soy sauce with a distinct taste of molasses. (When plain soy sauce is specified, use the familiar thinner version, such as Kikkoman.) Found in Asian groceries.

Fish Sauce (called *nam pla* in Thailand, *nuoc mam* in Vietnam, *tuk trey* in Cambodia, *patis* in the Philippines—its names are legion). A potent seasoning made from pressing the juices from salted anchovies. Not easy to take straight, but a surprisingly subtle flavor enhancer when used in cooking. Available in any Asian grocery store and many supermarkets.

Kecap Manis (ket-chup mah-niece). A condiment made from fermented soy beans and palm sugar. In its native Indonesia, it is used with the same abandon that we use . . . well, ketchup. The taste starts out like very salty blackstrap molasses and then moves into a riff of complex and unplaceable tangy notes. If you can't find it, mix palm sugar (see below) with dark soy sauce until the salt is balanced by the sweet.

Lemongrass. A tall, narrow grass with slender, razor-edged leaves. Its stalk has a distinct taste of lemon, without that fruit's acidity. Peel off the leaves down to the pale and tightly coiled stalk. Cut away a three-inch piece of this about an inch above the root end and discard the rest. This piece of stalk is very fibrous—if it is to be eaten, it must be minced or thinly sliced. When using it as a flavoring agent, though, simply flatten it a bit with the side of a knife and add it whole to the pot. Lemongrass can be found in supermarkets these days, but it is much cheaper in Asian groceries. Substitute strips of lemon peel.

Palm Sugar. A coarse-textured sugar made from the sap of the palmyra palm, usually sold as a solid mass in a package or jar, from which one hacks chunks and grinds them into a moist powder. It is not as sweet as cane sugar and possesses a slightly sour tang and sappy taste. Substitute raw cane sugar—especially one made from evaporated sugar cane juice.

Sambal Oelek. A fiery, bright-red sauce made from ground chiles (including seeds), vinegar, and salt. We buy Huy Fong Foods Rooster brand (look for the gold foil label) in an eight-ounce plastic jar. When we buy a new jar, Matt removes the seeds by pushing the sauce through a sieve, which makes it much easier to use. Substitute fresh hot chiles, seeded and minced, or powdered chile to taste.

Tamarind Paste. This is made by drying and compacting the pulpy contents of the pods of the tamarind tree. Squares of this, looking like thick slabs of fruit leather and colored a deep rusty red, can be found in any Asian grocery. The plum-like flavor is mild and fruity; what makes it special is its distinctive bright acidity. The dried product contains fiber and seeds, so it is necessary to dissolve the paste in a little hot water, pressing the soluble pulp through a sieve and discarding the debris. Substitute lemon or lime juice if these are not already called for.

Et cetera. Shallots are the universal substitute for the small, brown Bombay onions popular in Southeast Asian cooking. Small yellow onions may be substituted. Peanut oil is the cooking oil of choice in Southeast Asia—and for us, too—because of its clean, slightly nutty taste. Substitute the cooking oil of your choice. Unsweetened coconut milk—the coconut milk called for in the following recipes—is widely available in cans. Look for those containing no sweeteners or preservatives. We use Thai Kitchen brand. Unsweetened coconut flakes can usually be found for sale in bulk at natural food stores.

THE RECIPES

Marinating. The meat should be allowed to marinate for 1 hour or so at room temperature or 2 hours or more in the refrigerator (covered, you can leave it there overnight).

Substituting. Consult the glossary above for alternatives to ingredients that you can't find or don't see the point in purchasing. However, do note that these recipes have been crafted to show off the merits of those Southeast Asian ingredients Matt and I are particularly taken with—*kecap manis*, lemongrass, tamarind paste—and to bypass those—like galangal (ginger on a bad hair day)—that we aren't. None are expensive and all should be easy to find in a decent Asian grocery.

Skewering. Cut the meat into 1-inch squares, a little less than ½-inch thick. Skewer them together like slices of bread being turned back into a loaf. This gives you bite-size pieces that are charred around the edges but juicy and moist in the center. The meat should take up a third of the skewer; add too much and you'll find it hard to get everything evenly cooked—and plenty of handle makes them easier to manipulate.

Grilling. All the following satays should be grilled directly over glowing charcoal or, a distant second choice, 2 inches below a preheated oven broiler. (In this instance, snip off any exposed bamboo and turn the skewers with tongs.) Turn the skewers so that each side is exposed for about 2 minutes to the flame. Check for doneness by spreading two pieces apart with a knife blade: beef and lamb should be pink at the center; pork and chicken just past that point.

Portioning. Tailgaters may find that the skewers evaporate as fast as spilled ice on hot pavement, but served as the main course of a family meal (with plenty of peanut sauce to take up any slack), a pound and a half of meat should serve four. If offering satay as an appetizer, put less meat on each skewer and calculate serving six to eight.

Serving. As side dishes, we suggest rice or rice noodles and either a simple Thai cucumber salad (page 228) or a variety of plainly prepared summer vegetables—cucumber wedges, sugarsnap peas, parboiled green beans, etc. You might also have on hand a pitcher of iced tea or cold bottles of Singapore's Tiger beer, Indonesia's Bintang Pilsener, or Thailand's Siam Ale (all top-rated brews), and, naturally, coconut and/or ginger ice cream for dessert.

BEEF SATAY

FOR THE MARINADE:

2 teaspoons coriander seeds
1 small shallot, peeled and minced
1 garlic clove, minced
1 tablespoon minced fresh ginger
2 tablespoons *kecap manis*
1½ teaspoons minced lemongrass
1 teaspoon *sambal oelek*
1 tablespoon palm sugar
2 tablespoons peanut oil
½ teaspoon kosher salt, or to taste

1½ pounds beef (flank steak, chuck, or sirloin tips), cut into
     bite-size pieces (see above)
peanut sauce, curry-flavored (page 226)

Toast the coriander seeds in a hot, ungreased skillet until they release their aroma and begin to change color. When cool enough to handle, crush or process them into a coarse powder. Mix this with the remaining marinade ingredients in a bowl. Stir in the meat so that all the pieces are coated, and let marinate at room temperature for an hour or so. Thread meat onto skewers and grill over charcoal as directed above. Serve immediately with peanut sauce for dipping.

RATAMI'S LAMB SATAY

(Adapted from Rosemary Brissenden's *Joys and Subtleties: South East Asian Cooking*)

FOR THE MARINADE:

1 teaspoon tamarind paste
1 tablespoon hot water
2 garlic cloves, minced
½ teaspoon kosher salt, or to taste
2 medium or 1 large shallot, peeled and grated
1 tablespoon palm sugar
1½ tablespoons lemon juice
2 tablespoons *kecap manis*

1½ pounds lamb, cut into bite-size pieces (see above)
peanut sauce (page 225)

Dissolve the tamarind paste in the hot water and press the pulp through a sieve. Mix this with the remaining marinade ingredients in a bowl. Stir in the meat so that all the pieces are coated and let marinate at room temperature for an hour or so. Thread meat onto skewers and grill over charcoal as directed above. Serve immediately with peanut sauce for dipping.

PORK SATAY

(Adapted from Sri Owen's *Indonesian Food and Cookery*)

Sri Owen says that Indonesians don't often eat pork satay with peanut sauce, preferring to dip it into sambal kecap *instead—which, as it turns out, is an excellent alternative dipping sauce for any satay.*

FOR THE MARINADE:
2 garlic cloves, minced
1 tablespoon minced fresh ginger
1 teaspoon Chinese five-spice powder
1 tablespoon honey
1 tablespoon peanut oil
1 tablespoon *kecap manis*
2 teaspoons lemon juice

1½ pounds pork tenderloin, cut into pieces (see above)
sambal kecap (page 227)

Combine the marinade ingredients in a bowl, stir in the pork, and let marinate for an hour or so at room temperature, stirring occasionally. Thread meat onto skewers and grill over charcoal as directed above. Serve immediately with *sambal kecap* for dipping.

CHICKEN SATAY

We found two very similar marinades for chicken in Wandee Young and Byron Ayanoglu's Simply Thai Cooking *and in Bruce Cost's* Asian Ingredients, *each of which produced a very different but equally pleasing result. To try our adaptation of the Young-Ayanoglu version, add the ingredients from "either" to the rest in the list; to try our version of the Cost recipe, choose just the tamarind pulp in the "or" part.*

FOR THE MARINADE:
1 teaspoon each coriander seeds, cumin seeds, black
  peppercorns
1 tablespoon palm sugar
½ tablespoon fish sauce
2 large garlic cloves, minced
1 tablespoon peanut oil

EITHER:
1 tablespoon lime juice
1 tablespoon soy sauce
½ teaspoon turmeric

OR:

½ tablespoon tamarind paste dissolved in 3 tablespoons of
water, seeds and fiber strained out

1½ pounds boneless chicken thighs, cut into bite-size pieces
(see above)
peanut sauce with chiles and garlic (page 225)
tangy lime sauce (page 227)

Toast the coriander, cumin seeds, and black peppercorns together in a
hot, ungreased skillet until they release their aroma and begin to change
color. Pour them into a mortar or food processor and pulverize into a
powder. Combine with the other marinade ingredients in a bowl and
mix thoroughly. Toss in the chicken pieces and let marinate in the refrigerator for at least 2 hours. Thread meat onto skewers and grill over
charcoal as directed above. Serve immediately with peanut sauce and
tangy lime sauce for dipping.

SATAY PENTUL
(Adapted from David Burton's *Savouring the East*)

*In David Burton's account of this recipe, which he watched being pre-
pared in a family compound in Bali, the grandfather bashed the meat,
handful by handful, with the blunt end of a hatchet, for an hour. Then
he put it in a huge wooden mortar and pounded it with a pestle for another hour. Only then was it judged ready for seasoning and grilling.*

½ tablespoon tamarind paste
2 tablespoons hot water
1 teaspoon coriander seeds
2 garlic cloves, coarsely chopped
1 tablespoon finely minced fresh ginger
½ tablespoon *sambal oelek*
¼ teaspoon turmeric
½ tablespoon palm sugar
1 tablespoon soy sauce
½ teaspoon kosher salt

2 or 3 tablespoons unsweetened coconut flakes
1½ pounds ground chicken or pork

peanut sauce with shallots and tamarind (page 226) and/or
   sambal kecap (page 227)

Steep the tamarind paste in the water for 5 minutes. Strain. Toast the coriander seeds in a hot, ungreased skillet. In a mortar or food processor, blend the garlic, coriander, ginger, and *sambal oelek* into a paste. Turn this into a bowl, add all the remaining ingredients, and blend everything thoroughly into a sticky mass. Put the bowl in the refrigerator and let the contents cool and firm for at least an hour.

Form a golf ball–size amount of the paste around each skewer in the shape of a miniature hot dog. Grill over hot coals, turning often, until satays are dotted all over with crusty brown spots. Serve them with peanut sauce with shallots and tamarind and/or *sambal kecap.*

Cook's Note. Ordinary bamboo skewers don't have enough surface to hold the meat mixture fast. Look for stubbier skewers (about as thick as a pencil) or use chopsticks. (The mixture can also be shaped into patties and grilled like hamburgers.)

POTATO SATAY

Although Anya von Bremzen, author of Terrific Pacific—*among several other interesting cookbooks—told me that she remembered tasting a potato satay at an Indian hawker's stall in Penang, I had no luck turning up a recipe for one. However, potatoes take so well to that area's flavorings that I found it no problem to create a recipe of my own. Yellow-fleshed potatoes (like Yukon Gold) are ideal; calculate at least one large potato per person when this satay is the main course, half that when serving it with a meat satay.*

4 large yellow-fleshed potatoes, boiled whole in their skins
1 teaspoon each coriander seeds and black peppercorns
½ teaspoon curry powder
1 tablespoon lemon juice
1 garlic clove, minced

1 teaspoon kosher salt
1 tablespoon minced fresh ginger
1 tablespoon *kecap manis*
1 teaspoon *sambal oelek*

peanut sauce of your choice
    (pages 225–227)

Gently peel the potatoes and cut them into bite-size cubes. Toast the coriander and the peppercorns in a hot, ungreased skillet until the coriander seeds start to turn color. Pour them into a mortar or food processor bowl and process into a powder. Mix thoroughly with the other ingredients in a bowl. Stir in the potatoes and let everything marinate at room temperature for an hour or so. Then push the pieces gently onto thin skewers and grill until each side has lightly browned (don't let them burn). Serve with any peanut sauce.

DIPPING SAUCES

Probably the most popular street food, found everywhere, and with a variety of flavors depending upon the region, satays can be made with mutton, chicken, or beef. Regardless of which meat you prefer, it is the peanut sauce that defines the ultimate taste of a satay, and on this rests the success of any satay.
            —Copeland Marks, *The Exotic Kitchens of Malaysia*

Roasting the Peanuts. Although many recipes these days simply substitute peanut butter for peanuts in peanut sauce recipes, the sauce will be distinctly better—fresher flavor, more appealing texture—if you take the trouble to buy dry-roasted peanuts and grind them up yourself—or, if you can find raw peanuts, to roast them as well. To do this, add 1 tablespoon of peanut oil for every ½ cup of peanuts to a small skillet, pour in the raw peanuts, and heat them over a medium-hot flame. Shake the pan gently while they cook so that the peanuts are fried on all sides. When they turn a light tan (they won't have the golden sheen of deep-fried peanuts), turn them out onto a paper towel and let them cool. Then work them to a paste in a mortar or in a food processor set with a steel blade. The result should be smooth but slightly mealy, with bits of peanut all through.

Mix and Match. Our linking of each satay to a sauce is meant only as a suggestion—feel free to follow your own taste instead.

PEANUT SAUCE

(Adapted from Rosemary Brissenden's *Joys and Subtleties:*
South East Asian Cooking)

½ cup roasted peanuts, ground to a paste
1 large or 2 small shallots, peeled and grated
1 cup coconut milk
1 tablespoon palm sugar
1 teaspoon *sambal oelek*
1 stem lemongrass, bottom 3 inches only, sliced fine
salt and pepper to taste

Combine all the ingredients in a small pot and heat over a medium flame, stirring constantly. When the mixture reaches a simmer, remove from the heat. Stir in a little water if a thinner consistency is desired. Serve warm or at room temperature.

PEANUT SAUCE WITH CHILES AND GARLIC

½ cup roasted peanuts, ground to a paste
2 fresh hot chiles, cored, seeded, and minced
1 tablespoon minced fresh ginger
2 garlic cloves, minced
⅓ cup coconut milk
1 tablespoon peanut oil
1 tablespoon *kecap manis*
1 tablespoon fish sauce
1 teaspoon palm sugar
1 tablespoon fresh lime juice
½ teaspoon kosher salt
chopped fresh cilantro to taste

Put all the ingredients except the cilantro into a mortar or the bowl of a food processor and blend until smooth. Transfer to a small bowl and, when ready to serve, stir in the chopped fresh cilantro.

PEANUT SAUCE WITH SHALLOTS AND TAMARIND

1 tablespoon peanut oil
2 or 3 shallots, peeled and minced
3 garlic cloves, minced
1 tablespoon tamarind paste dissolved in ½ cup boiling water
2 to 3 tablespoons *sambal oelek*
1 stalk lemongrass (in this instance, the whole stem)
1 tablespoon minced fresh ginger
½ teaspoon kosher salt
1 tablespoon palm sugar
½ cup roasted peanuts, ground to a paste

Heat the oil in a small pot. Add the minced shallots and garlic and cook over low heat for 2 minutes, or until they are translucent.

Meanwhile, dissolve the tamarind paste in the boiling water, pressing the result through a sieve. Cut the stalk of lemongrass into 3 pieces and flatten them by pressing them under the side of a knife. Add the strained tamarind liquid, *sambal oelek*, flattened lemongrass, minced ginger, salt, and palm sugar to the pot with the sautéed shallots and garlic. Bring to a boil and simmer over low heat for 10 minutes.

Stir the peanut paste into the pot at the end of the cooking time and remove it from the heat. Fish out and discard the lemongrass and let the sauce rest at least 15 minutes before serving.

PEANUT SAUCE, CURRY-FLAVORED
(Adapted from Jackie Passmore's *Encyclopedia of Asian Food and Cooking*)

1½ tablespoons coriander seeds
⅔ cup roasted peanuts, ground to a paste
3 tablespoons *kecap manis*
½ teaspoon turmeric
2 teaspoons *sambal oelek*
1 teaspoon minced garlic
¾ cup coconut milk
2 teaspoons palm sugar
½ teaspoon salt
1 tablespoon lemon juice

Toast the coriander seeds in a hot, ungreased skillet, let cool, and crush to a powder. Combine this with the rest of the ingredients except the salt and lemon juice in a small pan and simmer for 3 minutes. Cool and stir in the salt and lemon juice.

SAMBAL KECAP

1 tablespoon *kecap manis*
2 tablespoons freshly squeezed lemon or lime juice
1 garlic clove, very finely minced (optional)
1 shallot, peeled and grated
1 to 2 teaspoons *sambal oelek*
pinch of salt

Blend everything together and serve.

TANGY LIME SAUCE

2 tablespoons lime juice
1 to 2 teaspoons fish sauce
1 tablespoon soy sauce
1 teaspoon *sambal oelek*
1 tablespoon palm sugar
4 sprigs fresh cilantro, chopped

Place all the ingredients except the cilantro in a small bowl and mix well. If necessary, adjust the balance of lime juice, fish sauce, *sambal oelek*, and sugar to taste. Do not mix in the chopped cilantro until the sauce is to be served.

Cook's Note. Without the fresh herb it can be kept for a week in the refrigerator.

THAI CUCUMBER SALAD
[Serves 4]

3 cucumbers, peeled
2 shallots, peeled
2 tablespoons kosher salt
½ cup rice vinegar
½ cup sugar
2 fresh hot chiles, stemmed, seeded, and diced
2 or 3 sprigs fresh cilantro, minced
½ cup roasted peanuts, chopped (optional)

Cut the cucumbers in half lengthwise and spoon out their seeds. Slice into crescent-shaped pieces about ¼-inch thick. Slice the shallots into the thinnest possible rings. Put the cucumber pieces and the shallot rings into two separate bowls. Toss each of them in a tablespoon of salt and let sit at room temperature for 30 minutes, stirring them occasionally.

Meanwhile, bring the rice vinegar to a boil. Remove from the heat and stir in the sugar until it has completely dissolved. Put this into the refrigerator to cool.

Wring out as much moisture as possible from the cucumbers and then the shallots in an old but clean dish towel. Mix everything together in the sweetened vinegar and serve at once. Add the chopped peanuts if not serving peanut sauce.

However we make our satay, there are certain seasonings that only imagination can supply—the sharp, whispery hiss and brilliant glare of kerosene pressure lanterns, the raffish smells of a Southeast Asian city street that at once beckon and repulse the appetite, the nighttime crowd—shopping, gossiping, snacking—that disgorges you when you stop to place your order, the rivulets of sweat that run down your back as you watch it cook.

Now, consider all this from the perspective of the satay. Its aroma has the power to pierce the tumult of sensory impressions; its spicy savor can drown it out entirely with the first mouth-filling, meaty bite. The satay as restaurant appetizer is a tasty triviality, a neutered remnant of the street vendor's vital original.

Making it ourselves, we bring back to life the blazing heat of fanned charcoal, the sizzle of the marinade as it vaporizes into the essence of itself, the intense aroma of the fragrant flares of dripping fat. And always the nervy mastery that satay-making requires; always the infinitesimal distance between success and ruin, a neatly flipped skewer and a painful burn. Get to this point and the scene I have described above is almost close enough to taste.

MASHED POTATOES

And if anyone thinks this amount of valuable space and number of words an extravagant tribute to pay to the dish in question— then he has never so much as made its acquaintance.
—Della Lutes, *The Country Kitchen*

A few nights ago, I entirely changed the way I make mashed potatoes. This may not surprise you, but it surprised me, because I was as certain as anyone needs to be that the way I usually prepared them was the best way there was—like so:

Peel the potatoes and cut them into large pieces. Place them in the steamer insert of a large saucepan, put about two cups of water in the bottom, cover, and bring to a boil. When the potatoes are completely soft all through but before they become mushy, remove the insert from the pot and pour out all but a quarter cup of the cooking liquid into a measuring cup. Then put the potato chunks into the pan, drop in a chunk of butter, and mash until the butter has melted and the potatoes are smooth and supple, working in as much of the reserved liquid as necessary, as well as salt and pepper to taste.

The result is soft but not without texture, full of potato flavor, and delicious. Consequently, for ever so long it's never occurred to me to do anything else.

Then, the other night, I was fixing supper—a fry-up of sliced bratwurst, onion, and cabbage—with mashed potatoes to be served on

the side. The cabbage requires a parboiling in a large pot of salted water to rid it of its slightly sulphurous undertones before it's chopped up
and added to the skillet (in this it is the reverse of the onion, which
needs to be fried before being added to liquid). And, lazily, not wanting
to dirty yet another pot, I dropped in the unpeeled potatoes too, leaving
them to percolate at the bottom, while the cabbage floated at the top.

Well, not just laziness. I had recently discovered that my own preferred potatoes for mashing—Yukon Gold—are remarkably easy to
peel after they've been boiled; something not true for other potatoes,
especially the red-skinned sort. Otherwise, in this instance I would have
peeled the potatoes first, one of those sensible decisions that often lead
to unremarkable results. Anyway, when a poke with a skewer revealed
the spuds were soft all through (this takes some time when you cook
them whole), I fished them out and, yelping a little from the heat,
peeled off the skin, put them in a bowl, chopped them up a bit with the
edge of a spatula to get things started, and then finished the job with
our waffle-faced masher.

Naturally, there was no potato water to thin them with, so, along
with the chunk of butter, I added some milk, just as my mother used to
do. I myself have always frowned on this, thinking that it "blurred" the
pure potato flavor. Well, forget that! Cooking them in their skins had
left them packed with the taste of spud, and deliciously creamy besides.
I said to Matt, as I set our plates on the table, "I think these are the best
mashed potatoes I've ever made."

•   •   •

Ordinarily the story would have ended right here, which wouldn't have
made it much worth reporting. But this experience, along with my comment to Matt, reminded me of one of the great moments in mashed potato meditations, which occurs at the beginning of Richard Olney's
autobiography, *Reflexions*.

> My first meal in Paris was in a glum little dining room for board-
> ers, in the Hôtel de l'Académie, at the corner of the rue de l'Uni-
> versité and rue des Saints-Pères. The plat du jour was "gibelotte,
> pommes mousseline"—rabbit and white wine fricassee with
> mashed potatoes. The gibelotte was all right, the mashed potatoes
> the best I had ever eaten, pushed through a sieve, buttered and

moistened with enough of their hot cooking water to bring them
to a supple, not quite pourable consistency—no milk, no cream,
no beating. I had never dreamt of mashing potatoes without milk
and, in Iowa, everyone believed that the more you beat them the
better they were.

There was a time when I would have felt, well, caught out by this
passage—an acolyte who had let a moment of weakness tempt him
from the true path. I have made and eaten those mashed potatoes; I
know how good they are. But I was ready for a change . . . just as, in
fact, Olney was himself. Young, in Paris, ready to be bewitched. And
here were these *pommes mousseline*, so different, so good, offering
themselves as the portal to a sea change in his opinions of what good
cooking was all about. He was, he now knew for sure, not in Iowa anymore. We are so used to this story, and from this particular perspective—an American in Paris—that we forget that it really is as much
about perspective per se as it is about culinary truth . . . or, perhaps,
about how much the two are inextricably tangled up together.

American country cooks are just as passionate about mashed potatoes as Richard Olney, and equally eloquent about the method he dismisses in the passage above. It only took a few moments of looking to
turn up several instances of this, starting with the testimony of Della
Lutes.

Now, mashed potatoes may be one of three things: the usual
soggy mess you encounter at most hotels and public eating places;
a little better quality met with in the home of the average cook; or
a light snowy drift of nutritive substance melting to the tongue,
sweet to the palate, welcomed by the stomach, and cherished in
memory.

To accomplish this miracle, a good quality of potato must be
chosen—of the later fall and winter varieties, and ripe. New potatoes should never be mashed. The potatoes should be peeled as
thinly as possible and thrown into cold water; then into boiling
water and boiled until quite done, but not broken. They are then
drained through a colander, and put back into the kettle in which
they were boiled, and which has been wiped dry. With a wire
masher, press them free from lumps. An old-fashioned wooden
masher is too severe in action, reducing the potatoes to pulp.

When the potatoes have been mashed, add one teaspoonful of
melted butter and one tablespoonful of cream to each cup of po-

tato—adding each gradually, with salt and pepper to season. Then with a wire whisk, or wooden spoon, beat them until they are light as a feather, white as a drift of snow, and as tempting as the apple was to Eve. Pile them in a serving dish, loosely, not packed or patted down with a spoon; dib a dab of butter here and there, sprinkle them gently with paprika, minced parsley, or chopped chives, and set in the oven for not longer than five minutes, or until the butter has melted.

I quote at length because the entire set of instructions demonstrates an instructive intensity of feeling. A page later, Lutes laments the decline of creamed asparagus ("I do not know whether people of to-day really do not care for [it], or whether a side dish and a spoon are so hopelessly out of date that the proper-minded modern housewife doesn't want to be caught [serving it]"), but she doesn't bother offering the recipe, let alone in such expansive detail.

Another instance is Ronni Lundy's fine book on Southern country cooking *Shuck Beans, Stack Cakes, and Honest Fried Chicken*, which devotes two-plus pages to mashed potatoes, including sidebars on the perfect pot for making mashed potatoes (can't buy it anymore) and the perfect masher (the waffle-faced one, not the curved-bar one). Lundy flatly states that her mother's mashed potatoes are "the finest mashed potatoes in the world." How come? "The secret is in the mashing, the whipping, and the butter—all done to excess and then some." Or as her mother puts it herself: "The more you beat 'em, the better they are."

Furthermore, Lundy's mother used a wooden spoon to whip them up. She would have no truck with a whisk or, especially, with an electric beater, used by more than one otherwise respectable Southern cook to lighten the load. "They just won't taste right." I don't know about you, but I'm a bit awed by the image of this white-haired old lady beating the dickens out of a large bowl of mashed potatoes with a wooden spoon. Farm families were big and they ate a lot, and this was merely—don't forget—a side dish . . . one that just happened to require biceps hard as baseballs and wrists of spun steel. If you think I'm exaggerating, just try it yourself. The first time I did, I had barely gotten started when I snapped the wooden spoon in half.

This is what I mean by perspective. These mashed potatoes emblemize an ethic that prided itself on hard physical work. There's not a hint of "you deserve a break today" in this kind of cooking, and it's a good reason why such a recipe wouldn't find much favor nowadays, delicious or no. After all, mashed potatoes are the epitome of comfort food, and this version just doesn't match the image that phrase is supposed to convey.

In this regard, they remind me of ironed sheets, which my mother probably still considers the height of homely luxury. Of course, most sheets now come out of the clothes dryer already "ironed," but that's not really the point. When she grew up, sheets, after they were washed, were fed through a clothes wringer, hung up to dry, and then ironed with a mangle. The sensation of climbing into bed between crisp, fresh sheets was the counterbalance to a lot of hard physical work. You need the one to truly relish the other.

Finally, my curiosity having been aroused, I wanted to track down an actual recipe for Olney's magical *pommes mousseline*. I couldn't find a recipe for them in his own work, but—by sheer blind luck—I did come across one in Raymond Sokolov's odd little book *How to Cook*. As a reporter for *Newsweek* in the mid-sixties, he was sent to Alsace to cover the awarding of a third (and highest) Michelin star to the Auberge de l'Ill. Sokolov's son, Michael, then an infant, wasn't ready yet to dig into foie gras baked in a brioche, but the chef knew just what to serve him—mashed potatoes. Sokolov writes, "But they called them *mousseline*, muslin. Those mashed potatoes deserved their French name, for they were as soft as fine sheets and as white and pure."

He then proceeds to give us the recipe: Quarter the unpeeled potatoes and boil them in just enough water to cover. Remove them when they are tender but before they turn soft, peel them while they're still hot, and push the pieces through a potato ricer. Put the result back into the pot and gently cook out any excess water. Then, with a whisk, beat the potato purée vigorously as you add first a chunk of butter and then scalded milk. "Add salt to taste and continue beating until the mashed potatoes are very light and almost frothy."

What, gentle reader, are we to make of that?

GO·FRY·AN·EGG

Anybody, almost, can fry an egg wrong.
—Martha McCulloch-Williams, *Dishes & Beverages*
of the Old South

It used to be so easy to fry an egg. After you lifted out the bacon from the skillet, you dropped in the egg and spooned the sizzling fat over the white. It took barely a minute to cook, and it was just the way a fried egg should be, with a brown-flecked, crispy undercoating, a tender field of fully cooked egg white, and, dead center, a liquid yolk that spilled out its deep yellow contents the moment you pricked it with a fork. More delicate appetites could request that the cook prepare it "over easy"—a task that requires dextrous spatula work. The yolk, neatly tucked beneath a blanket of white, still ran, if not quite as freely. And those who liked their egg yolks cooked through . . . well, I believe they used to be run out of town on a rail. (No, no. Let's just say that, for them, frying an egg has never posed a problem and never will.)

Today, of course, there is no bacon in the pan, and, to be honest about it, no egg either—at least not with any frequency. I rarely weigh in with nutritional advice: I write about what I like to eat, not what I think you (or I) ought to eat. However, in this instance, our subject is too entwined with the sometimes oblique influence of several decades of persistent propaganda to successfully separate it. However stubbornly you resist such advice, eventually it can wear you down. You start making compromises, often without noticing it. I have continued to eat eggs regularly, but, except for days when I'm feeling low, I have greatly cut down the butter/bacon/sausage quota, far beyond where I can fry my eggs in a flood tide of grease. And, like many people, lacking this assist, at first I found it nearly impossible to fry an egg in a nonstick pan with a slip of butter and produce, simultaneously, a firmly cooked white and a runny yolk, sunny-side up.

When I turned to my cookbook collection for some advice, I found that, for the most part, the problem was solved by sheer elision. The usually reliable Elaine Corn, for instance, devotes a whole page to frying eggs in her *365 Ways to Cook Eggs* but, when push comes to shove, leaves her reader in the lurch. "Remove from the pan when whites are completely set and yolks are nearly set and still very yellow-orange." Easy to say; not so easy to do.

The closest the French come to what we call a fried egg is the curiously named *oeuf sur le plat*. It is cooked in a bit of butter in a small heatproof individual gratin dish (*le plat*) or a tiny skillet made expressly for this purpose (it keeps the egg whites from spreading out, which they see as a sin). An *oeuf sur le plat* can be prepared either by baking it in the oven or by cooking it on top of the stove. In the latter instance, a lid is often slapped on the pan as soon as the eggs start cooking. The steam is thus contained and cooks the whites from the top. For the unskilled, the result is what is technically called steamfried eggs—identifiable by a glaze of white over the yolk . . . and by the flood of water that falls into the pan when you lift off the lid. Splitsecond timing can, it is true, overcome this, but that proved too much for me, at least first thing in the morning. So I tried to improve on the idea.

Initially, this meant putting a small cast-iron frying pan onto high heat a little before starting my eggs in another skillet over moderate heat. When the eggs were cooked on the bottom, I held the cast-iron skillet, now fiercely hot, directly over the eggs. This certainly worked: the whites solidified just seconds before the heat sufficiently penetrated the potholder to make me yelp and drop the skillet. Proximity to pain prompts refinement. I realized that if I left the toaster oven turned on after I removed my toast, I could use it as a salamander. Sliding in the pan of eggs the moment the uncooked whites began to glaze on top, I found that thirty seconds under the glowing toaster element rendered them perfectly done. (If you don't have a toaster oven, or one that can accommodate an 8-inch skillet—the right size for two eggs—preheating the broiler accomplishes the same trick.)*

• • •

> Fried eggs, according to the English way, are not to be thought of: they are a villainy. The egg is fried with a very little butter or bacon fat, in a large frying-pan—spreads out, and becomes on its edges thin and hard as parchment.
> —E. S. Dallas, *Kettner's Book of the Table* (1877)†

Naturally, at about the same time I had worked all this out, nutritionists began to realize that their demonizing of fat had had the unintended consequence of making us fatter (the equation fat = fat proved a bit simplistic) and may actually have harmed our health. The body needs fat, as long—it is now thought—as that fat isn't saturated, or, worse yet, hydrogenated. So, what had been thrown out the front door was now being gingerly let back in via the rear one. I could cook my eggs in a tablespoon or two of, say, extra-virgin olive oil, without any detriment to my health. Well, maybe.

The idea of cooking eggs in some medium other than butter or bacon fat is not as alien to the American breakfast table as it might at first seem. The only foreign fried egg dish to win wide popularity in this country is huevos rancheros, about which Bill and Cheryl Alters Jamison remark in *A Real American Breakfast*: "It's perhaps a prejudice

---

*Another way French cooks finish up an *oeuf sur le plat* is to use the point of a paring knife to poke holes in the white as it cooks, allowing the heat of the pan up to reach the surface of the egg. This gives the cooked white a tatty, patchwork look, like something proudly brought home by a five-year-old from kindergarten. But it works.

†Eneas Sweetland Dallas was born in Jamaica in 1828, came to England when he was four, and grew up to become a British literary critic, theorist, and, when he could afford to be, a bon vivant. He wrote much of *Kettner's Book of the Table* at café tables in Paris, when not forced by failing finances to reside in London. Kettner was a well-known Soho restaurateur of the time, and it is rumored that he paid Dallas in meals rather than cash to have the book identified as his. If Dallas had been given proper credit—it wasn't until the book was reprinted in 1968 that he was identified as its true author—he would today most likely be considered the father of literary food writing. His recipes are not only good but placed in a larger narrative that weaves together historical research, literary allusion, witty commentary, and very practical recommendations (for readers of that time, of course) regarding shops and suppliers. The book was an immediate success when it appeared in 1877, but Dallas received neither royalties nor regard, and died two years later in abject poverty. He was fifty-one.

from the years we've lived in the Southwest and traveled in Mexico, but huevos rancheros seems to us the perfection of fried eggs. Nothing brings out the earthy freshness of an egg better to us than the piquancy of a chile salsa and the corn tang of a tortilla."

While it's true that many Mexicans prefer to fry the eggs in lard rather than vegetable oil, the latter has become equally authentic—health concerns quite apart—now that good homemade lard has become more expensive and hence less freely used in that country.

HUEVOS RANCHEROS
[Serves 4]

When making this dish, I lean toward the more rustic (chunky) style of the tomato-chile sauce. The cherry tomatoes can be quickly prepared in a food processor fitted with a steel blade. Pulse them gently a few times—just enough to chop them up. It doesn't matter that some pieces are larger than others. I know that olive oil is rarely used in Mexican cooking, but I like what it does to this sauce.

THE NIGHT BEFORE, ROAST THE CHILES
AND PREPARE THE SAUCE:
6 to 8 red or green serrano chiles (see note)
1 tablespoon extra-virgin olive oil
1 small onion, finely minced
1 garlic clove, minced
1 pound cherry tomatoes, coarsely chopped (see note)
salt and powdered red chile, to taste

Heat a small cast-iron or other sturdy skillet over medium-high heat. Put in the chiles and cook, turning frequently, until they are blistered and spotted with black on all sides. Remove and let cool. When they can be handled comfortably, cut them in half lengthwise, remove the stem, core, and seeds, and coarsely chop them, skin and flesh together. Divide the chopped chiles in half, putting one portion in a small bowl in the refrigerator.

Heat the oil in a medium skillet. When it is hot, put in the minced onions and cook these, stirring, until they are translucent and start to brown at the edges. Add the minced garlic and cook for a minute or two more. Then add half of the minced chiles and the chopped tomatoes. Turn up the heat and cook, stirring constantly, until the tomatoes are fully cooked and reduced to a chunky sauce. Season to taste with the salt and powdered red chile. Remove to a bowl, let cool, cover, and refrigerate overnight.

Cook's Notes. Serrano chiles are moderately hot. For a gentler heat, substitute jalapeños. Cherry tomatoes give the sauce more body and more tomato flavor. However, 2 or so ripe ordinary tomatoes may be substituted.

THE NEXT MORNING, PREPARE THE HUEVOS RANCHEROS:
> tomato-chile ranchero sauce (above)
> 4 tablespoons peanut or other vegetable oil
> 4 medium-size corn tortillas
> 8 eggs
> ¼ cup crumbled queso fresco (see note)
> reserved roasted chile bits (above)
> chopped fresh cilantro
> refried beans (see note)

Preheat oven to warm. Put four 6-inch gratin dishes or similar-size plates in the oven to heat. Put the tomato sauce in a small pot and warm it up while preparing the tortillas and the eggs.

Heat the oil in a skillet. When it is hot, briefly fry each tortilla on both sides until well heated but not crisp. Use tongs to move each tortilla as soon as it is done to one of the waiting dishes in the oven.

Break the eggs into the hot oil. Fry these, spooning the oil over the whites to help them cook through. While the eggs are frying, remove the dishes from the oven. The moment the whites are cooked through, place 2 eggs on each tortilla. Then top with an equal portion of the sauce and the crumbled queso fresco, garnishing each with some of the reserved chile bits and the chopped fresh cilantro leaves. Serve with a scoop of piping hot refried beans on the side.

Cook's Notes. Queso fresco is a dry "squeaky" cheese, with a bland but rather salty taste. The usual substitute is Monterey Jack, but crumbled feta is closer to the original. Refried beans deserve an essay of their own. Until they get it, it's worth pointing out that some canned versions are not at all bad. Look for those made with as few ingredients as possible; better to add your own garlic and minced chiles than consume the dross that the canner tosses in. El Rio is a brand we use: just beans, water, soybean oil, and salt.

It's impossible to write about huevos rancheros without also mentioning a tasty variation from Jalisco, described by Diana Kennedy in *Mexican Regional Cooking*, called *huevo a la sorpresa*, or "egg surprise." To make it requires acquiring the knack for making a corn tortilla puff up when you're cooking it. This happens regularly when you don't intend for it to, but when you count on it happening, the kitchen god laughs. You'll find you have better success with freshly made corn tortillas. Otherwise it is a matter of speed and hot oil, because the tortillas won't puff once they're crispy. The best way to go about this is to practice getting them to swell while making huevos rancheros; once you feel confident, shoot for these.

FRIED EGG IN A TORTILLA POCKET
[Serves 1]

1 egg
salt and pepper to taste
1 teaspoon olive oil
1 fresh corn tortilla

Gently break an egg into a small juice glass and season it with salt and pepper. Heat a little olive oil in a skillet. When it is hot, slip in a fresh corn tortilla. Fry it until the edges just begin to dry out, then flip it over. Continue cooking it until the bottom begins to color. Flip it over again. At this point, the tortilla should puff up. Slice open the pocket just enough so that you can slip the raw egg into it from the glass. Reseal the pocket by pressing the edges together until they hold. Continue frying until the tortilla is golden brown. Quickly drain the tortilla on paper toweling and serve it with any or all of the accompaniments to huevos rancheros.

• • •

Spanish people have a weakness for fried eggs. They are not elegant and, being usually one of the cheapest meals available, cannot be said to enhance the social status of anyone who eats them in public. However, a Spaniard will always opt for a couple of fried eggs when at a loss for what to eat. All restaurants are ready for this emergency . . . In Spain the ability to fry an egg has long been considered 'the yardstick by which culinary skills are measured, and it is therefore most derogatory to remark that someone "doesn't even know how to fry an egg."
—Alicia Ríos, *The Heritage of Spanish Cooking*

The Spanish (and the French, when it comes to the *véritable oeuf frit*) have a somewhat more complex view than we regarding the art of frying an egg. For them a true *huevo frito* is cooked in deep hot fat— pretty much the way you would poach an egg in boiling water. Frying an egg this way is easier and certainly more exciting; instead of spreading out in a flat disk, the egg white instantly puffs up into a cloud-shaped mass. In seconds, the bottom has turned an appetizing brown. A quick flip over to finish off the top—*et voilà*. In less than a minute the egg is on your plate. And because it has no contact with the bottom of the pan, it remains compact, even kind of round if you are deft enough to perform the chefly trick of folding the white over the top of the yolk with a spatula or wooden spoon. The Spanish call these egg balls *huevos abuñuelados* (or "eggs turned into fried dough balls").

Admittedly, being rotund, crispy without, and tender within, these are a different animal from the usual (American) fried egg. I find them fun to cook and quite enjoyable to eat—pop one into a toasted roll and you have a killer fried egg sandwich. Nor are they, as you might expect, particularly greasy, since they cook almost instantly in the sizzling fat. And anyone who finds soft egg whites slightly queasy-making will adore them. (The yolk, of course, should remain runny.)

If there's anything not to like about them, it's that the process can be a bit messy. You can limit the splatter—but not eliminate it—by warming the eggs to room temperature before breaking them into the boiling oil. Fortunately, in the right pan (see below), the grease doesn't travel far; I get most of it by laying some butcher paper or a flattened paper bag down a safe distance from the burner.

You'll notice from the quotation above that the Spanish don't consider fried eggs as, especially, a breakfast dish but as an appropriate quick meal whatever the hour. This helps explain why fried eggs play a larger role in their cuisine than they do in ours, where, unfairly, they are unlikely ever to come to mind other than at breakfast (except perhaps at eateries that offer breakfast dishes all through the day). In any case, the Spanish argue about whether the best fried egg has *puntilla* (a crispy, lacy border) or not, and whether it is better to fry it with chorizo, which gives the egg whites a ruddy varnish, or *morcilla*, blood sausage, the soft texture of which better complements that of egg yolk. But of the many variations on this theme, my own favorite is *huevos fritos* served on top of a generous heap of *migas*, a kind of garlic-flavored crouton.

SPANISH FRIED EGGS WITH *MIGAS*
[Serves 4]

THE NIGHT BEFORE, START THE *MIGAS*:
8 ounces (about ½ loaf) stale bread (see note)
1 cup water
1 teaspoon kosher salt

Cut the bread, including its crust, into small cubes. Put these into a bowl. Dissolve the salt in the water and sprinkle this, bit by bit, over the bread, tossing the cubes as you do. Stop when the bread feels uniformly moist; don't let it get soaking wet. Use some of the remaining water to dampen a clean dish towel. Wrap the bread cubes in this and knot the ends together. Let this bundle sit for several hours (overnight) in the refrigerator.

THE NEXT MORNING, PREPARE THE *MIGAS*
AND FRY THE EGGS:
8 eggs
1 small yellow onion
1 garlic clove
1 small or ½ large red bell pepper, cored and seeded
1 small chile pepper, cored and seeded
2 or 3 sprigs parsley
1 cup extra-virgin olive oil

bread cubes prepared the night before (above)
1 teaspoon Spanish paprika
salt to taste

Put the eggs (in their shells) in a bowl and fill this with hot tap water. Set aside. Dice the onion, garlic, bell pepper, chile, and parsley. Heat 2 tablespoons of the olive oil in a large skillet. When the oil is hot, add the vegetables and sauté until the onion is translucent and the peppers are tender. Stir in the bread cubes and, gently turning them occasionally with a spatula, lightly brown them on all sides. As you do, sprinkle over the paprika, pinch by pinch, until all the cubes have been seasoned with it.

When done, the *migas* will be brown and crispy on the outside and mouth-meltingly tender within. Divide them among four shallow soup bowls while you heat the remaining olive oil in a high-sided 8-inch skillet. When the surface of the oil is shimmering, slip in the first egg. Once the whites have puffed up and the edges are crackly, briefly heat a skimmer or slotted spoon in the hot fat (otherwise the egg will stick) and either gently submerge the egg in the hot fat, or carefully flip it over, to finish cooking the egg white. All this should happen before a minute has elapsed. Slip the egg onto paper toweling to drain and proceed with the next one. When all the eggs are cooked, place them on top of the waiting bowls of *migas*, salt to taste, and serve at once.

Cook's Notes. Skillet: Choose an 8-inch skillet (or smaller) with high sides, since only one or, at most, two eggs should be fried at the same time. It needn't be expensive—I found a T-Fal skillet at Wal-Mart for $10.95 that is perfect for the task.

Cooking Oil: Use an inexpensive extra-virgin olive oil. Despite what you may have read, there is no problem using it for this kind of frying, and it imparts a delicious flavor to the eggs.

Eggs: Put these in hot tap water for a few minutes to warm them through before cooking them. As a safety precaution, it is wise to then break them into individual dishes (custard cups are perfect). Slide the eggs out of these into the hot fat.

Bread: This should be an Italian or French "country-style" loaf, made of only flour, salt, water, and yeast or sourdough starter, with a coarse, chewy interior. Note that to make proper *migas*, it must be a few days old.

As it turns out, olive oil is an excellent medium for frying eggs, even if you use just a few tablespoons. Frying eggs in browned butter has always raised the dish to a higher power, and extra-virgin olive oil's throaty edge turns out to be the perfect equivalent, as in this tasty concoction.

FRIED EGGS IN OLIVE OIL WITH CAPERS
[Serves 1]

2 tablespoons fruity extra-virgin olive oil
2 eggs
salt and black pepper to taste
2 pieces of hot toast
3 or 4 minced capers
1 teaspoon caper brine (see note)
pinch of hot red pepper flakes

Pour the oil into a skillet and heat it over a medium-high flame. When the surface of the oil shimmers, break in the eggs, spooning the oil over the whites to help them cook. Season with the salt and black pepper.

As soon as the eggs are done, remove them to the toast. If you wish, pour off some of the oil. Add the minced capers and their brine, along with the pinch of hot red pepper flakes, then turn up the heat a bit and swirl the mixture about for a minute to let most of the brine cook off. Pour this fragrant sauce over the eggs and serve at once.

Cook's Notes. Some minced fresh garlic stirred into the oil a minute before the eggs are done further enhances the dish. If caper brine is not to your taste, omit it and replace it with twice as much sherry vinegar.

In poorer areas of the Mediterranean, eggs often replace meat as the focal point of a dish. These are mostly scrambled but sometimes fried, as in the Greek *avga skordostoumbi*, where a garlicky tomato sauce is made in a skillet of fried potatoes and, when it has thickened, eggs are broken in and cooked sunny-side up. They are also eaten as street food, as in the following dish, the Egyptian Egg McMuffin.

FRIED EGGS WITH GARLIC AND MINT
[Serves 4]

2 loaves pita bread
4 garlic cloves, or to taste
2 tablespoons fresh lemon juice
4 tablespoons extra-virgin olive oil
8 eggs
½ teaspoon dried mint
salt and black pepper to taste

Preheat oven to 200°F. Wrap the pita together in aluminum foil. Put this bundle on a cookie sheet and let the bread warm in the oven.

Crush the garlic cloves and mix with the lemon juice. Heat the olive oil in a large skillet over medium flame. Add the garlic-lemon mixture, frying it until the garlic turns translucent. Slide in the eggs, as quickly as possible. Crumble the dried mint over them, then baste them with the garlic-and-lemon-flavored oil as they cook. Season with salt and pepper.

Remove the heated pita from the oven and cut each loaf in half around its circumference to make 4 disks. Slip two fried eggs onto each of these and drizzle with the cooking oil. Serve at once.

Cook's Note. If garlic in the morning seems a bit much, omit it and the mint, put the eggs directly into the hot oil, and pour the lemon juice over them as they cook. Baste with the cooking oil until done and serve on warmed pita as described above.

Naturally, other cooking oils can be used instead of olive oil, especially those that complement the taste of the eggs. For example, Cristine MacKie's remark in *Life and Food in the Caribbean* that "frying eggs in coconut oil is the finest way you can cook a fresh egg" got me to seek out some virgin coconut oil and try it.* She was right—if you love the

---

*My interest in coconut oil comes from the discovery that in Indonesia, Malaysia, and southern India, that oil is used to give dishes attractive and distinctive flavor notes—information that is rarely transferred to cookbooks written for American readers. Ordinary coconut oil is pressed from copra, the commercial term for dried coconut meat. "Virgin" coconut oil is extracted directly from fresh coconut milk, often by the small cooperatives where the coconuts are grown. The comparison with extra-virgin olive oil is not in the least far-fetched, since it, too, undergoes no further refinement, whereas "pure" coconut oil, like "pure" olive oil, is processed in a way that denatures the oil's character. Virgin coconut oil can be found in many

taste of coconut. For those who like it tempered with other flavors, I worked up the following dish, inspired by a Brazilian recipe, which works in the taste of coconut in a very delicious way.

FRIED EGGS WITH BANANAS, FRESH CHILES, AND ONIONS IN COCONUT OIL
[Serves 4]

2 firm ripe bananas
¼ cup virgin coconut oil (preferably) or peanut oil
1 garlic clove, minced
1 medium onion, finely chopped
4 to 6 serrano chiles, cored, seeded, and chopped
8 eggs
salt to taste

Peel the bananas and cut them into 1-inch rounds. Cut the center slices into four pieces and the end slices into two. Heat 1 tablespoon of the coconut oil in a large nonstick skillet over a medium flame. When the oil is hot, add the garlic, onion, and chiles. Once the garlic and onion have turned translucent, add the chunks of banana. Fry these, turning them gently and not too often, until their exposed surfaces have begun to brown.

Pour the remaining 3 tablespoons of oil into a separate skillet over a medium flame. When it is hot, break in the eggs. Fry these, spooning the oil over the whites to help cook their tops. When done, transfer to warmed plates and cover with the banana-chile hash.

Finally, this recipe. I like it because it is very good and because it is the reverse of a dish like huevos rancheros. Instead of being our own take on a foreign dish, it is an immigrant's take on one of our own dishes . . . and is refracted, therefore, through a very different culinary sensibility.

---

natural food stores or mail-ordered from Tropical Traditions. (Their website describes the traditional way this oil is produced.) P.O. Box 333; Springville, CA 93265; (866) 311-2626; www.tropicaltraditions.com.

Adapted from the recipe in Ken Hom's wonderful *Easy Family Recipes from a Chinese-American Childhood* for his mother's take on American fried eggs.

FRIED EGGS WITH OYSTER SAUCE
[Serves 2]

2 tablespoons peanut oil
2 scallions, trimmed and minced
4 eggs
salt and black pepper to taste
3 tablespoons oyster sauce

Heat a wok or large frying pan over high heat until it is hot. Add the oil; when it is very hot and slightly smoking, toss in the minced scallions and stir them well. Turn the heat down to low and crack each egg into the wok, keeping the yolks intact.

Continue to pan-fry the eggs over low heat until they are crispy and set. Salt and pepper to taste. Carefully remove the eggs from the wok with a spatula and let them drain on paper towels. Place them on a platter, drizzle with oyster sauce, and serve at once.

And so it goes. A fried egg may be a simple thing, but it is too good not to take seriously. Raymond Sokolov, in *How to Cook*, tells how the legendary French chef Fernand Point taught his apprentices how to fry eggs as their first lesson in cooking: "To impress upon them the delicacy of the process, he made them hold the skillet over a candle until its heat caused the whites to turn opaque." This entertaining image certainly makes the point, but it is, perhaps, a little . . . overearnest. Better to conclude with this evocative quote from Edouard de Pomiane, which will resonate with any fried-egg lover: "Salt. Eat, dipping your bread into the yolk, into the white, and into the butter. This is not being well brought up, but it is exquisite."

• • •

DO I DARE TO EAT AN EGG?

This may come as a surprise, but I am extremely suspicious about nutritional advice. The problem isn't that some of it is good and some of it bad but that it is nearly impossible to distinguish between the two. Because there is no unifying perspective to link the parts into a comprehensible whole, advice from one direction often contradicts that from another; what is emphatically asserted as incontrovertible at one point in time is, a little while later, quietly retracted.

Take eggs. Fifty years ago they were considered the perfect food, loaded with nutrition, easy for anyone, young or old, rich or poor, to afford, cook, and digest. Children, invalids, the elderly—eggs were what you fed them. Then the cholesterol scare arrived, and eggs—at least egg yolks—were vilified. Fortunes were made by selling products that contained egg whites only or that replaced eggs altogether with supposedly healthier facsimiles.

Then it was discovered that it's not so much the cholesterol as the saturated fat you ingest that puts your heart at risk. Eggs are high in cholesterol but relatively low in saturated fat, so the American Heart Association hemmed and hawed and finally said that it was probably okay to eat one egg a day (if you must . . .). More recently still, there has been some actual backtracking. In 2002, the American Council on Science and Health released a report that states in part:

> For most people, the avoidance of eggs is undesirable and unnecessary. It limits variety in the diet and keeps people from taking advantage of the benefits of eggs, including their high nutrient density, low cost, convenience, and usefulness in recipes. Excessively strong advice to minimize the use of eggs may be especially detrimental to people with limited incomes, who need low-cost protein-rich foods, and to elderly people, for whom the high nutritional value, low cost, ease of preparation, and ease of chewing of eggs are all important advantages.*

No doubt, by the time you are holding this book in your hands, all this will have been tossed into the blender again. However, what we can say with some amount of certainty is that eggs are loaded with nutrition,

---

*Meister, Kathleen, *The Role of Eggs in the Diet: Update* (New York: American Council on Science and Health, 2002).

affordable, easy for anyone to cook, and eminently digestible. But if it turns out they're not good for you—you might not want to eat them.

Unfortunately, this is not where our egg problems end. The FDA now insists that the way to ensure that an egg is completely safe from salmonella is to cook it until it turns to rubber. "You just need to cook your eggs thoroughly—no sunny-side up, no over easy," says the FDA Commissioner. "This is a case when it's better to be safe than sorry."[*] But is it? The Centers for Disease Control and Prevention estimates that one out of every twenty thousand eggs is contaminated with salmonella.[†] Statistically, this means that if you eat, say, two hundred and fifty eggs a year, you'll run into one contaminated egg every eighty years.

Those odds lengthen considerably if the eggs are fresh (buy locally), have been kept chilled until you eat them (the bacteria remain quiescent when cold), and have been heated throughout to 140°F for three minutes (at which point the bacteria die). Egg whites coagulate around 144°F, while yolks don't set until they reach at least 149°F. This means that if you get an egg out of the skillet as soon as the whites have set, you can still have a runny yolk while minimizing the risk of getting sick. Do I guarantee it? Of course not. But that's where I'm content to leave it . . . at least until I turn eighty.

THE GRIST ON GRITS

> When I first moved to Georgia [from Tennessee], I hated grits. But
> I finally found out, grits don't have a taste really. You have to add
> the taste. So you add salt and butter and gravy or whatever and
> hell, they're great.
>
> —Chet Atkins

Southerners, God bless them, can try one's patience sometimes, and
never more than when the talk turns to grits. It isn't only that they get
so high and mighty on the subject, implying that we Northerners just
don't "get" grits—but that they themselves are so often clueless about
them. True, they can dither endlessly about whether the word takes a
singular or a plural verb—as if anyone gives a damn.* And the same
blowhard who intones "grits is good" is, more often than not, perfectly
content to join the vast majority of his fellows in consuming a bowl of
something all but indistinguishable from, and certainly equally as char-
acterless as, Cream of Wheat. Hey, it isn't we Northerners who are
scarfing down the denatured, tasteless mush mass-produced by Albers,
Jim Dandy, Martha Washington, or Quaker Oats and piling on the butter and cheese that make it palatable.

In this regard, Chet Atkins is just telling it like it is. *Craig Clai-*

---

*You do? Well, some plural nouns—checkers, news—take a singular verb, while others—
pants, scissors—usually take a plural one. But there's still another group—means, proceeds,
headquarters—that can take either (although the fact that they end with an "s" makes us
nervous about using them with a singular verb). It's not grammatical law but usage that deter-
mines this. Grits is, grits are—it's your call.

borne's Southern Cooking has five recipes for grits, four of which call for at least a stick of butter and a cup of grated cheese and one, for grits casserole, which calls for nearly a pound of butter, a quart of milk, a cup of chopped Gruyère, and half a cup of grated Parmesan! Furthermore, there's not a recipe in the book for plain boiled grits. If Southerners want to know what Northerners think of when they hear the word "grits," I'll be glad to tell them: trouser buttons popping across the room.

I had my first bowl of grits in a bustling eatery in Deland, Florida, part of a breakfast order that also included eggs, fried ham, and biscuits. It was a decent enough meal, but there was nothing about the grits that caught my attention, let alone gave me the sense I had met a mate for life. And that would have been that, I fear, had I not, a good decade later, read Joni Miller's *True Grits: The Southern Foods Mail-Order Guide*, which, as the title suggests, treats the subject with genuine seriousness.

Unlike mass-produced grits, those from old-fashioned, small-scale Southern grist mills have not been stripped of the heart, or germ, of the corn, the part that's high in iron, niacin, and riboflavin. You can see for yourself that it's there—little dark speckles are the tip-off. These buff-colored grits have a rougher texture than fine-milled commercial grits; the flavor is straightforward, authentic, and full. When you're eating them you can really taste the corn, something that rarely comes through when you eat steel-ground grits. Cooked up, these artisanal grits will be homier-looking and -tasting and considerably thicker than commercial grits.

At the time I read Joni's book, Matt and I were living in Maine, and the sheer density of old-fashioned grits made them immediately appealing as winter breakfast fare. We ordered some from one of the mills she recommended. They were everything that she promised . . . and one thing she didn't mention: they took a devilishly long time to cook. The directions on long-cooking breakfast cereals do tend to shamelessly understate cooking times, but those that come with old-fashioned grits are often downright lies.

Even if you put them over a rip-roaring fire and stand there the whole time, stirring madly, they take a good forty minutes to become reasonably edible; at a safe-to-leave-them-unattended simmer, they can easily consume an hour. In days of yore, when a pot of grits was just one item in a breakfast symphony of frying, baking, and boiling, that didn't matter. But as the sole object of morning sustenance this endless stove time is, frankly, maddening.

I did eventually find a solution to this problem, which I'll share in a moment. The point here is that, having tasted the real thing, I wanted to find one. Good grits, it turns out, give you plenty to chew on. Their taste may hold a narrow place on the flavor spectrum, but that doesn't mean it's limited, especially if the grits are ground from white flint corn. Yellow stone-ground grits (if you can find any) give the taste buds an immediate hit of fresh corn, but the flavor quickly fades away. Conversely, the more delicate taste of white grits is surprisingly long lasting. You can take a spoonful and let it linger in your mouth a bit, just to savor it.

When other ground whole-grain products are cooked for eating, their flavor usually has grassy overtones and the texture a monotonous uniformity. Grits are different. Their flavor has a brightness to it, and the texture is complex. When whole dried corn is ground between cool, slow-turning granite millstones, not only are the grain's full range of nutrients and flavor nuances preserved, but the resulting consistency enrobes harder bits of kernel (the grits) in a delicate corn-flour mush (the tender heart).

When, recently, I discovered the following slow cooker–based "set and forget" cooking process, I started eating stone-ground grits for breakfast most days of the week. I don't deny that I add a few items to make sure I'm not deprived of my daily quota of saturated fat, but while these things heighten my pleasure, they are by no means the reason for it. This Northern boy simply loves his grits.

TRUE GRITS, MY WAY
[Serves 1]

Now, ideally, I would have a fuzzy-logic Japanese rice cooker to make my grits. But those are, alas, a bit pricey. So, instead, I use a 1-quart slow cooker that cost me five dollars, which I found at Wal-Mart one holiday season in a display of kitchen stocking stuffers. I've never seen it there since, but Rival sells a 1½-quart model (3215) that, though several times more expensive, has the advantage of a real glass lid and a removable insert with a nonstick coating (grits do stick). The following

*recipe slightly adapts the traditional 1-to-4 proportion of grits to water,
since more of the latter is absorbed during the long slow cooking.*

> ½ cup traditional stone-ground white corn grits
> 2¼ to 2½ cups water
> 1 teaspoon kosher salt
> 1 tablespoon butter
> "withs" (see below)

The Night Before: If you are using a slow cooker without a nonstick
surface, coat the bottom half of the pot with some of the butter. (This
won't keep the grits from sticking but will make it much easier to
scrape them away from the sides.) Put the grits in the slow cooker and
gently pour over the water. Use a skimmer to remove any chaff that
floats to the top. (Or leave it and get a little more fiber in your diet.)
Stir in the salt, drop in the rest of the butter, adjust the pot temperature
to "low" if you have that option (I don't), plug in the unit, and go
to bed.

The Following Morning: When you're ready for breakfast, use a
spatula to scrape away any grits that have stuck to the sides. Stir these
browned bits back into the general mass and get to work on the
"withs"—the things you're going to have with your grits. These might
include:

Cheese. For upscale treatment, stir in some grated Parmesan or aged
Cheddar; to go proletarian, melt in a slice or two of American cheese.
The point isn't to drown the grits but to just add to the pleasure of its
company.

Garlic/Fried Onion. Not, of course, garlic salt or powder or granules but the real thing, freshly minced or put through a press. Add this
when you start cooking the grits for a subtle presence or 20 minutes before you serve them for a more assertive one. Thai fried red onion
flakes, which are a prime reason for visiting Asian markets, make a
splendid last-minute addition to grits.

Eggs. Here I mean eggs cooked directly in the grits. Use a spoon to
hollow out an egg-size hole in the hot grits and break in the egg. If
cooking two, make a separate hole for the second. Cover up the egg(s)
with more grits and cook for another 20 minutes, or until the egg white
is firm. Spoon out whole or stir into the grits just before serving.

Sausage/Ham. Either of these can be added the night before, but I find the meat a little cooked out by morning. So, instead, I crumble some breakfast sausage into the steaming grits and let it cook another 20 minutes before serving, and treat little cubes of country ham (or ham fat) the same way.

Peanut/Coconut Oil. Instead of butter, I sometimes add a tablespoon of Chinese peanut oil, which has more of a peanut taste than the domestic type. Very tasty. So is coconut oil—remember, it used to be the secret ingredient that made movie theater popcorn so distinctly delicious.

CornNuts. Okay, I admit it, this is a tad weird. But one evening I had a fistful left over from a snack attack and impulsively tossed them in with the grits. They cooked into tender little nuggets that upped the corn flavor a notch.

GRIT CAKES

Put any leftover grits in the refrigerator. When it's time to make the cakes, heat some butter or peanut oil in a skillet, pat the grits into hamburger-size patties, and fry them until golden and crunchy on both sides. Give them at least 15 minutes on the first side before turning them over. Note that these can be called "cakes" only by stretching the definition: they keep falling apart and you keep coaxing them back into shape with your spatula.

A NOTE ON HOMINY GRITS

Growing up in the North as I did, for a long time I believed that grits were ground from dried hominy (dried corn from which the hulls have been removed by soaking in lye or hydrated lime). I was wrong. It may be that at one time folks who had to "crack" their grits at home (whence comes the epithet "cracker" as applied to rural Southerners) did so from hominy, since it was hullless and easier to shatter. But the grits produced by old-fashioned grist mills are ground from plain dried corn, with the coarsest pieces of hull removed by sifting. The term "hominy grits" remains in use probably because the inhabitants of South Carolina's low country have always called *ordinary* corn grits "hominy grits." They have their reasons for doing so, but it only further muddles the general understanding of the term.

As it happens, thanks to the Southern food authority John T. Edge, I did find one place—Anson Mills—that grinds dried hominy into grits. While their superb Carolina Whole Hominy Quick Grits are milled fresh from the field-ripened new crop corn, the miller, Glenn Roberts, has experimentally prepared hominy grits by soaking the same corn in a solution made with ash from a local barbecue pit (a nice touch), redrying it, and then cracking it into grits. Although he doesn't sell it retail, Roberts kindly sent me some to sample. If you like hominy, you'll like real hominy grits: the same alkaline-flattened corn taste, the same water-soaked-popcorn texture. It is also much tenderer and cooks more quickly. But you could get almost identical results by giving a drained can of hominy a quick whir in a food processor and heating it up on the stove. The result might be oddly tasty, but it really isn't *grits*.

Sources

All the following mills produce grits from whole dried white (and sometimes yellow) corn kernels. Consequently, these grits must be refrigerated or frozen on arrival. Each mill grinds its grits in its own way, so textures can vary from pleasantly coarse to noticeably creamy.

Adams Mill. Their coarse speckled white corn grits are topnotch and very reasonably priced. 146 Industrial Drive; Dothan, AL 36303; (800) 239-4233.

Anson Mills separates the germ and meal, sifts and cleans the latter, then mixes the germ back in by hand. The result, which they call "Antebellum Style," is uniquely creamy for stone-ground grits. They offer white or yellow, put up in 12-ounce bags, with a minimum order of 4 bags. Among their other products are grits made from heirloom rice. 1922-C Gervais Street; Columbia, SC 29201; (803) 467-4122; www.ansonmills.com (a very informative website).

Falls Mill powers 1,500-pound hand-quarried millstones with a 32-foot overshot waterwheel. Their white corn grits—which are my current favorite—come in 2-pound, 5-pound, and 25-pound bags. Mini-mum order is 10 pounds. I order two 5-pound bags and store one in the freezer. 134 Falls Mill Road; Belvidere, TN 37306; (931) 469-7161.

Logan Turnpike Mill, located in the North Georgia Mountains, is the source of the delicious old-fashioned speckled white grits sold by Hoppin' John's of Charleston, SC (www.hoppinjohns.com). They can also be ordered directly from the mill, yellow or white, in 2-pound and 5-pound bags. 3485 Gainesville Highway; Blairsville, GA 30512; (800) 84-GRITS (844-7487).

Further Reading

True Grits: The Southern Foods Mail-Order Catalog, by Joni Miller, is still in print and more reliable than you might imagine for a mail-order guide published in 1990. It also serves as a superb encyclopedia of Southern foods. Still, Joni, fans continue to hope for an update.

Good Old Grits Cookbook, Bill Neal and David Perry. The late Bill Neal provided the recipes in this jeu d'esprit, while David Perry supplied the introductory text. Dishes range from the basic—cheese grits, sausage fried grits, shrimp and grits—to such upscale eating as quail on little grits cakes. You'll also find directions for making an old-fashioned redeye gravy–style Southern breakfast and a chapter devoted to Southern hominy dishes.

"Stone-Ground Revival," *Saveur,* November 2003. An in-depth look at and a deeply felt salute to grits by Southern food writer John T. Edge.

HORIÁTIKI SALÁTA

The Greek salad we get all too often in mom-and-pop corner restaurants [is] made with wet iceberg lettuce, hard tomatoes, and canned California black olives, dressed with Wishbone Italian Low-Cal Dressing.
  —Nancy Harmon Jenkins, *The Mediterranean Diet Cookbook*

Greek salad became part of my life when I worked for a while in downtown Boston at the Massachusetts Department of Welfare. The office was situated at the edge of Chinatown, and I probably ate more lunches there than anywhere else—dry-fried beef *chow fun* becoming a pillar of my personal gastronomy—but there were other destinations as well. One of these was a Greek-run breakfast and lunch place about a block away. It's not there anymore and I don't remember its name—I may not have known it then—but I do remember being there perfectly well. To order takeout, you waded through a dense cluster of crowded tables to the cooks' station in the rear and gave your order directly to the first short-order cook who let you catch his eye.

Although Greek-run, this was by no means a Greek restaurant. Their usual dishes were that of the standard greasy spoon—pot roast, stuffed pork chops, lamb stew . . . anything that would sell and sit well in a steam table for a few hours. But they did offer Greek salad. There was nothing special about it—iceberg lettuce, onion rings, a few tomato wedges, and some scraps of green pepper. Some feta was scattered over the top along with a severely rationed number—three? four?—of Kalamata olives. This, with a hunk of French bread and a pat of butter, was yours for $4.95.

In other words, it was very much the sort of Greek salad—right down to the commercial Italian dressing—Nancy Harmon Jenkins accurately skewers in the quotation cited above. Even so, I liked it very much. I grew up in a world where what interest salads had was in what went on them. In my experience up until then, the classier the salad the creamier the dressing and the more additions there were to toss on top—bacon bits, seasoned croûtons, crumbled "bleu" cheese.

This Greek salad, it's true, had elements of this—the olives, the feta—but here there was no sense of a cloak of richness thrown over the boringly bland. Even in its diluted—and hence tamed—state, the salad seemed to me to be a kind of bear pit, where one strong flavor after another was tossed into the melée to duke it out with the rest.

I would eventually learn that good leaf salads are exactly like this, too; the dressing, as delicious as it may be, playing the role not of the elegant enhancement but the necessary referee, bringing order and cohesiveness to a collation of peppery, pungent, aggressively vegetative greens. But I didn't know that sort of salad then, and so this one got me to think. And it did so all the more because, even then, my digestive system had trouble dealing with raw onion and raw green pepper and my palate was slow to warm to the bitterness of imported olives and the sharp goaty saltiness of this Greek cheese. But in combination, somehow, it all made sense.

Furthermore, it became downright delicious when I pulled out most of the crumb from the accompanying piece of French bread (to be buttered and eaten as a kind of cake for dessert) and crammed the salad into the crust, transforming it—oxymoronically—into a Greek Italian. Do Hellenes themselves ever eat it this way? My sources don't tell me. But they ought to; it's that good.

• • •

> Saláta to most Hellenes means one seasonal vegetable, served raw or cooked, hot or cold, seasoned with olive oil and lemon or vinegar . . . Villagers walk for miles to pick wild greens—radikia, vrouva, vlyta, endidia, and scarollia—as a special tribute to visitors.
>
> —Vilma Liacouras Chantiles, *The Food of Greece*

The pleasures of bread and salad are celebrated elsewhere in this book—what matters here is that this simulacrum set me off on a life-long search for the real thing. Well, you might think, just close your eyes and grab any Greek cookbook on the shelf. Yes, that's so. But consider. Is it called "Greek salad" in Greece? Probably not, you would guess, and, in fact, in that country it is called *horiátiki saláta*, or, roughly, villagers' salad. But country folk don't call it that, and, chances are, they don't eat it, either. *Horiátiki saláta* is an urban fantasy of country life; it has a flavor that the Greeks taste but that a recipe can't convey: yearning for the countryside.

This phenomenon is hardly an alien one. When Matt and I took a trip to New Brunswick, Canada, several summers ago, we noticed any number of restaurants advertising "hearty farm breakfasts." Invariably, these proved to be as hearty and rustic as any city coffee shop's morning special: two eggs, two strips of bacon, two pieces of toast. At least *horiátiki saláta* will most likely be delicious; when urban Greeks dream of the countryside, it is with serious longing.

What the taverna version does do, however, is condense into a single dish the humble villager's entire meal—the saláta itself, plus olives and a wedge of cheese. In doing so, it not only changes the dish, but introduces a very different set of signifiers. A typical instance of a villager's meal might be a bowl of the earliest green beans, boiled and eaten with a dressing of the local olive oil, a spoonful or two of *skordaliá* (the pungent bread- or potato-thickened amalgam of raw garlic and walnuts). This, some bread, and some goat's cheese are plenty enough to make a satisfying supper.

Notice that here, connection is all concrete: the villager has picked the beans, cured the olives, knows the goat whence came the cheese. This particularity is such that the central dish—the salad—has no need of any recipe, nor would one even vaguely come to mind . . . no more than you or I want instructions to scratch our nose. If a passerby happened to ask what supper had been, there would be no trouble giving it a name: *fasoulákia me lathi*, green beans dressed in oil. But, as befits countrymen of Heraclitus, who observed that you can never step into the same river twice, the phrase would be understood as describing a dish that is in a state of perpetual—albeit gentle—flux . . . as any kind of cooking tends to be that is based on what is gathered from the garden that morning.

The word "salad," if we pursue it back to its etymological roots, means simply "eaten with salt," or, by extension, seasoned. Today, we think of salads as being refined, with their own plate, their own fork, their own course at dinner. But read *Acetaria*, John Evelyn's seventeenth-century "discourse of sallets," and you will see that our own bowl of greens once, too, evoked an idealized vision of rural life.* The Greeks are more attached to their countryside than we are, and their concept of salad, pure and simple, remains far closer to the origins of that word, a tiny step beyond the primitive forager's diet. How much civilization depends on that dribble of oil, that pinch of salt.

In contrast, the urban version, *horiátiki saláta*, is as civilized as you could want. It is powerfully evocative, to be sure, but it is still a defined entity, just one choice among many on the taverna's menu. In this kind of dish, the ingredients are subsumed to an idea, and it is that which holds our attention—first in its creation and then in the continual refining of it. On the other hand, that humble meal eaten by the villager exists at the very edge of unreflected thought, and the mind, when attempting to grasp it, finds it as slippery as a dream.

• • •

Knowing all this, I can look back at my initial encounter with Greek salad with fresh eyes. It is a particularly American experience to feel an almost wistful attraction to things from far older and more defined cultures than our own. That word "Greek" imbued this lunch-stop salad with a resonance that made it into something more than its paltry parts. Then again, perhaps it was partly my dissatisfaction with the salad's very slovenliness that drove me onward, like a blurry photograph that one struggles to bring into focus. If so, this lack of clarity would prove to be more important than any recipe, no matter how authentic, as a way to the heart of *horiátiki saláta*.

Because, as we have seen, what brings this salad to life is the tension it embodies between urban fantasy and rural pragmatism, between the emblematic flavors of Hellenic country life—the olives, the cheese, the sharp herbs—which never change, and the salad ingredients themselves, which remain in flux. Thus, the oft-encountered rule that lettuce does not belong in a true Greek salad can now be seen as both true and false. In the spring, when tomatoes are not to be found and lettuce is plentiful, the salad is made with it. In the late summer, when the lettuce bolts,

---

*John Evelyn (October 31, 1620–February 27, 1706) was an English writer, gardener, and diarist.

tomatoes come into their own. And for that time when both lettuce and tomatoes are available at the local market, they will wend their way together into the salad—as will other vegetables that happen to be there and happen to seem just right. To that end, the following recipes are meant merely as guides—this is a theme for which the variations are infinite.

GREEK SALAD, EASTER
[Serves 4]

1 large head romaine
4 or 5 scallions, trimmed of their ragged tops
a bunch of radishes, trimmed and sliced
1 large sprig fresh dill
2 or 3 sprigs flat-leaf parsley
¼ cup extra-virgin olive oil
1 tablespoon red wine vinegar
salt and black pepper
a dozen or so black or Kalamata olives, pitted
2 ounces Greek feta, cut into 4 slices

Core the head of romaine and discard the coarse outer leaves. Cut the tough end off the core and thinly slice the rest of it. Rinse the remaining leaves, drying them carefully afterwards. Stack up several similar-size leaves and slice them crosswise into ½-inch strips. Repeat this process until all the leaves have been cut. Put these and the slices of the core into a large salad bowl.

Cut the scallions, green and white parts both, into 3-inch lengths, then slice these into slivers. Add these and the radish slices to the lettuce in the salad bowl.

Strip the leaves of both the dill and the parsley from their stems. Roughly chop the herbs together and sprinkle over the salad.

Just before serving, mix together in a small bowl the olive oil, wine vinegar, a pinch of salt, and several grindings of black pepper. Toss the salad with it. Tear the pitted olives into pieces and scatter these over the salad as well. Divide among four salad plates and crumble a slice of the feta over each. Serve at once.

Cook's Note. Cos lettuce (after the Greek island Kos) is the Greek lettuce. Rena Salaman says that any other variety, outside of the mega-markets, is hard to find. However, a mixture of romaine and Bibb or Boston lettuce makes a pleasant variation.

GREEK SALAD, EARLY SUMMER
[Serves 4]

half of a small cabbage, shredded or chopped
a bunch of watercress or other peppery green, stemmed
several sprigs fresh cilantro, rinsed, patted dry, and stemmed
2 plump Kirby (pickling) cucumbers, peeled and sliced
3 large tomatoes, coarsely chopped
juice of ½ lemon
salt to taste
¼ cup extra-virgin olive oil
a dozen or so black or Kalamata olives, pitted
2 ounces Greek feta, cut into 4 slices

Put the cabbage, watercress, cilantro, cucumbers, and tomatoes into a salad bowl. Whisk the lemon juice, salt, and olive oil together in a smaller bowl until blended and toss the salad with it. Tear the pitted olives into pieces and scatter these over the salad as well. Divide among four salad plates and crumble a slice of the feta over each. Serve at once.

GREEK SALAD, FULL SUMMER
[Serves 4]

In Greece, according to more than one writer, the addition of lemon juice to this salad is done to individual taste by serving lemon wedges on the side. Of course, if you prefer, you can make the dressing with lemon juice directly, as in the preceding recipe.

1 pound or so red tomatoes, sliced in half and cut into
   wedges

1 red salad onion, very thinly sliced into rings
1 small, glossy green bell pepper, cored and thinly sliced
2 plump Kirby (pickling) cucumbers, peeled and sliced
¼ cup extra-virgin olive oil
a pinch of Greek oregano (see note)
4 to 6 capers, minced
salt and black pepper to taste
a dozen or so black or Kalamata olives, pitted
2 ounces Greek feta, cut into 4 slices (see note)
lemon wedges for serving

Combine the tomatoes, onion, green pepper, and cucumbers in a large salad bowl. Measure the olive oil into a smaller bowl and crumble in the oregano. Add the minced capers and salt and pepper, whisk everything together, and gently toss the salad with this dressing. Tear the pitted olives into pieces and scatter these over the salad as well. Divide among four salad plates and crumble a slice of the feta over each. Serve at once.

Cook's Notes. Optional additions to the above might include various chopped fresh herbs (cilantro, mint, flat-leaf parsley) and anchovy fillets. Also, some recipes suggest mixing a few green olives with the black ones. If you do, I would consider omitting the capers.

Greek Oregano: Wild Greek oregano, picked fresh, is so potent it can numb the tip of the tongue, and when dried retains an intensity of flavor and a pungent aroma that can fill a room when you crumble some leaves in your fingers. The best has the leaves still attached to their twigs. You can buy it in that form at most Greek markets and online at www.parthenonfoods.com.

Greek Feta: Within the European Union, the word "feta" is protected and can only be used when that cheese is made in Greece. It is more complex and better balanced (salty, tangy, sheepy) than imitations, and, of course, de rigueur for Greek salad.

> I always sprinkle the salad with oregano and pour quite a lot of olive oil over it. Fresh country bread dipped in the dressing and eaten with good-quality feta cheese is a taste I dream of all winter.
> —Aglaia Kremezi, *The Foods of Greece*

A NOTE ON GREEK MOUNTAIN TEA

> After the cooking herbs follow the ones that are used as tisanes.
> The most representative of these is called *agrio tsai tou vounou*
> (wild mountain tea—if translated literally). Every mountain in
> Greece seems to grow its *sui generis* tea: a very esoteric affair that
> can be identified down to an area by its special aroma.
> —Rena Salaman, *Greek Food*

The relative harshness of the Greek landscape seems ideally suited to
intensify the taste and aroma of the herbs that grow there—and what is
an herb, after all, other than an intensely aromatic plant? No one who
has grown their own oregano can have failed to notice how insipid it
is when compared to the fierce assertiveness of those scraggly wild
bunches gathered on a Peloponnesian hillside. This very strength has
meant that, historically, the Greeks have respected these plants more
for their medicinal values than their culinary ones. And so, although
they drink infusions of sage for chest colds and other ailments, they are
mildly incredulous when told that elsewhere it is used for cooking.

Greek sage leaves, brewed as a tisane, have for me all the charm of
a vermicide, but their "mountain tea"—*tsai tou vounou*—with its sil-
very, woolly leaves and clusters of tiny yellow flowers, takes that same
taste, gentles it, weaves in a hint of chamomile, and produces a brew
that is as soothing as it is genuinely good. It, too, is drunk by Hellenes
for its medicinal benefits—it is extremely rich in iron and is considered
an antipyretic, a perspirative, and a calmative—the perfect brew, in
fact, to sip at evening's end before heading off to bed.

Greek mountain tea can be found at Greek markets or online at
www.parthenonfoods.com. Look for packages containing the whole
stem, with leaves and flowers attached. Strip away about a tablespoon
of these, put them in a mug, and pour boiling water over. Brew for five
minutes, stirring in a teaspoonful of Greek thyme honey if you'd like to
add a little frosting to your cake.

FIORE DI FINOCCHIO

> Fennel pollen is one of the most exciting flavors of central Italian cooking and a well-kept secret . . . [It] is never sold commercially, which is why almost no one knows about it. Even in Sicily, where wild fennel grows with abandon and the green fronds are used in many dishes, no one has ever heard of using fennel pollen.
> —Faith Willinger, *Red, White & Greens*

Whatever else might be said about fennel pollen, it is certainly a secret no longer. And I suspect that the entire page Faith Willinger devoted to it in her book on Italian vegetable cooking had quite a bit to do with that. Her introductory sentence, quoted above, is the sort of statement that publicists kill for, all the more so since at the time it was written it was actually true—including the "almost no one knows about it" part. I wasted several hours going through our collection of Italian cookbooks to see if I could find a single mention of it prior to this one, and failed—even in the Tuscan ones (although I'm sure this omission will be rectified from here on in).

Before we move on to the "one of the most exciting flavors" part, it's worth noting that if anyone had written about wild fennel pollen a decade or so ago, the tone, even the import, of that mention would have been quite different. If someone decides to devote a whole page to an unknown, impossible-to-find ingredient, it's because their sixth sense says that its time has come. As with extra-virgin olive oil in the 1970s and balsamic vinegar a decade later, at a certain moment a willingness to pay what previously would have seemed an extortionate amount be-

comes palpable enough to be sniffed out by a food writer on the spot
. . . and, perhaps more important, by an adventurous entrepreneur.

In this instance, it was Ari Weinzweig, the guiding palate of Zingerman's Deli, in Ann Arbor, Michigan, who, in 2000—four years after
Red, White & Greens appeared (and two after *Flavors of Tuscany*, in
which Nancy Harmon Jenkins discussed the same subject with equal
fervor)—dropped by the butcher shop of Dario Cecchini, in Panzano, a
small Tuscan town. An enthusiast of traditional practices, Dario hand-
gathers, dries, and crushes the pollen-laden wild fennel flowers himself,
using the result to season cuts of pork.

When Ari asked about the possibility of purchasing the fennel
pollen alone, Dario showed him a baby-food-size jar, and Ari decided
he might as well buy two. After all, he wasn't in the neighborhood that
often. Dario filled the little jars and, with them, presented a bill that, incredibly, seemed in the vicinity of a hundred dollars.

> Not wanting to look like the ignorant American tourist I am, I
> reach into my pocket to get some money, hoping I have enough,
> all the while recalculating the conversion. For better or worse, my
> original calculation is about right. Whatever this fennel pollen is,
> it isn't inexpensive.

No joke. When this essay appeared in the November/December
2000 issue of *Zingerman's News*, their information-packed advertising
flyer, the price for 49 grams was $11, or $102 a pound. When this
book went to press, the asking price was $18 for 45 grams ($181 a
pound) and they had a hard time keeping it in stock. True, saffron is
more expensive still, but producing saffron is so labor-intensive that,
like true balsamic vinegar, you at least feel that you are paying for
something else besides the failure of supply to catch up with demand.

Wild fennel, which looks very much like dill (to which it is closely
related)—the same bright green, feathery leaves topped with spreading
umbrels of tiny yellow flowers—is native to southern Europe and
grows profusely there. Since turning its blossoms into *fiore di finocchio*
is no big deal, I don't doubt that Sicilian (or even Croatian) peasants
are already draping the outsides of their cottages with swags of the
stuff. If so, prices may well plunge in the foreseeable future—at least
for those who don't require the hand-plucked-on-Tuscan-hillsides seal
of authenticity.

(One of the places blessed with acres of wild fennel is California, and you can already buy the pollen from a company harvesting it there. But, like everything else with trendiness stamped all over it, California wild fennel pollen is even *more* expensive than the Tuscan version—a half-ounce tin for $7, or $224 a pound, which is really starting to nip at saffron's heels.)

Given all this, you might wonder if there is any point in spending twenty bucks for a tiny container of wild fennel pollen right now. Well, yes, there is—or at least I can tell you why I did. The stuff is truly potent. And, as Ari details, the effect doesn't exactly sneak up on you.

> With a certain swagger, [Dario] opens the jar and pushes it towards me to smell. I lean over to do so, but the aroma hits me long before I even get close. The smell of wild fennel pollen is, quite seriously, something else. The perfume fills the room rather quickly. Truth be told, in twenty years of cooking and traveling, I've never before, nor since, smelled anything quite like it. Its aroma is sweet, pungent, smelling intensely of everything great about fennel and then some. I haven't even eaten it yet, but on aroma alone, the stuff is amazing.

Up to now, quite frankly, the phrase "everything great about fennel" would have elicited an incredulous snicker from me. But wild fennel pollen takes that anise-drenched monotone and imbues it with a highly potent resiny complexity. While there truly is no easy comparison, my first sniff of wild fennel pollen did remind me of my first encounter with fresh basil, when before I had been familiar only with the one-dimensional flavor of the dried version. Then, as now, it was as if someone had flipped a switch and a black-and-white world was suddenly drenched in color.

• • •

> Fennel pollen is a typical Tuscan ingredient used throughout that region's repertoire of dishes, traditionally as a spice in the *salumerie* of Italy in salamis and sausages. Often applied as a rub for pork or poultry—mix it with rosemary and crushed garlic—it also combines well with other dried herbs and spices. Add it to fish soups or sprinkle it on roasted vegetables.
> —Rolando Beramendi, Manicaretti Imports

Once I tired of sniffing the container of wild fennel pollen that I had ordered from Zingerman's, I started using it in our cooking . . . cautiously. Even a tiny pinch made a spectacular match with sautéed zucchini.

GEMELLI WITH ZUCCHINI
AND ITALIAN SAUSAGE
[Serves 2]

2 medium zucchini
1 tablespoon kosher salt
2 tablespoons olive oil
1 large garlic clove, minced
¼ teaspoon wild fennel pollen (or twice that amount dried crumbled oregano)
¼ teaspoon powdered red chile
2 links sweet Italian sausage, casings removed
8 ounces gemelli or other short tubular pasta
Parmigiano-Reggiano
black pepper

Cut each zucchini into pieces that are approximately the length and thickness of the pasta you have chosen. Toss these in a bowl with the tablespoon of salt and let this sit for 30 minutes, turning it over occasionally. After 15 minutes, get a big pot of salted water for the pasta heating and continue with the recipe.

Put the olive oil, minced garlic, wild fennel pollen, and powdered red chile into a skillet, place this over medium heat, and cook until the garlic turns translucent. At the same time, break the sausage meat into bits and add these to the skillet. Stir occasionally to ensure that all the sausage meat is cooked through.

When the pasta water is about to boil, discard the liquid the salt has leached from the zucchini, spread an old but clean dish towel in the kitchen sink, and turn out the zucchini pieces onto it. Wrap them up in the cloth and twist this as tightly as you can, extracting every possible bit of moisture. This will be a surprising amount.

Put the pasta into the boiling water. Add the wrung-out zucchini to the skillet with the other ingredients and cook over medium heat, stirring frequently but gently, until the pasta is almost ready. Scoop out ¼ cup of the pasta cooking water and stir this in with the zucchini and sausage. Remove the skillet from the heat. Drain the pasta and divide it between two plates, topping each with a portion of the sauce. Serve with freshly grated Parmesan and lots of freshly milled black pepper.

We also liked the flair wild fennel pollen gave to such pasta regulars as fusilli with chickpeas and spinach (see our book *Pot on the Fire*, pages 203–204). And it added an appreciable depth of flavor to our butternut risotto (same book, pages 67–68). Furthermore, it called up some ideas for dishes all by itself, starting with:

FINGER-SUCKING SHRIMP
[A light meal for 2 (with salad); an appetizer for 4]

Note that you'll need to calculate in some marinating time when preparing this dish.

> ¼ cup olive oil
> 1 garlic clove, very finely minced
> pinch of wild fennel pollen
> ¼ teaspoon moderately hot powdered chile
> 1 teaspoon kosher salt
> black pepper to taste
> 1 pound large shrimp, unpeeled
> ¼ cup dry white wine
> torn chunks of country-style bread for serving

Put the olive oil, minced garlic, fennel pollen, chile powder, salt, and black pepper in an appropriate-size bowl. Set the shrimp in a sieve and quickly rinse them in cold water, shaking out as much excess liquid as possible. Turn the shrimp into the bowl and stir well to coat them all with the seasoned oil. Put the bowl in the fridge and allow its contents to marinate for 30 to 45 minutes.

Preheat a skillet for a minute over medium heat. Add the shrimp and the marinade, and sauté—turning them with a spatula—until they just turn bright pink. Add the wine, mix well, heat for 30 more seconds, then turn into shallow bowls. Serve with something to hold the discarded shrimp shells and with bread for mopping up the sauce.

• • •

Those fennel-pollen-seasoned pork cuts in Dario Cecchini's meat case also got me thinking. Nancy Harmon Jenkins published a very tasty-sounding pork roast flavored with it in *Food & Wine* a while ago, but we don't prepare a whole roast very often. Recently, though, Cryovac-packaged pork tenderloins have been on sale (buy one, get one free) at our local supermarket, and I had tried several ways of preparing these—slicing them into disks and pounding these into cutlets; marinating them and grilling them over charcoal—none of which resulted in any desire for an encore.

What, I wondered, would happen if I sliced the meat open into a long, thin slab, spread it with fennel-pollen-intensive seasoning, and rolled it up again? A simple trick—but, as it turned out, a very successful one, which I can happily recommend to you.

PORK TENDERLOIN *CASA NOSTRA*
[Serves 4 to 6]

2 pork tenderloins (about 12 to 16 ounces each)
1 large garlic clove, finely minced
1 teaspoon wild fennel pollen
½ teaspoon paprika or mild powdered chile
2 tablespoons very fruity extra-virgin olive oil
2 tablespoons good-quality balsamic vinegar
1 teaspoon kosher salt
freshly ground black pepper to taste
bamboo skewers for securing the meat
2 tablespoons butter or olive oil or a mixture of both

Trim off the tapered ends of each tenderloin, reserving these for another purpose. Divide the remaining pieces of meat into halves or thirds, cutting them crosswise to make equal-size cylinders. Using your sharpest kitchen knife, gently cut down about a quarter of an inch into the side of the first cylinder, then turn the blade and slice the meat as if you were using your knife to unroll it. If you accidentally cut through to the surface (or even slice off the piece entirely), just pretend you didn't and keep going. When you're done with both tenderloins, you should have four or six hankie-size rectangles of pork. Unless you're quite talented at this, they'll look a bit ragged, but no matter. This is a very forgiving dish.

In a small bowl, stir together the garlic, fennel pollen, paprika, olive oil, vinegar, salt, and black pepper, and brush this mixture evenly onto the upper surface of each piece of meat. Roll each tightly back up and secure the seam with a small bamboo skewer or similar object. (The advantage of using bamboo skewers is that you can snip off their excess length with a pair of scissors.)

Heat the butter and/or olive oil over medium heat in a skillet large enough to hold the pork roll-ups comfortably. When the fat is hot, add the meat. Turn it every 3 or 4 minutes, until all sides are nicely brown. Then lower the heat slightly and continue to cook until an instant-read thermometer inserted into the center of each roll-up (via one of its ends) reads 150°F to 155°F, or until a visual inspection shows the meat in the center to be a light pink. (Remember that the meat will continue to cook after it is removed from the heat.) As soon as the roll-ups are done, transfer them from the skillet to a warmed plate and let them rest for 10 minutes, covered with foil, before removing the skewers and serving.

• • •

Some final thoughts. I'm just as susceptible as the next guy to the tug of the new, especially to something that makes such a stunning first impression as wild fennel pollen. Even so, in my own opinion, it is closer to being another ingredient-of-the-minute (think pomegranate syrup) than a lasting influence on our cooking. When push comes to shove, it has the same limited range as any other herb, even if within that range it exercises genuinely transformational powers.

In this regard I think of oregano, an herb so familiar to us that, paradoxically, we have forgotten how good it can be. In Greece, where it is truly appreciated, it is gathered much as wild fennel is, in stalks with the just blossoming flowers still attached. These flowers are also full of pollen, and its resiny intensity can be equally provocative. There was a short time when you could purchase such hand-gathered bunches at most specialty food stores. But interest waned—and now, usually, you have to find a Middle Eastern import store to get hold of them or go online (for example, www.minosimports.com). Wild fennel pollen reminds us again that what we give to an herb in terms of respect, it gives back to us in potency and flavor.

Tasting Notes: Wild Fennel Pollen

Currently, wild fennel pollen comes from either Tuscany or California, where Sugar Ranch, a division of Pollen Collection & Sales, has made it a specialty. (Both Faith Willinger and Nancy Harmon Jenkins pointed to California, where wild fennel is a common weed, as a promising source for the pollen.)

Comparing the sample kindly provided to me by Sugar Ranch with Zingerman's Tuscan pollen, I found the former to be more visually attractive, its coarser texture revealing bits of the dried yellow flowers as well as pieces of green twig. But its aroma was monochromatically pungent of anise, with none of the heady complexity of the Tuscan variety. As far as taste was concerned, the Tuscan pollen was distinctly bitter, with overtones of anise, whereas the California pollen lacked any bitterness and tasted so strongly of anise that it was almost like licorice.

A possible explanation of this notable difference can be found in *The Oxford Companion to Food*, which distinguishes between two forms of wild fennel, the bitter and the sweet. (The fennel grown for its bulb, which is eaten as a vegetable, is separate again.) Bitter wild fennel is the plant that grows wild in Tuscany, whereas sweet fennel, which was domesticated from it, grows wild in California as an escapee from the gardens of Italian immigrants, who cultivated sweet fennel precisely because of its intensified anise flavor.

The choice is yours: do you want complexity or raw power? Or, to put it another way, how crazy are you about the flavor of anise? I'm not, and I don't believe that if my first encounter with wild fennel pollen had been the California pollen gathered by Sugar Ranch I would be writing about it now. However, they also sent me a sample of a farmhouse Monterey Jack flavored with their pollen, and I found it surprisingly good, if a little twiggy—much superior to the dill- and sage-flavored cheeses of the same ilk. So I'm keeping an open mind on the subject.

Sources

Wild fennel pollen can be found at many online specialty food purveyors, but the supply is limited and the importers few.

Zingerman's Deli. Hand-gathered wild fennel pollen from Tuscany. Powerful, complex aroma; taste is intriguingly bitter, with overtones of anise. Comes with recipes and helpful information. Zingerman's; 422 Detroit Street; Ann Arbor, MI 48104; (888) 636-8162; www.zingermans.com.

Sugar Ranch. Hand-gathered wild fennel pollen from California. Aggressive anise aroma and flavor, more potent but not as complex as the Tuscan variety. Comes with recipes and helpful information. Sugar Ranch; P.O. Box 608; Goshen, CA 93227; (800) 821-5989; www.fennelpollen.com.

Borghini Wild Fennel Pollen. Hand-gathered in Tuscany and imported by Manicaretti (a noted importer of Italian artisanal foods). Available from the Mount Horeb Mustard Museum; P.O. Box 468; Mount Horeb, WI 53572; (800) 438-6878; www.mustardmuseum.com. As of 2007, this costs $65 for a 200-gram (7.1-ounce) cellophane bag, which is a fantastic buy. But remember that a little of this seasoning goes a long way; unless you're a chef, 200 grams will last you a few years (although, divvied up in tiny jars, it would make for some excellent Christmas presents).

COOKED MIDNIGHT

Uncooked, rice is called *mai*; cooked, it is *fan*. Once cooked, rice was traditionally taken as food at least three times each day, first for *jo chan*, or early meal, either as congee or, if the weather was cool, cooked and served with a spoonful of liquid lard, soy sauce, and an egg. To eat rice is to *sik fan*, and there is, in addition to those morning preparations, *n'fan*, or "afternoon rice," and *mon fan*, or "evening rice." There is even a custom called *siu yeh*, which translates literally as "cooked midnight" and means rice eaten as a late evening snack. No time of any day in China is without its rice.

—Eileen Yin-Fei Lo, *The Chinese Kitchen*

Although there's no exact equivalent, the closest we come in this country to the casual everyday eating experience of the Chinese is when we attend a country fair or something like one, where inexpensive, open-air food stalls abound and masses of people stroll about, sampling from them as they go. Food courts aren't really the same, because you go there to eat, you buy food, you sit down and consume it, and you leave. Nor are food courts right outside your front door, so you can't slip into a bathrobe and duck outside for a quick bite before sleep. Nor do we have the tiny, hole-in-the-wall, single-dish snack joints that, in China, complement the stalls and expand the concept of snack without adding any inconvenience or expense.

In America, despite what we think, there's nothing casual about casual eating. Food, even snack food, comes well-wrapped, both physically and metaphorically. Those wrappings signal order, sanitation, property boundaries, and more. Imagine wandering into McDonald's for a bag of fries, crossing the street to Wendy's for a cheeseburger, and stepping into Burger King for a shake—even if this were your ideal fast-food feast, the effort involved in trying to assemble it would make the whole experience risible.

At home, snack makings are hidden inside cabinets and the refrigerator, where they're packaged up in bags, jars, boxes, aseptic containers. Consequently, the appetite isn't allowed to flow smoothly from the moment of hunger to that of fulfillment but is continually brought up short along the way, again like a dog on a leash. As a result, we end up spending more, eating more, and enjoying it less.

What is most obviously wrong here is the tyranny of portion control, especially when that controlling is done from far away and with intentions sometimes diametrically opposed to your own. Where food is cheap and packaging expensive, you are made to pay substantially extra for choosing just what you want, even if you're able to find an approximate fit in the mini-, maxi-, mega-sizes spread before you. And there's always the built-in tilt to persuade you to take just a little bit (or, in some instances, a whole lot) more.

But this is only the start of the story. In cultures where food is costly, great ingenuity is expended in spinning something out of nothing, in tempting palates with what, in our own culture, is often tossed into the rubbish bin. More expensive foods are prepared with the intent of making a little go a long way—compare a skewer of satay (in calories and pleasure) to a Big Mac or a Whopper.

These speculations came to mind as I was reading, in his eponymous *Jim Lee's Chinese Cookbook*, the author's account of growing up in a small village in the province of Canton. When he came home from school, he would head straight to the kitchen and to the rice pot, where he was almost sure to find some rice left over from the previous family meal: "I would scoop some into a large bowl, pour some peanut oil on it at random, then sprinkle some dark soy sauce on it and mix it well and have a feast! If they were available, and my hunger could wait, I chopped some scallions and sprinkled them on the rice. It needed nothing more."

To prepare this properly, the boy had learned that the oil had to be thoroughly stirred in first, to coat each grain of rice. Otherwise, when he added the soy sauce, it would be soaked up entirely by the first bits of rice it touched. Although Lee presents the dish in recipe format, it's clear that, as a boy, no such thing existed for him. The amount of each seasoning would depend on how much rice there was, his appetite, the presence of his mother in the kitchen. In other words, such thinking as he did was done through his hands, his eyes, his tongue.

One can see him at it, intently concocting, then happily eating, his impromptu creation. The image not only touches my heart and my appetite but also stirs my inner cook. I'm immediately drawn to dishes where the preparation and eating are a pleasingly inseparable whole, where the meal begins when the old rice pot is, once again, found to be a willing co-conspirator.

It goes without saying that the delicious phrase "cooked midnight" embraces a wide universe of which the following rice bowl recipes are just a part. I took that phrase for the title of this piece because as I leafed through our Chinese cookbooks, seeking out what they had to say about fried rice, I noticed that I kept coming across certain rice bowl dishes to which words like "bachelor," "late-night," "solitary," and the like were attached—dishes, in other words, that are for private eating, even when shared with family or friends. Rosa Chang, writing about her own youth at her family website, captures their intimate spirit to perfection:

> *Siu yeh*, or supper late at night, became a treat to look forward to, and night-time outings often ended with fried noodles brought home and eaten from their warm lotus leaf wrappings. *Siu yeh* could also be homemade and turned into Malayan versions of midnight feasts à la boarding school stories. The spice of it was the secrecy. Stealing into the kitchen, the four of us, led by Daai-Ga-Je, set the wok on the charcoal stove to fry rice or noodles. Plates of the forbidden food were stealthily carried upstairs with cups of Chinese tea, and a midnight feast was had, beyond the dreams of Enid Blyton. On an occasion to honour Didi's visit to the house, an over-enthusiastic stirring of the rice made a hole in the wok for which a confession had to be made to Mamma the next morning.

COOKED RICE SNACK
[Serves 1]

A recipe is hardly needed for this dish, but some encouragement might be: i.e., this is, in fact, really good. Lee writes that he was always curious to know what his Caucasian friends would think of it, since he could hardly serve it as a dinner dish. He found out when he encountered one of them, a restaurant cook, eating it. Surprised, Lee asked where on earth she had gotten the recipe. From you, she told him. He had described the dish to her years ago, and she had been making it for herself ever since.

> 1 bowl of cooked rice, at room temperature
> 2 tablespoons Chinese peanut oil (see note)
> 1 to 1½ tablespoons dark soy sauce (see note)
> 2 scallions, trimmed and minced

The rice should not be cold (i.e., not fresh from the refrigerator). Using your fingers or a soupspoon, break up any large clumps. Gently toss in the peanut oil, turning over the rice until it becomes a lightly glistening mass. Add the dark soy sauce drop by drop, stirring it in as you do. After 1 tablespoon has been added, taste the rice—if it needs more seasoning, add the rest in the same fashion. Finally, thoroughly mix in the minced scallion.

Cook's Notes. Chinese peanut oil has a more distinct peanut taste than American ones. It's available in Asian markets. Dark soy sauce can sometimes be oppressively salty. We prefer Pearl River Bridge Superior Dark Soy Sauce. If your digestive system objects to raw scallions, put them in a wok with the peanut oil, cook them gently for a few minutes, toss with the rice, and season with the dark soy sauce as directed.

HACKED MEAT RICE BOWL
[Serves 1]

All the recipes I know for this dish call simply for ground meat, most often beef. However, my guess is that hamburger, dangerously perishable as it is, is not something you find in most Chinese markets. And the dish tastes much better if you chop the meat yourself—the small amount called for here takes but a minute to mince, and it's enjoyable knife work.

> heaping ½ cup uncooked rice
> ¼ pound lean beef, pork, or lamb
> 1 teaspoon Chinese rice wine or dry sherry
> 1 teaspoon toasted sesame oil
> ¼ teaspoon kosher salt
> ¼ teaspoon sugar
> ¼ teaspoon black pepper
> 1 tablespoon light (ordinary) soy sauce
> 1 tablespoon finely minced fresh ginger

Put a scant cup of water in a small (1½-quart) saucepan and bring to a boil. Put the rice in a bowl and rinse it in two changes of cold water. Drain and add to the pot. When the water boils, reduce the heat to the lowest flame possible, cover, and cook for 13 minutes.

Meanwhile, use a cleaver or other knife to mince the meat. Mix it with the wine, sesame oil, salt, sugar, pepper, soy sauce, and ginger and form it into a thin patty a little smaller than the diameter of the rice pot. At the end of the 13-minute cooking time, uncover the rice and set the patty on top of it. Cover the pot with a folded napkin or dish towel and put the lid back. Cook for 2 more minutes, then turn off the heat. Let the covered pot sit for 15 minutes. At that point, gently break up and stir the meat into the rice and turn the mixture into a bowl.

CHINESE SAUSAGE RICE BOWL
[Serves 2]

Chinese sausages, about the size, shape, and, minus the ground chile, the color of a small pepperoni, are tightly packed with chunks of pork, pork fat, and, sometimes, duck liver. They have a sweet "Chinese sparerib" taste and a deliciously chewy consistency. Their fragrance permeates the rice while it cooks, which is why this is one of the most popular rice-bowl snacks. As a dinner dish, a whole sausage per person is often inserted into the rice and cut up by the diner. But for casual eat-

ing, it's simpler if the sausage is cut into shreds beforehand, as directed here.

> 1 cup uncooked rice
> 2 Chinese sausages, cut into slivers or shredded with a steel
> grater

Put 1⅔ cups of water in a small (1½-quart) saucepan and bring to a boil. Put the rice in a bowl and rinse it in two changes of cold water. Drain and add to the pot. When the water boils, reduce the heat to the lowest flame possible, cover, and cook until all the water on the surface of the rice has disappeared, about 10 minutes. Then lift the lid and distribute the bits of sausage over the rice, poking them down into it with the end of a chopstick. Re-cover and cook for another 5 minutes (for a total of 15). At that point, uncover again, place a folded napkin or dish towel over the rice, re-cover, and let sit off the heat for another 15 minutes. Serve.

Variation: Chinese Sausage with Green Peas. Either stir ½ cup freshly podded peas into the rice at the start of cooking or spread the same amount of thawed frozen green peas on top of the rice after the sausage has been poked in and mix them into the rice when it is done. Either way, I like to drizzle over some toasted sesame oil just before serving.

STIRRED EGG RICE BOWL
[Serves 1]

This dish is the epitome of rice-bowl dishes. Kenneth Lo says, in The Encyclopedia of Chinese Cooking: *"Rice cooked in this manner is often served to the very young, the aged, or the infirm . . . It is the sort of rice dish which is seen only in the most Chinese of surroundings, for example, in Chinese villages."*

> ½ teaspoon kosher salt
> heaping ½ cup uncooked rice
> 2 eggs
> 1 scallion, trimmed and minced

1 teaspoon toasted sesame oil
1 teaspoon Chinese rice wine or dry sherry
a drizzle of soy or oyster sauce to garnish

Put a scant cup of water and the salt in a small (1½-quart) saucepan and bring to a boil. Put the rice in a bowl and rinse it in two changes of cold water. Drain and add to the pot. When the water boils, reduce the heat to the lowest flame possible, cover, and cook for 13 minutes.

Meanwhile, beat the eggs gently with the minced scallion, sesame oil, and rice wine. At the end of the 13-minute cooking time, lift the lid from the rice and pour the beaten egg mixture over its surface. Cover with a folded napkin or dish towel and put the lid back. Cook for 2 more minutes, then turn off the heat. Let the covered pot sit for 15 minutes. At that point, gently stir the cooked eggs into the rice and turn the mixture into a bowl. Season with a drizzle of soy or oyster sauce and eat.

Variation: Stirred Egg with Crab. Stir half a small (6-ounce) can of crabmeat (drained) into the egg mixture before pouring it over the rice. Crab and egg is a favorite Chinese flavor combination, and canned crabmeat works nicely here.

SHANGHAI VEGETABLE RICE BOWL
[Serves 2]

This dish gets its name from a type of bok choy with light green stems that is very popular in Shanghai. Baby bok choy is a good substitute. Otherwise, use a smaller-size ordinary bok choy. Traditionally, this dish is made in standard rice-bowl fashion, with the vegetables cooked along with the rice. But the extra work required to make it as I do below preserves the crisp sweetness of the bok choy and makes for a livelier dish.

4 to 6 Chinese dried black mushrooms
2 or 3 baby green- or white-stemmed bok choy or 1 small
    regular bok choy, carefully rinsed
1 tablespoon lard or peanut oil
1 garlic clove, minced
½ teaspoon each kosher salt and black pepper

2 teaspoons toasted sesame oil
1½ cups cooked rice

Soak the dried mushrooms for 20 minutes in warm water to reconstitute them. Trim off and discard the stems. Coarsely chop the caps. After trimming away and discarding the very bottoms of the bok choy, coarsely chop the rest.

Heat the lard in a wok or frying pan over high heat. When it is at the verge of smoking, add the minced garlic. Stir this once or twice, then add the mushrooms, bok choy, salt, pepper, and toasted sesame oil. Stir-fry this until the bok choy is tender, from 2 to 3 minutes. Turn in the cooked rice and stir gently until the rice is heated through and everything is well mixed. Serve and eat at once.

CHILE BAMBOO RICE BOWL
[Serves 2]

Although this dish is ordinarily made with preserved (pickled) bamboo shoots, I substitute Taiwanese chile pepper–infused bamboo shoots packed in soy oil, to which I am completely addicted. Both can be found at Asian groceries, but, in a pinch, ordinary canned bamboo shoots can be used instead.

2 tablespoons each soy sauce and Chinese rice wine or sherry
¼ cup chicken stock or water
½ teaspoon sugar
1 tablespoon peanut oil (or chile oil from the jar of bamboo shoots)
2 scallions, trimmed and minced
½ tablespoon minced fresh ginger
¼ pound ground pork
¼ pound chile bamboo shoots, drained
¼ cup thawed frozen peas
hot, freshly cooked rice for two

Mix the soy sauce, rice wine, stock, and sugar together in a small bowl. Heat the peanut oil in a wok over high heat. When it is close to smoking, add the scallions and minced ginger and cook, stirring for several seconds, until the scallions have wilted. Add the ground pork and stir-fry, breaking it into bits with a spatula as it cooks. Add the bamboo shoots and the soy sauce mixture. Reduce the heat and simmer for 5 minutes. Stir in the peas and cook for another 2 minutes. Divide the rice into two bowls and cover with the contents of the wok. Serve at once.

FASOLIA GIGANTES

A sensational dish. Splendidly vegetarian, luxuriously rich, it makes one of the best meals served in Greek homes and it is customarily served as an appetizer in tavernas.

—Rena Salaman, *Greek Food*

I've written before that some new dishes enter my everyday cooking as if we've been friends for life, while others, for no good reason, have to wait for years. I'm aware of them, I'm attracted to them, I just don't make them. But there's at least one other category—dishes that I'm simultaneously attracted to and suspicious of, either because I just can't get myself to believe that they're as tasty as they're said to be or, more often, because they contain an ingredient or two about which I'm deeply ambivalent.

Fasolia gigantes plaki (roughly translated, *gigantes* beans baked with lots of garlic) is just the sort of dish I mean. Even ordering a pound of dried *gigantes* from a Greek food importer did nothing to push things along—the sack of them sat up in the cupboard for almost two full years before I got around to making the dish, and then only because Matt warned me that if I left them there much longer, they'd be beyond resuscitation. Just to prove her wrong, I soaked some overnight, and when it was clear they were still edible I had no choice but to follow through. Soaked dried beans wait for no man, procrastinators included.

Gigantes, if you're unfamiliar with them, are just what the name suggests: really, really big shell beans. If beans had titles, these would be the King, the Champion, the Dude. Cooked, you can eat them the way you eat olives or Brazil nuts, which is to say, not only with your fingers but one by one. And they're worth eating that way—especially as the Greeks prepare them to serve as a *meze*—because they have a smooth, soft texture, a delicately nutty taste, and tender skins.

The beans themselves, then, weren't why I hadn't made them. In fact, I've had a longtime love of butter beans, to which *gigantes* are just amiably hefty cousins. No, it was because the Greeks almost always bake them with tomatoes or, worse, tomato sauce or, worse still, tomato paste. The Greeks cook nearly everything with tomatoes. The only positive thing about this is that nothing catches my attention faster than when a Greek food writer admits to liking a dish better when made without them.

That's just what Aglaia Kremezi does in *The Foods of Greece*, writing about *fasolia gigantes plaki*: "These beans are usually baked in a spicy tomato sauce, but I prefer this simpler version, which is more common in northern Greece. The beans, scented with the garlic and dill, have a lovely sweet taste that they lose when tomatoes are added to the sauce."

Heart palpitating, I immediately copied out the recipe.

Alas, that same paralyzing ambivalence returned the moment I saw that her version contained fresh dill, or, more precisely, one and a half cups of it. I don't exactly hate fresh dill the way I do cooked tomatoes. But I've suffered enough from fresh dill–abused salmon (aka gravlax) in my life to think much of that herb anywhere outside a kosher pickle jar.

There was something else I didn't like about Kremezi's recipe: a tablespoon of dried mustard. That's yet another gravlax ingredient. Some Swedish chef must be on the rampage in Thessaloniki, I thought, meddling with innocent *gigantes* recipes. Those two items had incapacitated me for years. But now, the beans swelling in the soaking water, my back was up against the wall. I made the recipe.

Well, I was wrong about the dill but right about the dried mustard. It was just too harsh in this dish. But I knew immediately what I wanted to put in its place: green Greek olives. The very next day I went out and bought some. Now, if you've just made a face, I understand. Green olives are no special favorite of mine. But what is odd and remarkable about *gigantes plaki* is how it takes aggressive ingredients like fresh dill and green olives and works them together in a completely delicious way. The bean's mellow-tasting meatiness embraces those strong flavors and smothers them in a big bear hug.

It helps, too, that the usually strident herbaceousness of the dill meets its match in the tonic bitterness of the green olives, the texture of which also melds well with that of the beans. Finally, the sweetness of the onions brings it all into harmony, while the plenitude of garlic, after long cooking, provides its usual delicious savory depth. In short, besides making a wonderful appetizer, it's also a great vegetarian main course, served over rice.

GIGANTES PLAKI WITH DILL AND GREEN OLIVES
[Serves 6 to 8 as an appetizer, 4 as a main course]

Fasolia gigantes are inexpensive and easy to order online (at, for example, www.greekinternetmarket.com) if your local Middle Eastern grocery doesn't carry them. Alternatively, you can substitute dried butter beans (aka large white lima beans) or even, in a pinch, canned ones. However, gigantes truly are one of a kind, and they make this dish shine. It's worth the effort to get them.

1 pound *gigantes*, picked over, washed, and soaked overnight
¾ cup good fruity olive oil
1 tablespoon dried Greek oregano, crumbled
2 large onions, cut into small dice
4 to 6 garlic cloves, minced
1 hot red pepper, stemmed, seeded, and minced, or
    ½ teaspoon hot powdered chile
1 small bunch fresh dill, washed, stemmed, and minced
¼ cup coarsely chopped green olives
1 cup dry white wine
salt to taste

Put the beans and their soaking water into a pot and bring to a boil. Skim away any scum that floats to the surface and, after 10 minutes, lower the heat and cover. The flame should be just high enough to keep the pot gently bubbling. Cook for 1 hour all told, then check one of the beans. They should be edible by now but not quite cooked through (a little coarse-textured). If not, cook them another 10 minutes or so. Then drain them, reserving their liquid.

Preheat oven to 300°F. Pour the olive oil into a large skillet and heat over a medium flame. Crumble in the oregano, then add the onions and, after 5 minutes, the garlic, hot pepper, and beans. Sauté everything for another 5 minutes, turning with a spatula so the beans are well coated with the seasoned oil. Set aside about 1 tablespoon of the minced dill and stir the rest into the bean mixture along with the chopped olives.

Transfer the contents of the skillet to a small bean pot or covered casserole. Pour over the wine and salt to taste, starting with ½ teaspoon. Finally, pour over the bean liquid and, if necessary, a little more water so that the beans are just covered. (They shouldn't be swimming in liquid.)

Cover the pot and put it in the preheated oven. Bake for 1 hour, or until the texture of the beans is quite smooth. *Gigantes plaki* can be served hot or at room temperature. Before bringing it to table, sprinkle with the reserved dill.

● ● ●

But don't think you've eaten gigantes until you've had them in the Akrolimnia Taverna in Psarades—Greece's only settlement on Megali Prespa, most of which belongs to Albania and Macedonia. These are a staple meze in tavernas throughout [Greece], but nowhere have I had better.

—Diana Farr Louis

[At Zeus, a restaurant near the Acropolis], tables are all outdoors, and the place usually isn't very crowded . . . Try their gigantes, a traditional Greek appetizer, which is better here than anywhere else I've had it.

—Jon Corelis

Once you start poking around in Greek travel books or, for that matter, websites (whence the above quotations), you discover that *gigantes*—and especially *gigantes plaki*—often stand out in the recollections of dishes eaten in Greek restaurants. This may be partly due to the fact that you expect a huge bean to have a pretty potent flavor (they don't call broad beans "horse beans" for nothing), so it always comes as a pleasant surprise to be reminded how suave and subtle *gigantes* actually are.

However, I think it's more likely that enterprising Greek tavernas vie with each other to offer a memorable version of a popular but all too often lazily prepared dish. Now that I've been turned on to it myself, I was rather upset that Diana Farr Louis, author of the near-impossible-to-find *Feasting and Fasting in Crete* (Kedros, 2001), didn't have the wits to wrestle the recipe away from the proprietor of the Akrolimnia and share it with us.

If I were a food writer of the alpha type, I'd have felt obliged to head off to Psarades to get it myself. I'm not, though, so I did a little thinking, instead. If the best *gigantes* in Greece are grown in the north, perhaps it might be worth doing a little exploring a little further north still—across the border in Macedonia.* I took down the few Balkan cookbooks we possess and quickly turned up a little gem of a bean dish from that country in Maria Kaneva-Johnson's *The Melting Pot: Balkan Food and Cookery*, called *tavche gravche* (literally, "clay-casserole-cooked beans"). This is what it evolved into in our kitchen.

TAVCHE GRAVCHE
[Serves 4 as a main course]

Despite much trying, I haven't turned up any specific evidence stating that tavche gravche *is made with* gigantes, *good as this dish is when prepared with them. Consequently, cannellini are perfectly appropriate. Just remember cannellini require longer cooking.*

1 pound *gigantes* or cannellini beans, picked over, washed,
    and soaked overnight
¼ cup olive oil
2 tablespoons dried bread crumbs
2 or 3 medium onions, chopped
2 or 3 garlic cloves, minced
1 to 2 teaspoons hot powdered chile

*That is, the part of what was once Yugoslavia that has adopted this name—a fact that has angered the Greeks, who have laid claim to the geographic designation "Macedonia" since the days of Alexander the Great, and have been very huffy about this.

leaves of 1 sprig mint or basil, torn to bits
1 teaspoon kosher salt
black pepper to taste
1 large tomato, cut into thin slices
½ cup chopped pickled red peppers (see note)
minced parsley for garnish
a bowl of gherkins, and bread for dunking

Drain the beans, empty them into a saucepan, and cover them with fresh water. Boil them rapidly for 10 to 15 minutes, skimming away any scum. Then reduce the heat to a simmer and cook the beans until they are soft but still intact. For *gigantes*, this will take about 1 hour or so, depending on their age; for cannellini beans, from two to three times longer. Turn the beans into a casserole, about 10 inches in diameter, reserving their cooking liquid.

Preheat oven to 325°F. Heat ½ tablespoon of the olive oil in a small skillet. Mix the bread crumbs into the hot oil, stirring until they have absorbed it. Then, continuing to stir occasionally, sauté the bread crumbs until golden over low heat. Turn into a small bowl.

While the bread crumbs toast, heat another tablespoon of the olive oil in a larger skillet. Add the chopped onions and garlic and sauté until the onions are wilted and have begun to brown. Add the powdered chile, torn bits of herb, salt, black pepper, and the bean cooking liquid. Stir this up, cook for another minute, then pour it over the beans.

Top the casserole with the slices of tomato and scatter around the bits of pickled pepper. Drizzle over the remaining olive oil and sprinkle with the bread crumbs. Bake in the preheated oven for an hour, or a little longer if needed for the tomatoes to lightly brown. Bring the casserole to the table after sprinkling minced parsley over the top. Serve with gherkins and bread.

Cook's Note. Pickled Peppers: Middle European preserved foods—from Poland all the way down to Croatia—seem to have become a commonplace in supermarkets, at least in New England. If pickled red peppers aren't available where you live, substitute a 6-ounce (or so) jar of roasted red peppers.

The use of pickled peppers in this dish is another example of how *gigantes* provide a mellow background for all sorts of vivid flavors. Re-

cently, our local Stop & Shop, already designated as "Super," metasta-
sized again, adding, among other things, a franchised Boston Market
prepared food section and a huge aisle-long appetizer bar offering a
wide range of imported olives of all hues, some filled with various stuffings; marinated mushrooms, artichokes, and mixed vegetables; roasted
garlic and peppers; and on and on. Just the sort of things, I thought, to
be tossed with some home-cooked *gigantes*, chopped raw onion, some
minced fresh herb, fruity olive oil, and lemon juice. The beans would
go with any of them and keep the nosher from getting mouth fatigue
from all those brazen flavors.

On the other hand, *gigantes* are quite satisfying as a nibble all by
themselves, if the seasonings bring some livening savor to the dish, as in
the following recipe. As indicated, the results can also be served over
rice or a stubby pasta like gemelli or fusilli.

GIGANTES PLAKI WITH GARLIC AND THYME
[Serves 6 to 8 as an appetizer]

1 pound *gigantes* or butter beans, picked over, washed,
    and soaked overnight
½ cup extra-virgin olive oil
4 to 6 garlic cloves, minced
2 bay leaves, broken in half
1 sprig fresh thyme or 1 teaspoon dried
1 teaspoon crushed hot red pepper flakes
1 teaspoon kosher salt
black pepper to taste

FOR GARNISHING:
1 small red salad onion, chopped small; flesh of 1 small red
    bell pepper, diced; 1 celery stalk, diced; 8 Kalamata olives,
    pitted and chopped; juice of 1 lemon; 1 tablespoon
    chopped parsley and/or chopped fresh mint

Drain the beans and discard the soaking liquid. Heat the olive oil in
a thick-bottomed saucepan. When it is hot, turn down the heat to
medium low. Add the drained beans, then the garlic, bay leaves, thyme,

red pepper flakes, salt, and black pepper. Let this cook for 10 minutes, turning the beans over gently so they are coated with the oil and seasonings.

Add enough water to just cover the beans. Bring to a very gentle simmer and, with the cover slightly ajar, cook the beans for about 1 hour, stirring them every 20 minutes and adding a little more water if necessary. The liquid should be reduced to a sauce-like consistency, and the texture of the beans should be quite smooth.

Finally, gently stir in the chopped onion, red bell pepper, celery, and olives, followed by the lemon juice. Taste for seasoning. Remove from the heat and transfer to a serving bowl. Let everything cool down to room temperature, stirring occasionally. Sprinkle with the minced parsley and/or mint just before serving.

RANDOM RECEIPTS

Over the years, I've noticed that I've never written about a lot of interesting dishes simply because they didn't fit into a larger theme or seem worthy of an entire essay. So, recently, I've begun writing about various cooking adventures that simply resulted in a dish that pleased Matt and myself. Of course, it's not in my nature to present a recipe without conveying something of how I happened to choose it and how I went about shaping it to my taste . . .

NOT EXACTLY ECUADORIAN SHRIMP CEVICHE

For experienced cooks, reading recipes in newspapers can be a frustrating pastime. I was reminded of this when, glancing through the *Boston Globe* food pages, I happened across a recipe for "Ecuadorian Shrimp Ceviche." Despite the fact that shrimp is far and away this country's favorite seafood,* Matt and I don't eat it much. In New England, most of the year, you can only buy shrimp frozen,† and freezing any seafood tends to wash out its flavor, leaving you with what seems a lackluster

---

*According to the National Fisheries Institute, the average American ate 4.2 pounds of shrimp in 2004, a record.
†Fresh shrimp caught in the Bay of Maine used to be a winter treat here. This winter, due to depressed prices, Down East shrimpers couldn't give them away—no suppliers would touch them.

simulacrum of the real thing. However, I do like shrimp, and I thought that a ceviche might be a way to get closer to the taste and texture of fresh shrimp—so I read through the recipe.

Whenever I do this, several parts of my personality start gabbing all at once. Already we've heard from Mr. Easily Beguiled, compulsive recipe reader. At this point, though, he is quickly elbowed aside by Mr. Practical Shopper, who, as usual, has done a fast calculation of what this dish is going to cost. (The following list omits, of course, things we already have at hand, like salt, olive oil, etc.)

2 pounds unpeeled large shrimp:	$18.00
1 orange, juiced:	.65
1 cup coarsely chopped parsley:	1.00
1 cup coarsely chopped cilantro:	1.50
1 tomato, chopped:	1.00
1 red onion, halved:	.75
3 limes, halved:	2.37
1 avocado:	1.50
plantain chips for garnish:	1.29
Total:	**$28.06**

"Over twenty-five bucks for an *appetizer*?" he snorts. "What personage are we expecting for dinner? The Pope?" I point out mildly that shrimp is often on sale this time of year; that for Matt and myself, I would be using only half the called-for amount; and that I was planning to serve it over rice as a main course (not, it would turn out, a good idea). Also, I could probably omit one of the limes, the parsley, and the plantain chips.

But now a very indignant Mr. Culinary Know-It-All interrupts.* "Stop me if I'm wrong," he hisses, "but isn't a ceviche a dish of marinated *raw* seafood?" I nod. "Well, the first thing this recipe does is sauté the shrimp for *five minutes*. Plus," he sniffs, "it calls for three heaping tablespoons of ketchup. How Ecuadorian is *that*?"

I sigh. It's a vice of his to assume that other cuisines answer to a higher calling than our own. I wouldn't be in the least surprised if Ecuadorians, like everyone else in the civilized world, use ketchup with feckless abandon. However, the point about ceviche seemed well taken,

---

*That irritating nag, Mr. Food Poisoning Alert, has been temporarily silenced by the fact that the shrimp in question were previously frozen. Between you and me, I don't really know positively that raw "pickled" shrimp is safe to eat, but that seems to be the general consensus.

so I decided to do a little research, both in our own South American cookbooks and on the Internet.

Ecuador, it turns out, is one of the world's largest shrimp producers, and the country has practically all but trademarked shrimp ceviche. Perhaps because of this very fact, recipes for the dish have little unanimity, although all have an obvious family resemblance. Even the question as to whether to cook the shrimp first ranged all over the map, from no cooking at all to a serious ten-minute boiling. And, when it came to what ingredients to include, the recipes ran the gamut from the short and spartan to the impossibly over-the-top.

This meant that I was able to rule out several versions right away, like the one that called for the zest of six oranges (yeah, right) and another that called for twelve ingredients in the marinade itself, including Dijon mustard, Worcestershire sauce, and—heh—a quarter-cup of ketchup. More problematic, however, were the recipes that attempted to cope with necessary ingredients that are almost impossible to find in the United States.

The most important of these is the acidic juice of citrus fruit, which, along with salt, is what "cooks" the seafood in a ceviche. Ecuadorians use their native lemon or the sour orange. Both are more acidic than ours, and so the recipe writers mostly resort to using a citrus blend— lime and lemon for one, and lemon and orange for the other. I've been in this situation before, and I've decided that a mix of juices leaves the dish with an unsatisfactory generic citrus taste. So, as I usually do, I cast my lot with the familiar Persian lime.

Having factored all this in and worked up a preliminary recipe, I did a trial run. The results didn't really sweep me away. Acid-cooked seafood is, in taste, closer to the raw than to the cooked, which, with shrimp, means delicate almost to the point of faint. If shrimp flavor is what you want, the best way to get it remains, at least for this cook, to sauté them in their shells and eat the result with your fingers (see recipe on page 269).

Quite possibly, the reason for parboiling the shrimp when making this ceviche is simply to get more of their flavor into the dish. But, for me, the persuasive reason for leaving them uncooked except by the marinade was the resulting taut and chewy texture. (It reminded me a bit of periwinkles, which, long ago on the Maine coast, I used to gather at low tide and boil up for supper.) In other words, shrimp ceviche offered the sort of deliciousness that comes from learning how to match the featured ingredient's assertive consistency with a careful balancing of the other flavors so that they enhanced rather than drowned out its delicate taste.

To accomplish this, I had to do two things. First, I had to tame the sulphuric acridity of the raw onion, and I found an Ecuadorian cooking site that taught me how. Next, I had to stop skimping on the lime juice. Originally, given that limes were seventy-nine cents each, I had used just enough to cover the shrimp, thinking that would be enough. But the salt leached enough liquid from the onion and the shrimp that it diluted the lime juice. Even after twelve hours, not only had the transmutation barely taken place, but the flavors had failed to harmonize.

Consequently, the next time around, I bought a container of Minute Maid frozen lime juice. It was made from concentrate, but pure and unadulterated, and it tasted just fine. For the price of less than three limes, I could use as much as I needed, with plenty left over for the next time. And, after I made the second batch, I knew for sure that there would be a next time—and another after that. This time, the flavors linked arms, the shrimp was a pleasure both to taste and to chew, and the onions got along with everyone.

ECUADORIANESQUE SHRIMP CEVICHE
[Serves 4 as an appetizer]

Ecuadorians serve this ceviche with lard-toasted dried corn kernels (see lengthy commentary below). But for this norteamericano, good tortilla chips are not only a more accessible substitution but are delicious with the dish and make it easier to eat. And if you're looking for an excuse to party, just set out a bowl of this ceviche, another of guacamole, the tortilla chips, and lots of ice-cold beer.

    1 small red onion, very thinly sliced
    ½ tablespoon sugar dissolved in 1 cup water
    1 pound frozen large shrimp (31/35 count), defrosted
    ½ cup lime juice, freshly squeezed or from concentrate
    ½ medium green bell pepper, finely diced
    2 red jalapeño peppers, finely diced

1 small garlic clove, very finely minced
1 teaspoon kosher salt
a good grinding of black pepper
leaves from 6 to 8 sprigs fresh cilantro, minced
white corn tortilla chips for serving

Soak the sliced onion in the bowl of sugared water, stirring occasionally, while you prepare the other ingredients.

Peel the shrimp and cut each one in half. Put the shrimp, lime juice, green pepper, jalapeños, garlic, salt, pepper, and the onions (drained) into a nonreactive bowl and stir up well. Then pack into a quart-size ziplock plastic bag and seal it up. (The bag is optional, but it helps ensure a thorough marination.) Place this (in a bowl) in the refrigerator. The shrimp will be ready in an hour and will sustain maximum goodness for up to four hours.

To serve, strain off and discard the marinade (see note), put everything else into a bowl, sprinkle with the minced cilantro, and let come to room temperature.

Cook's Note. After I drained off the marinade I stuck my finger into it and tasted it—not bad. So I poured it over crushed ice along with a tot of rum, stirred well, added a few cilantro leaves for garnish, and drank. Sort of like a shrimp-based Bull Shot. Tasty and *¡muy potente!*

A Note on *Maiz Tostado*

In the wondrous ways of our contemporary world, an Ecuadorian grocery opened up in the town next to ours while I was working on this piece. Ecuador Andolino is only a little larger than a walk-in closet, and, even so, its limited wares are spread out to fill empty shelves. What Ecuadorians miss from the home country isn't necessarily what newcomers to the cuisine would want to find: lots and lots of packaged cookies and pastry and candy, Ecuadorian pasta, and hundreds of compact discs and videos. But you can also find flours milled from fava beans and purple corn, exotic herbal teas (although none made with coca leaves), canned South American fruit,* and, happily, big packages

---

*I fell into conversation with Tony Garay, the store's affable proprietor, about two jars of unfamiliar native fruits—*tomate de arbol* (tree tomatoes) and *babaco*. Mr. Garay was hard-of *maiz tostado*, the dried corn kernels that are toasted, then served as an accompaniment to many dishes or eaten by themselves as a snack.

Actually, the shop offered two sizes of this: *maiz tostado* itself, noticeably oversize kernels of white corn, and *maiz chulpe*, smaller kernels of yellow corn. Toasting these kernels is nearly identical to making popcorn (although it can also be done in a deep-fat fryer, or, as the Indians did before the Spanish arrived with pigs, with no fat in clay pots stuck in hot coals). I heated a tablespoon of fat in a two-quart saucepan over a medium flame, sprinkling in half a teaspoon of fine sea salt, then adding one cup of the dried kernels. I covered the pan, gave everything a shake, and let the kernels heat. Pretty soon, there was the familiar—if unexpectedly leisurely—sound of corn popping.

Maiz tostado takes longer to burst open than popcorn, so to prevent the kernels from burning, you have to keep tossing them, one hand securing the lid, until the noise stops. Let the pan sit unopened for a minute or two (there are always a few after-the-fact explosions), then lift up the cover and peek in. Be prepared for a surprise: despite all that popping noise, nothing will seem to have happened.

Look closer. The kernels have not only turned a toasty brown but have swelled up and burst open—they just haven't "popped." What you get when you toast this kind of corn is essentially a pot full of "old maids." But where those are usually hard and tough, the large kernels of *maiz tostado* are crispy on the outside and tender within. In fact, the texture reminds me of roasted chestnuts, and the taste less of popcorn than dryish cornmeal mush. According to Maria Baez Kijac, in *The South American Table*, "Tostado is an integral part of the Ecuadorian *hornado* (roasted leg of pork) and *fritada* (fried pork chunks)." I can

---

pressed to characterize the flavor of these, especially *babaco*. But he did say that he liked to empty a jar of that fruit into a blender and whiz it up into a sort of breakfast smoothie. Once home, I both read up on and took a sample bite from each of the jars. *Tomate de arbol* remain a bit of a puzzle—only barely sweet, they taste like a tomato that just lost a fistfight with an unripe mango. But *babaco*—wow! A species of papaya that is distinctive enough to have its own name, it offers up a deliciously delicate papaya flavor, touched with pineapple and banana. Thirty seconds in the food processor melded the fruit slices and their light syrup into a mildly sweet, fruit-nubbled purée, unusual, filling, and very good. I was aware of the passion denizens of the tropics have for fruit blender drinks, but not that these could be made with canned fruits—and that's the only way to get hold of a lot of native varieties, Southeast Asian ones included.

easily see substituting it for hominy in a dish like *pozole*, but the kernels are a bit too mealy for me to totally enjoy as a snack.

On the other hand, the smaller kernels of *maiz chulpe* toast into something that is just as tender as *maiz tostado* but also thoroughly, deliciously crunchy—as well as bursting with flavor. (CornNuts, which are made by deep-frying kernels of an American strain of the same corn, are somewhat similar but lack *maiz chulpe*'s tenderness and fresh, punchy flavor.) Kijac says that Bolivians serve slices of cheese with toasted corn, but melt thin slices of Monterey Jack or another mild cheese on top of a plate of just-toasted *maiz chulpe*—and what you have is, without a doubt, the ultimate corn snack.

Sources: South American Groceries Online

Since Latin American cooking hasn't yet become trendy enough to catch the interest of gourmet sites, you'll find you have to do a little digging to locate things like canned native fruits or *maiz*. Perhaps the best of the lot is www.amigofoods.com, which breaks down its offerings by country. There you can buy my favorite variety of *maiz tostado*, La Cholita brand *maiz chulpe*. Another site worth a visit is www.latinmerchant.com, which offers two other kinds of Peruvian-grown *maiz tostado*. Both are sold under the Amazonas label—giant white *maiz cancha cuzco* and the rather smaller yellow *maiz cancha amarillo*. As for the two South American fruits in jars that I mention above, I couldn't find any sources at all. This is probably all for the best, because nothing beats checking out these foods at your local Latin American grocer. And if you're nervous about finding your way about, pick up a copy of Linda Bladholm's *Latin and Caribbean Grocery Stores Demystified*. It has 400 entries and 200 illustrations, and the text is clearly written and encouraging—the best sort of guide for anyone entering their local *mercado* for the first time.

THE RIGHT STUFF

The budget-constrained *bec fin* could do worse (although, it should be added, not much worse) than to periodically check over the pickings at the local liquidator warehouse store's "gourmet" shelves. These fascinating emporiums are the last station on the line for the unsold and the unsalable, whether these be grayish-colored green peas in glass jars from Bulgaria, ornate flasks stuffed with chile peppers, carrot chunks, green olives, and garlic cloves, or tiramisu-flavored sponge-cake rolls (think Little Debbies for Eurotrash).

Our own emporium of this sort is Big Lots, and this is where I go to stock up on packages of Wasa flatbread ($1.49) edging up to their sell-by date; jars of pungent black olives from Argentina (99¢); and, recently, imported from Turkey, some large, flat cans of zucchini stuffed with rice ($1.99). I bought the last with no other anticipation than of having something different for my midnight snack. But when I dug into them—straight from the can—the very first mouthful unexpectedly seized hold of my imagination.

If you had been there looking down into the can with me, you would have seen, neatly pressing against each other, six rounds of zucchini, open mouths facing up, each stuffed with seasoned rice. This sight was, in fact, very appetizing itself, and when I dug in my spoon and took a bite, I felt a very childlike delight in how easily the spoon slid through the cooked squash (as it wouldn't have if the can, say, held stuffed grape leaves). I also loved the play of soft textures against each other—the almost mushy rice, the slight but noticeable resistance of the zucchini.

All that kept it from ringing the bell was the washed-out flavor, not all that unexpected given that canned zucchini isn't exactly renowned (although, saints preserve us, it does exist). I was convinced that if I could figure out a recipe, I could make it all work out.

The version I present here was assembled from an assortment of Turkish and other Middle Eastern cookbooks, with some finishing touches all my own. When Matt saw the first attempt, fresh from the oven, she remarked that she could tell just by looking at it that this was my kind of dish. There is something about mixing things into rice that has an almost magical power over me, and our history together is studded with them, starting with the Cajun boudin I made from scratch for our first supper together, and followed by dirty rice, fried rice, duck hash . . . the list goes on and on.

Also, like other of my favorite dishes, this one appeals by being conceptually simple while offering an amazing potential for variation, even in its essential elements. You could, for instance, replace the rice with dried bread crumbs, or substitute small eggplants or large chile peppers for the squash. And, as for the flavorings, choices range from chopped celery to black olive bits, baby peas, capers . . . even morsels of dried fruit. Once you set this dish in play, you'll find that, as much as appetite, fascination with its possibilities will bring you back to it again and again.

ZUCCHINI STUFFED WITH RICE
[Serves 2 or 3 as a meal, 4 as a side dish]

Middle Eastern cooks use a variety of corers to hollow out vegetables for stuffing. I traced two of these down, ordered them, and found them next to useless. I also tried a boning knife and a screwdriver, and only just managed to restrain myself from attempting the job with an electric drill. What works best for the job, I discovered, is a nested set of circular biscuit cutters. They not only create a perfect round but let you pop the core right out. If you don't have a set (and this is a great excuse to get one), a paring knife is the distant second choice.

> 6 zucchini, 6 to 8 inches long, as tubular as possible
>   (see note)
> 6 tablespoons extra-virgin olive oil
> 1 teaspoon kosher salt
> 1 heaping cup uncooked long-grain white rice
> 1 large garlic clove, finely minced
> 1 bunch scallions, ragged tops trimmed off, coarsely chopped
> 4 sun-dried tomatoes, cut into bits (see note)
> 1 or 2 green jalapeño peppers, diced
> a handful each fresh parsley and dill, finely chopped
> 1 tablespoon freshly squeezed lemon juice
> 1 cup boiling water seasoned with 1 teaspoon kosher salt

Trim the ends from the zucchini and discard. Slice them into 4 rounds and cut out the center of each, leaving a ¼-inch shell. Chop up and reserve the removed pulp.

In a deep 10-inch skillet, heat all but 1 tablespoon of the olive oil over a medium flame. Add the salt, then the rice, and sauté for 5 minutes, stirring the while. Don't let it brown. Add the minced garlic, chopped scallions, and dried tomato and jalapeño bits, and sauté another 2 or 3 minutes, until the garlic is translucent and the scallions wilted. Stir in the zucchini pulp and continue to cook, while mashing with a fork until it is soft and incorporated with the other ingredients.

Taste for salt, adding more if desired. Pour in ½ cup of water and bring this to a boil. Cover, reduce the heat to low, and simmer until all the liquid has been absorbed. Mix in the chopped parsley and dill and the tablespoon of lemon juice.

Meanwhile, preheat oven to 350°F. Use the reserved olive oil to grease the bottom and sides of a casserole wide enough to hold all the zucchini rings and set them in place, hollowed part facing up. A tight fit is great but not necessary.

When the stuffing mixture is cool enough to handle, spoon it into the zucchini rings and—if there's some left over—into the interstices between the rings. Pour over the salted boiling water, cover, and bake in the oven until the zucchini rings are tender and the rice entirely cooked, about 45 minutes.

Cook's Notes. Zucchini: In my test runs, I tried substituting summer squash and Cubanelle peppers for some of the zucchini; both were delicious, although it's harder to find tubular summer squash. In the summer, when yellow zucchini is available at the local farmers' markets, it will make an equally nice contrast.

Sun-Dried Tomatoes: Very often, recipes call for currants in this dish, and, while for years and years I had a box of these aging quietly in the pantry, I no longer do. Other recipes call for adding fresh tomatoes. Because I had the sun-dried tomatoes on hand, this seemed an easy way to kill two birds with one stone. Feel free to add a smallish chopped fresh tomato and/or a small scoop of currants, if you prefer.

A Note on *Taze Fasulye*

While researching this dish, I became curious about what other stuffed vegetables were imported from Turkey. I found a site online offering several,* and ended up ordering some, along with a can of Türkili

---

*There are, it turns out, more than a few sites offering Turkish foods, but the one with the best assortment of canned goods at near–Big Lots prices was www.yiyelim.com. However, before you rush over to your computer, I should note that the entire site is in Turkish. After discovering that pushing buttons at random wouldn't get me what I wanted, I located a Turkish-English online dictionary—www.seslisozluk.com. With that and some careful exami-

brand *taze fasulye* ($1.99)—a mélange of green beans, red bell pepper, tomatoes, and onions in a tomato-based sauce. When the can arrived, I saw that the green beans were actually Romano (sometimes called Roma or Italian) beans—flat, thick-skinned green beans that, in my experience, offer more to chew than to taste. In this context, however, they were delicious—perhaps, I thought, because they held up better than ordinary green beans to factory processing. And if that was so, perhaps plain old frozen Romano beans could produce a version just as tasty—and almost as easy to make.

The "almost as easy" part of this was abetted by two habits I've fallen into. One is to cut up a lemon, separate the slices with plastic film, and keep these in a ziplock bag in the freezer for when I need some fresh lemon juice or a bit of lemon peel.

The other is to snap up passably decent red (or yellow or orange or green) bell peppers when these appear on the produce section's markdown rack ("not our best but still good"). As soon as I get them home, I core, stem, and seed them, and slice the flesh into strips. These I fry in a tablespoon or so of olive oil, with some minced garlic and a good pinch of salt. Prepared this way, they will last at least a week in a bowl in the refrigerator, finding their way into egg dishes, sandwiches, and soups.

With these at hand, making the salad really was a snap, but even without them the effort is well worth it. The frozen Romano beans had an appealing meaty texture, and sautéing (rather than boiling) them retained more than a sufficient amount of fresh green-bean taste. Just remember that the flavors improve if the salad is allowed to sit for an hour or so, then stirred well and served at room temperature.

---

nation of the photographs of various canned items, I was able to assemble a pretty tasty order. I especially recommend the somewhat caloric but delicious Türkili *patlican kizartma* (fried eggplant slices in a flavorful sauce of green pepper and tomato), $1.99; Sera *pazi sarmasi* (bulgur-stuffed chard leaves), $2.14; the same brand's *patlican dolma* (eggplant stuffed with rice and currants in tomato sauce), $2.19; and Baktat *dolma biber* (small, rice-stuffed peppers), $1.99—and there are many other items I'm looking forward to trying. Note that shipping will add about a dollar a can to your order. Finally, if wrestling with Turkish is not your idea of a good time, you can find similar items similarly priced (just not so many) at their sister English-language site, www.turkishfoodstore.com, or at www.turkishtaste.com, in the "ready to eat" section. Strangely (maybe), not one of the places I visited sold cans of stuffed zucchini (*etli kabak dolmasi*).

ROMANO BEAN SALAD
[Serves 4 as a side dish or salad]

1 small (or ½ large) red bell pepper, cored and seeded
1 small onion
1 garlic clove
2 tablespoons extra-virgin olive oil
1 lemon slice or ½ tablespoon red wine vinegar
2 plum (cooking) tomatoes, cut into chunks
1 pound bag frozen Romano green beans
⅛ teaspoon ground allspice
salt and black pepper to taste

Cut both the red pepper and the onion into strips about the length of (but somewhat narrower than) the Romano beans. Mince the garlic.

Heat the olive oil over medium-low heat. Add the prepared bell pepper, onion, and garlic, and stir to mix well. Sauté these for 15 minutes, or until the pepper skins are tender. Lower the heat if necessary to keep the onion or garlic from getting brown.

Cut the lemon slice (if using) in half. Add these (or the wine vinegar) and the tomatoes to the skillet, followed by the beans. Stir together with the skillet contents and continue cooking—again, occasionally stirring—until the beans are heated through and have become tender (but not soft).

Sprinkle over the allspice, season with salt and black pepper to taste, and toss well. Remove the skillet from the heat and either serve immediately or, preferably, after the dish has ripened at least half an hour.

TWO SOUPS

Both of these soups are prepared in a very similar fashion; both are hearty and uncomplicated; both show how the seemingly mild flavor of potato can make a stunning marriage with sharp-edged greens. The reason I've brought the two recipes together here is to demonstrate how the different character of the two greens—the escarole with its hint of bitterness, the bok choy with its peppery cabbage tones—led me to different choices with regard to most of the flavorings. The making of both these soups may seem overly fussy, but I found that I needed to go about it this way to coax out what are, after all, rather delicate flavors and to protect them from being overdiluted and overcooked.

POTATO AND ESCAROLE SOUP
[Serves 4]

4 medium-size Yukon Gold potatoes, washed but unpeeled
2 teaspoons kosher salt
2 tablespoons extra-virgin olive oil, plus more for serving
1 or 2 garlic cloves, finely minced
½ teaspoon hot red pepper flakes
¼ teaspoon dried oregano
black pepper to taste
2 celery stalks
1 large yellow onion
1 head escarole
¼ cup white wine

Put the unpeeled potatoes in a medium saucepan and barely cover them with water. Add a teaspoon of the salt. Bring the water to a boil, then cover loosely, and reduce the heat so that the water remains at just a simmer. Cook for about 45 minutes, or until a bamboo skewer or similar implement can easily be poked through the entire potato.

Pour the olive oil into a large soup pot and put it over a low flame. Add the minced garlic, hot red pepper flakes, oregano, the rest of the salt, and a few grindings of black pepper. Cut the celery stalks at an angle into V-shaped bite-size pieces and add these to the pot. Now cut the onion in half, then slice each half into bite-size pieces as well. Add these to the pot, stirring a bit to separate the onion pieces. Cook all this gently in the open pot, giving them an additional stir every few minutes, until they are tender.

Strip the leaves from the head of escarole and wash them carefully in a basin of water. Trim and discard the discolored end from the bottom of the core and cut what remains into slices. Add these to the soup pot, then tear the leaves into large bite-size pieces, collecting them in a bowl. Include among them, whole, any immature leaves at the center.

When the potatoes are done, remove them with a slotted spoon to a cutting board, reserving the cooking water. Slice them in half and gingerly strip off their skins. (I eat these right then with a pinch of salt and a dab of butter.) Cut the potatoes into bite-size chunks and add these to the soup pot. Pour the white wine over and stir well, so that the potatoes are coated with the wine and the seasoned olive oil. Continue cooking, stirring gently, for 5 minutes.

Pour in the reserved potato water, then add the escarole, handful by handful, stirring each in before adding the next. Raise the heat slightly and cook the soup until the escarole is wilted and soft, another 3 minutes or so. By now enough of the potato will have dissolved to produce a thickish broth. Taste this for salt, adding more as necessary, then ladle everything into soup bowls, dressing each with a little swirl of olive oil before bringing them to table.

Cook's Note. Those who shudder at the notion of a meat-free main-course soup are welcome to thickly slice a few links of precooked (and appropriately seasoned) chicken sausage and add these to the pot at the same time as the cut-up potato.

POTATO AND BOK CHOY SOUP
[Serves 4]

4 medium-size Yukon Gold potatoes, washed but unpeeled
2 teaspoons kosher salt
2 tablespoons extra-virgin olive oil
1 or 2 garlic cloves, finely minced
½ teaspoon black mustard seeds
black pepper to taste
1 large yellow onion, chopped
1 medium-size head bok choy, washed and trimmed
8 ounces fresh or frozen green peas
minced leaves of several sprigs flat-leaf parsley

Put the unpeeled potatoes in a medium saucepan and barely cover them with water. Add a teaspoon of the salt. Bring the water to a boil, then cover loosely, and reduce the heat so that the water remains at just a simmer. Cook for about 45 minutes, or until a bamboo skewer or similar implement can easily be poked through the entire potato.

Pour the olive oil into a large soup pot and put it over a low flame. Add the minced garlic, mustard seeds, the remaining teaspoon of salt, and several grindings of black pepper. When the garlic is translucent, add the chopped onion, stirring after a minute or so to separate its pieces. Cook these gently in the open pot, giving them an additional stir every few minutes, while you prepare the bok choy.

Remove the leafy stems of the bok choy from its core. Rinse everything gently in cold water. Cut away and discard the bottom ¼ inch of the core, then slice the rest of it into coins. Add these directly to the soup pot. Now trim the leaves from the white stems and cut the latter into bite-size pieces, slicing at an angle so that they are more triangular than square. Finally, stack together and slice the leaves into a chiffonade, collecting these and the cut-up stems in a large bowl.

When the potatoes are done, remove them to a cutting board. Add the peas to the cooking water. If these are frozen, turn off the heat. If they are fresh, gently cook them until tender. Slice the potatoes in half and gingerly strip off and discard their skins. Cut them into bite-size chunks and add these to the soup pot. Sprinkle over the minced parsley and continue cooking for 5 more minutes, turning the potatoes over with a spatula so that they are coated with the seasoned olive oil and mustard seeds.

Now add the bok choy, handful by handful, stirring each in before adding the next. Finally, turn in the peas and the reserved cooking liquid. Raise the heat slightly and cook the soup until the bok choy stems are succulent but still crisp. By now enough of the potato will have dissolved to produce a thickish broth. Taste this for salt, adding more as necessary, then ladle the soup into bowls and serve.

NINE-HOUR SHOULDER OF LAMB

The shoulder is by far the most versatile of all the cuts of the lamb and like its counterpart in the beef, the chuck, offers some of the greatest money-saving potential for any consumer willing to spend a little time learning all of the many things that can be done with it.

—Merle Ellis, *Cutting-Up in the Kitchen*

Several years ago, I was persuaded to prepare that French classic *gigot à sept heures*—leg of lamb cooked for seven hours. As promised, the meat was tender enough to eat with a spoon, but that hardly offset the fact that it was on the far side of well done, the dullest sort of gray, to the eye and to the mouth. For a person who likes his leg of lamb just a nudge past rare, the results of this technique were, if not exactly a sacrilege, certainly nothing I wanted to eat.

However, tenderness definitely trumps rareness when the subject is shoulder of lamb, a cut that, in the ordinary course of events, I have found little use for. The truth is that lamb is expensive, either because it's plainly pricey—as with loin chops, leg roasts, and a rack of ribs—or because of a large amount of waste. Lamb shanks are mostly bone, lamb breast is mainly bone and fat, and lamb shoulder chops are a medley of these plus sinew and cartilage, with some meat struggling to keep them all apart.

You might wonder, this being so, why these cuts of lamb aren't sold at a more appropriate (i.e., much lower) price—or, for that matter, why the cheaper cuts of lamb have become harder and harder to find. Lamb kidneys never seem to be around these days, and I can't remember the last time I saw lamb breast, which I regularly prepared back in the seventies. As for lamb neck bones, lamb tongues, or lamb liver—you'd think they'd found a way to breed sheep without those things.

However, the reason has nothing to do with genetics and everything to do with the meat business. Twenty-five years ago, supermarket meat departments bought lamb by the whole or half carcass, and butchered it themselves. Cuts like lamb breast and shank were priced low because they had to sell them. Now, they order only the cuts customers will buy and price them accordingly. Consequently, where previously buying a package of lamb shanks was doing the butcher a flavor, if any show up in the display case these days, the butcher considers this a favor that he's doing *us*.

Recently, however, I got into experimenting with lamb shoulder chops, first separating out the meat from the dross, then stewing these chunks for several hours at a very low temperature. The result was more than encouraging—it got me wanting to apply the method to a whole lamb shoulder roast.

If you haven't heard of such a thing, you aren't alone; I can't recall ever seeing one during my entire cooking life. Still, Merle Ellis had an illustration of one in his tome of butcherly wisdom, *Cutting-Up in the*

Kitchen, and that was good enough for me. When lamb shoulder chops went on sale for $1.99 a pound at our local Big Y, I paid a visit to "Sam," the store's head butcher.* I wish I had brought Merle along with me. "Sam" seemed rather flummoxed when I asked him for a lamb shoulder roast, and what he eventually handed over the counter resembled not at all the neatly trimmed roast pictured in the book—it was just a plain ol' ragged, four-pound hunk of meat.

However, I just cut or pulled away all the fat I could, rubbed the rest with some marinade, and slid it into a very slow oven. It took nine hours to reach the point where a skewer could easily be poked right through the roast. Then it was merely a matter of searching out the meat. After I removed a thick layer of fat and cut free a number of various-size bones, I found I had a goodly amount. Furthermore, it was moist, flavorful (muttony, yes, that too, but not nearly as gamy as shanks can be), and, best of all, mouth-meltingly tender. Indeed, with a little effort, you could eat it with a spoon.

SLOW-COOKED SHOULDER OF LAMB
[Serves 4]

Unless your butcher is willing to do some serious trimming, I'd recommend erring on the generous side and purchasing a pound of shoulder for each eater you plan to serve.

two dribbles plus ¼ cup extra-virgin olive oil
1 large or 2 medium yellow onions, chopped
6 garlic cloves
a pinch plus 1 tablespoon kosher salt
leaves from a sprig fresh rosemary or pinch of dried
½ tablespoon coarsely ground black pepper
½ teaspoon hot red pepper flakes
4 pounds lamb shoulder, trimmed of excess surface fat
½ cup dry red wine
½ tablespoon flour, for the gravy

---

*"Sam" is in quotes because, for reasons that one can only guess at, the supermarket's management encourages customers to call *all* Big Y butchers by that name.

Preheat oven to 175°F. Use a dribble of olive oil to lightly grease the bottom of a stewpot large enough to comfortably hold the lamb shoulder. Put the pot over a low flame, add the chopped onion, and sauté gently until translucent.

Flatten each of the garlic cloves with the side of a chef's knife or cleaver. Anoint these with a pinch of salt and a dribble of olive oil. Then sprinkle the rosemary leaves over. Mince everything together.

In a small bowl, put the ¼ cup of olive oil, the remaining salt, the black pepper, and the red pepper flakes. Add the minced garlic-rosemary mixture and mix into a slurry. Using your fingers, rub this into all exposed areas of the lamb shoulder, working it gently into any crevices. (This not only flavors the meat but adds some potent antibacterial protection during the slow rise to cooking temperature.)

Pour the wine over the sautéed onions, place the meat into the pot on top of them, cover, and put into the preheated oven. Let it cook undisturbed for 9 hours.

When the cooking time is over, take the pot from the oven and the cover from the pot. Let the meat sit for 15 minutes, then carefully transfer it to a cutting board. Cut the meat away from the bones, at the same time discarding as much fat as possible. Cut large pieces of meat into slices.

Meanwhile, see if the cooking liquid needs to be skimmed of fat. (Because of the low cooking temperature, much less fat is rendered.) If so, remove it. Put the pot over a medium flame, then make a gravy by delicately sprinkling in the flour and stirring this for 5 minutes until it is thoroughly incorporated and the liquid has thickened into a gravy. (If the gravy seems too salty, thin it with up to half a cup of water or milk.) Pour this into a gravy boat and serve at once with the meat and whatever else you've planned for supper.

Cook's Note. If you'd prefer to separate the meat from the fat and bones before cooking it rather than afterwards, do so, cutting large pieces into smaller chunks. Put these in the bowl with the marinade, toss to coat well, and turn everything into the stewpot. Cover and cook as directed above, except for a total time of 8 hours instead of 9. During the last hour of cooking, you may, if you wish, sauté bite-size pieces of carrot and peeled potato in a large skillet in a few tablespoons of seasoned olive oil until cooked through. Add the finished lamb pieces and the pot liquid and serve as a lamb stew. (However, don't add the raw vegetables to the stewpot with the lamb, because, even after 8 hours, they won't be ready to eat.)

BRIAMI

> We ate [*briami*] with a local family in the village of Mounthros, about an hour's drive from Rethimno, under the coolness of the huge plane trees in their sloping hilly terrace, backed by the monotonous resounding cascading of the cold crystal water of the mountain waterfalls for which the village is well known.
>
> —Rena Salaman, *Greek Food*

I first came across *briami* in an issue of *MealTicket*, Malika Henderson's cleverly named journal on travel and food that accomplishes what many try to do and few succeed at: matching intelligent, evocative prose with equally striking photography.* In that issue she documented a visit to the Greek island Lesvos, and although she described many meals she ate there (recipes also provided), her pleasure in *briami*—*briam*, she calls it, as do many Greeks (and some Greek cookbooks)—was so transparent that she got me interested in it myself.

I'm glad she did. *Briami* is one of those rustic dishes whose recipe can never be pinned down because every cook takes the basic idea—slices of potatoes, zucchini, tomatoes, and onions mixed in herb-flavored olive oil and baked until tender in the oven—and goes her own way with it. The dish appears in six or so of my Greek cookbooks, and the version in each was so different from the others that the total effect was one of suggestion rather than direction.

Furthermore, the aspect of *briami* that immediately seized my attention the first time I made it was that as it baked it filled our apartment with a wonderful aroma of hot tomatoes. This was not at all like, say, a pasta sauce cooking, and it was somehow redolent of my childhood, although I couldn't place how. Matt suggested scalloped tomatoes, and as soon as she said it I knew that she was right—even though I hadn't tasted these . . . even thought about them . . . for many decades. Scalloped tomatoes is one of the delicious but irredeemably old-fashioned

---

*MealTicket; P.O. Box 778; Woodacre, CA 94973; (415) 847-6083. Find out more by visiting her website, www.mealticketnews.com.

Yankee dishes that my grandmother adored, and you could easily apply the same comments to it that Della Lutes makes about creamed asparagus (see page 233).

On its home turf, *briami* is a summer dish, not only because it is made with that season's vegetables but because it is light and usually eaten at room temperature—ideal, that is, to make ahead in the cooler part of the day. Or, even better, have someone else do this. In *The Foods of Greece*, Aglaia Kremezi writes: "During our summer holidays, we used to prepare this classic dish early in the morning. We would leave it with the village baker on our way to the beach, then pick it up on the way home. The top was always a little burned, but that did not spoil the taste."

As such, it is often eaten with bread and cheese on the side—Rena Salaman, enjoying it on that shaded terrace in Mounthros, had it with homemade Myzithra, a soft, white, unsalted sheep's milk cheese, "deliciously rich and melting in the mouth in a slow process of over-lapping waves of pleasing tastes." It is also easy to imagine this summery version of *briami* served as a side dish with grilled lamb or fish.

None of this means that you won't want to eat it in winter. On the contrary, that summery aroma, that wealth of summer vegetables, brings with it a flood of evocative suggestion that wraps you in its own kind of warmth. Our cold-weather version, meant to be eaten hot, takes a cue from scalloped tomatoes—the topping of rich, crunchy bread crumbs. Breaking through this to reveal the steaming mélange of vegetables beneath makes the whole thing seem so cold weather–worthy that you might almost wish for a snowstorm to put it to the test.

Finally, it came to me that if the Greeks eat *briami* in summer with slices of soft fresh sheep's milk cheese, why not in winter, to match the season, eat it with fried hard sheep's milk cheese? *Saganaki*, that tasty taverna *meze*, the Hellenic version of toasted cheese, is one of my favorite treats, but it rarely fits in with what I'm preparing at home. This means that I never get to eat it, apart from a visit to a Greek restaurant. Here was a meal that literally demanded it . . . and since all the preparation work for the *briami* was already done, provided no distractions to keep me from getting it right.

WINTER *BRIAMI*
[Serves up to 4]

*This is a dish very much given to casual proportioning. I make it fre-
quently and never the same way twice—but each time veering a little
closer to my own notions of perfection. For example, early on I decided
to parboil the potatoes because uncooked spuds take forever to cook in
a casserole and for this dish to be at its best, they need to be buttery
soft. I also eschewed salting and wringing the zucchini because the dish
needs its copious supply of liquid. Greek cooks add all variety of summer vegetables (and fresh herbs) to the dish, most notably eggplant and
okra, but we just found they made it slimy. The roasted peppers, a
salute to colder weather, are great. And if I have to limit my advice to
one rule, it would be: Don't skimp on the olive oil—the dish thrives
on it.*

> 2 medium onions
> 2 garlic cloves
> 6 tablespoons extra-virgin olive oil plus 1 teaspoon
> 1 teaspoon dried Greek oregano
> ½ teaspoon hot red pepper flakes
> ½ cup homemade dried bread crumbs (see page 206)
> 2 or 3 medium zucchini, ends trimmed
> 2 large Yukon Gold potatoes, parboiled and peeled
> 2 or 3 vine-ripened tomatoes
> 1 6-ounce jar fire-roasted red or yellow peppers, drained
> several sprigs flat-leaf parsley, minced
> 1 teaspoon kosher salt

Preheat oven to 400°F. Coarsely chop the onions and mince the garlic.
Heat 4 tablespoons of the olive oil in a medium skillet and sauté the
onion until it is translucent, then mix in the garlic, oregano, and red
pepper flakes. In a separate, smaller skillet, gently heat the bread
crumbs in the remaining 2 tablespoons of olive oil, stirring to distribute
the oil evenly. Let these darken slightly but not toast.

Meanwhile, slice the zucchini into thin rings. Cut the potatoes in
half and then into slices about ¼-inch thick. Treat the tomatoes the
same way. Cut the roasted peppers into bite-size pieces. In a large mix-

ing bowl, toss all this gently together with the sautéed onion-garlic mixture. Use the teaspoon of olive oil to grease a medium gratin dish and fill this with the vegetables, packing them down gently. Scatter the bread crumbs over evenly.

Cover loosely with a piece of aluminum foil and bake for 40 minutes. Then remove the foil and continue baking until the casserole is hot and bubbling throughout and the crumbs are a toasty brown, about another 20 minutes. Even in winter you should let the *briami* cool for at least 15 minutes before serving it—just out of the oven the interior is mouth-burningly hot.

SAGANAKI
[Serves 2]

Like briami, saganaki *is more an idea than a recipe, a chunk of molten cheese served in a small, two-handled gratin dish (it is from this that* saganaki *takes its name). This version goes the extra kilometer and gives it a hot, crispy, golden crust as well. The trick is to have the cheese very cold and the frying oil very hot. The Greeks have other cheeses that can be prepared this way, but Kasseri, a salty hard cheese made of goat's or sheep's milk, is the easiest one to find.*

> 6-ounce piece of Kasseri
> cornstarch for dredging
> 4 tablespoons extra-virgin olive oil
> warmed plates
> lemon wedges

Cut the cheese into 4 slices about ½-inch thick and slip these into the freezer for at least 30 minutes. When ready to prepare the dish, sift a few tablespoons of cornstarch onto a plate. Rinse each slice of cheese under cold water, shaking it free of excess moisture, and set it down into the cornstarch. When all the slices are on the plate, sift more cornstarch on top to coat.

Meanwhile, heat the oil in a (preferably) cast-iron skillet large enough to comfortably hold all the cheese. When the oil is very hot—almost but not smoking—add the slices of cheese, tapping each as you lift it from the plate to dislodge any loose cornstarch. Quickly grill the cheese until the bottom of each slice has turned golden and its center has begun to melt, about 3 minutes. Then gently turn each over and grill the other side until it is crusty and golden, about 3 minutes more. Transfer to the warmed plates and serve at once with the lemon wedges.

TORTA FREDDA GIANDUIA

While I was researching *bagna caôda* for the essay that starts on page 8, I came across the following Piedmontese dessert in Ada Boni's groundbreaking *Italian Regional Cooking*. My eye was drawn to it because of the word *gianduia*—that highly addictive flavor combination of roasted hazelnuts and chocolate, most often encountered in this country as a silky-textured confection. But this turned out to be something very different and, if possible, even more delicious—a dense, chewy, chocolate-and-hazelnut-intensive, brownie-like torte. Here's the version we worked out.

· [Serves 6]

4 ounces (about ½ cup) hazelnuts, preferably skinned
2½ ounces (squares) unsweetened chocolate
1 large egg plus 1 large egg yolk
½ cup sugar
pinch of salt
5 tablespoons butter
4 ounces Petit Beurre cookies, crushed (see note)
unsweetened whipped cream for garnish

Preheat oven to 350°F. Put the hazelnuts in an ungreased pan and toast them gently for about 5 or 6 minutes, or until lightly browned. Don't let them get too dark or they will have an acrid taste. Let them cool and chop them, not too coarsely but not into a powder, either.

Grate the chocolate using either a four-sided box grater (the small shredding holes work best) or a food processor fitted with a grating disk.

Put the whole egg, egg yolk, sugar, and pinch of salt into a small mixing bowl. Whisk the mixture by hand until it becomes very light and smooth. Now whisk in the grated chocolate.

Melt the butter in the top of a double boiler. When it has completely liquified, remove the top section, set it on a towel (the bottom of the pan will be wet), and whisk in the egg-sugar-chocolate mixture. Put the top section back and continue to whisk the mixture over low heat for 5 minutes, allowing it to thicken. It is ready when the furrows made by the whisk hold their shape for several seconds and the mixture resembles a soft buttercream.

Use a spatula to gently but thoroughly fold in the chopped hazelnuts and crushed cookies. Turn the resulting chocolate-y mass onto a plate and gently shape and flatten it with the spatula until it is more or less square and about the thickness of a brownie. Put it in the refrigerator and let it chill for an hour or so before serving. Slice it into six pieces and top each with a dab of unsweetened whipped cream.

Cook's Note. Petit Beurre: We used LU's French-made Le Petit Beurre, which had the simplest ingredient list of any in our supermarket. If you can find that brand, a quarter-pound is about 13 or 14 cookies.

THE COOK CONCOCTS
HIS MIDNIGHT SNACK

Breakfast usually has at least a slender thread attaching it to the conventional, since beyond our eating of it wait the sobering demands of the day. Midnight snacking, however, situated just this side of dreams, is driven by the dangerously combustible combination of solitude, fatigue, and starvation. It is often a no-holds-barred affair. This is made all the worse for me because I regularly find myself more awake before bedtime than I have been all day. My mind, especially, gets energized the moment it starts riffling its way through the refrigerator, or even, occasionally, the garbage pail (see "Cilantro Sandwich" and "Smoked Kielbasa–Casing Po' Boy" below). The results may occasionally fall flat, but the search is never less than serious, and driven by forces not all that easy to explain. Sometimes I think it's the body's attempt to balance out what's been eaten earlier in the day; other times, it seems as if my system needs a stultifying jolt of fat in order to gear down for sleep. Whatever the reason, the ride is always an interesting one—as you'll see from perusing these entries from my online midnight snack diary.

BAKED FAT

Matt and I use smokehouse-aged country ham to add savor to many of our dishes, and the last time I ordered it, I got a half ham from Burger's Smokehouse—sliced there, then packaged in several Cryovac packets. Although the photos of the ham slices at their site always show relatively lean cuts, there is, in fact, a lot of fat on country hams, and most of this I trimmed away when I cut up the ham to add to a pot of red beans or some butter bean soup.

I baked the discarded fat trimmings in a 350°F oven for about an hour, until there was a lot of rendered fat and the pieces themselves had turned a dark golden color. At that point I removed the strips of baked fat (and rind) to drain on a paper napkin and poured the fat into a little dish for making fried eggs and such.

You might ask—what's the point of trimming away the fat if you're going to eat it anyway? Frankly, this is a very misguided question. First, by removing the fat from the ham, I'm reclassifying it from "meal food" to "snack food." When I eat it as a snack, I won't be eating some *other* high-calorie item along with it, like a bowl of salted-in-the-shell peanuts. Second, to my mind, it is one of the most delicious things in the world. Crusty, salty, edged with chewy bits of rind, its deep succulence is the savory eater's equivalent to an old-fashioned lump of divinity fudge.

SAUTÉED SPINACH STEMS

This falls more into the category of "cook's treat" than it does "midnight snack," because it's usually something I cook up for myself to eat while I'm preparing supper. Still, I don't have a "Cook's Treat" diary (nor would it make much sense to start one, since usually these are too ephemeral to keep track of. I'm not going to stop cooking and run to the computer to write a note about a scrid of beef tendon I've trimmed away and then decided to dip in salt and chew), so I decided to stick it in here.

This night we had a heap of spinach from a local farmers' market, and it had a lot of stems. As I picked through the leaves and washed them, I cut off a bunch of the largest stems and set them aside. Then, late in the evening, I put them in a skillet with a thin slice of sweet butter, a pinch of salt, and some pepper, along with two tablespoons of water. I covered them with the pan lid and cooked them for four or five minutes over medium-high heat, until the water had mostly evaporated and the stems were tender but not mushy. Then I took a spatula and tossed them around so they were all coated with the pan butter, turned them into a dish, and I had my midnight snack.

There's a reason for doing this. Spinach stems are much less acidic than spinach leaves—they have that distinctive spinach flavor without the bite. In a word, their taste is *delicate*, and you miss that if you cook up leaves and stems together. (Of course, you also miss it if, like some people, you cut off the stems and throw them away.) I won't say that they're better . . . No, damn it, I *will* say it: I'll take a bowl of these over ordinary spinach any day of the week—if they're prepared like this, of course.

BAGEL *MIT WIENER SALSWASSER*

Up until a few years ago, one of my duties during my visits to my mother in Maine was to drive her to the Navy commissary at the Naval Air Station Brunswick so that she could stock up on discount groceries. Military commissaries are just like supermarkets of a certain vintage (with close to the same prices); the one difference is that there's been a considered effort to find foods to fit their customers' taste. Since many military people have been stationed in Germany, the commissary carries a surprisingly large selection of German foodstuffs—including, in this one, two brands of frankfurters in tall glass jars. I prevailed on my mother to buy me one of them: "six snappy, spicy, tender Deutschlander."

These franks turned out to be skinny and eight inches long, their flavor pretty much identical to your average American hot dog. The best thing in the jar was the brine these wieners came in, so I decided I had to think of something appropriate to do with it. From a strictly practical point of view, the best way to put it to use would have been to add it to the liquid in a pot of baked beans, or perhaps use it as the base for some homemade sauerkraut. However, the franks were bought as potential midnight snacks, and I felt obliged to use the brine for the same purpose. Hence the creation of the "bagel *mit wiener Salswasser*."

You might want to know how to make this delicacy, on the off chance you mistakenly purchase a jar of these things. To start, remove and discard the wieners. Cut a pumpernickel bagel in half and thoroughly soak both halves in about half a cup of the *wiener Salswasser* (hot dog brine to you). Melt a large pat of butter in a skillet over medium heat and then gently place the sopped bagel halves, cut side down, into it.

Let them sizzle there for at least five minutes, or until the cut surface of the bagel has crisped up and is tinged with a golden fried color. Then turn the halves over and—while the other, round side crisps up—spread the tops with some slices of a slightly pungent cheese. A good *Bierkäse* would be perfect; so would Esrom or, in a pinch, Havarti. Plate up, dress it with a squirt of deli mustard, and chow down. And, whatever else you might think about it (pretty damn delicious, I hope), you'll have to admit this: you've never tasted anything quite like it.

SWEET CORN AND MILK

I actually prepared this midnight snack for Matt. I cut the kernels from two ears of fresh-picked corn and scraped the pulp from the third ear, after cutting through all the kernels with the tip of a knife. I blended the kernels and the pulp together, mixed in a cup of milk, a pinch of salt, and a dash of Jamaican hot sauce. Then I gently heated it up in a saucepan, just enough to have to blow on the first few spoonfuls to cool them, and served it up.

MYSTERY MEAT

The label on the package read "Delmonico Country Style Beef Rib Bone In," and the price was $6.99 a pound discounted from $10.99 a pound. Each rib weighed about ten ounces, and, despite the label, one of the pieces was boneless. There was enough here for supper for two, but Matt is not especially fond of gristly chunks of beef, and the price of the package I had my eye on, despite the discount, was a little more than what I allow for a snack. Hmm. Well, there *is* the "experimental foray" budget, and this surely fell into that classification. The meat slid into the cart.

Still, the question remained: What the hell had I bought? So when I got home I turned to my trusty (invaluable, really) copy of Merle Ellis's *Cutting-Up in the Kitchen*. The supermarket was having a sale on boneless rib-eye steaks and, as I suspected, Delmonico steak is another term used to describe these. Although Ellis doesn't say so, by comparing the cuts of meat with the illustration he provides, I was pretty sure what I had was what butchers call "cap meat" or "rib lifters"—the

piece of meat left on the rib when the rib eye is cut away. These are often sold as boneless short ribs, and the meat is not as tender as the rib-
eye steak itself is. But, as Ellis remarks, "they are tender enough,"
especially because these were well marbled and cut from the small end
of the rib.

It was sort of like getting everything I really love about a steak—the
crispy fat on one side, the meat close to the bone on the other, without
all the meat in the middle. Not that I don't like that, too. I do. But since
this cut made a full portion and then some, I didn't particularly miss
the "only meat" part, either. Next time I'll restrain myself and only eat
one rib at a time, which will drive the portion price down very close to
snack territory. That way I'll be able to eat dinner. (This was not a midnight but a midafternoon snack, given the problems with grilling late at
night when you live in an apartment house.)

KHAI PEN

My own guess is that this phrase, translated from the Laotian, would
read something like "a walrus sneezed on it"—with the "it" being a
kind of flavor-treated papery seaweed that is deep-fried until crisp. The
person who sent this to me—who, in this instance, would probably
like to remain anonymous (right, Minnie?)—actually smuggled it from
Luang Prabang into Australia. She raved about how delicious it was, although her comment that "you can just feel the minerals diving into
your system!" should have alerted me to the fact that her idea of
"yummy" as applied to snack food might be different from my own.

Anonymous also insisted that the odd bits that I suspected had
emerged from the maw of a walrus (and, not to put too fine a point to it,
its nostrils as well) were in fact bits of chopped garlic and dried tomato.
Maybe. But that's *not* what they looked like or tasted like, which is seaweed with a delicate coating of chawed-on fish scraps and walrus
phlegm. Don't mistake me—the flavor was far from rank. Think of rice
paper that has been dipped in seawater and then deep-fried, and you get
the idea: crispy, wispy, with a hint of the sea. But any gustatory pleasure
came from the sesame seeds (if that is indeed what they were), and if I
want to enjoy those, I don't need to go fry up a batch of seaweed first.

Have you noticed that when it comes to nonmeat Asian snacks, one's usual response is, "Hey! That's not as bad as I thought it would be!"? Think edamame. Or Japanese rice crackers: "There must be *something* here worth eating," you think, then heave a sigh of relief when you come across a peanut.

However, I draw the line this side of seaweed. Quite honestly, walrus hankie scrapings are the least of it. Having lived a good while on the Maine coast, with its red-tide warnings, the occasional oil slick, semitreated effluent, and wall-to-wall flotsam of the most repulsive sort, I don't find the idea of eating seaweed all that appetizing.

For me, at least. When *Saveur* magazine published its 2003 annual list of the foodie Top 100, item 52, under the heading BETTER THAN PO-TATO CHIPS, turned out to be Korean toasted laver, which looks suspiciously like *khai pen* minus the contribution from the walrus. *Saveur*'s annual listing is always worth a read, and my own guess is that in this instance the editors simply didn't notice that a word had fallen out of the headline. It should have read: BETTER THAN KOREAN POTATO CHIPS. Then it all makes sense.

HEADCHEESE

The world is generally divided into two groups when it comes to head-cheese: those who have never heard of it and those who have and wish they hadn't. However, there are exceptions. I became one when I noticed, waiting for a slice of pancetta for a pot of Tuscan beans, that the deli counter sold three different versions, a high-end headcheese from Boar's Head (except maybe I should write "low-end," since a lot of the meat in it is merely ham), where everything is bound together in lovely clear gelatin and dotted with bits of sweet red pepper. Then there are two locally made, much cheaper versions, packed with such totally noggin ingredients as pig snout and pork tongue. The difference between these last two is that one is made with beef blood (red version) and one not (white version).

I like them both, but Matt has threatened to leave me if I bring the blood version home one more time. Also, to be honest, there's that pesky matter of mad cow disease. While blood is not, per se, the riskiest part of the animal to eat, it comes in contact with the animal's nervous-system tissue, especially during the slaughtering process. Headcheese is enough of a risk without the blood—it is made from meat that lies very close to the brain and it is extracted by unskilled laborers who have no encouragement to be careful—but it is made from pork, not beef, and pigs, so far, seem exempt from the disease.

Okay, so what's to like? First of all, as cold cuts go, headcheese is the low-cal king; about the only thing less fatty than a pig's tongue is its tail. It's chewy without being gristly; it tastes meaty and offal-y at the same time, strangely elegant for such scrappy stuff. Each slice is at once an intricately designed mosaic of ivory, pink, and mottled shades of red . . . and undisguisedly made up of chunks of pig that the eater would otherwise never see, let alone put to mouth. Finally, headcheese is resolutely honest in a deli case where the "rare" roast beef seems as much a triumph of chemistry as cooking and not a ham on the counter looks anything like what Dad once carved at Sunday dinner.

CILANTRO SANDWICH

This is the sort of casual midnight snack that is so impromptu that it barely makes it into consciousness. It was made from the remains of a bunch of cilantro after we had used as much of it as we thought wise in an Indian dish of potatoes, tomatoes, and chickpeas. The rest was heading straight for the landfill, but I rescued it at the last minute, tossed it in some olive oil, minced garlic, salt, and pepper, piled it between two slices of bread, and ate it. I don't think I could face a cilantro salad—maybe nobody can, since I can't remember ever reading of one—but the bread mellows that rabid herb perfectly, the same way it does watercress. Next time I may have the patience to pull off some of the more gangling stems, but, on the whole, I would call this a success.

HOT DOG WITH NORWEGIAN POTATO FLATBREAD

It is a little-known fact that Norwegians eat their own weight in hot dogs every month. Okay, I lie—but they come close. Furthermore, they like to eat them in an easy-to-make potato flatbread called *lompe*

(pronounced "lumpy." Okay, I lie again. I don't know how it's pronounced). I found a recipe for this, which was a simple matter of mashing a large, baked Maine potato (russets would probably work well,
but not waxy varieties) with a pinch of salt, mixing in a heaping tablespoon of flour, and quickly kneading it into a soft dough. This I divided
in two, then patted the first half between two sheets of waxed paper
into a pretty thin pancake. I slid it into a hot, lightly greased skillet and
cooked it about five minutes to a side, until both sides had an appetizing dappling of brown.

I flipped the pancake onto a plate, rolled it up around a hot frank
dressed to the max (i.e., with everything except the shrimp-mayo concoction you get in Norway, for which I couldn't find a recipe), and ate
it. It tasted pretty much as good as it sounds, which is darn fine. Better
still, there was enough dough left over to do it again.

SWEDISH MEATBALLS

In the early days of my career as a food writer, long before I moved to
Maine and met and married Matt, there would be periods of time—
anywhere from a day to a week—when I would be too depressed to
cook for myself. This was a time when I was beyond broke (one of the
reasons for my depression). On such evenings, I would wander over to
the supermarket and root around in the frozen-food aisle for something
very cheap that might also actually be edible. (Remember chicken and
beef potpies?) Budget Gourmet's Swedish meatballs with noodles in
cream sauce quickly became the meal for these occasions, often for several days running. If I wanted to treat myself, I would eat two containers instead of one. (They were $1.29 apiece then, and on sale could cost
under a dollar.)

The only explanation I can offer for this, apart from the fact that I
did enjoy them, is that I've never liked anything with tomato sauce,
thus eliminating most of the Budget Gourmet line. In fact, at least in a
state of depression, there was very little in the frozen-dinner aisle that
seemed worth choosing over starvation, not counting the occasional
louche urge that propelled me home with frozen fried-chicken drum-
mettes (the meaty joint of a chicken wing, and one of the great marketing terms of the twentieth century). Frozen fried chicken tastes as if it

were made from some alternative-universe fowl that resembles the original only in skeletal structure, which can be a source of amusement if you're in a certain kind of mood.

Jump to the (almost) present. One day I noticed that one of our local supermarkets had put the entire Budget Gourmet line on sale, so much so that they cost just what they did back in 1983! Wow! All that time and the brand was still around! And still sold in a no-frills heat-and-eat cardboard package! Could it be that they still sold *Swedish meatballs*? I bent down to scrutinize the containers, which were stuck way down on the bottom shelf of a freezer unit, a few inches higher than the floor. Yup—there they were, looking exactly the way I remembered them, and they proved to taste just the way I remembered, too. No messing with the old corporate recipe.

The Swedish meatballs were still good, frozen-dinner style; the egg noodles coated in white sauce remained a mystery. They would be okay if they came in a cooking pouch that could be immersed in boiling water. However, they sit in a cardboard tray that spends half an hour in the oven, with a corner torn open so the steam can escape. The problem is that parts of the noodles get dried out during the baking, becoming tough and dry. It doesn't spoil the meal, but it doesn't exactly enhance it, either.

Furthermore, eating these, I found myself counting the number of meatballs in the container: I think there were five or six. Wouldn't I be happier with just a plate of meatballs—hold the noodles and white sauce? You bet. And, miraculously, the same supermarket was having a sale on frozen Swedish meatballs, pure and simple (if I can use that phrase to describe a product with an ingredient list as long as your arm). So tonight I had a plate of thirteen (baker's dozen) heated in the oven on aluminum foil, and eaten with a toothpick (which, after all, is how Swedish meatballs are *supposed* to be eaten).

Update 2006. When I went to the Budget Gourmet website to see if they offered a meatball count ("Now with *seven* meatballs"), I discovered that the line has been purchased and renamed—hold on to your hat!—*Lean* Gourmet. I stopped reading; I didn't want to know another thing.

BOK CHOY

Let's get vegetarian for a change. I love bok choy, and I love it so much stir-fried in peanut oil and a little oyster sauce (oops, there goes the vegetarian part) that it would appear more often on the midnight menu if it didn't call for a bit more effort than I usually care to expend. Even so, every now and then I come across a head of bok choy with my name written on it—small and crisp, with unsplit, bright white stalks—and I have to take it home and cook it up and eat it all myself.

I do this in a large wok. I put a tablespoon of peanut oil, a tablespoon of soy sauce, half a tablespoon of oyster sauce, a dash of hot sauce, and half a tablespoon of natural sugar granules into the bottom and heat this gently while I chop up the bok choy into bite-size pieces, keeping the stalk pieces separate from the leaf pieces. When the oil is hot, I stir in the chopped stalks and let them cook until they are tender but still crisp. Then I add the leaf pieces and stir them about until they wilt. Finally, I add a few drops of sesame oil (really—two or three drops does the trick) and pour it into a bowl. It's truly delicious, and if you're watching a video with your mate you can eat it with your fingers. (If he/she looks askance, just point out, "Hey, no crumbs!!")

The only other thing I might do is mince a garlic clove and add it at the very start, but this is really pushing the envelope for a snack. Maybe I should just flatten it with the side of a cleaver, toss it in, and then save it for last, ending the snack with a knockout blow to the taste buds.

SMOKED KIELBASA–CASING PO' BOY

A little while ago I bought a Luhr-Jensen electric fish smoker, which I've been using to smoke everything except fish. The company would probably deplore my use of it as a barbecue pit (you have to know what you're doing and they don't need the lawsuits), but the low heat ensures the slow cooking over smoldering wood that produces the best kind of smoked meat. Among the various items I've smoked in it—baby back ribs, pork neck bones, chicken thighs, slabs of choice beef top round, etc.—one of my favorites is smoked kielbasa sausage. There are some local artisanal kielbasa makers here in the Pioneer Valley, and they turn out a good product.

However, they have failed to take the final step, which is to peel off the natural casing *before* the smoking process. I then hang the denuded sausages from a hook at the top of the smoker and bathe them through the afternoon in hickory smoke. I usually do two at a time, which leaves behind a whole lot of casing. Now, one's first impulse might be to sweep the whole lot into the trash. But that would be a big mistake. However carefully you pull the casing off, little bits of meat inevitably stick to it, so we're not talking pure intestine lining here.

In fact, I noticed that I was nibbling away at the stuff as I was peeling it off. And I thought if it's not bad like this, it might be pretty tasty fried up in a little bacon fat with some sliced onions and heaped onto a bun. So I took my Chinese cleaver and cut the casing up into thin strips, to make it easier to eat. Since a kielbasa is already fully cooked, there was no need to worry about cooking time: I just kept stirring it until the onions were done and the casing was crispy, say ten to twelve minutes. Then I heaped it on a bun and, in the spirit of the thing, seasoned it with a generous smear of Pulaski Polish-Style Mustard with Horseradish.

Fried kielbasa casing makes a pretty fantastic sandwich. It's tender but crispy and chewy—something that's usually hard to attain in a cold cut—and the frying brings out the meaty savor and delicate spicing of the kielbasa itself. The fried sliced onion rounded it all off. In fact, it's so good that you could build a franchise around the idea—the Scrappy Boy—although you probably won't.

A final note: Yeah, I was a little nervous about what my digestive tract would do when it found itself on the receiving end of two kielbasas' worth of bacon fat–fried casings. But, no problem. After all, it's handled a lot worse.

COOKING THE BOOKS

HAVE IT YOUR WAY

Hundreds of millions of people buy fast food every day without giving it much thought, unaware of the subtle and not so subtle ramifications of their purchases. They rarely consider where this food came from, how it was made, what it is doing to the community around them. They just grab their tray off the counter, find a table, take a seat, unwrap the paper, and dig in. The whole experience is transitory and soon forgotten. I've written this book out of a belief that people should know what lies behind the shiny, happy surface of every fast food transaction. They should know what really lurks between those sesame-seed buns.
—Eric Schlosser, *Fast Food Nation*

A few blocks from where we live are two small old-fashioned grocery stores, State Street Fruit and Serio's Market. Because Northampton is a college town and the college itself is also close to both stores, these markets possess a certain panache that otherwise they most likely would not. State Street Fruit has an excellent wine store attached to one side and a well-stocked delicatessen to the other; Serio's has a full-service meat counter in the back and, in season, fills the front of the store with local vegetables and fruits. This display soon spreads out onto the sidewalk, to tables heaped with sweet corn, tomatoes, and, for the briefest of moments, fresh-picked asparagus, strawberries, and raspberries.

Places like these were one of the reasons we came to Northampton, and so it is all the more puzzling, even shocking, to me how rarely we shop there, especially when you consider that when we first moved

here, I felt their proximity would allow us to escape the depressing vap-
idity of the chain supermarkets on the outskirts of the city. Even so, old
patterns soon asserted themselves, and now we do almost all our food
shopping at Stop & Shop and Big Y, stopping at the local stores maybe
once a month—except during the summer—always for specific purchases, not for general shopping. I would estimate that we spend a dollar there for every twenty-five dollars we spend at the supermarket.

Why is this the case? And why did I start thinking about this as I
read my way through *Fast Food Nation* by Eric Schlosser, a no-holds-
barred exposé of the havoc wreaked by fast-food chains on our personal health and well-being and the social and ecological fabric of first
our country and then the entire world. There's no doubt the book
struck a nerve. Not only was it a runaway bestseller and made into a
movie, but references to it and excerpts from it have since appeared
everywhere, from the national media to the local press.

Understandably so. The book is a compelling read, offering a stag-
geringly unsettling look at a world that, as much as it impinges on most
of our lives, usually manages to remain just beyond our ken. All of us,
of course, are familiar with the experience of the fast-food restaurant itself. But Schlosser pursues the fries back to the potato farm, the burger
back to the cattle ranch, the neighborhood McDonald's back to its ges-
tation at corporate headquarters—to the decisions that put it here, not
there, that carefully crafted every item on the menu, that worked out
each piece of equipment and exactly what sort of person would be
hired to operate it.

The book is, in fact, a paean—albeit a mostly inadvertent one—to
American ingenuity. By this I'm not only referring to the relatively innocent mechanical cleverness that can come up with high-powered
guns that shoot a steady stream of peeled potatoes through slicing
blades to create mountains of French fries in a matter of minutes. No, I
also mean the sort of resourcefulness that is endlessly adept at finding
ways to end-run the government regulations it can't trample over, that
crushes unions in order to replace good jobs and decent working conditions with badly paying and often horrifically dangerous ones . . . and
manages even to extract tax credits for doing so.

Fast Food Nation presents a strong and persuasive case for public
concern about the real cost of the food served at McDonald's, especially that of the meat. Schlosser details the corporate meat-buying

strategies designed to give ranchers and poultry raisers the short end of the stick, often making them tenant farmers on their own land. He takes us to processing plants that have been redesigned so that the work can be done by minimally trained migrant workers, who are quickly shunted back to Mexico when they are injured on the job. And, in each step of the process, he reveals how these plants are paring the safeguards against food contamination to the very quick.

> The slaughterhouse tasks most likely to contaminate meat are the removal of an animal's hide and the removal of its digestive system. The hides are now pulled off by machine; if a hide has been inadequately cleaned, chunks of dirt and manure may fall from it onto the meat. Stomachs and intestines are still pulled out of cattle by hand; if the job is not performed carefully, the contents of the digestive system may spill everywhere . . . At the IBP slaughterhouse in Lexington, Nebraska, the hourly spillage rate at the gut table has run as high as 20 percent, with stomach contents splattering one out of five carcasses.

It will be the rare reader who does not blench at Schlosser's description of the disgraceful working conditions in these slaughterhouses, feel for those whose sad lot it is to work in them, and put the book down wondering about the state of at least some—and perhaps much—of the meat that emerges from them.

Even so, Schlosser began to lose this reader when, on the strength of isolated incidents of food contamination, he contends that both the meat-packing and fast-food industries have turned the act of eating meat into "a form of high-risk behavior":

> The war on foodborne pathogens deserves the sort of national attention and resources that has been devoted to the war on drugs. Far more Americans are severely harmed every year by food poisoning than by illegal drug use. And the harms caused by food poisoning are usually inadvertent and unanticipated. People who smoke crack know the potential dangers; most people who eat hamburgers don't.

Now, there does seem to have been a dramatic rise in food poisoning over the past fifty years. Currently, one out of every four of us suffers an attack of it each year, and at least one out of every two hundred of those who do will require medical treatment. However, whether you are likely to suffer that attack from eating at a fast-food restaurant—and, especially, from eating the meat there—is, at best, a matter of debate. An article in *The New York Times* (March 18, 2001) on the increase of food poisoning noted that "at least 80 percent of food-related illnesses are caused by viruses or other pathogens that scientists cannot even identify" and observed that while

> much of the fear surrounding food safety focuses on meat and poultry, especially beef, the General Accounting Office estimates that 85 percent of food poisoning comes from the fruits, vegetables, seafood and cheeses that are regulated by the FDA and claim a larger share of the American diet each year. And poisoning from such foods can be every bit as deadly as that from meat and poultry.*

Considering that the average American is more likely to be killed by an automobile while out on a walk than by food poisoning—and that the odds of either are infinitesimal—it might make the most sense to treat the occasional bout of intestinal distress as one more toll exacted by contemporary life rather than as an omen of impending disaster. The problem is that we live in a world rife with potential calamities, and we don't seem to be especially adept at predicting those that will actually happen—be they killer African viruses or an end-of-millennium worldwide computer meltdown.

For a book like *Fast Food Nation* to be effective, it must do more than make us feel outrage at the villainy it discloses; it has to successfully define a problem that can actually be solved and point us in the direction of a workable solution. And once Schlosser turns his attention from the meat-packing industry to our national infatuation with fast food, it seems to me that he conspicuously fails to accomplish either.

---

*Readers will think immediately of the fresh spinach scare in the fall of 2006, which killed three people and sickened more than 200, costing the industry millions of dollars before the source of the contamination was located. But the real problem is persistent food poisoning in raw vegetables that is too low-level and too random to successfully fight—except by just not eating the food. As long ago as January 2001, the *Wellness Letter* from the University of California, Berkeley, was warning its readers: "Don't eat raw sprouts, especially if you are elderly or have an impaired immune system. And don't feed sprouts to young children. Salmonella and *E. coli* bacteria in sprouts have made thousands of Americans sick . . . In healthy people these bacteria can cause diarrhea, nausea, cramps, and fever for several days; in high-risk groups the symptoms can be life-threatening."

Whatever we may think ourselves, there is certainly no doubt that most of the world equates America with fast food; whether, because of this, they think we live in heaven or hell seems to be a toss-up. Either way, Ronald McDonald has become the human face of American-style free enterprise. What is so remarkable is how quickly all this has come about. *Fast Food Nation* is worth reading alone for its careful detailing of how the right entrepreneur at the right time with the right product and the right technology can change America overnight. Just as Bill Gates recognized the importance of someone else's idea, pounced on it, and turned it into Microsoft, so did Ray Kroc see in the McDonald Brothers Burger Bar Drive-In and its Speedee Service System way back in 1954 a concept that would come to profoundly change this country's eating habits.

I was in my twenties before I saw my first McDonald's and almost thirty before one was reasonably close to where I lived. New England, of course, was dotted all over with individual hamburger stands and fried-fish places, as well as chain restaurants like Howard Johnson's and Friendly's. These, too, served popular, easy-to-eat dishes where the potatoes were always fried and the meat or seafood most often came in a bun. But they also had table service and real menus, which, however limited and standardized, proffered what seems a veritable cornucopia of choices compared to fast-food restaurants today.

I had just learned to drive about the same time that McDonald's began springing up here and there in the far western part of Massachusetts where I was teaching at a small boarding school—and it was a particularly happy afternoon when I would pack my tiny Triumph Herald convertible with students and head off for the nearest one, a twenty-mile drive away. Those were the days when the golden arches spanned the entire building, making it probably the only example of Googie architecture in all of Berkshire County.* Who knew that this

---

*If you've never seen the original McDonald's, with its roof-topping golden arches, the sixty-foot-high neon sign with Speedee the Chef (yes, there was a McDonald's before Ronald McDonald), and the red-and-white-striped tile exterior, the company still operates one in Downey, California. Opened in 1953, it is now on the National Register of Historic Places. McDonald's maintains it just as it was, with walk-up windows and outdoor seating. Employees wear the fifties-style uniforms of paper hats, white shirts, and bolo ties and serve up the

exotic was in fact a sort of restaurant kudzu—tenacious, hardy, all but impossible to uproot—that would soon crowd the more fragile indigenous eateries right out of the New England landscape?

What I did know was that I was completely enchanted with what I found there. My first order of fries was a culinary epiphany—flavorful, salty, and deliciously crispy, they seemed in a class by themselves. (As, indeed, they were: French fries were a passion for the chain's founder, Ray Kroc, and he relentlessly sought out ways to perfect them.) I also loved the Big Mac. After years of fighting to get my hamburgers dressed with mayonnaise, here was one that already came with something better. And, as a savory breakfast lover, I became an immediate fan of the Egg McMuffin and, later, of their sausage in a biscuit. I never made a trip anywhere that didn't start with breakfast at McDonald's.

Still, a meal there remained an exception to the rule. When I worked in downtown Boston, there were more interesting eating places to explore; when I moved to Maine, none of the McDonald's were conveniently close. In any case, by this time, my delight in fast food had begun to wane. The fries never recovered after McDonald's kowtowed to the diktats of the health police and stopped frying their potatoes in (mostly) beef fat. For similar reasons, the hamburgers became universally overcooked, bland, and, most fatally, mushy—until it was nearly impossible for the palate to tell the burger from the bun.

There's a difference between happy food and food that makes you happy. For some of us, all it takes is time to learn how to distinguish between the two: the immediately satisfying, repeatedly experienced, eventually becomes cloying, even in the best of circumstances. However, it turns out that for a lot of people that very feeling of surfeit is a comfort hard to surrender, and a glance back into our nation's history may help explain why.

Solvency is what makes America the place it is. Ours is a nation based on the fluidity of money: the excitement that comes when it washes into our lives and the fear when it washes out; the freedom it brings by leaching out, if not utterly dissolving, the competing and more traditional claims of family, religion, political belief, ethnicity, and race. This also makes our country, even during the most peaceful of times, a stressful place to live.

---

original menu of hamburgers, cheeseburgers, fries, and old-fashioned milkshakes (along, of course, with Big Macs and Happy Meals).

Over the centuries, Americans have tried a multitude of nostrums to deal with this stress, but none have had the unwavering popularity of tobacco and alcohol. Visitors to this country in the nineteenth century regularly commented on the presence of spittoons in the highest reaches of society and the brown stains on the floor everywhere else. They also noted the enormous amount of hard liquor consumed here; it was not in the least uncommon to wash supper down with a bottle of whiskey. Until Prohibition, the national hangouts were the beer garden and the saloon.

Gradually, it became the general consensus, at least among those who concerned themselves with such matters, that all this drinking and spitting was both unhealthy and disgusting; it destroyed families and tore unsightly rents in the national fabric. The reformers, of course, set out to battle alcohol and chewing tobacco, not the reason people resorted to them. That, it was believed, was the consequence of weak moral fiber, and those who indulged simply needed to be protected from themselves.

As it happened, at the height of this prohibitionist fever, refined sugar became a generally affordable commodity, and temperance unions enthusiastically touted root beer and ginger ale as ideal substitutes for their alcoholic counterparts. Whatever effect this had on alcohol consumption, the switch to soft drinks did wonders for the amount of sugar we began to consume . . . as the replacement of chewing tobacco by the more genteel cigarette did for the national intake of nicotine. After all, women, for the most part, neither chewed tobacco nor frequented saloons, but they felt quite at home in the ice cream parlor and, more and more, with a pack of cigarettes.

Men, however, did not take much to the ice cream parlor—the public place of soda consumption and the temperance answer to the saloon. Coffee, not Coke, has always been the male alcohol substitute of choice, and men tended to patronize greasy spoons where they could always get a cup of joe and something to eat, whether that was a doughnut or a bowl of beef stew. If they felt like a soda, they bought one from a dispensing machine. These male hangouts, for which I know no truly accurate term, could be distinguished from restaurants by the fact that, whatever the hour, there would be several men sitting at the counter, smoking cigarettes and nursing a cup of cold coffee.

Even eating places that accommodated both sexes tended toward segregation—not only of men from women but of young from old. Go into, say, the local Howard Johnson's and you would find men mostly gathered at the counter, while families, women, and teenagers occupied the booths. What you had was a hybrid eatery, a greasy spoon joined at the hip to a soda fountain. These places were pleasant enough, but they had no clear identity of their own and, to the extent that they tried to find one, ended up doing nothing very well.

McDonald's revolutionized the fast-food business by rejecting the hybrid eatery for something subtly but profoundly new: an eating place modeled on the dining experience where we first learned the pleasures of the mealtime break—lunch in the school cafeteria. We would arrive there hungry, to be sure, but mostly pumped full of pressure from the self-control required to sit still through a morning's worth of classes, and desperately seeking release. At the school cafeteria you ate fast, talked fast, bussed your table, and left on the dot—which is to say you did what you were supposed to do and still managed to have a good time. What better definition of "fast food" could there be?

Fast-food places are painted in the same bright colors, and they offer the same limited range of choices on the menu, the same uncomfortable but ultra-sturdy and ultra-cleanable seating. They enfold us in an entirely familiar universe, where we experience the same controlled but nevertheless joyous sense of release. And, also like the school cafeteria, they offer us an eating environment in which there are no lingering memories of smoking a cigarette or downing a glass of beer. At McDonald's or Burger King or Wendy's, there is no taste of the historical past, only of our own.

A fast-food outlet is certainly an eating place, but it is not quite the same thing as a restaurant. However convivial the occasion, the focal point at the latter is the meal; at the former, the food is often the means rather than the end—which is why, unlike most restaurants but like most roadhouses, fast-food parking lots are always full of cars. Eating, like drinking, is an activity that all of us can enjoy, that requires no talent or expertise, and that is social by its very nature. It provides a natural excuse for people to gather together, enjoy themselves, and simply relax.

In other words, just as we don't go to a tavern for a drink of water, neither do we head for Kentucky Fried Chicken to eat a salad—those things may refresh the body, but they do nothing for the spirit. We go to a fast-food place for that comforting sense of pleasure that comes from eating a lot of fat, usually with a large chaser of sugar on the side. That you've also quenched your thirst or eaten lunch is just a bonus, or, perhaps, an excuse.

You would have to go back to the Middle Ages to find a public house that offered an equal welcome to men, women, and children, and the same measure of pleasure to all—and for a pittance that even the meanest purse would find hard to begrudge. And, as at the ancient public house, what you imbibe at McDonald's is—unlike coffee, tobacco, or hard alcohol—actually nutritious. A dark, rich ale is full of food value, and many a peasant made a meal of it; the buzz it provided was no more debilitating than the one we get from our morning double espresso. However, as intoxicants go, the stuff served in fast-food restaurants doesn't even warrant a PG rating—if you consider it an intoxicant at all.

In McDonald's, then, America has finally found the ideal temperance saloon: no alcohol, no tobacco, and—even better—no faint odor of either lingering in the woodwork like a sad ghost mourning lost times. On the contrary. Democratic, cheerful, and well-lit, offering a helping of prosperity to all who enter, watched over by a cheerful motley fool who is loved by children and a threat to no one . . . what could be a more appropriate—or more appropriately chosen—emblem of the American way of life? Isn't all this good?

Apparently not. In the past two decades, fat and sugar have joined alcohol, tobacco, and recreational drugs on the list of dangerous substances, and fast-food places receive no more quarter from today's neo-prohibitionists than saloons got from Carrie Nation. For Eric Schlosser, it isn't only the threat of food poisoning that justifies a national war on fast food; McDonald's and its ilk are corrupting our youth and making all of us grossly fat.

• • •

The aesthetics of fast food are of much less concern to me than its impact upon the lives of ordinary Americans, both as workers and consumers. Most of all, I am concerned about its impact on the nation's children. Fast food is heavily marketed to children and prepared by people who are barely older than children. This is an industry that both feeds and feeds off the young.

—Eric Schlosser, *Fast Food Nation*

I read several reviews of *Fast Food Nation* before I started working on this piece, and I was interested to note that a majority of the reviewers made a point of saying that they rarely, if ever, ate fast food, which is also the case with the author (although he gamely downed some while doing his research). In fact, it is worth observing that (apart from college students) the people who regularly eat fast food are not going to read this book, while those who do read it—myself included—rarely visit the places that sell it and, when they do, don't much identify with their fellow customers.

Fast-food meals are a commonplace in our society, to be sure—but they are much more of a commonplace for some of us than for others. Apart from those accompanying children—90 percent of America's kids between the ages of three and nine visit a McDonald's every month—and those who have simply acquired a taste for the food, I, like many others, have always thought that the lower you go down the financial scale, the more regular the visits to McDonald's or Burger King or Kentucky Fried Chicken become.

I was wrong, and my error reflects a class prejudice that I'm ashamed I didn't have the wit to challenge. A study on fast-food consumption in America that appeared in 2003 in the *Journal of the American Dietetic Association*[*] reported that the consumption of "fast food was lowest among people 60 years of age and older and among people with a household income of 100% of the poverty threshold or less." Furthermore, it suggested that (brace yourself) "the results from this study suggest that more education may be associated with fast-food consumption," at least up to a point. The report does add that "fast-food use may decline at the highest levels of education" (which one might guess to mean the levels of the authors themselves). However, for adults, the defining factors seem to be mainly "convenience and a busy lifestyle." No wonder that the authors conclude that fast-food consumption in the United States can only grow.

This casts a bit of doubt on the notion that the clientele of fast-food places are unwitting victims of corporate malfeasance. They are neither

---

[*] "Fast-food consumption among US adults and children: Dietary and nutrient intake profile," Sahasporn Paeratakul, M.B.B.S., Ph.D.; Daphne P. Ferdinand, M.N., R.N.; Catherine M. Champagne, R.D., Ph.D.; Donna H. Ryan, M.D.; George A. Bray, M.D. October 2003, vol. 103, no. 10.

stupid nor ignorant. The worst you can say about them is that they've been offered a deal too good to refuse, which is simply a characteristic of life in America today.

Furthermore, I think Schlosser oversimplifies when he writes about how fast-food franchises mistreat their mostly teenage employees by giving them meaningless work and paying them poorly for doing it. Here, he sounds like someone who never had to find a part-time or summer job. When I was sixteen, I would have considered finding a job at a place like McDonald's a stroke of fantastic good luck. In the late 1950s, unless you had connections or a Horatio Alger work ethic, you were very lucky to find any sort of regular job at all. Most likely, you spent your summer dragging the family lawn mower around the neighborhood. These days, kids can often pick and choose, and those who have been there know that this means something—even if, to others, the choices appear universally bad.

Similarly, he makes much of the fact that soft drink companies have been negotiating to install soda machines in public schools in exchange for substantial financial payments that are no doubt very welcome to cash-strapped school systems. Obviously, those who are well off needn't stoop to such measures, and readers of *Fast Food Nation* will most likely congratulate themselves for having aggressively sought out school districts where this sort of desperation is unimaginable.

However, what interested me about this phenomenon was something else. When I was in high school, I got an allowance of ten dollars a month. Others of my friends may have done better than that, but not so that I noticed and felt deprived. I rationed that money very carefully and was only occasionally willing to drop a dime into a soda machine. I got a lot more mileage out of a roll of Life Savers or, a little later, a pack of cigarettes (which then cost 25¢!). It's not likely that the Coca-Cola folks would have considered winning the right to put a soda dispenser in my high school the equivalent of a license to print money.

By the same reasoning, if these days teenage boys drink twice as much soda as milk, whereas twenty years ago they drank twice as much milk as soda, the point is that neither then nor now did they ever pay for the milk. This statistic, then, tells us at least as much about the amount of money in teenage pockets and their attitudes toward spending it as it does about the success of saturation advertising over the vulnerable teenage psyche.

Our ever-increasing rate of sugar consumption, especially in the form of soft drinks, is one of the worrying statistics that Schlosser attempts to tie to the fast-food industry. At the turn of the last century, the average consumption was 5 pounds per person a year. Twenty years ago, it was 26 pounds. Today, despite diet sodas and the like, the average American adult consumes about 64 pounds* of sugar and the average American teenage boy, 109 pounds, about half of which comes from soft drinks. In fact, these are the single biggest source of refined sugars in the American diet.† Soft drinks today are the fifth-largest source of calories for adults. For adolescents, the figures are much higher: they provide 9 percent of boys' calories and 8 percent of girls' calories. And these percentages are triple (boys) or double (girls) what they were thirty years ago.

This state of affairs explains a paradoxical statistic regarding this nation's fat consumption: between 1965 and 1995, the proportion of fat in the average American diet fell dramatically, from 45 to about 34 percent. This is only 4 points higher than the 30-percent limit set by government dietary guidelines. So, why do we keep getting heavier and heavier? Well, because we're actually eating more fat than ever before. The percentage has dropped because we're devouring an even greater number of carbohydrates, and many of these calories come from plain old sugar—or, more accurately, the less expensive corn sweeteners that have increasingly replaced sugar as the empty carbohydrate of choice in the American diet.

This increase in our consumption of fatty and sugary foods is perhaps Schlosser's favorite cudgel for pounding the fast-food industry, and again it does not seem to be—evidenced by both his personal appearance and the absence of any such admission within the pages of his book—a problem he has experienced himself. However, I have, and it may cast a little illumination on what he chooses to describe as our

---

*Those who follow such things will know that this is a conservative estimate. According to U.S. Department of Agriculture data, sugar consumption in 1999 was 158 pounds per person, with consumption rising every year but one since 1983. But this figure is based on the total amount of sugar available in wholesale channels, making no adjustment for food that is made but not sold and food that is sold but not eaten.

†They are also a significant source of caffeine. Six out of the seven most popular soft drinks contain it, and while Coke and Pepsi both make a caffeine-free version of their colas, these account for only about 5 percent of cola sales.

"obesity epidemic" for me to describe something of my own struggle
with weight control.

• • •

> Obesity is now second only to smoking as a cause of mortality in
> the United States . . . Obesity has been linked to heart disease,
> colon cancer, stomach cancer, breast cancer, diabetes, arthritis,
> high blood pressure, infertility, and strokes. A 1999 study by the
> American Cancer Society found that overweight people had a
> much higher rate of premature death. Severely overweight people
> were four times more likely to die young than people of normal
> weight . . . Young people who are obese face not only long-term,
> but also immediate threats to their health. Severely obese Ameri-
> can children, aged six to ten, are now dying from heart attacks
> caused by their weight.
>
> —Eric Schlosser, *Fast Food Nation*

Ironically, it was just at the time that my interest in fast food faded that
my own weight problem turned from a niggling annoyance to a genuine
cause of concern. It might seem perfectly natural—perhaps even desirable—for a food writer to be on the hefty side. But in my case it wasn't
the pleasure I take from eating that made me fat. No, I lost control of
my weight when I had gave up smoking; it is as simple and as complicated as that.

I started smoking so long ago that I hardly remember why I wanted
to do so—and why so passionately—but I know that when my parents
said that I could begin on my sixteenth birthday, when it became legal
for me to do so, I had secretly started months before that date.

Much has been made about the pressures of cigarette advertising,
but in the late 1950s what most likely influenced my own decision to
smoke was that virtually every photograph of an actor or literary figure
showed them puffing on a pipe or dangling a cigarette from their
mouth: Albert Camus, Jean-Paul Sartre, William Faulkner, Humphrey
Bogart, Bertrand Russell, James Dean. And this was the result of no
tobacco industry conspiracy. In those days to smoke was to signal an
obscurely defined but obviously resonant nexus of personal qualities:
seriousness, toughness, self-reflectiveness.

This was not just a matter of style. Nicotine is a superb spur to intellectual effort, simultaneously stimulating the mind and relaxing the body. This was something I needed very much. Always when I write or talk I am filled with anxiety, and nicotine, enhanced by a good dose of caffeine, helped me deal with this. I couldn't sit down in front of a type-writer without lighting a cigarette. Giving this habit up was the hardest thing I ever did in my life. Twice I stopped for a year or more and then began over again. And when I quit for good, it would be years before I threw away the pack of cigarettes in my freezer that I kept there so I could occasionally take one out just to hold and, especially, to smell.

To help me with this struggle, I had a small container of party straws, cut to cigarette length, on my desk, and in the first year or so I chewed my way through package after package of them. Unfortunately, this wasn't all I was chewing on. Where before I would smoke and read, now I would snack and read. Where before I smoked when I met with friends to talk, now I found myself meeting them in restaurants or inviting them over for meals. Usually, I didn't eat while I wrote, but I would often go into the kitchen after a difficult session and scarf down anything I found there.

As it happened, I smoked my last cigarette (and last pipe of to-bacco—which had remained my real love) just before some major changes shook up my life. I left the woman with whom I had been liv-ing for ten years in order to begin a relationship with Matt; I quit my job so I could write full-time.

For the next two or three years, I was surviving financially by the very skin of my teeth, more months than I want to remember paying my rent with a credit card check. I would lie awake for hours, night after night, twisted into knots by anxious worrying. During this period of high stress my weight shot up about fifty pounds. Before I gave up smoking I weighed 195; now I weighed a little under 250. And in that vicinity, despite much effort, I remain today.

Worst of all, after more than twenty years, I still miss smoking. Hardly a day goes by when I don't think about trying nicotine gum; my favorite pipes are tucked away in a box somewhere, not because I plan to ever smoke them again but because I had become too attached to them to throw them away. If I am at all typical of the antismoking cam-paign's successes, then something is wrong with the campaign itself.

Don't mistake me. I'm glad I no longer smoke. I have no intention of ever smoking again. But my experience with the cost of giving it up has made me wonder this: Would I be better off if, back in 1983, instead of quitting, I had simply switched to some more benign nicotine-dispensing device, be it patch or chewing gum? It isn't that I think these things are without risk—I just wonder how those risks stack up against those I run by being "pathologically obese."*

Such nicotine products are punitively priced precisely to keep them from being used as a smoking substitute, but this hasn't stopped people from doing just that. In fact, I wouldn't be surprised to learn that the category of "ex-smoker" embraces a rather large but low-profile number of, especially, nicotine-gum chewers, who, after all, can truthfully claim to be "tobacco-free."

Those who study our obesity epidemic have recently come to the conclusion that the only real solution to the problem is to convince people not to get fat in the first place. This makes sense, because once you get fat it is very, very hard to become thin again. Fat, to the body, is money in the bank—once a nice amount is safely stashed away, it fights like hell to hold on to it forever. Had I switched from smoking to nicotine gum, today I might weigh, say, 215 pounds—overweight to be sure, but not morbidly so. But I didn't, and here I am.

However, you could just as easily argue that the only real solution to nicotine addiction is to keep people from smoking in the first place, and how realistic is that? Despite massive expenditure, legislation, and impressive lawsuit victories against tobacco companies, between 1988 and 1996 there was a 30 percent increase in teenagers who try smoking at least once and a 50 percent increase in those who admit to daily use.

Schlosser doesn't discuss our national nicotine addiction in *Fast Food Nation*; people don't smoke in Burger King. But isn't it possible that if the increases in teenage sugar and cigarette consumption are so eerily similar, the reason may lie in the fact that their effects are very much the same—especially when that sugar is combined with fat? Fat has always been sugar's amiable abettor, whether the two are combined in ice cream or sugar-glazed doughnuts, or eaten as companions, as with a double cheeseburger and a large Coke. The sugar charges you up

---

*That is the term used to categorize anyone who is 30 percent heavier than their recommended weight, and I do occasionally ask myself how objective this medical classification is. After all, heavy as I am, I still resemble a lot of my fellow citizens. If I am *pathologically* obese, what is the person who weighs double their recommended weight? Or triple it?

even as the fat soothes you and calms you down—which is pretty much the effect that nicotine has. Except that nicotine doesn't make you fat.

The teenagers I know lead far more complicated lives than I did at sixteen, when adolescence was awash with boredom and empty time. If they are drinking more soda (and, increasingly, booze) and smoking more cigarettes, it's because their time is too booked up; these days, kids hold parties just so they can talk to their friends in person rather than online with Instant Messenger. Obviously, a lot of them will be drawn to anything that promises to slow time down or speed it up or—perhaps best of all—to do both at once. In this regard, fast food, like smoking, like soft drinks, is really a means to an end.

In any case, Schlosser's charge that McDonald's is brainwashing today's children into becoming fast-food customers for life does not ring true to me (however much McDonald's might wish it were so). What I see instead is that the more money kids have to spend, the more they have schooled themselves at an increasingly younger age to resist being manipulated as to how to spend it. They are quite savvy about relegating most advertising to background noise, and they can surely take in their stride schools with soda machines . . . even—as may soon be the case—Wendy's or Abercrombie & Fitch outlets. In this world of seemingly unfettered prosperity, the meaning of the phrase "substance abuse" has taken on a whole new dimension.

• • •

> Pull open the glass door, feel the rush of cool air, walk inside, get in line, and look around you . . . Think about where the food came from, about how and where it was made, about what is set in motion by every single fast food purchase . . . Then place your order. Or turn and walk out the door. It's not too late. Even in this fast food nation, you can still have it your way.
> —Eric Schlosser, *Fast Food Nation*

Thus the concluding paragraph of *Fast Food Nation*, an encapsulation of the author's solution to our dilemma: "Just say no." If we Americans join together and refuse to eat fat- and sugar-laden food produced by poorly paid employees out of riskily processed foodstuffs, McDonald's and company will be forced to change their ways. We can win this battle one determined consumer at a time.

Even taken at face value, this solution leaves a bad taste in the mouth. Do you casually toss the wrapper of the candy bar you've just eaten onto the sidewalk as you stroll through town? No, and neither do I. But I don't notice that our effort has much affected the nation's litter problem. And it never will, not when for every ounce of trash we dispose of properly, a ton of it is being pressed into a mostly indifferent public's hands.

How many people who tell kids to just say no to drugs have been swept into that maelstrom themselves? It's easy enough for Eric Schlosser to urge us to give up fast food; if instead he had looked into the mirror and told himself, "Just say no to simplistic solutions to complicated problems," he would have written a much more interesting book.

This is the crux of the problem as I see it: How do you say no to fat when you live in Fat City? If body heft were the nation's only weight problem, most of us would still be in reasonable shape. But our personal amplitude is just one manifestation of the curious era in which we find ourselves. Peasants lived in a world where the cycle moved from fast to feast and then quickly back again. In the industrial world, the cycle moved more slowly, but when the pendulum swung, it swung hard. In these postindustrial times, it creeps so sluggishly that it can sometimes seem to be barely moving at all. Perhaps a downswing in the market will change all this, but somehow I doubt it. The empire of affluence has gotten too large and complex to be felled with a single blow.

Not all share in the overabundance of our times, of course, and those who do don't share in it equally. But there it is, even so. New houses can't be too big; shopping malls can't have too many outlets—it isn't just soft drinks that come super-size these days.

Every time we shop, in theory we face two distinctly different sorts of choice: (1) whether to purchase something as opposed to nothing (just say no), and (2) whether to purchase this thing instead of that thing. These days, we are less likely to even consider the first and ultimately more important kind of choice, and not necessarily because we intentionally resist doing so. The more money we have to spend, the more those who want to take it from us become adept at making every shopping decision fall into the "this or that" category.

In 1999, I bought a new computer, an Apple PowerMac G4.* My

---

*This essay was written in 2003, when the G4 was already getting long in the tooth. Now (in 2007), it is all but obsolete.

old one was only three years old, but it was starting to have problems
dealing with updated versions of some of the programs I regularly use.
This was one reason I persuaded myself to step up, but another was
that the new computer was twice as fast as the old one and it cost five
hundred dollars less. Furthermore, it cost about a thousand dollars less
than my first computer, a MacPlus.

In fact, the G4 is so much more powerful than the MacPlus—in
storage capacity, processing speed, available memory—that comparing
the two is almost risible. It would be like dropping off a fifteen-year-old
Ford Fairlane at the junkyard and picking up a brand-new BMW for a
third less than I had originally paid for the Ford—if, that is, the BMW
had a cruising speed of ten thousand miles an hour and drove all day
on a cup of gasoline.

However, although it doesn't show it, my new computer is substantially overweight. It has much more power than I need, and the programs that I run on it are capable of doing far more complicated things
than I'll ever ask of them. But if I could pay for exactly the amount of
computing power and software complexity I need, such a computer
would actually cost much more than this one, because the companies
who make these things would sell far fewer of them.

If the world of computers seems too esoteric to you, consider shopping for clothes. Twenty years ago, purchasing a new shirt was an
event, at least for a guy like me; today, it is almost a habit. I recently
stopped at a Filene's Basement outlet to buy some socks and came
home with an armload of shirts as well—so handsome and so affordable . . . how could I resist? To make room for them in the closet, I
dropped off a few of the older, not so handsome ones at Goodwill, and
I wasn't the only one waiting for a chance to get at their line of collection boxes.

We Americans discard so much new clothing that Goodwill doesn't
know what to do with it; the poor in this country just can't absorb it
all. So, tons of wearable clothes are bundled up and sent off to Third
World countries (which is why you see African slum kids wearing
Metallica T-shirts). Perhaps some actually end up getting worn by the
folks who originally made them, in—to take three of my own shirt la-
bels—Costa Rica, Bangladesh, or Indonesia. Smudging the line between
need and want, it seems, can let you have your cake and eat it, too, at
least for the short term.

Commentators often wryly observe that gasoline in this country costs less than seltzer, but they rarely ponder why, more often than not, seltzer costs more than Coca-Cola. The reason is that if bottlers priced seltzer at a dime a bottle, it's unlikely we would buy more than we already do. We have a pretty clear idea of how much seltzer we want to drink, regardless of what we pay for it. Fill up the cellar and you won't be buying any for a long, long time. But buy a load of discounted bottles of Coke and you'll find yourself reaching for it more often, especially if it's in one of those super-cheap two-liter bottles that go flat in a couple of days.

When McDonald's first appeared, it priced its hamburgers at 15¢ apiece, and people lined up to buy them by the bagful. It was like having Happy Hour every day, all day long. Since then, though, this strategy has evolved. Now, you pay a lot for the basic item, and get a substantial price break if you'll spend still more. When I was a teenager, a Coca-Cola bottle held 6.5 ounces and cost a dime; today, the standard can holds 12 ounces and costs up to ten times as much. But if you buy a two-liter bottle on sale for 99¢, the cost of 6.5 ounces is about what I paid in 1961 (less, factoring in inflation). Similarly, customers at McDonald's are regularly urged to "super-size" their order—a 12-ounce ("child-size") drink costs 89¢, while a drink 350 percent larger (the 42-ounce "super-size") costs $1.59, a mere seventy cents more.

Smart shopping? You tell me. But there's no doubt at all that it's smart selling. Just say no? Sorry, that's not how today's brand of prosperity works. To survive and prosper, consumer-oriented companies have had to learn to keep us spending long after the reasonable response would once have been to cry "Enough!" And they do that by making the choice always seem to be between this and that, child-size or super-size, and then, if possible, make us opt for the "bargain."

This brings me back to the question I posed myself at the start of this piece. Ask me why I shop at the megamarket in the strip mall instead of the neighborhood grocery store and I'll tell you that I save money shopping there and am offered a wider range of choices. In fact, I doubt that either of these things is true.

Supermarkets are extremely skilled at letting you "save" money on individual items and still emptying your wallet at the checkout counter. Even if you wanted to, you couldn't spend the same amount at the local grocer; he just doesn't have the space—or the marketing tools—to accomplish it. And, although this isn't as immediately obvious, you could argue that the supermarket presents you with fewer choices than the neighborhood grocery. The latter constantly makes you choose between buying or not buying, because there's a good chance that the local grocer won't have what you're looking for or he will have it but it won't be in good enough condition or will cost more than you planned to spend.

This means making a kind of hard decision that the supermarket almost never requires. There, if this cut of meat is too expensive, that one is priced just right. If the oak-leaf lettuce looks a little wilted, the romaine in the next bin has just been put out. At the supermarket, you find yourself choosing not only between this and that but, as often as not, both this *and* that—which can barely be called choosing at all.

True, if I stay too long at the supermarket I get slightly nauseous, but a visit to the local market has an even more repellent quality—it leaves me bored. I no longer know how to find pleasure in the choices it offers, no matter how admirable some of them may be. I feel the same way in small-town bookstores, with their racks of greeting cards, shelves of gift items, and walls of special-interest magazines. I spent an hour in one recently while my mother kept a medical appointment and finally, overcome with an eerie sort of claustrophobia, had to finish the wait outside in the December Maine cold. I escaped this world forty years ago, and nothing is going to drag me back.

This is why I love Barnes & Noble. Those fortunate enough to live in cities with excellent bookstores may view that company as a dangerous carnivore, but as far as I'm concerned it can gobble up as many Mr. Paperbacks and Waldenbooks as it wants. Okay, I'm swept in the door by the alluring number of choices, the anonymity, the false but still soothing sense of saving money even as I'm spending more. The difference is that there is sufficient serious reading matter on offer here to form a counterweight to the meretricious stuff that so easily sucks my wallet free of change. At Barnes & Noble, my punch-drunk parental self and my overindulged baby self can actually relax and talk to each other—and make some selections that I'm still okay with when I get my purchases home.

Similarly, there is a new breed of supermarket—among them Fairway Market in New York City and Whole Foods, just about everywhere—that by refusing to infantilize the shopping experience in the name of profit offers us a complex arena of organic vegetables, humanely raised meat, farmhouse cheeses, and so on, where our moral intelligence can at least find a foothold.

I'm not arguing that Barnes & Noble or Whole Foods is somehow equivalent to a first-class independent bookstore or local market. Things change—sometimes for the better—but they never change back into what was. This is equally true for people. I read recently that high schoolers no longer try out for the baseball team but for specific positions on it, and go to special camps where they can train for these—catcher, pitcher, first baseman. Same kids, same game, but, at the same time, not.

Specialization is evolution's answer to overcrowding—find a niche and make it your own—and "niche" is the buzzword of today, a major conceptual force in everything from computer businesses to marketing techniques to fad diets. If you're overwhelmed by the wealth of choices available to you, you'll find yourself tempted simply to shut the door on a host of them, and at an increasingly younger age. One response to chronic glut is selective revulsion: eating no meat, drinking no caffeinated beverages, wearing no synthetic fabrics. In fact, the wildfire popularity of *Fast Food Nation* could be seen as an example of this—selective revulsion can sometimes prove to be very contagious.

I suppose in a way you could call this the somewhat reluctant "No, thanks" version of "Just say no," and I, for one, have gotten rather familiar with it. I now say "No, thanks" to fast food, television, dessert, most restaurants, most movies, most prepackaged foods, and to most soft drinks as well—a whole aisle of them in the supermarket and only a few that are fit to drink. These things bore me; they've toyed too long with my interest and worn it out.

Such decisions have made my life more tolerable, but they have generally come too late to be considered solutions to anything. I can't read fast enough to keep up with the books I buy; I can't burn fat fast enough to keep up with all the food I consume; and I can't wear out my clothing fast enough to keep my closet trim. And I'm not altogether sure I want to. If history teaches us anything, it is that you should try to learn to live with your problems if you can—because, more often than not, you're going to like living with the cure even less.

If the choice I'm being offered—as it increasingly seems—is between being a fat fat person and a thin fat person, I'll take the first option, please. True, I'll continue trying to make myself into a semi-demi fat person, but I've lived long enough to no longer confuse the thin person

I left behind with the person I will become if I ever return to what I still think of as my "original" weight.

Meanwhile, to Eric Schlosser, I say: Don't worry. America may be fast-food nation today, but it's all too likely that it will be Prozac nation tomorrow. Instead of the beer gardens that Prohibition killed forever, the coffee bars, ice cream shops, and, finally, the fast-food places, those always slightly tawdry but very human gathering places that were devised to replace them—we'll be offered a calming yet energizing and altogether legal pharmaceutical. It won't be habit-forming or lead to weight gain or cause any form of cancer or encourage aberrant behavior. It will be great; we'll all be Ronald McDonald; and we'll miss fast-food nation like you wouldn't believe.

A DIFFICULT MAN

In the morning, we drank bowls of black coffee on the terrace and she asked why I was staring so intently into my bowl. At first I couldn't answer because it was an unconscious thing—finally, I explained that all the vineleaves and skyscape were so beautifully reflected in dark light on the surface of my coffee, a sort of distillation of memory and eternity . . .

—Richard Olney, *Reflexions*

Arthur Koestler, confronted by a fan who stammered on and on about the honor of meeting him, is said to have replied sardonically that "to like a writer and then to meet a writer is like loving goose liver and then meeting the goose." This is one of those clever remarks that wrap a hat pin in the soft cloth of self-deprecation—"You are a fool," it says, "to want to meet me, and I would be even more of a fool to want to meet you." In other words, "Please leave me alone."

Novelists, of course, would be nothing if they weren't self-absorbed, but it may come as a surprise to learn that food writers are often even more so. This is because one of the most important purposes of the kitchen is also one of the least acknowledged—to serve as an escape hatch from the chatter in the living room. Like the writer's den, the kitchen is a blame-free haven where the exhausting demands of human interaction can be replaced with the soothing company of, in the one instance, words, and in the other, carrots and onions. Food writers get to have their cake and eat it, too.

This is meant as an observation, not a criticism (I mean, look who's talking). After all, self-absorption is what allows some food writers that uncompromising attention to technique and others that unalloyed susceptibility to pleasure—and, in a very special few, the eerily successful combination of the two—which makes their writing so enjoyable. Even so, there is apt to be a jolt when the same writer turns his or her gaze away from the cooking pot and glances up into the mirror.

Self-absorption is not the same thing as egotism, the maniacal self-regard of the average super-chef. We are led to the mirror not to be asked to admire what we see but to be taken on a tour of every flaw, pimple, and flake of dead skin—and made to experience the sharp stab of anguish each provokes. The same sensibility that we enjoy so much when it concerns itself with food can bring us up short if we choose to follow it when the cook steps out of the kitchen.

This, at least, is the likely experience of anyone picking up Richard Olney's *Reflexions*, his autobiographical ruminations. Olney, who died in 1999 at age seventy-one, is the author of such classic cookbooks as *Simple French Food* and *Lulu's Provençal Table* and of two definitive studies of French wine, *Yquem* and *Romanée-Conti*; he also conceived and then directed the production of the infinitely valuable twenty-seven-volume Time-Life Good Cook series. Olney—along with Patience Gray—has also served as a kind of patron saint for my own food writing. However, after reading *Reflexions*, I have had to cast about for a different word—dæmon, perhaps—since, although my admiration for him remains undimmed, I have to admit that his prospects for sainthood are, at best, problematic.

For most of his life, Olney was an indefatigable letter writer, especially to members of his family, and it is obvious that he initially intended to use the letters (all carefully saved, it seems) as the raw material for an autobiography along the lines of his friend James Merrill's *A Different Person*—a candid account of a young gay man's coming-of-age in the 1950s. The first hundred or so pages of *Reflexions* are just that, and finely crafted and entertainingly bitchy as well, with James Baldwin, W. H. Auden, Kenneth Anger, James Jones, and other less famous friends and acquaintances sketched with a portraitist's keen if not always flattering eye.

Indeed, Olney's original ambition was to be a painter, and as the paintings—portraits all, a few in color—reproduced in the book show, he had the talent to do it.* At the age of twenty-four, he left the United States to sail to France—and for all intents and purposes never came back. He found cheap passage on the *De Grasse*, the oldest and slowest ship on the French Line, and equally modest accommodations at the Hôtel de l'Académie, a student hotel.

Elsewhere in this book (see page 231), I quote his account of his supper there. It's hard to imagine someone who spends his first meal in Paris deconstructing the mashed potatoes becoming anything other than a food writer, but in fact it happened as if by accident, a melding of chance events and randomly made friends. How he became one is by itself a fascinating story, and the curious will find it all spelled out in these pages, as is the entire arc of his amazing if always relatively obscure career.

Unfortunately, only the truly curious will be likely to make the effort. It isn't as if the rewards aren't there—Olney's book is studded with passages of brilliantly evocative prose, some describing now-forgotten restaurants, others recording simple but carefully crafted meals, still others cataloguing Olney's encounters with an extraordinary range of fine French wines.

In addition, anyone with a taste for food-world gossip will find they can stuff themselves to surfeit here. With Olney, you were either a member of the enchanted circle—Elizabeth David, Simone (Simca) Beck, Alice Waters, Lulu Peyraud, Sybille Bedford—or else a potential threat. As such, you would be treated first with suspicion and then—

---

*In the Summer 2006 issue of *The Cincinnati Review*, his brother, James, offers an informative meditation on this part of Olney's life, centered on four portraits that he painted of his Parisian landlady, Mlle Marty, over a span of twelve years. Mlle Marty was a character-and-a-half. An actress manquée, she detested her stuffed-shirt bourgeois neighbors and was delighted to have a tenant like Richard to flaunt in their faces—an American, an artist, and gay, with—frosting on the cake—a black lover. James Olney writes of her and her relationship with his brother with bemused affection, and uses it as well to cast perspective on Richard's development as a painter. The last portrait of the series, painted during Richard's leisurely five-year relocation to his new home in Provence, shows Mlle Marty fading into shadow—indeed, she was devastated by his leaving and died within the year once he was truly gone. Mlle Marty was by no means a pretty woman, and had self-pretentions that could easily be mocked, but Olney captures her honestly and appealingly as a woman whose self-regard fails to disguise her vulnerability. James Olney writes interestingly about the connections that link Richard's painting and his food writing. But surely the nub of it is right here—the capacity to recognize the sensual and then to coax it out from hiding, be it in a woman of a certain age or a freshly dug bunch of turnips.

suspicions being almost always confirmed—without mercy. His portrait of James Beard is devastating, and he makes short shrift of many other food-world eminences as well: M.F.K. Fisher ("empty-headed, has no palate, and her writing is silly pretentious drivel"); Craig Claiborne ("silly but harmless"—the harmless part would later be struck, after a conspicuous snub). And on and on.

This is at once refreshing and disturbing—refreshing because it brings into the open a cottage industry of maliciousness that in the food world is almost always *entre nous*; disturbing because Olney seems oblivious to the fact that, far from settling old scores, the damage he is doing is almost entirely to himself. And this isn't because he's nasty; it's because he never really admits how unpleasant he himself can be. The terrible rages, the drunken misbehavior, the caddish mistreatment of others, are cruelly observed in everyone but himself. The result will leave a bad taste in any but the most indulgent reader's mouth—a taste not entirely alleviated by the many moments of tenderness, affection, and vulnerability that these pages also reveal.

The word "reflections" is particularly apt for the title of an autobiography—meaning as it does both meditative observations and images taken straight from life, which—as Olney himself puts it in the quotation at the beginning of this essay—combine to create a "distillation of memory and eternity." The problem is that about a third of the way through the book, it seems he was no longer able to continue the hard—but up to then very successful—work of recasting raw experience into carefully considered prose that gives the book's title its point.

Instead, he cobbles the rest of the book together by taking excerpts from his copious stash of letters and connecting them with short stretches of "I went here, I did that" narration. The letters, in other words, are left to carry the weight of the story . . . something letters should almost never be allowed to do. Written in the heat of the moment and without thought of their impact on anyone but the addressee, they easily veer from agitated vehemence to obsessively detailed minutia (in Olney's case, a listing of practically every bottle of wine he ever drank in France).

Once this happens, the book simply escapes the control of its author . . . and the reader becomes a passenger on a ship where another storm is blowing in and the captain has once again locked himself in his cabin with a bottle. There are warnings early on that this is not going to be an easy trip. Olney seems helplessly attracted to hysterics, in his lovers as well as his friends, people who use acting out, often savage acting out, as a way of controlling others.

The passages describing their behavior can be almost unbearable to read, especially since Olney seems incapable of putting a decisive end to a bad situation—as he is also unable to do in similarly perverse business relations, such as the one he had with Time-Life Books during the production of the Good Cook series. His stormy relationship with the French chef Georges Garin, which spans much of the book, eventually becomes so excruciatingly painful and violent that the reader can't help wondering if it really is nothing more than a friendship gone bad—if not, it is a friendship that makes your usual soap opera plot seem like so much marshmallow fluff.

Why go on reading? There are a number of reasons. First, Olney was an active and ultimately a prominent participant in the French wine and food scene for almost half a century. He knew personally the great chefs and the great vintners; he went everywhere; he tasted everything—and he kept careful notes that, read together, provide a peerless record of French gastronomy. Furthermore, the book's narrative, self-serving though it often may be, has the tortured power of a Tennessee Williams play—or, really, several Tennessee Williams plays, staged back to back.

Finally, Olney was one of the greatest food writers who ever lived, and probably the best American one. Unlike M.F.K. Fisher, he was a brilliant cook; unlike almost anyone else, he was never so rigorous as when he cooked for himself or a casual gathering of friends in the rustic kitchen of his hillside Provençal home in Solliès-Toucas. Thus, while you are hardly surprised by his detailing in *Reflexions* the preparation of a pot-au-feu for the *Club des Cent*, an exclusive Parisian gastronomic group, it is an unexpected treat to have him happily recounting the making of a homely lunch for three:

> Nora was in Solliès for a few days at Easter time. Gisou joined us for the Easter weekend. Wild thyme was in flower everywhere and shoots of wild asparagus were pushing up daily on the hillside. We lunched on wild asparagus omelettes, swelled and golden, semi-liquid inside, and salads composed of tender garden lettuces, rocket, salt anchovies maison, grilled, peeled and seeded peppers, green sweet shallots, green beans . . .

Such descriptions—and you will find many in these pages—are often superior to any recipe, the author's obvious pleasure in the dish giving the reader an encouraging push without the burden of nagging instruction: "The shrimp were grilled dry in fiercely heated frying pans thickly layered with coarse sea salt, less than a minute on one side, then on the other, only until the translucent shells turned pink and opaque; I have never since prepared them any other way."

Interestingly, the cooking this passage describes was performed not by Olney himself but by Alice Waters; the shrimp were part of a supper she cooked at Solliès-Toucas for a crowd of guests, including Lulu and Lucien Peyraud. Alice's daughter, Fanny, made the tomato salad. The atmosphere conveyed is one not only of happiness but of harmony— you leave the book feeling that anyone who wanted to could find a way to join in the cooking. Olney may have been difficult and self-absorbed, but when it came to the pleasures of the kitchen, he never comes across as hogging the stove.

On the contrary: In one of my favorite passages in *Reflexions*, Olney tells of a visit by a nephew, Christopher, who comes for a three-week stay the summer before his last year of college.

> The day before leaving, Christopher realized that he needed a cooking lesson. He loved the slices of rustic sourdough bread that I grilled, rubbed with garlic, dribbled with olive oil and cut into small squares to accompany pre-dinner drinks and he thought the flat zucchini omelette (shredded zucchini, salted in layers, squeezed, sautéed in hot olive oil, stirred into eggs, beaten with chopped butter and fresh marjoram, returned to the hot pan with more olive oil, Parmesan grated atop and finished beneath a grill) was very special. He returned to Rochester and proudly treated the family to olive oil-anointed garlic crusts and zucchini omelettes.

The teacher's pride is touchingly palpable, not least because of the innocence of the student and the magic simplicity of the dish. Someone who knew him well once described Olney to me as the nicest unpleasant man he had ever met. There are worse epitaphs—indeed, this is one that the recipient would probably have secretly relished himself.

AMERICAN EATS

When I first learned that John T. Edge was planning a series of books on such emblematic American vernacular dishes as fried chicken, apple pie, and hamburgers and fries,* I groaned aloud. You name the dish—these, particularly, but also the BLT, macaroni and cheese, brownies, hot dogs, and on and on—and it's been done and done again. We're flooded with single-subject cookbooks that come to praise but end up smothering their subject in sticky bandages of disingenuous enthusiasm and insulting recipes.

However, now that Edge's books have begun to appear, I find them valuable, even unique. That's because he actually sets out on the road to find out how Americans of every sort are trying to find a viably commercial way to keep these dishes alive. He does fill out the story with some serious research into the historical and culinary back files, but at the heart of these books is not a search for recipes (although he includes many fine ones) but a desire to connect with the passion of people determined to do things right.

They've become a rare breed. Out in the real world, the last time I had a truly memorable piece of fried chicken was in New Orleans over twenty years ago. A slice of apple pie with a flaky, tasty crust hasn't come my way in ten years, maybe more. Well-made fries (crispy, meaty, with an identifiable potato flavor) do occasionally pop

---

*The series continues, but at the time I wrote this, they included *Fried Chicken: An American Story*; *Apple Pie: An American Story*; and *Hamburgers & Fries: An American Story*.

into my life, but, on the other hand, I've completely given up on hamburgers.*

Many blame the fast-food franchises for this, but that's a bit like blaming the buzzards for the carcass. Who today—possessing the talent and the smarts to do it right—would see in a fried-chicken shack a promising way to earn a living? The odds are so much stacked against it: the inordinate amount of start-up capital, the ever-constricting health regulations, and the difficulty of finding workers willing to do hard work for low pay.

Should these innocents go ahead anyway, they find they have to fight off the temptations of a debased restaurant industry touting the profit margins of frying mediums that never turn rancid; patented seasoned coatings; prepared mixes and fillings and crusts; precut fries and preshaped patties. Then, finally, they find themselves butting heads against the eating habits of more than one generation who find goodness less in taste than in the persistent persuasiveness of hype.

Edge rightly considers the few who have overcome all (or at least most) of this impossible battle as heroes of a sort, and it's the primary reason why no fast-food franchises make it into his books. You may meet *customers* who are passionate about what they find there, but I challenge you to find an employee who feels that way. What makes his writing different from others who trod this path is the respect he has for those who work on the other side of the counter of the places he's tracked down.

They are, to be sure, an unusual bunch. There's the amazing Chef Luciano, proprietor of Chicago's Gourmet Fried Chicken, who was called to the trade by an epiphany of revulsion over a Kentucky Fried Chicken ad; Anissa Mack, a performance artist, who put freshly baked apple pies on the windowsill of a quaint little house one summer to see what would happen (among other things, children camped outside her door with forks in hand); Don Taylor Short, owner of a Maid-Rite hamburger franchise, who refuses corporate pressure to use their commissary-issued, vapor-locked bags of seasoned, cooked beef. He leads Edge down to the basement where hang a dozen or so quarters of

---

*I stopped ordering them when I realized that I had switched over to cheeseburgers because hamburgers no longer had any real juiciness to them—for me, the whole point of a hamburger is lost when no meat juices go dribbling down your chin.

Iowa beef. "This one," he says, "came from a country fair; it was raised by some teenager . . . We don't have need for bags of beef."

These books are surely worth obtaining for their recipes—fantasy apple pie with biscuit-bowl crust, onion-fried shore chicken, Hawaiian local burger—but it will be the quest itself that will leave you trapped in your armchair, eyes wide, occasionally bursting out laughing. For example, Edge got it into his head to search around for fried chicken that's been smoked before being batter-fried, having tasted pork ribs prepared that way at Little Dooey's in Columbus, Mississippi.

I doubt that deep-fried barbecue ribs are a staple at very many BBQ joints, and it's no surprise that deep-fried smoked chicken is impossible to find. However, on a visit to Los Angeles, he learned that a place called Stevie's sold it. However, when he got there, he discovered that they no longer did. Dejectedly, he asks the cashier why. Her answer: "Liquid smoke got too expensive."

The humor in that reply has an ironic edge to it that underlines the fact that Edge's trips around the country weren't all smooth sailing. He is a writer who unflinchingly factors in the amount of bad food he has had to eat in order to find the few dishes that shine. This separates him from Jane and Michael Stern, who cover much the same territory. The sun shines everywhere in their writing, and if you follow in their footsteps, you soon discover why—a depressing lack of discrimination.

However, even those willing to seriously weed out the good from the bad can be brought up short when the good itself is worryingly problematic. Take, for instance, an apple pie. It is, in essence, a marriage of apple and sweetener and crust. Each of these is a heavily freighted subject, plenty enough to absorb the mind of the serious pie maker . . . but not, these days, most customers.

Instead, it's the apple pie enhanced with Red Hots that draws them in—as do, apparently, cheese-straw apple pies, pecan apple rye pies, and "Green with Envy Chile Pies." This is an age where flavor has to be shoved into most people's mouths and set on fire before they pay attention. You can't deal honestly with commercial cooking, high or low, without taking this into account. And you can't hope to eat out much without learning to live with it.

Our vernacular cooking has always been best when our native ingenuity made something out of nothing because nothing was the only thing there was. Pies made the most of what was cheap or free—the fruit, the lard—and made do with just a little of what wasn't—the sugar and flour. The fried-chicken shack, for example, came to the fore once chicken became cheap and the deep-fat fryer provided the means of offering it in a delicious form with no serious outlay of cash. Put a griddle beside the fryer, and you can start selling hamburgers and fries.

Unfortunately, now that the same ingenuity has set out to tackle unimaginable abundance, inspiration is *still* pushing to make something out of nothing—not because of the limitations of scarcity but because selling nothing as something turns out be where the real profits lie. The temptations to do so are insidious and aggressively marketed, and, worst of all, they're contagious . . . and all but inescapable in almost any place you choose to eat.

More than any other writer on this subject that I know, Edge sets all these cards on the table and shows you how he plays them, while still managing to make the game attractive enough to draw you in. Here, for instance, is his description of the grill cook at Jay's Jayburgers in Los Angeles, going deftly about his business.

> He trowels a spoonful of cumin-scented chili onto the bottom bun in the same manner a mason applies grout to brick, drapes a slice of cheddar across a double-decker of half-inch patties so that the cheese binds one layer of beef to the next, toasts the top bun to ensure that, even upon prolonged contact with a sheath of lettuce, the bread will not turn to mush; and wraps the burger in a paper envelope designed to contain errant globs of condiment. It seems as though he does all of these things at the same time. Every effort—every ingredient—is employed with a kind of architectural intent that yields a burger of eminent portability.

This passage, and many another like it in these three books, makes you feel both hungry and unchauvinistically—which is to say, complicatedly—American.

LOOSE CANON

American cooking, as it is now and has been for at least half a century, answers a question that most of us never thought to ask: How can millions of people, most of them strangers to each other, products of different social, ethnic, and economic backgrounds, manage to create what we might call a shared culinary commons—a place where we can all sit down and find something good to eat.

There's no doubt that we've done this. Get in your car and drive one, two, three, four hundred miles in any direction, and you'll come across a grocery store where you'll have no problem filling your shopping cart or a restaurant offering dishes that, if not exactly familiar, are hardly strange.

This, if you stop and think about it, is a rather amazing state of affairs. Even if readers of this book, who have at least that much culinarily in common, were extensively polled, the result would, I suspect, uncover no more than a handful of dishes we prepare in more or less similar ways. This isn't because we're so different, each from the other, but because we have so many choices—and because so many conflicting forces (and impulses) propel us in contrary directions.

Elsewhere in the world, a country's signature dishes are emblematic of the best of the cuisine: France's pot-au-feu, Greece's moussaka, Mexico's *mole poblano*. But in America, the reality is that the more a dish is commonly shared, the more likely it is to be the choice of those who can't do better . . . and so regularly dine on Campbell's chicken noodle soup, Kraft macaroni and cheese, Dinty Moore beef stew, Table Talk blueberry pie.

The way shared taste works in America is more complicated than in more traditional societies, and it gets more so with each passing year. Take music, for example. In the last decade or so, I've become oblivious to whatever the top ten hits of the moment are, or even if there still is such a thing. I have more satisfying ways of finding music. Because of that, the likelihood of my meeting someone who has more than a couple of the same CDs I own is highly unlikely. In fact, if I know anyone who has the same CDs as I, chances are I gave them to him, or he gave them to me—or that this is a "hot" CD that somehow managed to connect with us both, the latest from Bob Dylan, Bonnie Raitt, or the Boss.

Of course, the idiosyncratic cooking in my household, where tamales are sometimes served at breakfast and scrambled eggs and *peperonata* on rice eaten for supper, probably has less in common than most with what the neighbors are putting on the table. But what little I know about how other people cook leads me to believe that it isn't a shared repertoire of dishes that stitches us all up in a common cuisine.

Of course, we do share common ingredients, culinary forms (casseroles, stews, roasts), and recognizable rhythms of daily eating (breakfast, lunch, supper, snacks). But for critics of American cooking, our lack of a coherent collection of prized national dishes leaves it trapped in adolescence, at once too anarchic and too jejune. It needs to go to college and major in the classics. This at least is what Raymond Sokolov proposes in his latest book, *The Cook's Canon: 101 Classic Recipes Everyone Should Know,** which its dust jacket proclaims to be "a liberal arts education for the palate."

> By definition, you can't have a canon unless you decide what is canonical.
>
> —Raymond Sokolov, *The Cook's Canon*

Unfortunately for his argument, Sokolov starts off by shooting himself in the foot. "Canon" has many meanings, but in this context it denotes an assemblage of authentic or exemplary texts. The Jane Austen

---

*I should point out that one of his 101 recipes is for macaroni and cheese, and that Sokolov sticks some skewers into me regarding my own version, before he goes on to present his own. He isn't the only one to think that my version is the one the new champ has to knock out of the ring; *The New York Times* took it on in its food pages on January 4, 2006. I take this as a compliment, but, even so, caveat lector.

canon is comprised of those works indisputably written by her. The Western Canon traces the evolution of the modern sensibility through our civilization's seminal works. What lies at the core of this understanding is a sense of direct, perceivable connection—from Shakespeare to Milton to Wordsworth to Tennyson to Hardy to Lawrence. If the connection seems trivial, the writer, no matter how good, is not included.

Following from this, it's easy to conceive of any number of culinary canons, even in the United States. Regional cooks could, for instance, agree on a canon of traditional Yankee or Carolina Low Country dishes, as rough around the edges as these might be. The operative word here, though, is "agree": You don't "create" canons; you codify them. Sokolov is simply wrong when he presents a canon as a matter of personal taste: "Professor X has his favorites. Professor Y has his."

In truth, the creation of a canon requires precedent and scrupulous debate. Sokolov refers to the deliberations of the Council of Trent (1546) as establishing "a canon of officially anointed books to include in the Catholic Bible," but seems unaware that the council's considerations were based on the determinations of centuries of church thought. Naturally, there are always some questionable works that don't quite make it into the canon but also refuse to go away—such as a newly discovered, unsigned poem possibly written by Shakespeare. It is *then* that the opinions of Professors X and Y enter the scene, and in hot debate.

Sokolov looks to France for his inspiration, a country that *can* boast of a culinary canon, and asks why we Americans can't create a similar (or, because we can draw on so many different traditions, an even better) one of our own. He, of all people, should know the answer. In 1976, he wrote *The Saucier's Apprentice*, a carefully thought-out primer on classic French sauces, replete with diagrams showing where each sauce fits into its family tree.

That book was possible because French cooking springs from a largely coherent culture, one of the manifestations of which is a passion for codifying. The French have done this to their language, their literature, their wine, and certainly to their cuisine.

Consider, for example, one of my favorite cookbooks, Robert Courtine's *Cent Merveilles de la cuisine française*,* which tells the story

---

*An English version was published in 1973 by Farrar, Straus and Giroux, as *The Hundred Glories of French Cooking*.

of the hundred dishes the author considers *la crème de la crème* of French cuisine. In doing so, he manages to condense the cultural history of French cooking into dishes still being prepared in the present day. He doesn't even bother to present this as a canon. As a French gastronome, Courtine simply embodies one. *"La cuisine française? C'est moi!"*

But things work differently here in America. Once, inspired by Courtine, I proposed a book to be called *The Hundred Glories of American Cooking*. But the publisher took two years before finally accepting my proposal, and by then I had decided it wouldn't be worth the effort. American cooking is as much about the dishes we don't have in common as about the ones we do.

The Cook's Canon is a perfect example of this paradox. Here, at random, is a sampling of its recipes:

> sauerbraten
> savarin *valaisanne*
> shepherd's pie
> shrimp, crab, and okra gumbo
> sole meunière
> soufflé
> Southern fried chicken
> spaghetti alla carbonara
> standing rib roast with Yorkshire pudding
> steak au poivre
> strawberry preserves
> suckling pig
> Szechwan dry-fried beef
> tamales *con rajas*
> tempura
> terrine of foie gras

What such a gathering suggests is exactly the idiosyncratic opinions of Professor X and Professor Y—or, more specifically, of Professor S. It matters little that Sokolov prefaces each recipe with an explanation as to why this particular dish (and his version of it) made it onto his list. If he had happened to choose 101 entirely different recipes, his introductions to those would be just as convincing . . . and no more canonical. Without meaningful connection, there's just no canon here.

In his introductory essay, Sokolov compares his book to "a traditional survey course in the humanities, a book about the 'Western' heritage." Well, at my age, I've made less than half the dishes Sokolov lists. And, apart from reminding me of some others that, like *tripes à la mode de Caen*, I'd like to get around to preparing someday, I found only two or three unfamiliar recipes that I had any inclination to try.

Sokolov might well accuse me of not aspiring to culinary literacy, which certainly could be true. However, I can still remember how soporific those courses on the history of civilization often were—and how the anthologies with which they were taught debased and trivialized great literature by jamming together a chunk of this with a piece of that. Similarly, Sokolov's book reminds the reader not so much of the glories of great cuisine as of those old-fashioned "continental" restaurants where *moules marinière* rubbed shoulders with *risotto alla Milanese* and *paella valenciana*.*

As a corrective to all this, compare Sokolov's effort to Auguste Escoffier's magnificent *Le guide culinaire*—a book that presents a precise encoding of more than five thousand recipes from the French classical tradition. The purpose of that book was to help chefs perfect what they already knew and to show them how familiar dishes had direct links to others that they had yet to prepare.

For Escoffier, everything is meaningfully connected because the book articulates something that already exists and with which its practitioners are intimate. Sokolov, conversely—and perversely—has assembled a collection of recipes that have little connection with each other and so offer the cook no entry into a greater whole.

This isn't to say that, taken one by one, Sokolov's recipes aren't interesting. After all, he was once food editor at *The New York Times* and has authored several well-regarded food books. But this less justifies his effort than puts it in its place. Despite his ambitions for it, *The Cook's Canon* turns out to be just another cookbook.

---

*Of course, it also reminds one of a certain genre of cookbook, those that purport to collect "the world's greatest recipes." Recently, fresh life has been breathed into this genre by David Rosengarten's *Taste: One Palate's Journey Through the World's Greatest Dishes*, and Anya von Bremzen's *The Greatest Dishes! Around the World in 80 Recipes*. Both have qualities that lift them above Sokolov's: Rosengarten's for the depth with which it treats each recipe, and von Bremzen's for its verve and the freshness of many of her choices.

THE COOK AND THE GARDENER

Three or four years ago, Faber and Faber published a small book entitled *Pampille's Table: Recipes and Writings from the French Countryside.* I happened across an advertisement for it—it got very little press coverage—that showed a picture of a sweet-looking book jacket, on which I could make out the enticing description "a translation and adaptation of Marthe Daudet's 1919 classic *Les Bons Plats de France.*"

I got hold of a review copy . . . but then found myself presented with a dilemma that I was never able to satisfactorily resolve. This was a book that demanded two reviews, each of which nullified the other: one about what the book contained—a collection of classic dishes from turn-of-the-century *cuisine bourgeoise,* ably adapted for American home cooks; the other about what the book should have contained but didn't—the story of Marthe Daudet, whose pen name was Pampille.

This wasn't because of any ignorance on the part of the editor/translator, Shirley King. She had already written *Dining with Marcel Proust,* and it was likely while researching that book that she encountered *Les Bons Plats de France.* Not only is Pampille mentioned by Proust in *Remembrance of Things Past* but she was the wife of one of his closest friends, Léon Daudet. Daudet was among the greatest gastronomes of his day (he gets a paragraph in *Larousse gastronomique*; she gets a line);*

---

*Daudet was famous for seasoning his journalism with wittily culinary turns of phrase: Renan was "gracious with lust and sauce"; Briand started to "wriggle like shellfish sprinkled with lemon"; Clemenceau was "as appetizing as a cabbage soup thick enough to hold the spoon of eloquence upright without any other support."

he was also a founder of and regular contributor to *L'Action française*, the reactionary, ultranationalistic, and virulently anti-Semitic Parisian daily. And it was as a regular column in this publication that Pampille's culinary writings first appeared.

One sympathizes with Shirley King's dilemma. To tell the book's real story would be to cast, at best, a certain ironic perspective on those "recipes and writings from the French countryside." Say nothing, however, and the subtitle raises questions—Whose recipes? Whose writings?—that the book is now unable to answer. *Pampille's Table* sank without a trace.

At first glance, Amanda Hesser's *The Cook and the Gardener* seems an entirely different proposition. It is an ambitious, glamorous, and very handsomely produced book, with lovely sepia illustrations by Kate Gridley, and is full of freshly conceived and carefully detailed recipes. It has been rapturously received by the food press and is doing quite well in the bookstores. And, given the story it tells, one can almost imagine a movie in the works as well.

Here's how it would go: A young, talented American chef-in-training—Jennifer Aniston, say, or Claire Danes—takes the job as cook at a seventeenth-century château in rural Burgundy. She is warned by the estate's mistress, Anne Willan (Miranda Richardson), herself a famous culinary figure, to keep her distance from the bad-tempered old gardener, Monsieur Milbert (Anthony Hopkins), who, with his frumpy but good-hearted wife, Madame Milbert (Joan Plowright), provides the château with its vegetables.

Of course, the plucky young cook—knowing the importance of being on friendly terms with the gardener, but also because her curiosity is piqued—gradually wins the old couple over, so much so that by the end of her stay she is regularly watching the French version of *Jeopardy* with them (and amazing them when she shouts out a right answer). She then goes on to write a lovely cookbook inspired by their friendship as well as all the fruits, vegetables, and other foods the old curmudgeon brings her (a love interest, I know, is needed here, but surely someone— Orlando Bloom? Matthew McConaughey?*—is waiting in the wings).

• • •

---

*As things turned out, it was Mr. Latte.

Roger and Francine Milbert came to work at the Château du Feÿ in 1977, after a life spent farming a rented plot of land a few miles away. They had just reached their sixties; their children had not been interested in farming; and after years of raising cows and tilling their land with a horse and plow (which M. Milbert did to the very end), the life of custodian/gardener at a château must have seemed more like a form of retirement than a new job. They were both very energetic, as M. Milbert—seventy-nine years old when Hesser knew him—remains to this day, perhaps in part because gardening is his life and at the Château du Feÿ he has been able to push vocation into avocation. With a free rein and no necessity to turn a profit, he is essentially being paid to play in the garden.

Actually, "obsess" would be the better word. M. Milbert is a fatalist and homegrown philosopher, a fountain of folk wisdom. Sayings predicting bad news are spoken with particular relish: "*Brouillard en mars, gelée en mai*" ("Fog in March, frost in May"). He is weatherwise; he religiously plants by the cycles of the moon. Like many gardeners, he has never met a seed he didn't like; his garden is scattered with oddments, like the Texas bluebells sent him by a previous visitor. (Before sowing, he says to the seeds, rather enigmatically, "*Poussez si vous voulez, si vous ne voulez pas, restez*" ["Grow if you will; if you won't, stay put"].) And, like most good gardeners, he frets . . . and frets . . . and frets:

> Meanwhile, his fruit trees did suffer during the frost. It was a good thing he wasn't in the garden to see their flower buds suspended in crystallized ice shells. Eventually they also recovered, blossoming by midmonth, but not without some drama from Monsieur Milbert. Unfailingly gruff, he cursed his way through the entire episode. It was painful to watch, a man distraught, standing solemnly over his baby peach tree. He was convinced the entire crop would fail. I tiptoed around, exaggerating my gratitude for every herb or vegetable I found on the kitchen counter. We didn't talk fruit.

The more ambitious the gardener, it has to be said, the greater the problems, because there is so much more to go wrong. M. Milbert struggles with freak bad weather, fickle plants, rampant weeds, and hordes of field mice. He plants wheat between the rows of radishes so

THE COOK AND THE GARDENER

that the mice will eat the one and leave the other alone, only to arrive one morning to discover they have eaten everything—wheat, radish tops, and a row of fresh peas. "*Ils massacrent tous!!*"

Hesser's writing shines when she and M. Milbert are in the garden together; I can't imagine any fellow vegetable gardener not being enthralled by these sections, one for each month of the year. (Enthralled, but also a little frustrated—absurdly, the book contains no diagram of the garden's idiosyncratic layout.) Hesser weaves into her prose a gradual accumulation of tiny details, until eventually it takes on something of the character of its subject:

> Late June yielded a crowded, cluttered mess of beauty. Beneath the clutter was a decided order and arrangement to all the rows, trees, and shrubs that spattered across Monsieur Milbert's canvas. Sorrel, parsley, and spinach formed definitive sections in the large beds; the currant bushes alternated colors along a path; the peach trees slouched lightly, shading the sage in the corner and protecting the young cabbages from the unforgiving summer sun.

• • •

Unfortunately, Hesser's gimlet eye doesn't always show a heart to match, especially toward Mme Milbert. Unlike her almost preternaturally spritely husband, Mme Milbert is not what she once was, as recently as ten years earlier, when Anne Willan wrote this description of her in *La France Gastronomique*:

> Following tradition, Madame Milbert looks after the poultry yard, raising a flock of chickens and seething hutches of rabbits, each more endearingly fluffy than the last. Her rabbit terrine is a perfect blend of gamey richness . . . In spring she dries lime flowers for herb tea, in summer she sits in the shade, shelling beans and peas by the hour, while in autumn it is the turn of wild chestnuts, gathered from the avenue outside the gate.

The portrait that Hesser paints of the poor woman when she encountered her could be of someone else entirely: "I saw little of Madame Milbert. She had spent so much time inside in recent years that she had lost her strength with age . . . waiting for [her husband] to return. She watched television, she chewed gum. She prepared meals and kept a hawk eye on the gates to the château." Cruel but accurate description is one thing—as when Hesser describes her coming out of her cottage "outfitted in her blue housedress and ratty cardigan sweater draped over her pot belly, socks pulled to the knee"—but unsupported suppositions are another. How does she know that Mme Milbert has lost her strength from spending too much time inside rather than the opposite—that she spends so much time inside because her health is failing?

Although Hesser is well aware that Mme Milbert is weak and her eyesight is bad, she simply cannot bring us into the Milberts' home without observing, again and again, how filthy the floor is or how grease-coated the kitchen walls. And when Hesser notes that Mme Milbert once did work outside, she portrays the situation so: "Monsieur Milbert has always raised rabbits—and chickens . . . He would feed the animals but he didn't have the heart to kill them. That was Madame Milbert's job. And from what I've heard, she did it coolly, without flinching." Here, Hesser puts M. Milbert in charge of the rabbits and chickens—contrary to what Willan wrote—only to give poor Mme Milbert another jab of the needle as well by reducing her role to that of the merciless executioner.

At first, I was puzzled by all this—what had the old lady done to deserve this treatment? But then I noticed that Hesser treats M. Milbert the same way, only more circumspectly. She writes about catching him taking the first radishes (and other vegetables) for himself instead of hurrying them over to the château. She makes a point of revealing his ignorance of the famous *potager* at the Château de Villandry, in the Torraine. (Her remark that "for a French vegetable gardener, not knowing of Villandry is like a tennis player never having heard of the French Open" is as condescending as it is untrue.)

So, while her notion of putting M. Milbert at the center of this book was in its way an inspired one, the same act, without her realizing it, reveals its essential shallowness. Hesser had come to the château in pursuit of a career, and had the cleverness to spot the literary value of the old peasant couple she found there. She used them and then discarded them, without ever really getting to know them at all.

• • •

Amanda Hesser began her culinary career working at Boston restaurants and bakeries at night while attending college by day (and at one

point studying with the food historian Barbara Wheaton). After gradu-
ation, she did a stint with Dan Leader at Bread Alone before heading to
Europe, thanks to a scholarship from Les Dames d'Escoffier. There she
worked in bakeries in Germany, Switzerland, Rome, and Paris. Then,
more Italy, more France, until she accepted a job as personal cook for
La Varenne founder Anne Willan, her family, and the many guests at
Château du Feÿ, where she also assisted her employer with the research, recipe development, and editing of two cookbooks.

For the Milberts, despite their proximity to all this, it might as well
be happening on another planet. They remain rooted, thanks in part to
the traditional roles they have come to play at the château, in what the
French call *la France profonde*—deep France, let's say—that fading rural universe where time does not advance but, like a patient donkey,
slowly pulls round the great wheel of the year.

Here, change is a matter of season, not ambition, and the Milberts
are no better equipped to understand what Hesser is out to make of her
life than she is to understand what they have made of theirs. Probably,
they don't much care. After all, there have been many Amanda Hessers
flitting in and out of their lives and bean rows over the years, visitors
who are ultimately little more to them than a mildly annoying species
of garden pest.

And to her, they are . . . what? Picturesque, amusing, the real thing
that so few tourists ever encounter, and, best of all, ideal theme material for a potential book. At the same time, they are dirty, unlettered,
unappreciative, greedy, and—what all this essentially adds up to—*poor*,
a category to which she unhesitatingly assigns them early in the book.
Why? Because, to her, they *look* poor. But they don't, really—they look
and act like the old French peasants they are. True, the Milberts are not
avid consumers, but maybe that's because they're quite content to make
do with little in order to have all the more to sock away under the mat-
tress.

Perhaps Hesser finds it so difficult to empathize with the Milberts'
peasant ways because she is so acutely aware of the social stigma attached to them. All those mean little digs—at the drunken son-in-law,
at Mme Milbert reaching covetously for another jar of the author's jam
(they must *drink* the stuff, she thinks), at their habit of retreating indoors with closed shutters when the weather grows hot, "as if it were a
scare of some sort"—are gestures of dissociation. They make crystal
clear that it is Mme Milbert, especially, and not she who, in my dictio-

nary's second, figurative meaning of "peasant," is "an uneducated person of low social status."

Hesser uses M. Milbert's garden and its produce to emblematize the subject of *The Cook and the Gardener*—the importance of seasonality in good cooking, of making the most of what is best at that particular moment of the year. This is hardly a novel idea, but few have been in a better position to put it into practice. After all, she doesn't have to grow this food or even shop for it; it just appears like magic every morning on the kitchen table.

The trouble is that everything is a little *too* easy for her. Perhaps because Willan writes for an American audience and so keeps her kitchen well stocked with the range of international ingredients that we take so much for granted—walnut oil, balsamic vinegar, ricotta salata, preserved lemons, pancetta, and the like—which move directly into Hesser's own recipes. The result is that seasonality in *The Cook and the Gardener* has more the feel of a California farmers' market than of a Burgundian *potager*.

Sautéed green tomatoes with lime; zucchini-lemon soup; red snapper sautéed with fennel seeds, tomato, and vermouth; mixed-mushroom bulgur; beets roasted with raspberry vinegar—what do the Milberts have to do with food like this? The answer is: not a thing. And by putting the Milberts so squarely at the center of the book, Hesser unintentionally allows them to undermine its theme by their wholehearted rejection of her cash-intensive culinary philosophy.

M. Milbert will have nothing to do with the harvesting of tender baby vegetables; it goes as much against his peasant grain as would eating a hen before it has stopped laying eggs. "Seasonality" to M. Milbert means spending a good proportion of his gardening time growing and storing the foods that will keep him and Mme Milbert fed during the garden's time to sleep and renew itself. Most importantly, the Milberts' almost animal appetite for the genuinely seasonal produce of the garden—sweet peas, raspberries, new potatoes—is a sober reminder that if this is the only time you're able to enjoy them, the moment can be almost lamentably brief.

The watchword of this sort of seasonality is, above all, economy. The reason that M. Milbert crushes his apples into cider and from that distills his own calvados and that Mme Milbert plucks thousands of linden flowers and then dries them in wicker baskets in the attic over the chicken coop is because by doing so they can enjoy them for free. For them, time is easier to spend than money. For us, of course, the reverse is true.

The quandary that *Pampille's Table* presented was that for the book to be accepted for what the publisher wanted it to be, the circumstances of its creation had to be kept hidden. Amanda Hesser, of course, is no Marthe Daudet, and the moral flaw that lies at the heart of *The Cook and the Gardener* is there for anyone who wishes to see. Hesser put M. Milbert at the center of this book not because she wished to bring *him* to life but because she found in him a foil who would bring *her* book to life. It is Beauty and the Beast all over again, but without the romance. In the end, it's all about Beauty, and it leaves a sour taste in the mouth.

WORK ADVENTURES
CHILDHOOD DREAMS

Have a room of your own and keep the key to the door in your
pocket or something like that, said Jung.
—Patience Gray

Fascicoli, the author calls them (the English word is "fascicles")—
pieces of writing too allusive to be called essays, too coherent and
carefully crafted to be called fragments. Instead, bursts of thought,
dreams, memories, propel us to mysterious destinations along routes
full of sudden, unmarked curves. Their titles—"Patron Saint and Patron," "About Your Journey and Mine," "Other Worlds and Other
Rooms"—often serve more as punch lines than as guideposts, and they
certainly give you no hint at all of a prose style that can catch you up
and spin you along like a leaf in a freshet, making you dizzy with pleasure just when you most ought to be paying attention to the lie of the
shore.

Notice, for instance, how in the following passage the reader is unexpectedly, unexplainedly flipped back in time as well as distance—the
chill of the evening reminding the writer of totemic transitions in the
landscape on the drive north from Italy.

We reached Paris at night and slid into the last parking space outside Napoleon's Circus. It was July, a Sunday, cold, and most
of the bars on the boulevard were closed. Sunflowers stop at
the Bouches-du-Rhône and the gold corn had turned green on
the way.

Patience Gray and her late husband, Norman Mommens, are planning to spend the night with their friend, Wolfe. After climbing up five flights of stairs to his garret apartment, they discover that no one is at home. Norman, exhausted, is content to just sack out on the floor, but Patience is drawn to the open window on the landing by a turtle dove's soft purring call (calling to mind the "snoring whirr" of turtles, on a spring evening, "by Apollona's shingle-choked river-mouth").

The window opens onto the narrow inside courtyard, and she can see that a window to Wolfe's apartment has been left open, "strung with a stave of laundry lines on which a random assemblage of clothes-pegs were marking time." She slips out of her sandals and onto the "cat-run ledge," and cautiously makes her way to the window, climbs through, and opens the door for Norman.

> The extraordinary disorder of the claustrophobic little room! When two people get inside they have at once to sit down on the bed to make way for the piano, the extendable table, the records, the coffee grinder, the eau de vie, and the books and music standing out in cantilevered piles. The bed, a 1930 piece, was inextricably combined with a varnished credenza motorstyled, a rented room's pretence to stabilize pills, postcards, alarm clock, theatre programmes and Galerie Daniel Cordier's mescalin emanations.
>
> Feasts on Sundays, one could see that. An enamelled iron casserole was squatting on the piano lid with the remains of some appetizing fish congealing among Biennale catalogues and discs. A huge bottle of Cent'Erbe—Venice's lagoon-green medicinal liqueur—and a full glass were fighting on the table with three white china mazagrans, a fallen rose, a blanched carnation. No blood but a lot of green liquor had been spilt. What looked like a cast-iron astrolabe was swinging its handle in the mess and a lot of ice was melting in an aluminium pot-au-feu on the floor. Goncharov, Rimbaud and Stendhal signalled from the bed. Maria Callas, her photograph blown up to life size, dominated the scene, with the last act of La Traviata on the record player, and the green walls pinned to the eyebrows with Normaniana.

If you don't quite follow all this, I'm in your company. At least I could look up "mazagran" in the dictionary (once I figured out the right one to consult—I finally found the word in a fat French one, which told me only that it is a kind of goblet), but for the most part we readers are left to work things out as best we can. The author is the last one to spoil an effect with an explanation.

It probably rarely occurs to her to do so—publishing her own writing, she has no anxious editor eager to meddle with her sinewy, enigmatic sentences. But it is also a mark of respect for the reader in a time when almost all writing is addressed to the lowest possible common denominator. Her voice seems to speak to us from another time, or perhaps from another universe, rather than from just another country. I find the result as cleansing as it is stimulating, the pleasure-pain of a swim in a mountain stream.

Work Adventures Childhood Dreams was published in a limited edition under the imprint of Rolando Civilla's Edizioni Leucasia di Levante Arti Grafiche. The production was closely supervised by the author, whose presence can be felt in the typeface, the book's spacious and attractive design, and especially in the nature, placement, and profusion of the illustrations (many of them by her, many others photographs of Norman's sculptures).

The outcome is something that is not only handsome and unique but in shape, design, and content the perfect companion to the author's *Honey from a Weed*, a food book that also issued from that other universe. In these pages, you return to the same place, the same sensibility; only the subject is different. The other book gave us the cooking and the eating; here are the work and the days, the memories and the dreams. Otherwise, the contents are exactly the same, a complex intellectual energy brought to heel by irreducibly simple things—two bottles on a work table, a local neighbor seeking a replacement for a stolen statue of a saint, a laurel-wood plank found in a cowstall, an unanticipatedly pure bar of silver (the author works with both precious and wholly mundane metals)—and what happens next. This, I can promise, will be what you least expect.

• • •

You may wonder, reader, why an appreciation of this book, which had few copies printed, which is now nearly impossible to obtain, and which is not at all concerned with food, appears in these pages. Patience and I wrote each other regularly after I published my review of *Honey from a Weed*, and that correspondence blossomed into an epistolary friendship (she had many of these), with an occasional letter from Norman.

However, it distressed Patience that I was not more of a culinary activist in the vein, say, of the Slow Food movement. And she lost all hope for me after I wrote "Have It Your Way," the first essay in this section, thinking it a paean to the pleasures of fast food. She was a Christian, and was drawn to those who possess an active inclination to do good (in the largest sense of that word). My own deep fatalism, and the related irony that propels that essay, was something that she could not (or would not) understand. I realized, eventually, that trying to explain myself only made matters worse. We continued to write occasionally, but the distance was always there. She died on March 10, 2005, without our ever achieving a true reconciliation.

This essay, on her last book, gave Patience great pleasure, and for that reason, especially, I place it here. She and Richard Olney were my two lodestars, and it seems fitting, in this volume, to make my goodbyes to both.

BIBLIOGRAPHY

Abdennour, Samia. *Egyptian Cooking: A Practical Guide*. Cairo: American University in Cairo Press, 1984.

Aharoni, Israel, and Nelli Sheffer. *Eating Alfresco: The Best Street Food in the World*. New York: Harry N. Abrams, 1999.

Albertini, Massimo. *Pasta & Pizza*. New York: St. Martin's Press, 1977.

Alford, Jeffrey, and Naomi Duguid. *Hot, Sour, Salty, Sweet: A Culinary Journey Through Southeast Asia*. New York: Artisan, 2000.

———. *Seductions of Rice*. New York: Artisan, 1998.

Anderson, Jean. *The American Century Cookbook*. New York: Clarkson Potter, 1997.

———. *The Food of Portugal*. New York: Morrow, 1986.

Anderson, Patrick. *Snake Wine: A Singapore Episode*. London: Chatto & Windus, 1955.

Andrews, Colman. *Catalan Cuisine*. New York: Atheneum, 1988.

———. *Flavors of the Riviera*. New York: Bantam, 1996.

Arnold, Sam'l P. *Eating Up the Santa Fe Trail*. Niwot: University Press of Colorado, 1990.

Artusi, Pellegrino. *The Art of Eating Well*, trans. Kyle M. Phillips III. New York: Random House, 1996.

———. *Science in the Kitchen and the Art of Eating Well*, trans. Murtha Baca and Stephen Sartarelli. New York: Marsilio, 1997.

Asada, Mineko. *Rice Bowl Recipes: Over 100 Tasty One-Dish Meals*. Tokyo: Graph-Sha Japan Publications, 2000.

Bar-David, Molly Lyons. *The Israeli Cook Book*. New York: Crown, 1964.

Barron, Rosemary. *Flavors of Greece*. New York: Morrow, 1991.

Bayless, Rick, with Deann Groen Bayless. *Authentic Mexican: Regional Cooking from the Heart of Mexico*. New York: Morrow, 1987.

Beard, James, and Sam Aaron. *How to Eat Better for Less Money*. New York: Appleton-Century-Crofts, 1954.

Bettoja, Jo, and Anna Maria Cornetto. *Italian Cooking in the Grand Tradition.* New York: Dial Press, 1982.

Bhumichitr, Vatcharin. *Vatch's Thai Street Food.* San Diego: Laurel Glen, 2002.

Bianchi, Anne. *From the Tables of Tuscan Women.* Hopewell, NJ: Ecco Press, 1995.

———. *Zuppa! Soups from the Italian Countryside.* Hopewell, NJ: Ecco Press, 1996.

Bittman, Mark. *Fish: The Complete Guide to Buying and Cooking.* New York: Macmillan, 1994.

Bladholm, Linda. *The Asian Grocery Store Demystified.* Los Angeles: Renaissance Books, 1999.

———. *Latin and Caribbean Grocery Stores Demystified.* Los Angeles: Renaissance Books, 2001.

Boni, Ada. *Italian Regional Cooking.* New York: E. P. Dutton, 1969.

Brissenden, Rosemary. *Joys and Subtleties: South East Asian Cooking.* New York: Pantheon, 1971.

Brown, Dale, and the Editors of Time-Life Books. *The Cooking of Scandinavia.* New York: Time-Life Books, 1968.

Brown, Lynda. *The Cook's Garden.* London: Century, 1990.

Bugialli, Giuliano. *Bugialli on Pasta.* New York: Simon & Schuster, 1988.

———. *The Fine Art of Italian Cooking.* New York: Quadrangle/Times Books, 1977.

Burton, David. *Savouring the East.* London: Faber and Faber, 1997.

Caggiano, Biba. *Trattoria Cooking.* New York: Macmillan, 1992.

Cannon, Poppy. *The Can-Opener Cookbook.* New York: Thomas Y. Crowell, 1952.

Cao, Guanlong. *The Attic: Memoir of a Chinese Landlord's Son.* Berkeley: University of California, 1996.

Casas, Penelope. *¡Delicioso! The Regional Cooking of Spain.* New York: Knopf, 1996.

Chamberlain, Lesley. *The Food and Cooking of Eastern Europe.* London: Penguin, 1989.

Chantiles, Vilma Liacouras. *The Food of Greece.* New York: Atheneum, 1975.

Chao, Buwei Yang. *How to Cook and Eat in Chinese.* New York: John Day, 1945.

Claiborne, Craig. *Craig Claiborne's Southern Cooking.* New York: Times Books, 1987.

Coe, Sophie D. *America's First Cuisines.* Austin: University of Texas, 1994.

Corn, Elaine. *365 Ways to Cook Eggs.* New York: HarperCollins, 1996.

Cornfeld, Lilian. *Israeli Cookery.* Westport, CT: Avi, 1962.

Cost, Bruce. *Asian Ingredients.* New York: Quill, 2000.

Courtine, Robert. *The Hundred Glories of French Cooking.* New York: Farrar, Straus and Giroux, 1973.

———. *La Vraie Cuisine française.* Paris: Marabout, 1963.

Covarrubias, Miguel. *Island of Bali.* New York: Knopf, 1937.

Dallas, E. S. *Kettner's Book of the Table.* Facsimile of the 1877 edition. London: Centaur, 1968.

Darrow, Diane, and Tom Maresca. *The Seasons of the Italian Kitchen.* New York: Atlantic Monthly Press, 1994.

David, Elizabeth. *Italian Food.* New York: Penguin, 1963.

Davidson, Alan. *A Kipper with My Tea.* London: Macmillan, 1988.

———. *North Atlantic Seafood.* New York: Viking, 1979.

———, ed. *The Oxford Companion to Food.* Oxford: Oxford University Press, 1999.

Davis, Irving. *A Catalan Cookery Book.* Totnes, Devon, UK: Prospect Books, 2002.

Del Conte, Anna. *Gastronomy of Italy.* London: Bantam Press, 1987.

della Croce, Julia. *Pasta Classica.* San Francisco: Chronicle Books, 1987.

Dent, Huntley. *The Feast of Santa Fe: Cooking of the American Southwest.* New York: Simon & Schuster, 1985.

Der Haroutunian, Arto. *Middle Eastern Cookery.* London: Century, 1982.

Dods, Margaret Lees. *The Cook & Housewife's Manual.* Edinburgh: Simpkin, Marshall, 1828.

Edge, John T. *Apple Pie: An American Story.* New York: Putnam, 2004.

———. *Fried Chicken: An American Story.* New York: Putnam, 2004.

———. *Hamburgers & Fries: An American Story.* New York: Putnam, 2005.

Ellis, Merle. *Cutting-Up in the Kitchen.* San Francisco: Chronicle Books, 1975.

Escudier, Jean-Noël, and Peta J. Fuller. *The Wonderful Food of Provence.* Boston: Houghton Mifflin, 1968.

Evelyn, John. *Acetaria: A Discourse of Sallets.* Facsimile of the 1699 edition. London: Prospect Books, 1982.

Field, Carol. *Celebrating Italy.* New York: Morrow, 1990.

Field, Michael. *Michael Field's Cooking School.* New York: Holt, Rinehart and Winston, 1965.

Filkins, Dexter. "Europe's on Notice: Don't Mess with Our Lunch." *The New York Times,* June 24, 2003.

Fisher, M.F.K. *How to Cook a Wolf.* New York: Duell, Sloan and Pearce, 1942.

Franz, Carl. *The People's Guide to Mexico.* Santa Fe, NM: John Muir, 1995.

Gale, H. Frederick. "China's Growing Affluence: How the Food Markets Are Responding." *Amber Waves,* 1:3 (June 2003), pp. 14–21.

Gambera, Armando, ed. *Ricette delle osterie d'Italia.* Bra, Italy: Slow Food, 1998.

Gargan, Edward. *The River's Tale: A Year on the Mekong.* New York: Knopf, 2002.

Ghedini, Francesco. *Northern Italian Cooking.* New York: Hawthorne, 1973.

Gilbert, Fabiola Cabeza de Baca. *The Good Life: New Mexico Traditions and Food.* Santa Fe, NM: San Vicente, 1949.

———. *Historic Cookery.* State College: New Mexico College of Agriculture, 1946.

Goria, Giovanni. *"La Bagna caôda."* www.atasti.it/goria/bagna.htm.

Grant, Rose. *Street Food.* San Francisco: Crossing Press, 1988.

Gray, Patience. *Honey from a Weed.* London: Prospect Books, 1986.

———. *Work Adventures Childhood Dreams.* Presicce, Italy: Edizioni Leucasia, 1999.

Grigson, Jane. *Fish Cookery*. Harmondsworth, England: Penguin, 1975.

———. *Jane Grigson's Fruit Book*. New York: Atheneum, 1982.

———, ed. *The World Atlas of Food*. New York: Simon & Schuster, 1974.

Harland, Marion. *Marion Harland's Complete Cook Book*. Indianapolis: Bobbs-Merrill, 1903.

Harris, Valentina. *Recipes from an Italian Farmhouse Kitchen*. New York: Simon & Schuster, 1989.

Hazan, Giuliano. *The Classic Pasta Cookbook*. New York: Dorling Kindersley, 1993.

Hazelton, Nika. *The Regional Italian Kitchen*. New York: Evans, 1978.

Helou, Anissa. *Mediterranean Street Food*. New York: HarperCollins, 2002.

Hess, John L., and Karen Hess. *The Taste of America*. New York: Grossman, 1977.

Hesser, Amanda. *The Cook and the Gardener*. New York: Norton, 1999.

Hillman, Howard. *Great Peasant Dishes of the World*. Boston: Houghton Mifflin, 1983.

Hom, Ken. *Ken Hom's Chinese Kitchen*. New York: Hyperion, 1994.

———. *Easy Family Recipes from a Chinese-American Childhood*. New York: Knopf, 1997.

Hongwiwat, Nidda. *Thai Fried Rice*. Bangkok: Sangdad, 1996.

Hosking, Richard. *A Dictionary of Japanese Food: Ingredients and Culture*. Tokyo: Tuttle, 1997.

Howe, Robin. *Balkan Cooking*. London: Deutsch, 1965.

———. *Greek Cooking*. London: Deutsch, 1969.

Hsiung, Deh-Ta. *The Chinese Kitchen*. New York: St. Martin's Press, 1999.

James, George Wharton. *New Mexico: The Land of the Delight Makers*. Boston: Page, 1920.

Jamison, Cheryl Alters, and Bill Jamison. *The Border Cookbook*. Boston: The Harvard Common Press, 1995.

———. *The Rancho de Chimayó Cookbook*. Boston: The Harvard Common Press, 1991.

———. *A Real American Breakfast*. New York: Morrow, 2002.

———. *Texas Home Cooking*. Boston: The Harvard Common Press, 1993.

Jaramillo, Cleofas M. *Genuine New Mexico Tasty Recipes*. Santa Fe, NM: Seton Village Press, 1942.

Jelani, Rohani. *Malaysian Hawker Favourites*. Singapore: Periplus, 2001.

Jenkins, Nancy Harmon. *The Mediterranean Diet Cookbook*. New York: Bantam, 1994.

Johnson, Samuel. *A Journey to the Western Islands of Scotland*. London: Stahan & Cadell, 1791.

Jones, Robert F. *Deadville*. New York: St. Martin's Press, 1998.

Kaneva-Johnson, Maria. *The Melting Pot: Balkan Food and Cookery*. Totnes, Devon, UK: Prospect Books, 1999.

Kasper, Lynne Rossetto. *The Italian Country Table*. New York: Scribners, 1999.

Kelly, R. Talbot. *Burma, Painted and Described*. London: A. & C. Black, 1905.

Kennedy, Diana. *The Art of Mexican Cooking*. New York: Bantam, 1989.

———. *The Cuisines of Mexico*. Rev. ed. New York: Harper & Row, 1986.

———. *Mexican Regional Cooking*. New York: Harper & Row, 1984.

———. *My Mexico: A Culinary Odyssey*. New York: Clarkson Potter, 1998.

Kerr, W. Park, Norma Kerr, and Michael McLaughlin. *The El Paso Chile Company's Texas Border Cookbook*. New York: Morrow, 1992.

Kijac, Maria Baez. *The South American Table*. Boston: The Harvard Common Press, 2003.

Kochilas, Diane. *The Greek Vegetarian*. New York: St. Martin's Press, 1996.

Kramer, Matt. *A Passion for Piedmont*. New York: Morrow, 1997.

Kremezi, Aglaia. *The Foods of Greece*. New York: Stewart, Tabori & Chang, 1993.

———. *The Mediterranean Pantry*. New York: Artisan, 1994.

Kurlansky, Mark. *Cod: A Biography of the Fish That Changed the World*. New York: Walker, 1997.

Lamb, Venice. *The Home Book of Turkish Cookery*. London: Faber and Faber, 1969.

Lantermo, Alberta. *Piemonte in Bocca*. Milan: Il Vespro, 1976.

Larkom, Joy. *Oriental Vegetables*. New York: Kondansha, 1991.

Lassalle, George. *East of Orphanides*. London: Kyle Cathie, 1991.

Lebovitz, David. *Room for Dessert*. New York: HarperCollins, 1999.

Lee, Calvin. *Chinatown, U.S.A.* Garden City, NY: Doubleday, 1965.

Lee, Calvin, and Audrey Evans Lee. *The Gourmet Chinese Regional Cookbook*. New York: Putman 1976.

Lee, Jim. *Jim Lee's Chinese Cookbook*. New York: Harper & Row, 1968.

Lesem, Jeanne. *Preserving Today*. New York: Knopf, 1992.

Leung, Mai. *The Chinese People's Cookbook*. New York: Harper & Row, 1979.

Levy, Faye. "Felafel Fetish." *Jerusalem Post*, June 5, 1998.

Li, Shu-Fan. *Hong Kong Surgeon*. New York: Dutton, 1964.

Lin, Hsiang Ju, and Tsuifeng Lin. *Chinese Gastronomy*. New York: Harcourt Brace Jovanovich, 1969.

Lin, Tsuifeng, and Hsiang Ju Lin. *Secrets of Chinese Cooking*. Englewood Cliffs, NJ: Prentice Hall, 1960.

Lo, Eileen Yin-Fei. *The Chinese Kitchen*. New York: Morrow, 1999.

Lo, Kenneth. *Chinese Cooking on Next to Nothing*. New York: Pantheon, 1976.

———. *Chinese Regional Cooking*. New York: Pantheon, 1979.

Loomis, Susan Hermann. *Italian Farmhouse Cookbook*. New York: Workman, 2000.

Lorde, Audre. *Zami: A New Spelling of My Name*. Watertown, MA: Persephone Press, 1982.

Lundi, Ronni. *Shuck Beans, Stack Cakes, and Honest Fried Chicken: The Heart and Soul of Southern Country Kitchens*. New York: Atlantic Monthly Press, 1994.

Lutes, Della. *The Country Kitchen*. Boston: Little, Brown, 1936.

MacKie, Cristine. *Life and Food in the Caribbean*. New York: New Amsterdam, 1992.

Malka, Victor. *Israel Observed*, trans. Jean Joss. London: Kaye & Ward, 1979.

Manjón, Maite. *The Gastronomy of Spain and Portugal*. New York: Prentice Hall, 1990.

Margaret, Len. *Fish & Brewis, Toutens & Tales, Canada's Atlantic Folklore-Folklife Series*, vol. 7. St. John's, Newfoundland: Breakwater, 1980.

Mariani, John. *America Eats Out*. New York: Morrow, 1991.

Mark, Theonie. *Greek Islands Cooking*. Boston: Little, Brown, 1974.

Marks, Copeland. *The Exotic Kitchens of Malaysia*. New York: Donald Fine, 1997.

Marks, Gil. *The World of Jewish Cooking*. New York: Simon & Schuster, 1996.

Martini, Anna. *The Mondadori Regional Italian Cookbook*. New York: Harmony, 1982.

Mayson, James. *Street Food from Around the World*. Bath: Absolute, 1998.

McCulloch-Williams, Martha. *Dishes & Beverages of the Old South*. Facsimile of the 1913 edition. Knoxville: University of Tennessee, 1988.

McDermott, Nancie. *Real Vegetarian Thai*. San Francisco: Chronicle Books, 1997.

McNeill, F. Marian. *The Book of Breakfasts*. London: Alexander MacLehose, 1932.

———. *The Scots Kitchen*. London: Blackie & Son, 1929.

Middione, Carlo. *La Vera Cucina: Traditional Recipes from the Homes and Farms of Italy*. New York: Simon & Schuster, 1996.

Miller, Keith Ruskin. *Indonesian Street Food Secrets*. Portland, OR: Hawkibinkler Press, 2002.

Mowe, Rosalind, ed. *Southeast Asian Specialties: A Culinary Journey Through Singapore, Malaysia and Indonesia*. Cologne: Könemann, 1998.

Moffitt, Bruce C. "Menudo." www.premiersystems.com/recipes/mexican/menudo .html.

Morphy, Marcelle, Countess. *The Best Food from Italy*. New York: Arco, 1954.

Morash, Marian. *The Victory Garden Fish and Vegetable Cookbook*. New York: Knopf, 1991.

Morse, Kitty. *The Vegetarian Table: North Africa*. San Francisco: Chronicle Books, 1996.

Norman, Jill, ed. *Masterclass: Expert Lessons in Kitchen Skills*. London: Jill Norman & Hobhouse, 1982.

Novas, Himilce, and Rosemary Silva. *Latin American Cooking Across the U.S.A.* New York: Knopf, 1997.

Oliver, Sandra. *Saltwater Foodways*. Mystic, CT: Mystic Seaport Museum, 1995.

Olney, Richard. *Lulu's Provençal Kitchen*. New York: HarperCollins, 1994.

———. *Reflexions*. New York: Brick Tower Press, 1999.

Ommanney, F. D. *Fragrant Harbor: A Private View of Hong Kong*. London: Hutchinson, 1962.

Ortiz, Elisabeth Lambert. *The Complete Book of Mexican Cooking*. New York: Evans, 1967.

———. *The Food of Spain & Portugal*. New York: Atheneum, 1989.

Owen, Sri. *Indonesian Food and Cookery*. Totnes, Devon, UK: Prospect Books, 1986.

Parsons, Russ. "The Dinner Pot: Take My Casserole . . . Please." *Los Angeles Times*, January 20, 1994.

———. *How to Read a French Fry*. New York: Houghton Mifflin, 2001.

Passmore, Jacki. *The Encyclopedia of Asian Food and Cooking*. New York: Hearst Books, 1991.

Peterson, Joan, and David Peterson. *Eat Smart in Indonesia*. Madison, WI: Ginkgo Press, 1997.

Peyton, James W. *El Norte: The Cuisine of Northern Mexico*. Santa Fe, NM: Red Crane, 1990.

Pilcher, Jeffrey M. *¡Que vivan los tamales!* Albuquerque: University of New Mexico, 1998.

Plagemann, Catherine. *Fine Preserving*. Berkeley: Aris, 1986.

Plotkin, Fred. *Recipes from Paradise: Life and Food on the Italian Riviera*. Boston: Little, Brown, 1997.

Pomiane, Edouard de. *Good Fare: A Code of Cookery*. London: Gerald Howe, 1932.

Preston, Mark. *California Mission Cookery*. Albuquerque, NM: Border Books, 1994.

Priestland, Gerald. *Frying Tonight: The Saga of Fish & Chips*. London: Gentry, 1972.

Rector, George. *Dine at Home with Rector: A Book on What Men Like, Why They Like It, and How to Cook It*. New York: E. P. Dutton, 1937.

Reynolds-Ball, E. A. *Unknown Italy: Piedmont and the Piedmontese*. London: A. & C. Black, 1927.

Rhodes, Gary. *More Rhodes Around Britain*. London: BBC Books, 1995.

Ríos, Alicia, and Lourdes March. *The Heritage of Spanish Cooking*. New York: Random House, 1992.

Roden, Claudia. *The Book of Jewish Food: An Odyssey from Samarkand to New York*. New York: Knopf, 1996.

———. *A Book of Middle Eastern Food*. New York: Knopf, 1972.

Rogers, Ann. *A Cookbook for Poor Poets and Others*. New York: Scribners, 1966.

Rombauer, Irma, and Marion Rombauer Becker. *The Joy of Cooking*. Indianapolis: Bobbs-Merrill, 1951.

Root, Waverley. *Food*. New York: Simon & Schuster, 1980.

———. *The Food of Italy*. New York: Atheneum, 1971.

Root, Waverley, and the Editors of Time-Life Books. *The Cooking of Italy*. Foods of the World Series. New York: Time-Life Books, 1968.

Rosengarten, David. *Taste: One Palate's Journey Through the World's Greatest Dishes*. New York: Random House, 1998.

Salaman, Rena. *Greek Food*. Rev. ed. New York: HarperCollins, 1994.

Saveur Magazine Editors. *Saveur Cooks Authentic French*. San Francisco: Chronicle Books, 1999.

Scaravelli, Paola, and Jon Cohen. *Mediterranean Harvest*. New York: Dutton, 1986.

Schlosser, Eric. *Fast Food Nation: The Dark Side of the All-American Meal*. Boston: Houghton Mifflin, 2001.

Schwartz, Arthur. *Naples at Table*. New York: HarperCollins, 1998.

So, Yan-kit. *Yan-kit's Classic Chinese Cookbook*. New York: Dorling Kindersley, 1993.

Sokolov, Raymond. *The Cook's Canon: 101 Classic Recipes Everyone Should Know*. New York: HarperCollins, 2003.

———. *How to Cook*. New York: Morrow, 1986.

———. *The Saucier's Apprentice: A Modern Guide to Classic French Sauces for the Home*. New York: Knopf, 1976.

Solomon, Charmaine. *Charmaine Solomon's Encyclopedia of Asian Food*. Singapore: Periplus, 1996.

Spencer, Evelene, and John N. Cobb. *Fish Cookery*. Boston: Little, Brown, 1921.

Steinberg, Rafael, and the Editors of Time-Life Books. *Pacific and Southeast Asian Cooking*. New York: Time-Life Books, 1970.

Steingarten, Jeffrey. *The Man Who Ate Everything*. New York: Knopf, 1997.

Stobart, Tom. *The Cook's Encyclopedia: Ingredients and Processes*. New York: Harper & Row, 1981.

Tausend, Marilyn. *Cocina de la Familia*. New York: Simon & Schuster, 1997.

Thompson, Sylvia Vaughn. *The Budget Gourmet*. New York: Random House, 1975.

———. *Economy Gastronomy*. New York: Atheneum, 1963.

Thorne, John. *Home Body*. Hopewell, NJ: Ecco Press, 1997.

———. *Simple Cooking*. New York: Penguin, 1987.

Thorne, John, and Matt Lewis Thorne. *Pot on the Fire*. New York: North Point Press, 2000.

———. *Serious Pig*. New York: North Point Press, 1996.

Tracy, Marian. *Casserole Cookery*. New York: Viking Press, 1942.

Tropp, Barbara. *The Modern Art of Chinese Cooking*. New York: Morrow, 1982.

Vester, Bertha Spafford. *Our Jerusalem: An American Family in the Holy City, 1881–1949*. Garden City, NY: Doubleday, 1950.

Villas, James. *Crazy for Casseroles*. Boston: The Harvard Common Press, 2003.

von Bremzen, Anya. *The Greatest Dishes! Around the World in 80 Recipes*. New York: HarperCollins, 2004.

von Bremzen, Anya, and John Welchman. *Terrific Pacific Cookbook*. New York: Workman, 1995.

Ward, Artemas. *The Grocer's Encyclopedia*. New York: James Kempster, 1911.

Willan, Anne. *Château Cuisine*. New York: Maxwell Macmillan, 1992.

———. *La France Gastronomique*. New York: Arcade, 1991.

———. *French Regional Cooking*. New York: Morrow, 1981.

Willard, Pat. *A Soothing Broth*. New York: Broadway, 1998.

Willinger, Faith. *Red, White & Greens: The Italian Way with Vegetables*. New York: HarperCollins, 1996.

Wilson, C. Anne. *The Book of Marmalade*. Rev. ed. Philadelphia: University of Pennsylvania Press, 1999.

———. *Food and Drink in Britain*. London: Constable, 1973.

Witty, Helen. *Fancy Pantry.* New York: Workman, 1986.

Wolfert, Paula. *The Cooking of South-West France.* New York: Dial Press, 1983.

Wright, Clifford A. *A Mediterranean Feast.* New York: Morrow, 1999.

Wright, Jeni, ed. *The Encyclopedia of Asian Cooking.* London: Octopus, 1980.

Yoshida, George. *Hawaii's Best Cookbook on Fried Rice.* Honolulu: circa 2000.

Young, Wandee, and Byron Ayanoglu. *Simply Thai Cooking.* Toronto: Robert Rose, 1996.

Zeng, Xiongsheng. "Huang-Lu Rice in Chinese History." *Agricultural Archaeology* 1998(3): 292–311.

Zimmerman, Sybil. *Israeli Cooking on a Budget.* Jerusalem: Jerusalem Post, 1978.

Zuckerman, Larry. *The Potato.* New York: North Point Press, 1999.

INDEX

Chinese, rice bowl with, 278–79
Chinese, wok-fragrant fried rice
 with, 161–63
grits with, 253–54
Italian, pasta with zucchini and,
 268–69
Saveur magazine, 322
Savouring the East (Burton), 222
scacciata, 146
scallions
 bagna caôda with, 21–22
 somen noodles with, 73–76
Scandinavian food, 193
 see also Norwegian food
Scaravelli, Paola, 68
Schlesinger, Sarah, 36
Schlosser, Eric, 331–35, 339–43, 345–
 47, 351, 352
school cafeterias, 338
Schwartz, Arthur, 36, 198, 200*n*
Science in the Kitchen and the Art of
 Eating Well (Artusi), 112
Scotch broth, 84
Scotch whiskey, morning dram of, 43–
 45
Scots Kitchen, The (McNeill), 57
seasonality, 374
Sea and Sardinia (Lawrence), 120
seaweed, 321–22
Sebastian, John, xxvii
Sephardic Jews, 184
Serio's Market (Northampton, Massa-
 chusetts), 331
Seville oranges, 42–43, 49
shallots, peanut sauce with, 226
Shaw, Diana, 36
Sheffer, Nelli, 152*n*
Sheraton, Mimi, 28
Short, Don Taylor, 360
shrimp, 358
 ceviche, 291–95
 finger-sucking, 269–70
 de Jonghe, 129–30
 wok-fragrant fried rice with, 163

Shuck Beans, Stack Cakes, and Honest
 Fried Chicken (Lundy), 233
Silva, Rosemary, 92
Simple Cooking (food letter), 35, 41
Simple French Food (Olney), 354
Simple Thai Cooking (Young and
 Ayanoglu), 221
Singapore, 209, 219
slada matecha, 153
slaughterhouses, 333
Slow Food movement, 15, 379
smoked meats
 deep-fried, 361
 marrowbones from, 6–7
 see also ham
snack foods, tempo of eating, 104
snails, 153
Snake Wine (Anderson), 208
soda, *see* soft drinks
soft drinks, 337, 346, 347, 351
 in public schools, 341
 sugar in, 342
 Turkish, 107
Sokolov, Raymond, 234, 247, 364–
 67
somen noodles, 70–71, 75
 with beef, 75–76
 with chicken, 73–74
Sontag, Susan, 36
Soothing Broth, A (Willard), 77–
 78
soup
 bread and tomato, 146
 cabbage and dumpling, 135
 canned, 86–87, 127, 130–31, 133
  (*see also* Campbell's soups)
 minestrone, 109–24
 pepper pot, 79–87
 potato, 302–305
 snail, 153
 tripe, 79–99
soupe au pistou, 116–17
South East Asian Food (Brissenden),
 225